THE ACADEMY OF INTERNATIONAL BUSINESS

Published in Association with the UK Chapter of the Academy of International Business

Titles already published in the series:

International Business and Europe in Transition (Volume 1)
Edited by Fred Burton, Mo Yamin and Stephen Young

Internationalisation Strategies (Volume 2)
Edited by George Chryssochoidis, Carla Miller and Jeremy Clegg

The Strategy and Organization of International Business (Volume 3)
Edited by Peter Buckley, Fred Burton and Hafiz Mirza

Internationalization: Process, Context and Markets (Volume 4)
Edited by Graham Hooley, Ray Loveridge and David Wilson

International Business Organization (Volume 5)
Edited by Fred Burton, Malcolm Chapman and Adam Cross

International Business: Emerging Issues and Emerging Markets (Volume 6)
Edited by Carla C. J. M Millar, Robert M. Grant and Chong Ju Choi

International Business: European Dimensions (Volume 7)
Edited by Michael D. Hughes and James H. Taggart

Multinationals in a New Era: International Strategy and Management (Volume 8)
Edited by James H. Taggart, Maureen Berry and Michael McDermott

International Business (Volume 9)
Edited by Frank McDonald, Heinz Tusselman and Colin Wheeler

Internationalization: Firm Strategies and Management (Volume 10)
Edited by Colin Wheeler, Frank McDonald and Irene Greaves

The Process of Internationalization (Volume 11)
Edited by Frank MacDonald, Michael Mayer and Trevor Buck

International Business in an Enlarging Europe (Volume 12)
Edited by Trevor Morrow, Sharon Loane, Jim Bell and Colin Wheeler

Managerial Issues in International Business (Volume 13)
Edited by Felicia M. Fai and Eleanor J. Morgan

Anxieties and Management Responses in International Business (Volume 14)
Edited by Rudolf Sinkovics and Mo Yamin

Corporate Governance and International Business (Volume 15)
Edited by Roger Strange and Gregory Jackson

Contemporary Challenges to International Business (Volume 16)
Edited by Kevin Ibeh and Sheena Davies

Resources, Efficiency and Globalisation (Volume 17)
Edited by Pavlos Dimitratos and Marian V. Jones

The Rise of Multinationals from Emerging Economies

Achieving a New Balance

Edited by

Palitha Konara
University of Huddersfield, UK

Yoo Jung Ha
University of York, UK

Frank McDonald
University of Liverpool, UK

and

Yingqi Wei
University of Leeds, UK

palgrave
macmillan

First published 2015 by
PALGRAVE MACMILLAN

Palgrave Macmillan in the UK is an imprint of Macmillan Publishers Limited, registered in England, company number 785998, of Houndmills, Basingstoke, Hampshire RG21 6XS.

Palgrave Macmillan in the US is a division of St Martin's Press LLC, 175 Fifth Avenue, New York, NY 10010.

Palgrave Macmillan is the global academic imprint of the above companies and has companies and representatives throughout the world.

Palgrave® and Macmillan® are registered trademarks in the United States, the United Kingdom, Europe and other countries.

ISBN: 978–1–137–47310–3

This book is printed on paper suitable for recycling and made from fully managed and sustained forest sources. Logging, pulping and manufacturing processes are expected to conform to the environmental regulations of the country of origin.

A catalogue record for this book is available from the British Library.

Library of Congress Cataloging-in-Publication Data

Konara, Palitha.
    The rise of multinationals from emerging economies : achieving a new balance /
Palitha Konara, Yoo Jung Ha, Frank McDonald, Yingqi Wei.
        pages cm. — (Academy of International Business (UKI) series)
    Includes bibliographical references and index.
        ISBN 978–1–137–47310–3 (alk. paper)
    1. International business enterprises – Developing countries. I. Title.

HD2932.K66 2015
338.8'891724—dc23   2014049543

In Memory of Professor Alan Rugman

*This book is dedicated to the memory of Alan Rugman,
who sadly died in July 2014. Alan, in addition to being one of the
most important contributors to the development of international
business theory, was a staunch supporter of the AIB UKI
Chapter. His support for the annual conference and the doctoral
symposium as well as his robust and humorous comments
on papers will be greatly missed. Alan's substantial contribution to
international business theory will of course be an enduring legacy.*

Contents

List of Figures

List of Tables

Foreword

The 41st Annual Conference of the Academy of International Business (AIB) UK & Ireland Chapter was held at the University of York, 10–12 April 2014. This book contains records of keynote speeches and special sessions on key topics, as well as a selection of some of the best papers presented at the conference.

The name and theme of the conference was 'Achieving a New Balance: The Rise of Multinationals from Emerging Economies and the Prospects for Established Multinationals'. The keynote speeches by Professors Peter J. Buckley (University of Leeds) and Jean-François Hennart (University of Tilburg) were on issues connected to the conference theme. The talk by Professor Buckley focused on what we could learn from the methodologies of business history to help to enhance the depth and scope of research on international business. Professor Hennart's presentation centred on the adequacy of current theory, in particular the OLI paradigm, to help us to understand outward FDI from emerging economies. Records of the keynote speeches are included in this book.

The conference met at an opportune time to consider the implications for MNEs of the possibility of Scottish independence. Following an idea suggested by Professor Alan Rugman the conference chairs arranged for a panel of experts to discuss key issues likely to arise from this. As there are many separatist movements among both advanced and emerging economies, an investigation of the implications of the creation of new small economies that are committed to integration into the global economy is an important area of study for international business. The book contains a chapter with a record of the talks given by the experts with comments on some important implications of separatist movements for international business research. The conference continued the tradition of providing special sessions on important areas in our field of study. One of the special sessions continued the work begun at the Liverpool conference in 2012 to help develop interaction between economic geography and international business researchers. This session, led by Professor Gary Cook and Dr Jennifer Jones, included contributions from leading researchers in economic geography and international business, and a record of this session is included as a chapter in the book. The other chapters in the book represent some of the best papers presented at the conference and cover a series of important topics connected to the theme of the conference.

I hope you find this book to be informative and useful, and I hope it encourages you to get involved with the work of AIB UK & Ireland Chapter. The AIB UK & Ireland web site (http://www.aib-uki.org/) provides a wide range of information about the chapter and matters of interest to international business scholars.

Heinz Tüselmann
Chair of AIB UK & Ireland Chapter
Manchester Metropolitan University Business School

Notes on Contributors

Maria L. Allen is Senior Lecturer in Strategy and International Business at Manchester Metropolitan University Business School. Her research focuses on firm strategies and their institutional settings. She has published in international business, human resource management and political economy journals and in a leading handbook on comparative institutional analysis. Her work has been recognized by awards at Academy of International Business (UK & Ireland Chapter) conferences.

Tahir Ali is Assistant Professor of International Business at the University of Vaasa, Finland. His research focuses on international joint ventures, international strategic alliances, managing inter-partner relationships, the role of trust, relational risk, conflict resolutions strategies, complementary capabilities, culture, control and performance measurement in international joint ventures.

Matthew M.C. Allen is Senior Lecturer in Organization Studies at Manchester Business School. He coordinates the Knowledge, Technology, and Innovation conference track for the Society for the Advancement of Socio-Economics. He has published in leading international journals, such as *Socio-Economic Review* and *International Journal of Human Resource Management*. He has held visiting appointments at the European University Viadrina, Frankfurt (Oder), Germany, and the University of Applied Sciences, Düsseldorf, Germany.

Joseph Amankwah-Amoah is Assistant Professor of Management at Bristol University. He holds a PhD from the University of Wales Swansea. His research interests include organizational failure, strategic renewal, global business strategy, lateral hiring and the airline and solar PV industries. He has published articles in journals such as *International Journal of Human Resource Management, Business History, Group & Organization Management, Journal of Business Research, Thunderbird International Business Review, Strategic Change* and *Journal of General Management*.

Svante Andersson is Professor of Business Administration at Halmstad University. His areas of research include international business, marketing and entrepreneurship. He has published in journals such as *Journal of Business Venturing, Journal of International Marketing, International Marketing Review, European Journal of Marketing* and *International Studies in Management and Organization*. He has extensive international experience as an export manager and as a guest teacher/researcher.

Frank Barry is Professor of International Business and Economic Development at Trinity College Dublin. He has published extensively on topics in international trade, foreign direct investment, economic development and the Irish economy.

Grahame Boocock is an honorary fellow in the School of Business and Economics at Loughborough University. After some years working for a major UK clearing bank, Grahame switched careers to move into the higher education sector in 1983. He spent 25 years at Loughborough as a lecturer and then as a senior lecturer in banking and entrepreneurship before retiring from a full-time role at the end of 2012. He also spent a year as a visiting professor at the University of Northern Malaysia. He has published widely over the years, and his research interests include risk finance for SMEs, government support for SMEs and entrepreneurial learning.

Peter J. Buckley, OBE, FBA is Professor of International Business, Founder Director of the Centre for International Business, University of Leeds (CIBUL) and the Business Confucius Institute at the University of Leeds, and Cheung Kong scholar chair professor at the University of International Business and Economics (UIBE), Beijing. He was president of the Academy of International Business (2002–2004), served as immediate past president (2004–2006), and was chair of the European International Business Academy (2009–2012). He has published over 190 refereed articles and around 50 books. He holds a PhD in economics from Lancaster University and honorary doctorates from the University of Uppsala, Sweden, and Lappeenranta University of Technology, Finland.

Liam Campling is based at the School of Business and Management, Queen Mary University of London, where he convenes an MSc in international business and politics and teaches modules on world economy & development and business & society. His research interests are on multinational firms and the world economy, the politics of international trade relations, commodity chain analysis and the political economy and ecology of development.

Gary Cook is Professor of Economics and Head of Economics, Finance and Accounting at the University of Liverpool Management School. His main area of research is into industrial clusters, with current research themes including regional differences in cluster performance, the influence of MNE location within clusters and entrepreneurship. His other main area of interest is in the economic analysis of insolvency law, with particular interest in rehabilitation procedures for financially distressed small firms.

Nigel Driffield is Professor of International Business at Warwick Business School, University of Warwick. He is a member of the Business and Management

REF panel 2014 and a member of the editorial review board of *JIBS*. His previous post was as a reader at the University of Birmingham. Nigel has published extensively in leading journals in the areas of FDI and economic development. He has held four ESRC awards and currently holds a Leverhulme Fellowship, looking at the interactions between multinationals location strategy and economic development.

Natasha Evers is Lecturer in Marketing at the National University of Ireland, Galway. She holds a PhD and M.Econ.Sc. from University College Dublin. Her expertise lies in international marketing, entrepreneurship and commercialisation of innovation. She is lead author of *Technology Entrepreneurship – Bringing Innovation to the Marketplace* (Palgrave, 2014). Her work has appeared in *Journal of International Marketing*, *International Marketing Review*, *Entrepreneurship and Regional Development* and *Journal of Small Business & Entrepreneurship*.

Yoo Jung Ha is Lecturer in International Business at the York Management School, University of York, UK. She holds a PhD from The University of Manchester and an MPhil from The University of Oxford. Her research interests include technology spillovers, the impact of activities by multinational enterprises on host countries, innovation strategy at the subsidiary level and interaction between the multinational enterprise and its environment. She has published in *International Business Review* and *Asian Business & Management*.

Jean-François Hennart is Emeritus Professor of International Management at Tilburg University and an extramural fellow at its Centre for Research in Economics and Business. He works in the Department of Business Management at the Faculty of Economics of the University of Pavia in Italy, is Professor of Strategy and International Business at Queen's University Management School in Belfast, UK and is a distinguished visiting professor at the Lee Kong Chian School of Business at Singapore Management University. His research focuses on the comparative study of international economic institutions such as multinational firms, joint ventures and alliances, and modes of foreign market entry. His work has been published in *Journal of International Business Studies*, *Strategic Management Journal* and *Journal of Economic Behavior and Organization*, among others. He is a fellow of the Academy of International Business and of the European International Business Academy. He holds a PhD in economics from the University of Maryland and an honorary doctorate from the University of Vaasa.

Martin Hess is Senior Lecturer in Human Geography in the School of Environment and Development, University of Manchester. Prior to joining Manchester, he worked at the University of Munich, Germany, where he also obtained his PhD. Having held a visiting scholarship at the University of Hong Kong 2001–2002, he also spent three months in 2011 working as a visiting scholar at the International Labour Organization in Geneva.

Jennifer Johns is Senior Lecturer in International Business at the University of Liverpool Management School. She trained as an economic geographer, completing her PhD at the University of Manchester before moving to the University of Liverpool. Her research interests include the spatialities of international business, global production networks and the dynamics of industrial clustering.

Ziko Konwar is Lecturer in International Business at Sheffield Business School, Sheffield Hallam University. He has recently completed a PhD in international business from Bradford University. His research interests are in the assessment of productivity effects of knowledge transfer in MNC affiliates and the role of sub-national locations and institutional differences in FDI-mediated knowledge spillovers.

Palitha Konara is Lecturer in International Business at the University of Huddersfield Business School, UK, where he convenes an MSc in international business management and an MSc in international business with financial services. He holds a PhD from the University of York and a master of research degree in international business from the Lancaster University. His current research interests include investigating the determinants of foreign direct investment with special focus on language, human capital and political instability. His research also examines the impact of foreign direct investment on host economies and performance of foreign and local firms in host countries.

Olli Kuivalainen is Professor of International Marketing and Entrepreneurship in the School of Business at Lappeenranta University of Technology, Finland. His expertise covers broad areas of international business, entrepreneurship, marketing and technology management and their interfaces. Before joining academia Olli worked in a consultancy company. He has published in journals such as *Journal of World Business, Journal of International Marketing, International Business Review, Technovation, International Marketing Review, International Journal of Production Economics* and *Journal of International Entrepreneurship*.

Jorma Larimo is Full Professor of International Marketing at the Faculty of Business Studies, University of Vaasa, Finland and a part-time professor at the Faculty of Economics and Business Administration, University of Tartu, Estonia. He is the vice dean of the Faculty of Business Studies and director of the Doctoral School of the University of Vaasa. His main research areas are internationalization of SMEs, acquisition and international joint venture strategies and performance and entry and marketing strategies in CEE countries. He is an active member of several academic associations, and his research has been published in several edited books and international journals, including *Journal of Business Research, Journal of International Business Studies, Journal of*

International Marketing, Journal of World Business, International Business Review, Management International Review and *Journal of Global Marketing*.

Yong Kyu Lew is Assistant Professor of International Business and Strategy at Sejong University, Seoul, South Korea. He received his PhD from the University of Manchester. His research interests include inter-firm governance issues in strategic alliances, and capabilities and knowledge transfer in developing economies. His recent work has appeared in *Long Range Planning, International Business Review* and *Global Strategy Journal*.

Xiaohui Liu is Professor of International Business and Strategy at the School of Business and Economics, Loughborough University. She received her PhD from the University of Birmingham. Her main research interests include knowledge spillovers, human mobility, innovation and the internationalisation strategies of firms from emerging economies. She has published widely with publications in the *Journal of International Business Studies, Strategic Management Journal, Research Policy* and *Entrepreneurship Theory and Practice*, among others. She is senior editor of *Management and Organization Review* and advisory editor of *Research Policy*.

Brad MacKay is Professor of Strategic Management and head of the Strategy and International Business Group at the University of Edinburgh Business School. Brad previously held the post of assistant professor in the School of Management at the University of St Andrews. He has published in a range of journals, and he is an ESRC senior fellow in the Scotland Analysis programme.

Frank McDonald is Professor of International Business at the University of Liverpool, UK. His previous posts include Manchester Metropolitan University, University of Hull and the University of Bradford. Frank was chair of AIB UKI (2005 to 2008), and he is currently co-chair of the British Academy of Management Special Interest Group in International Business and International Management. He holds visiting appointments at Copenhagen Business School and ESC Rennes. He has published in the areas of MNC strategy and employee relations in multinational corporations in journals in international business, economic geography and HRM.

Huu Le Nguyen works as an assistant professor in the Department of Marketing, University of Vaasa, Finland. He is an active researcher in the field of international business. His research interests are strategic alliances and international joint ventures, conflict management in partnership, post-acquisition strategies, competitive strategies and strategies of firms in recession. He has presented papers at AIB, AOM, EURAM and IMDA. He has published articles in *International Journal of Business and Management, International Business Research, Transnational Management Journal*, and *Journal of General Management*, among others.

Jeong-Yang Park is Assistant Professor of International Business Strategy at Nottingham University Business School, University of Nottingham. She was awarded her PhD in management from the University of Edinburgh. Jeong-Yang also holds an MSc from Imperial College London and a BSc from University College London. Her current research is grounded principally in international strategic alliances and approaches to the internationalisation process.

Vijay Pereira is Senior Lecturer in International and Strategic HRM and Leader in Knowledge Services (Human Capital Development) at Portsmouth Business School, University of Portsmouth, UK. He has published in journals such as *Journal of World Business, International Studies of Management and Organization, Culture and Organisation* and *International Journal of Indian Culture and Business Administration*. He previously worked in consulting and industry. He is also the area/associate editor (OB/HRM) of *Journal of Asia Business Studies*.

Duncan Ross is Senior Lecturer in Economic and Social History at the University of Scotland. Duncan is an expert on Scottish economic history, including multinational corporations and FDI in Scotland and banking in Scotland. He was editor of *Financial History Review* (2004–2009) and has numerous publications in the areas of economic history in banking and of multinational corporations.

Alan Rugman was Professor of International Business and Head of International Business & Strategy at Henley Business School, University of Reading. Previously, he had held tenured appointments at the University of Oxford, Indiana University, and the University of Toronto and visiting appointments at Harvard University, Columbia Business School, UCLA and other leading universities in North America, Europe and Asia. Professor Rugman published numerous books and refereed articles examining the strategies and performance of the World's 500 largest multinational enterprises. He was also a consultant to leading MNEs, to the Canadian Government during the negotiations for NAFTA and to the United Nations.

Peter Scott is Senior Lecturer specialising in Employment Relations at Portsmouth Business School, University of Portsmouth, UK and has previously taught and researched at a number of UK universities. He has published in journals including *Industrial Relations Journal, Economic and Industrial Democracy* and *New Technology, Work and Employment*.

Vikrant Shirodkar is Lecturer in International Business at the University of Sussex School of Business and Management. He completed his PhD in Management at the University of Kent in 2012. He is mainly interested in the way the firm-level resources, institutions and external dependence conditions shape the strategies of foreign firms in the context of emerging economies (particularly India). His research examines the political strategies of multinational enterprises and foreign direct investment in the context of emerging economies.

Rudolf R. Sinkovics is Professor of International Business at Manchester Business School (MBS), where he is currently director of MBS-CIBER (Centre of International Business Research) and serves as director of research for MBS. He has previously held a number of visiting scholar positions, including at Michigan State University, and the University of Oklahoma, USA and at the University of Otago at Dunedin, New Zealand. He received his PhD from Vienna University of Economics and Business (WU-Wien), Austria.

Chengang Wang is Senior lecturer in the School of Management, Bradford University. His main research is in the areas of foreign direct investment, international trade and economic development. His research has appeared in academic journals including *British Journal of Management*, *Cambridge Journal of Economics*, *Journal of International Business Studies* and *World Development*.

Yi Wang is a postdoctoral researcher in International Marketing at the Faculty of Business Studies, University of Vaasa, Finland. His research interests focus on FDI entry mode strategy and survival of foreign subsidiaries operating in China. His research has been published in *Journal of Global Marketing*.

Yingqi Wei is Professor of International Business at Leeds University Business School, University of Leeds, UK. Her main research areas are foreign direct investment (FDI), international trade and economic development, with a focus on the determinants and impact of inward FDI in China and the internationalization of Chinese firms. Yingqi has published in various journals, including *Journal of International Business Studies*. She is also a recipient of best paper award in Academy of International Business (UK & Ireland) conference, Academy of Marketing conference and International Journal of the Economics of Business.

Stephen Young is Professor of International Business at the University of Glasgow. He has previously held posts at the University of Paisley and at Strathclyde University. He has had visiting appointments at Louisiana State University, the University of Texas and Georgetown University. He has been an adviser with UNCTAD, OECD, ILO and the US Department of Commerce and a specialist adviser to two UK House of Commons Select Committees on Inward and Outward Investment, and was a founder member of the High Council for Foreign Direct Investment in Portugal. Stephen has published widely in leading journals on topics connected to international business and international economics.

Huan Zou is Senior Lecturer in International Management at the Department of Financial & Management Studies, SOAS. She received her PhD from Manchester University. Her research focuses on mainly international market entry strategies, international acquisitions, international entrepreneurship and venture capital in emerging markets. She has published widely with publications in *International Journal of Research in Marketing, International Business Review, Journal of World Business, Management International Review, International Marketing Review* and *Asia Pacific Journal of Management*.

Introduction: The Rise of Multinationals from Emerging Economies – Achieving a New Balance

Palitha Konara, Yoo Jung Ha, Frank McDonald and Yingqi Wei

The spread of particularly American multinational enterprises (MNEs) in the first half of the last century marked an increasing domination of the world economy by these firms. In the second half of the twentieth-century the dominance of American firms was challenged by a wave of MNEs from Europe, Japan and Newly Industrialised Economies. At the turn of the century it is, however, a group of rather 'unexpected' firms, such as Embraer, Huawei and Tata, from emerging economies that have stamped their mark on the world stage. Since then more MNEs from emerging economies are joining their ranks. The rise of emerging economy MNEs (EMNEs) has coincided with a shift in many aspects of production from industrialised countries to emerging economies and the accelerating dispersion of international R&D activities. In some emerging economies, this process is accompanied by the rise of a type of state capitalism. These changes pose challenges and bring opportunities for all participants in international business, including EMNEs themselves, developed economy MNEs (DMNEs), governments and multilateral organisations such as the World Trade Organization (WTO).

The prominence of emerging economies has altered the current balance in international business activities. The characteristics of emerging economies, such as institutional systems and factor market conditions, have influenced the scope of strategic options of these EMNEs (Hoskisson, et al, 2013; Lu, et al, 2014; Meyer, et al, 2009). For DMNEs, emerging economies pose various challenges, including escalating rivalry and high volatility requiring DMNEs to innovate their business models to capture new market opportunities that emerging economies offer (Hoskisson, Eden, Lau, Wright, 2000; Ramamurti, 2012; Tan, Litschert, 1994). There is a dynamic co-evolutionary path between DMNEs and the external environment in emerging economies. Foreign MNEs operating in emerging economies influence business practices of firms and entrepreneurs in the host country and initiate dynamic co-learning processes even before they enter into competition in the global markets (Beamish and Berdrow, 2003; Cantwell, et al, 2010; McKelvey, 1999). Thus, the growing integration of emerging economies into the global economy has profound implications for the strategies and operations of both DMNEs and EMNEs. Moreover, the ways MNEs react and contribute to the development of this new global environment exercise significant influence in the development of the home bases of both DMNEs and EMNEs.

The aim of this book is to enhance our understanding of the changing international landscape and the implications for the world economy in general and for EMNEs and DMNEs, national governments and multilateral organisations. A number of important questions arise from these new developments. Does the balance of power change between rising EMNEs and established DMNEs in areas such as positions in the value chain and centres of R&D and innovation? Do the types of relationships emerging between governments and businesses lead to excessive state involvement in the development of EMNEs? Do EMNEs have significantly different strategic and operational orientations from DMNEs? How will EMNEs affect the strategies and operations of DMNEs? Are there significant implications of these developments for international business theories and concepts? This book examines some of these issues.

This volume contains selected research papers presented at the 41st Academy of International Business (UK & Ireland) Conference held at the University of York in April 2013. Part I of the book consists of three chapters based on the keynote speeches and two special panels. Chapter 1 provides records of the keynote speeches given by Peter Buckley and Jean-François Hennart. Buckley discusses how some of the methods used by historians are important and relevant to international business research. It is followed by Hennart, who critically reviews the current literature about the rise of EMNEs and discusses why not all EMNEs are resource-poor. Chapter 2 contains summaries of presentations by experts on the implications for international business of separatist movements using Scottish independence as an example. Chapter 3 is a record of a panel session on developments in international business and economic geography.

The remainder of the volume focuses on key issues connected to the central themes of the conference. The topics covered in three sections consider major aspects of the new balance in international business: 1) the driving force of success and failure of EMNEs; 2) the survival (performance) strategies of DMNEs in emerging economies; 3) the influence of the presence of foreign operation on local firms and entrepreneurs in the emerging economies.

The chapters in Part II focus on the salient role of home or host countries' institutional factors as well as firm-level factors in the internationalisation of EMNEs. In Chapter 4, Matthew Allen and Maria Allen examine the role of institutions in both home and host countries in shaping the patterns of investments by EMNEs. Based on the analysis of company, industry association and government documents as well as newspaper and analysts' reports, they illustrate how German institutions, particularly political authorities' financial support, influence the emergence and development of firms in new industries, and the potential sale of those companies to overseas rivals, including those from emerging economies. The chapter emphasises the role of host country and home country institutions in shaping the development of EMNEs by examining how support from home country institutions and specific host country conditions enables foreign firms to acquire German solar PV firms that have superior technological capabilities. Their analysis, which draws on the resource-based view of the firm as well as comparative institutional analysis, therefore helps to account for the uneven geographical spread of organisational capabilities as well as the expansion patterns of EMNEs.

In Chapter 5, Pereira and Scott investigate the evolution of indigenous and overseas influences upon the internal human resource management (HRM) practices of Indian-owned MNEs, using a longitudinal qualitative case study of a major human resource offshore outsourcing firm. Pereira and Scott identify four main drivers of HRM change operating over three temporal phases. According to this research, indigenous influences on HRM have some resilience, but they gradually transform through absorption of certain Western 'high performance' techniques to synthesise progressively a 'cross-vergent' human resource regime, subsequently re-exported throughout the firm. Such hybrid HRM regimes are increasingly synchronised with distinct business strategies underpinned by growth and internationalisation of the firm, so 'Westernisation' or 'Indianisation' alone are unlikely to triumph.

In Chapter 6, Amankwah-Amoah examines how domestic support can become a source of liability. By considering a plethora of research examining the benefits of government support for state-owned enterprises (SOEs), the research emphasises that existing literature has failed to recognise how domestic support can become a liability. In the chapter, a novel concept of 'the liability of domestic support' is developed to articulate how government support for SOEs can create conditions for business failure to occur. By analysing the cases of Air Afrique, Nigeria Airways and Ghana Airways, the research identifies factors which helped to create the conditions that allowed inefficiencies, mediocrity and incompetence inherent in SOEs to thrive, which ultimately led to their respective demises.

Part III deals with the topics of survival (performance) strategies of DMNEs in emerging economies. In Chapter 7, Wang and Larimo examine the survival of subsidiaries established by Nordic MNEs in China. Wang and Larimo develop their hypotheses based on transaction cost economics and resource-based and institution-based views. Using 405 subsidiaries established in China by Nordic MNEs in the period of 1982–2012, the results indicate that the host country experience, firm size, industry growth in the number of firms and the later stage of institutional transitions are positively associated with subsidiary survival. Furthermore, the degree of product diversification is negatively related with subsidiary survival. The findings further point out the positive interaction between R&D intensity and degree of product diversification with subsidiary survival.

In Chapter 8, Nguyen, Larimo and Ali assess how control position strategy of MNEs and cultural distance between international joint venture (IJV) partners influence the selection of conflict resolution strategies (CRS) of MNEs in their attempt to solve conflicts with their local partners. Furthermore, they investigate the relationship between different CRS of MNEs and the performance of IJVs. The empirical evidence, based on a survey of 89 Nordic MNEs, shows that there are strong links between control position strategies of MNEs and the selection of their CRS. The strategies selected, in turn, have strong influence on IJV performance. The findings further reveal inter-action effects relating to cultural distance between partners, control strategies of MNEs and CRS. They conclude their chapter with theoretical and managerial implications and propose new opportunities for further research of CRS in IJVs.

In Chapter 9, Shirodkar investigates the determinants of MNEs' collective action in India. Using resource dependence theory and notions of path dependence, this chapter attempts to explain that two factors – (1) the crit-icality of locally available resources and (2) the strong local business ties/networks – are important determinants of MNEs' collective action in emerging economies. The tests of the hypotheses use a sample of 105 foreign-owned subsidiaries in India. The results indicate that MNEs that depend on local resources and those that have developed strong local business ties are more active in collective action. The findings contribute to the factors that affect MNEs' political activities in emerging economies.

Part IV embraces the topics of dynamic interaction between foreign and local firms. In Chapter 10, Zou, Boocock and Liu explore how human capital affects entrepreneurs' responses to conflict. Adopting a qualitative analysis, this chapter integrates the human capital and conflict management literature to examine the factors that cause conflict in the entrepreneur-venture capit-alist (E-VC) relationship in China and to investigate how entrepreneurs with different degrees of human capital respond to conflict. The findings reveal that communication barriers and different goals and value systems are the main sources of conflict between Chinese entrepreneurs and foreign VCs. They further show that entrepreneurs with start-up experience are more likely to adopt collaborative and competing strategies, and hence, they have a more positive and productive attitude towards conflict with VCs. Inexperienced entrepreneurs, however, tend to use passive accommodating and avoiding approaches that create problems in the E-VC relationship.

In Chapter 11, Park, Ha and Lew explore the conditions under which IJVs can develop joint absorptive capacity across foreign and local parents. They identify inter-organisational learning processes for co-learning and an iterative feedback system for dynamic learning, and they show how both can lead to the creation of joint absorptive capacity. Fine-grained documentation of processes of dynamic co-learning establishes how IJVs avoid unplanned, premature termination and co-create knowledge on a sustainable basis. Overall, they show that IJVs that implement dynamic co-learning can shape the co-evolutionary path of foreign and local firms before they go on to compete in broader global markets.

In Chapter 12, Evers, Kuivalainen and Andersson examine how the nature of the industry, or the industrial environment in which the firm operates, can affect the internationalisation of the new venture. They investigate the role of industry influences in terms of geographical scope, entry strategy and inter-nationalisation speed. The chapter presents some insights into the industry idiosyncrasies and international new ventures (INVs) and a conceptual framework identifying key industry variables to aid further examination of the role of industry factors on INV internationalisation processes and strategies. Thereafter, by formulating propositions on how industry specifically affects the internationalisation process of the INVs, they provide a platform for further studies in the domain of international entrepreneurship.

In Chapter 13, Konwar, McDonald, Wang and Wei consider the effects of foreign ownership mode on FDI spillovers in India. Unlike previous studies, the chapter examines all of the major forms of foreign ownership and uses an improved system to define ownership. Furthermore, by using a dataset of large firms, they reduce the problems of capturing the influence of the absorptive capacity of domestic firms on spillovers. This study provides an improved way, from that used in previous studies, of identifying the effects of ownership on spillovers, and it finds evidence that majority owned joint ventures and wholly owned subsidiaries result in positive spillovers, but minority joint ventures do not. A conceptual framework provides an outline of the key processes at work in generating spillovers under different foreign ownership modes. The chapter draws some policy implications for emerging economies from the results.

In conclusion, this book offers some insights at the new balance, namely the rising power of EMNEs, the need for novel approaches by DMNEs to retain competitive advantages and the co-evolutionary process in which MNEs interact with external environments to produce forces driving significant changes to the global economy.

References

Beamish, P., Berdrow, I. (2003) 'Learning From IJVs: The Unintended Outcome'. *Long Range Planning*, 36(3), 285–303.

Cantwell, J., Dunning, J.H., Lundan, S.M. (2010) 'An evolutionary approach to understanding international business activity: The co-evolution of MNEs and the institutional environment'. *Journal of International Business Studies*, 41(4), 567–586.

Hoskisson, R.E., Eden, L., Lau, C.M., Wright, M. (2000) 'Strategy in Emerging Economies'. *Academy of Management Journal*, 43(3), 249–267.

Hoskisson, R.E., Wright, M., Filatotchev, I., Peng, M.W. (2013) 'Emerging Multinationals from Mid-Range Economies: The Influence of Institutions and Factor Markets'. *Journal of Management Studies*, 50(7), 1295–1321.

Lu, J., Liu, X., Wright, M., Filatotchev, I. (2014) 'International experience and FDI location choices of Chinese firms: The moderating effects of home country government support and host country institutions'. *Journal of International Business Studies*, 45(4), 428–449.

McKelvey, B. (1999) 'Avoiding Complexity Catastrophe in Coevolutionary Pockets: Strategies for Rugged Landscapes'. *Organization Science*, 10(3), 294–321.

Meyer, K.E., Estrin, S., Bhaumik, S.K., Peng, M.W. (2009) 'Institutions, resources, and entry strategies in emerging economies'. *Strategic Management Journal*, 30(1), 61–80.

Ramamurti, R. (2012) 'Competing with emerging market multinationals'. *Business Horizons*, 55(3), 241–249.

Tan, J., Litschert, R.J. (1994) 'Environment-strategy relationship and its performance implications: An empirical study of Chinese electronics industry'. *Strategic Management Journal*, 15(1), 1–20.

Part I
Keynotes and Panel Sessions

1
Keynotes

Peter Buckley and Jean-François Hennart

This chapter presents the keynote speeches delivered by Peter Buckley (University of Leeds) and Jean-François Hennart (University of Tilburg) in the Academy of International Business, UK & Ireland Chapter Annual Conference in April 2014. The session was chaired by Yingqi Wei (University of Leeds) (co-chair of the conference).[1]

Buckley on 'historical research methods in international business'

Good morning, it is a particular pleasure for me to be here because I am a graduate of York University. It is also appropriate that I am talking about historical research methods because of course I did my degree a long time ago. When I was here last time, I went to look for the university that I knew and it is buried in a much bigger institution, but it is a pleasure to be here and at the annual conference of AIB UKI. I am talking today about something rather different, or something completely different, as Monty Python might say: Historical Research Methods in International Business.[2]

I've always had an interest in history, and I read a lot of history, which shows what a sad individual I am. It occurred to me that the methods that history used and the methods that international business use have a lot in common and I was looking for issues that are relevant and where we can draw from what historians have done. History and international business are very different subjects as we will see, but what I am trying to do is to look at the parts of historical research and the methods of historical research that can be relevant to international business. So, I thought I would start off on a really positive note! Here is one from Kogut and Rangin (2006): 'For the general public methodological discussions are tedious. Worse – methodologists often render interesting topics into lifeless entities'. So, I propose to give a really tedious talk and make it as lifeless as possible![3]

Just to mention a few points about the kind of philosophy that underlies the way that historians approach research. Historians (and international business scholars) have very different views (on some key concepts), especially about causation. Historians and social scientists including international business take very different views about causation, such as what is endogenous and what are the dependent and independent variables. And the whole approach of history is actually very different as we will see.

One of the phrases that is used of historical research methods is the difference between 'cartography' where you are trying to be very precise and produce a precise map of history and what happened, versus 'landscape painting' where you are trying to give a general overall impression of what happened and trying to obtain a picture of the reality, in the way that an artist sees a landscape. Here you can see the difference of approaches that historians take. Some historians want to be very precise and measure things as we will see. Cliometrics and economic histories are of this type. Other historians want to give an overview and insight – and sometimes an idiosyncratic insight.

Path dependency is a very important issue for both historians and international business scholars. A lot of people have written about path dependency, and this is one of the areas of very deep water that I find myself getting into. There are lots of really important things being written on path dependency with equations that take up pages about how sensitive events are to initial conditions and what makes the difference.

The final thing is propulsion and periodisation – that can be translated as what leads to growth and how we decide particular époques, how do we put things in different periods, which is very important to historians in defining themselves. So, those are some of the underlying philosophical issues that arise with regard to both history and international business.

I wish to focus on some of the methods of history that I think are important to international business. I hope it is relevant to our own work in international business. I will focus on sources and analysis of texts, time series analyses, comparative methods, counterfactual analysis, the unit of analysis and finally one which is a bit of a catchall – history, biography and the social sciences, which is about the relationship between individuals and wider causes. I think all of these issues from (the discipline of) history have relevance to international business.

The first point is *the sources and analysis* of texts. When historians think about text, not only are they necessarily talking about a written piece of information. They could also be considering oral history, about the way people explain their lives or the issue that we are talking about and on how reliable are eyewitness accounts. Historians have spent a lot of time on this because there are stories, particularly of battles, where an individual was involved in a battle. We might think the best way of explaining a battle is to go to and see what an individual thought about that battle. It doesn't need much imagination to see that an individual in a battle may be one of the worst people to explain what happened because the fog of war may make their record of the battle not be relevant to the overall issues of how the battle was fought. Is that at all relevant to the way that we international business scholars look at how managers view the battles they are part of? Does a manager see the whole of a battle? Do we often take a manager to be all-thinking and all-seeing and take their word as given? Is that right? We may also consider artefacts – the Bayeux Tapestry is one of the best sources about the conquest by William the Conqueror over Harold, so we have got a wide range of sources that we could use to consider big defining events.[4] Do we in international business necessarily always use all possible sources including artefacts, and, if we do, how much authority do we give to them? Should we be investing in these 'artefacts' sources that we use – interviews of managers, texts of managers, company reports, whatever we call them with authority? Historians ask questions of their artefacts – what is their provenance, and how internally reliable are they? Do international business researchers always ask these types of questions of the 'artefacts' that they use in their research? Typically, historians will ask of a text some key questions. When was it written or produced? Where was it written or produced? By whom? What pre-existing material was there? Has it got integrity? Has it got credibility? And I have added one, which is the translation issue. When we translate as we do in international business, how reliable is the translation? So, we have a whole set of questions. When we approach evidence, when we present evidence, are we as rigorous as we should be in asking all those questions of the evidence that we get? And finally what about the material that is not in archives? If we are business historians, as some of us in this room are, we could look at the archive. (For example,) we could look at the archive of Marks & Spencer's on Leeds University campus. We could go into the archives, but of the materials that are included in the archive, how much of them depict the whole of the story? There has been a lot of work done in history on what has been called 'subaltern studies'. When you look at the story of India, for example, who wrote that story? The Raj, or the British essentially wrote the story of India but they only wrote certain Indians into the story and others were left out. So historians have spent time trying to look for evidence that is outside the archive as a criticism, as a counterweight. Perhaps we in international business should be doing that as well.

Time series analysis: there is a whole lot to say about this, but I have time for only a brief overview of this complex issue. Of course, historical variation is one of the most important things in international business. There have been stacks of articles in, for example, Journal of International Business Studies (JIBS) about endogeneity, methods from history, economic history, computerable general equilibrium models, longitudinal qualitative research and all methods on which we could draw. There is an interesting quote from British philosopher and historian Isaiah Berlin: 'history details differences amongst events, sciences focus on similarities'. We are often looking for regularities. However, there is an argument that perhaps it is the differences, the outliers, the non-standard things that we should also be looking at. My argument would be we should pay a lot of attention to the way historians have dealt with differences between events in the past.

Comparative methods are absolutely central to international business. The very word 'international' means 'comparative', you are comparing nations in this case. Nations are not always the right measurement as we will see in a minute. There are three key measures that we can take – all of which are used in history. The first comparative method includes the comparison across space – for example, to compare the IBM subsidiary in America with its subsidiary in India at a point in time. Then there are comparisons over time, so that we may look at the growth/decline in IBM's subsidiaries in different locations over time. Finally, there is the counterfactual, controversial issue of asking 'what if?' What if IBM had not done certain things? What if Tata had not bought Land Rover? So, the issues of comparison across space and over time and counterfactual comparisons are absolutely central to international business studies.

The second comparative method is natural experiments, where we can actually look at a situation where the experiment has occurred in the real world. One of the classic examples of this was a study by Kogut and Zander of the Zeiss company. Zeiss, a German company, was split in two by the Iron Curtain. So, you can compare Zeiss in East Germany with Zeiss in West Germany, and we have a natural experiment where there is the same starting point, the same company in a different context. It would be absolutely wonderful if you could find examples of those kinds of real world examples – of a company with the same starting point but with some sort of a split that leads to different trajectories from the starting point. Normally, international business scholars will compare subsidiaries in different countries and hold constant a lot of the things that are likely to affect subsidiary behaviour and outcomes. This is statistical control rather than experimental control. Typically, international business scholars use statistical control. We measure things via statistics, but experimental control is a more rigorous and sometimes more revealing method of controlling for different conditions. We cannot always use the experimental method but, where we can, we can have different means of controlling for other factors likely to affect behaviour and/or outcomes.

The final thing is about qualitative comparison. This comes from an ancient British genius named George Boole, who invented this way of thinking about comparison.[5] So let's say we have the argument that there are three causes leading to an effect. Let's say we are going to argue that Japan developed rapidly because it had business groups, company unions and the zaibatsu system. How

Table 1.1 Truth table for a three cause proposition

Condition			Outcome
A	B	C	1 or 0
0	0	0	0
0	0	1	?
0	1	0	?
1	0	0	?
1	1	0	?
1	0	1	?
0	1	1	?
1	1	1	1

do we prove this? Let's see Table 1.1. We need cases where one or two of those things are relevant. If none of them are relevant, we need a case where none of them occur and presumably the outcome is zero. Indeed, we actually need eight cases to be able to show that these three events were the reason for the outcome. So, if the outcome is one, the three events are on the bottom line and we need that whole array. That helps us in designing case studies. I often get this question: how many case studies do I need? How many students have come and asked you that? Well, here is a possible answer. If you have got three causes, you need eight cases with all those different factors. So, you don't have to do thousands and thousands of cases. If you can choose your eight cases, you have got a case for your argument.

Now I would like to move on to *counterfactual analysis*, the 'what if' question. This is another area where I rather fell into a big argument. There is a book called *Archduke Franz Ferdinand Lives! A World without World War I.*[6] This is a counterfactual history. It is an attempt to work out what would have happened if the bullet had missed him (Archduke Franz Ferdinand) in Sarajevo. World War I would not have happened. If World War II would not have happened, Hitler would not have controlled the Third Reich and the Holocaust would not have happened and so on. Here is another book that criticises counterfactual history – it is called *Altered Pasts: The Counterfactuals in History.*[7] The book has the image of an astronaut on the moon and the Chinese flag on his right side. So, what would have happened if China had landed on the moon, not America? Counterfactual history can be absurd as, for example, Niall Ferguson's recent BBC programme on what would have happened if Britain had not entered World War I. There are also all kinds of issues raised in counterfactual history about the role of individual agency and about the deep causes of large and significant events. There are, however, some less ambitious attempts in business history to look at the historical alternatives approach: The argument, for example, that technological determinism may not be as strong as business historians typically take it to be. For those of us who are fairly long in the tooth, we can remember the alternative position, the argument about what would have happened if a firm from country A had not invested in country B. There is a lot of work on that, and this goes back to Fogel's analysis of American railways where he was asking the questions about what would have happened if the American railways had not been built, whether growth would have been as fast, and so on.[8] What Fogel did was to specify an alternative where a system of canals did the work that was actually done by the railways. Another wonderful attempt at doing this is Mark Casson's alternative railway system for the UK, complete with timetable. This is not about imagining lots of changes. It is actually using an alternative by more carefully specifying what did happen, and I think that is far more acceptable than the rather wild assertions of alternative history based on grand and sweeping generalisations, which is common in much of literature on contemporary history.

Let me consider next the issue of *the unit of analysis*. We have huge issues in international business about the unit of analysis. So do historians. Historians have looked at all kinds of different levels global history, national history, and so on. A relatively recent fashion is micro-history, looking at very small units, peasant communities and small communities to try to look at what happened to them and to create the sort of total history on a micro scale. We have exactly the same type of problems. The list here is actually from a paper I did with Don Lessard from MIT Sloan School of Management. We looked at different levels of analysis: manager, subsidiary, firm, economy, region, world economy and we might add to that the network and the value chain. If we are looking at one of those levels, how do we control for the others, how do we look at interactions, and what is the right level to look at the causation we are searching for? These are really important questions in specifying a setup of research and a doctoral thesis.

Another unit of analysis issue links somewhat to the *what if* thing because the what if thing is often about a great man, it usually is a man, it's not very often a woman, a great man, say Napoleon. What would have happened if Napoleon had lost? What would have happened if Franz Ferdinand had not been shot? Historians tend to attribute a great deal to individual agency. International business scholars have the same tendency. We have a tradition of attributing things to heroic businesspeople. Richard Branson comes to mind. This raises the question – what is the role of individual agency versus underlying forces? A very profound and a very important question. I could not resist this one: An example of the best of the best. This is from a sports history showing just how incredible some individuals are in the arena of sport. Some people will make the argument it is just the same in business: there are some people who are so much better than everybody else. I am not sure I believe it, but I am going to put forth the argument that some people are so much better than everybody else that they really change things. That score of Bradman is unbelievable,

4.4 standard deviations above the mean of test cricket as batsmen![9] That is phenomenal. Of course, it is an accident of history that Bradman was not an Englishman, but accidents do happen. So, what is the independent variable? Is it individuals who make a difference? How do we specify the independent variable? If we have very sensitive dependence on initial conditions, maybe individuals can and do make a difference. I think that there is a lot more to say about this issue of the role of the individual agent in outcomes, and perhaps international business scholars should more adequately address this issue.

Finally, I think the longer I have explored history the less satisfied I become about many things in our approaches in international business. We need to give greater consideration to a number of factors, and we can learn from historians. We need a critical approach to text and all our sources. We need to think about the roles of contingency, choice and agency. We need to look at the interaction of history and geography because context is absolutely crucial for both international business and history. There is a different debate about the role of history and international business and influence in policy. Both communities think they have got a problem in having sufficient influence on policy. We might think about why that is, especially with the growing implications of research for impact on policy makers. This issue, however, requires more time than we have available in this session, but this issue does need to be addressed. I finish by returning to Kogut. Remember that quote form him at the beginning of my talk, about how dull and boring this was going to be. I hope it has not been quite that bad. Here's another quote from Kogut: 'It is one of the best kept secrets of research that a methodological contribution is the most powerful engine for the replication and diffusion of an idea'.[10] If there is any truth in that, I recommend that you look at historical methods. Thank you.

Hennart on 'why the OLI paradigm cannot explain the rise of emerging market multinationals?'

I am not going to talk about historical methods. I guess this is clear to everybody. I am going to talk about the future. I am going to talk about emerging market multinationals (EMMs). Especially, I am going to talk about the contrast or contradiction between the rise of EMMs and some of the most established theories in international business. I decided as I was coming to the UK that I should talk about Dunning's Ownership, Location, Internalisation (OLI) paradigm (Dunning and Lundan, 2008). Basically what I want to ask is how does one explain foreign direct investment by EMMs and what can we say about it. Do we have a theory that actually can predict the future of EMMs? Why do they exist and what is likely to be their position in the next 20 years? By emerging market multinationals I mean firms which are based in what we call the emerging markets, and that is the BRICS and VISTA countries.[11]

Three main types of investment are made by EMMs. Two of them can be explained rather easily by extant theories, such as the transaction cost theory of the multinational enterprise (Hennart, 1982). One of the types of investments they make is natural resource acquisition, and we can explain such investment by the fact that they are developing very rapidly, and they need natural resources; and some of those natural resources they cannot obtain through market processes or long-term contracts. The other type of investment that EMMs make is in the servicing of their exports, and here again we can explain such investments by the fact that they cannot rely on independent distributors and therefore must integrate vertically to service their exports effectively. I think those investments are pretty easy to understand. What is less easy to understand, especially given the theories that we have and especially given OLI theory, is the fact that they make investments in developed markets, which take the form of acquisition of technology-intensive firms and of the setting up of greenfield R&D subsidiaries. I will explain in a minute why this is a bit puzzling given most existing theories of international business.

First of all, let me have a quick refresher of OLI theory, and I want to point out one particular aspect of OLI theory, which I think has not been very well understood. The OLI theory is, I think, a very intuitive theory. It basically says that for firms based in one country to undertake value-adding activities in another country, there must be three conditions. The first condition is that the firm that makes the investment must have some kind of strong ownership advantages, or firm-specific advantages (FSAs). Typically, those are thought to be intangibles, new technologies, new trade names, reputation. Such advantages could actually be incorporated into exports, and this actually would not lead to foreign direct investment. Hence the second condition, for foreign direct investment is that these intangibles must be bundled with factors of production located outside the country of the innovator. So, we have what are called location advantages, or country-specific advantages (CSAs). Here we are talking about natural resources, a customer base and other types of location-based advantages – for example, R&D spillovers. Now this actually leads to a firm locating activities outside its home country, which incorporate intangible resources. The first two conditions are compatible with the possibility that the innovator franchises or licenses to a local producer. The third condition for foreign direct investment that has direct ownership of some kind is that those intangibles must be internalised. So there are three conditions for a firm that's based in one country to own value-adding activities in another country to serve customers in that country or to serve customers in another country.

Now, it is generally understood by most people that EMMs have very weak technological advantages and very weak brands. When I show pictures of brands owned by EMMs and I ask the audience to which company they belong, most of the time people do not know. They say they have no idea. Even in countries such as the US, you show them, for example, the logo of Baidu, and they will not know this company, even though it has by far the largest market share for search engines in China. If you show them a picture of the Flying Pigeon logo, they basically draw a blank.[12] So clearly, those firms do not have strong O advantages (strong FSAs). Here is a sample of some of the writings of some of the major authors who have talked about EMMs: Mathews (2006) says they are 'resource poor', Luo and Tung (2007) write that they are 'at a competitive disadvantage', and for Rugman (2009) they have 'not developed sustainable firm-specific advantages'. So all these authors agree that EMMs do not have strong FSAs. That is of course a bit of a problem because OLI theory states that O advantages, or FSAs, are a necessary condition for foreign direct investment. So, why then are EMMs investing abroad?

I think there are three types of explanation. The first one, which Alan Rugman has pioneered, is to say that EMMs are a flash in the pan. They are just supported by CSAs. However, CSAs, as I will explain in a minute, are actually hypothesized by OLI theory to be available to anybody operating in that particular market. The argument is that EMMs are also fuelled by easy credit, so they will disappear as emerging economies mature. Hence, Alan Rugman's question made in 2009: when will China generate its own world-class MNEs? The answer for Rugman is not for 10 or 20 years. The second explanation, which Alvaro Cuervo-Cazurra has pioneered, is that EMMs may not have traditional FSAs, but they have a particular type of FSAs. Cuervo-Cazurra has a piece on this in which he has a long list of very specific advantages owned by EMMs.[13] I do not want to go into details on this. To summarise, Cuervo-Cazurra says that EMMs know how to operate in an environment with weak institutions. I would add 'formal' to this because I do not think China or Brazil has weak institutions; they have weak formal institutions. In this view firms in emerging economies know how to operate in those environments, leading them to have advantages over developed market multinationals in their home markets. The third explanation is the one put forth by Mathews. He basically says we have to throw away OLI and replace it with LLL.[14] OLI is unable to account for EMMs because EMMs do not have the FSAs that the theory actually predicts. Mathews says EMMs are multinationals because they go abroad to acquire O advantages. That is basically what his LLL theory is about. They go abroad to acquire resources, not to exploit them.

I find all those explanations unsatisfactory. The Rugman's view – I think that EMMs have actually done well overseas and will continue to do well overseas. If you look – and I could go into great details and numbers – at firms like Huawei, Lenovo, Haier, those firms are actually doing well overseas. Haier is the largest producer of appliances in the world. Lenovo is the largest producer of computers in the world. If you look at firms like these, not only are they strong in their home market, but they are also very strong competitors internationally. The Cuervo-Cazurra explanation does not account for the fact that

EMMs not only invest in other emerging markets; they also invest successfully in developed markets. So, the advantages that they have are not only advantages which allow them to compete in their home market; they are also much more general advantages. The explanation by Mathews – well it is nice to say you go abroad to acquire advantages, but it is a bit like saying you join the Tour de France to learn how to ride a bicycle. The problem is, of course, while you are is busy learning through exploration, there are firms going for exploitation in your home market. So, it is a bit difficult to start learning while having to compete at the same time. If you do not know how to ride a bicycle, and you compete in Tour de France, you will crash before the end of the Tour. You will not be able to compete in these circumstances. I think this LLL theory sounds fine, but there is a big gap into it: how do EMMs manage to get the time, the space and the resources to be able to acquire competitive advantages?

My point here is that all of this misunderstanding comes from a particular feature of OLI theory. If you look carefully at OLI theory, it does not handle the O and the L advantages in a purely symmetrical way. The O advantages are actually firm specific. The L advantages are country specific, which means they are basically assumed to be available for everyone. As Dunning and Lundan (2008: 6) have written, 'L advantages are specific to a particular country while available to all firms' while Lessard and Lucea (2009) state that 'country-specific advantages [O advantages] are common to all firms located in a country'. So, L advantages in the OLI model are actually CSAs. They are not firm-specific advantages. They are available to anybody located in that country to acquire on an equal basis. This I think is the flaw in OLI theory. My point is that EMMs are not resource poor. They are only resource poor if you discount L advantages, but they do have privileged access to L advantages in their home locations. This gives them advantages that are possibly stronger than the O advantages. In other words, the control of L advantages is as strategic asset which may offset the lack of O advantages. In a full model, which I will call a bundling model, we need to model the transactional capabilities, or the transactional aspects, not only of O advantages but also of L advantages. We need therefore to treat O advantages and L advantages in a purely symmetrical way. When we do that, we come up with a totally different conclusion. I am therefore going to make the point that to produce in any market, you need to link O advantages, or FSAs, with L advantages, or CSAs. You need to merge imported intangibles with local assets. Local assets could be land, natural resources, access to customers, access to government permits, and so on. My point is that if you look at modes of entry, and if you look at owning equity, in other words who ends up owning the investment, the optimal outcome is one which maximises the rents available from bundling. How do firms maximise the rents available from bundling? Well, they minimise the cost of bundling the assets together. The assets that need to be bundled can be

		Knowledge held by the MNE	
		Easy to transfer	Difficult to transfer
Distribution held by local firm	Easy to transfer		3 MNE is sole residual claimant = wholly-owned affiliate of the MNE
	Difficult to transfer	2 Local firm steals, rents or buys knowledge from the MNE =: wholly-owned local firm	4 Joint venture between MNE and local firm

Figure 1.1 Optimal bundling in emerging market (e.g. China)
Source: Adapted from Hennart (2009).

traded on various markets: the market for assets, the market for the service of the assets and the markets for the firms in which the assets are embedded. The optimal outcome is the one that optimally minimises the cost of bundling those assets or maximises the rents of bundling them.

So, I propose a very simple model where I have two types of assets: technology as an intangible and access to distribution (Figure 1.1).

I assume that technology can either be traded on efficient markets or be traded on inefficient ones, depending on the characteristics of the technology. Distribution can also be traded on efficient markets or inefficient markets, depending on the characteristics of the distribution process. Bundling can be effected either through the market or through hierarchy – that is, it can be achieved by some type of equity arrangement. The rules for optimal bundling is that the party contributing the asset, or the capability, which is the hardest to measure – the hardest to control – should be the party owning the equity. Intuitively, you can see why this is the case. Assume, for example, that a firm requires two members, an innovator and a marketer. Assume that the innovation process is very specific, and you can easily control the innovator. The marketing aspect, however, is very creative; therefore, it cannot be easily controlled. Then the marketer should own the firm and hire the innovator. Assume the opposite – the innovating part of the business is creative and difficult to control, but the marketing side is routine, and it is easy to control. Then the innovator should own the firm and hire the marketer. If both are very difficult to monitor and control, they both should be co-owners of the firm. That is basically the intuition behind the model.

In terms of modes of entry, the issue is who owns the business. Here we are situated in an emerging market. Assume that we have two types of goods, or assets: knowledge held by the MNE and distribution held by the local firm in the emerging country. Knowledge can be easy or hard to transfer. By easy to transfer I do not mean appropriability. I mean that it is rather well protected by intellectual property rights and that it can it be easily licensed and therefore easy to transfer. If technology can be easily stolen, it is also easy to transfer. Difficult to transfer means it is tacit; it is not licensed; and it is not imitable. Consider, for example, distribution: it can be easily transferred, in the sense that there are many distributors available on the market, and they can be controlled easily by the manufacturer. Distribution can, however, be difficult to transfer. This is the case when it needs to be owned by the manufacturer or there are few possible existing distributors. The manufacturer may have to undertake distribution for some administrative or strategic reasons, but it may be difficult to actually implement an effective distribution network due to, for example, poor knowledge or access to important resources in the host location. That is what I mean by 'difficult to transfer'.

If you look at the OLI model, it considers only cases where local resources are easy to access, but the resources of the MNE are actually hard to transact. The internalisation condition means that the innovator must actually own the goods and services in which its innovation is embedded. So, in the OLI case we are only in the right end column of the 2x2 matrix of Figure 1.1. The knowledge held by the MNE is difficult to transfer, but all the local assets that you need to sell in the local market are actually available on an equal basis relative to local firms. In that case the MNE owns all the equity, and the only case that it ends up joint-venturing is when it considers it too costly or too risky to have full ownership. In my bundling model shown in Figure 1.1 on the other hand, the reason why the multinational needs to joint-venture is because it needs to give equity to the local firm to be able to access its distribution services. In this model there is actually a space for local firms because in the case where local assets are hard for the multinational to access but technology is easy for the local firm to access, you will have only local firms. In this model there is space for local firms alongside MNEs as well as a space for joint-ventures between local firms and multinational firms.

The bundling model (Figure 1.1) illustrates the challenges for MNEs and local firms.

The challenge for MNEs is to access local resources, which they can do either through greenfield investment or by acquiring existing local firms. The challenge for local firms is to access intangibles which are held outside the home

		Knowledge held by the MNE	
		Low bargaining power (many substitutes)	High bargaining power (few substitutes)
Distribution held by local owner	Low bargaining power (many subsitutes)	1. Consumers capture most of the value of the bundle	3. MNE captures most of the value of the bundle
	High bargaining power (few substitutes)	2. local firm captures most of the value of the bundle	4. MNE and local firm share the value of the bundle

Figure 1.2   Division of the gains of selling the bundle in an emerging market
Source: Adapted from Hennart (2012).

country. They will do this through many means, one of them of course being acquiring foreign firms and setting up of R&D labs in foreign countries. This can be considered as a giant bargaining game. The question becomes – who is likely to be in the best position in the quest for complementary resources, the local firm or the MNE? In this model it all hinges on the relative difficulty for local firms to acquire technology versus MNEs' ability to acquire complimentary local resources. In that game I will bet on the emerging market local firms as opposed to the multinational firms for reasons I will explain in a minute.

Emerging market firms are not resource poor. They are actually resource rich because their resource is the control of local assets which are difficult in many cases, not in all cases, of course, for MNEs to access. The OLI paradigm describes only one of the three cases of Figure 1.1 I have looked at. It is a special case where FSAs are difficult to transact because they are proprietary to the MNE, while local assets are easy to access. The implication of the model is that owners of local asset own equity wherever those assets are more difficult to access than knowledge and that they will access intangibles through foreign investment on international markets. This is one of the ways in which they acquire them, but not the only way. They will become foreign direct investors in only one specific case. They can acquire technology at home, for example, through joint-ventures with foreign firms in their own country. They also can acquire technology through contracts – that is, they can license it. They can also steal foreign technology. They will make foreign investments only when the technology is most efficiently acquired in a foreign location. Thus, foreign investments will occur when technology is strongly embedded in firms that are not located in their own country, when the labour that they need to hire for their R&D centres cannot be moved to your own country, or when externalities of research make it more efficient for them to locate their R&D subsidiary in a foreign country as opposed to at home.

In answer to the question I raised about why EMMs go abroad to acquire knowledge, the bundling model I have presented is compatible with Mathews' LLL model. There is, however, this question: can they actually afford those foreign direct investments? We have to look at who captures the gain of putting together the bundle of local assets and foreign assets in the foreign market. This is a straight bargaining game. The party who actually captures the gains of the bundle is the party whose own assets have fewer substitutes; it also happens to be the party who owns the equity. You can have a different matrix where you look at who is going to get the most value out of the bundle (Figure 1.2). You have to ask yourself, does the knowledge held by the MNE have many substitutes, in which case the MNE has low bargaining power? Or does it have few substitutes, in which case the MNE has high bargaining power? Then you can ask: does distribution – or any other local asset – have many substitutes, or does it have few substitutes? If it has many substitutes, then of course the local firm will have low bargaining power. If it has few substitutes, the local firm will have high bargaining power. When both part parties have low bargaining power, the consumer is the one getting most of the gains. When the MNE has high bargaining power – that is, when there are few substitutes for its technology – the MNE will capture most of the value of the bundle. When the local firm has assets which have few substitutes, then the local firm will capture most of the gains of the bundle. When both assets have few substitutes, then we have a typical joint-venture where the two parties, the MNE and the local firm, will actually share the gains from the bundle.

When do local owners of complementary assets have a strong bargaining power? There are many reasons why in many emerging markets local firms have monopolised the access to inputs. Just to take one example: in many countries where Roman law is the basis for the legal system, the state has the monopoly ownership of resources below the ground. Only in Anglo-Saxon law does the owner of land above ground also have the right to resources below the ground. In all Roman law countries, and that is all Latin America and all of Europe (except for the UK and Ireland), the state has the ownership of any sub-soil resources. This is a built-in monopoly, and of course, that also applies in previously communist countries. There are other reasons why local actors may have monopoly power. One of them of course is that local firms are incumbent, and in many emerging markets access to many local resources was denied to foreign investors until very recently. In China access to distribution was actually forbidden to foreigners until 1986; that is quite late in the game. Local firms actually did not wait for MNEs to line up distribution systems and to line up customers. Once there are established and strong distribution systems, buyer switching costs rise, and this leads to some measure of monopoly power. This will not last forever, but it is a first mover advantage in distribution, and it is a very powerful weapon. Does Microsoft offer the best software product in the world? I think we all will agree this is not the case. Does Microsoft have an overwhelming share of software in PCs? The answer is yes, because they were first. They monopolised access to software by preloading it into new computers. Once a firm has an installed base, it has very strong monopoly power.

An answer for MNEs that face distribution monopolised by local firms is to buy these local firms, be they either distributors or manufacturers that have integrated distribution systems. Therefore, MNEs can potentially jumpstart the process by acquiring existing local firms that control distribution. Unfortunately, in many emerging markets there are problems with making acquisitions because there are few firms to acquire, and governments often prevent MNEs from acquiring them. A third problem is that very often local firms are highly diversified and highly vertically integrated into assets which the MNE does not want. For example, in China many firms traditionally operated not only manufacturing plants but also dormitories, residences, and power plants because of inefficient markets. Many of these local firms are not specialised, in contrast to what you find in many Western countries where firms specialise, thereby allowing MNEs to buy exactly what they want. Making acquisitions in emerging markets, however, quite often involves acquiring of a bundle of assets that the MNE does not want, making it an unwieldy acquisition. I have called this the digestibility problem.

I also believe that the bargaining power of owners of FSAs, especially intangibles, is very rapidly declining. One reason for this is that in many emerging markets effective intellectual property protection is very weak. An example of this is Daewoo's Matiz car and the Cherry QQ (a Chinese car). They say you can take the door from a Matiz and put it on a QQ, they are so similar. There are many other examples of this type of problem with protection of intellectual property.

Catching up is not the same thing as innovating. People in the West are mistaken. They assume that EMMs must match the expenses and the trouble of innovating Western firms, but all that is needed is imitation; there is no need for innovation. With control of distribution, a firm can make a huge amount of money. All that is needed is to be as good as your competitors. Imitation costs about 60 per cent of innovation, so even if a firm starts from scratch they can imitate an existing innovation at 60 per cent of the cost, if not less. We need to be careful to not exaggerate the progress that an emerging market firm must have to make to be able to actually compete with a Western firm. No need for trial and error, they can actually start from scratch, which is a good advantage. Innovation in markets for technology is helped by codification. A good example of this is the mobile phone. By the beginning of this century, all the parts needed for a mobile phone had become available on world markets. All a firm needed to do was is to put them together. This allowed Chinese mobile handset makers to capture in 2003 fifty-five percent of the market for mobile phones in China. They were able to get local market share because they knew better what Chinese customers wanted (polyphonic ringtones, for example) (Zeng and Williamson, 2007).

It is possible to hire international specialists that have the benefit of expatri-ates who have been trained in Western countries free of charge. The people running Ali Baba started their career in Silicon Valley and moved back to China with ideas and training. There is an efficient market for corporate control in developed countries. There are very few restrictions on buying firms, so it is much more efficient for Chinese firms to acquire knowledge through acquisi-tions than it is for Western firms to acquire distribution through acquisitions of emerging market firms.

There is not a level playing field in this area. We do not have time to consider this in depth now, but I looked at cases written on emerging market firms – Huawei, Haier, and Bimbo – the latter a firm you probably do not know but which is the largest seller of baked goods in the world and is based in Mexico. There are other examples: Vale, formerly CVRD, a firm that extracts iron ore; Arçelik, a Turkish firm that makes white goods; and Lenovo, the Chinese computer manufacturer. In all cases I found that the firms got started by con-trolling distribution in their own market and got resources out of that; and with those resources they went on a buying spree and bought Western tech-nology to actually achieve parity in terms of technology. In the case of Lenovo, it based its power and its ability to gain resources and to finance foreign acqui-sitions, including the acquisition of IBM's PC division, on its dominance of the Chinese distribution network, and once it did that, it had money that it could then invest in acquiring state-of-the-art technology from the outside. We know they have contracts with human resource consultants and with adver-tising and design agencies, and of course they acquired the R&D labs of IBM's PC division.

The international oil industry provides a good example of the relative bargaining power of local firms vs. MNEs (Figure 1.3).

Here we have the benefit of a very long track record. There are two types of players in the oil industry: the majors and the national oil companies (NOCs). The NOCs control oil and gas deposits. What do the MNEs have? In theory they have control of technology. In fact, most of technology now is owned by the oilfield service firms. These firms will sell state-of-the-art technology. They sell to NOCs state-of-the-art technology which actually is better than the one that

		Knowledge held by MNEs	
		Easy to transfer	Difficult to transfer
Oil reserves held by local firms	Easy to transfer		3 MNE is sole residual claimant = wholly-owned affiliate of the Oil majors
	Difficult to transfer	2 Local firm steals, rents or buys knowledge from the MNE =: wholly-owned NOCs	4 Joint venture between oil major and NOC

Figure 1.3   Optimal bundling in an emerging market: the international oil industry

the major MNEs have. So, the major MNEs no longer own technology, because they no longer control the technology. Technology has now become highly competitive, but the ownership and the control of the oilfields remains in the hands of emerging market governments – of Saudi Arabia, of Iran, of Mexico, of Brazil. What is the result? The result is that while 85 per cent of oil and gas reserves were controlled by the oil major MNEs in the 1950s, today it is 10 per cent. Six of the ten largest oil and gas firms are now NOCs. In the case of the oil industry, the power has shifted from the Western MNEs to the local firms owning the natural resource. Location advantages have not made those local firms resource poor. Control of local resources has made those firms extremely rich, and this wealth allows them to acquire technology, which is now sold on a competitive basis worldwide.

My point is that control of local resources has in some cases, but not in all, allowed local firms to obtain the resources which they then have used to acquire technology from the outside. They have built a market base, and then from that they have been able to compete in world markets. We can see that very clearly in the case of Lenovo, first control of the domestic market and then access of state-of-the-art technology and now worldwide competition with Dell and Hewlett-Packard and others.

So, this is basically what I wanted to say. The picture I draw from this is much rosier for EMMs, but it is also much less rosy for Western MNE. Some of the arguments that I made today are in a paper that I published in the Global Strategy Journal in 2012.[15]

Notes

1. Footnotes are added by editors.
2. 'And now for something completely different' is a phrase used by British comedy group Monty Python, highlighting a major transition within the show.
3. Kogut, B., Rangin, C. (2006). 'Exploring complexity when diversity is limited: Institutional complementarity in theories of rule of law and national systems revisited'. *European Management Review*, 3(1), 44–59.
4. Bayeux Tapestry is an embroidered cloth which depicts the Norman conquest of England when in 1066 William the Conqueror defeated King Harold of England – one of the defining moments in English history.
5. Boole, G. (1854) *An Investigation of the Laws of Thought: On Which are Founded the Mathematical Theories of Logic and Probabilities.* London: Walton and Maberly.
6. Lebow, R. N. (2014) *Archduke Franz Ferdinand Lives! A World without World War.* Houndmills, Basingstoke: Palgrave Macmillan.
7. Evans, R. J. (2014) *Altered Pasts: Counterfactuals in History.* London: Little Brown.
8. Fogel, R. W. (1964) *Railroads and American Economic Growth: Essays in Economic History.* Baltimore: Johns Hopkins University Press.
9. Donald George Bradman (1908–2001), an Australian cricketer.
10. Kogut, B. (2009) 'Methodological contributions in international business and the direction of academic research activity'. In A. Rugman (Ed.). *Oxford Handbook of International Business* 2nd edition. London: Oxford University Press, p. 711.
11. VISTA countries are Vietnam, Indonesia, South Africa, Turkey, and Argentina. BRICS countries are Brazil, Russia, India, China.
12. Flying Pigeon is a Chinese bicycle company.
13. Cuervo-Cazurra, A. (2012) 'Extending theory by analyzing developing country multinational companies: Solving the Goldilocks debate'. *Global Strategy Journal*, 2(3), 153–167.
14. LLL is Linkage, Leverage and Learning. Mathews, J. A. (2006) 'Dragon multinationals: New players in the 21st century globalization'. *Asia Pacific Journal of Management*, 23, 5–27.
15. Hennart, J.-F. (2012) 'Emerging market multinationals and the theory of the multinational enterprise'. *Global Strategy Journal*, 2(3), 168–187.

References

Dunning, J. H., Lundan, S. M. (2008) *Multinational Enterprises and the Global Economy.* Cheltenham, UK: Edward Elgar.
Hennart, J.-F. (2012) 'Emerging market multinationals and the theory of the multinational enterprise'. *Global Strategy Journal*, 2(3), 168–187.
Hennart, J.-F. (2009) 'Down with MNE-centric theories! Market entry and expansion as the bundling of MNE and local assets'. *Journal of International Business Studies*, 40, 1432–1454.
Hennart, J.-F. (1982) *A Theory of Multinational Enterprise.* Ann Arbor: University of Michigan Press.
Lessard, D., Lucea, R. (2009) 'Mexican multinationals: Insights from CEMEX'. In R. Ramamurti and J. Singh (Eds). *Emerging Multinationals in Emerging Markets.* Cambridge: Cambridge University Press.

Luo, Y., Tung, R. (2007) 'International expansion of emerging market enterprises: A springboard perspective'. *Journal of International Business Studies*, 38, 481–498.

Mathews, J. (2006) 'Dragon multinationals: New players in 21st century globalization'. *Asia-Pacific Journal of Management*, 23, 5–27.

Rugman, A. M. (2009) 'Theoretical aspects of MNEs from emerging countries'. In R. Ramamurti and J. Singh (Eds). *Emerging Multinationals in Emerging Markets*. Cambridge: Cambridge University Press.

Zeng, M., Williamson, P. (2007) *Dragons at Your Door: How Chinese Cost Innovation is Disrupting Global Competition*. Boston: Harvard Business School Press.

2

Implications for International Business of Separatist Movements: The Case of Scottish Independence

Frank McDonald, Frank Barry, Nigel Driffield, Brad MacKay, Duncan Ross, Alan Rugman and Stephen Young

Introduction

In September 2014, the people of Scotland will vote in a referendum proposing that Scotland should become an independent country. If voters in Scotland accept the proposal, Scotland would become a new country. The White Paper containing the case for independence (Scottish Government, 2013) clearly states that an independent Scotland would continue to be an open economy. In these circumstances, foreign direct investment (FDI) both inward and outward, and foreign trade, would be central to the Scottish economy. In effect, a yes vote leads to the creation of a new small developed economy that is heavily integrated into the global economy. In different parts of the world, separatist movements are seeking to break away from the countries they currently are part of, for example, Wallonia and Flanders in Belgium, Catalonia, and the Basque Country in Spain, Quebec in Canada, various parts of Indonesia and in many other places. International business research has not investigated the implications for FDI and trade of the possibilities of successful separatist movements creating new small open economies. It is possible that a number of new small open economies could emerge in the coming years. There is research, but not much, on existing small open economies and FDI and trade (Barry and Kearney, 2006; Hooley et al, 1996). This work reveals that small open economies can prosper and attract considerable volumes of FDI that often stimulates exports. Membership of regional integration bodies (Buckley, et al, 2001) and the existence of exporting advantages, and/or rare and desirable resources (Gammelgaard, et al, 2009), may offset the disadvantages of smallness for integration into the global economy. The small amount of research on international business and small open economies cast some light on possible implications of successful separatist movements, but the implications of breaking away from larger economies and of creating and sustaining a successful small open economy are largely unknown.

The events leading up to the referendum in Scotland provide an opportunity to highlight some of the key issues on the implications for international business of separatist movements. Currently, there is very little published material on the implications of Scottish independence for international business activities (Young et al, 2014). At the suggestion of the Alan Rugman, the chairs of the Academy of International Business, UK & Ireland Chapter Annual Conference in April 2014 (Yingqi Wei, University of Leeds and Frank McDonald, University of Liverpool) arranged a special panel to discuss the international business implications of Scottish independence. The panel's members were Alan Rugman University of Reading), Frank Barry (Trinity College Dublin), Nigel Driffield (University of Aston), Brad MacKay (University of Edinburgh), and Stephen Young (University of Glasgow). This chapter offers the presentations given by the five speakers and concludes with a summary of the views presented by the speakers with some indications of the implications for international business of separatist movements.

Alan Rugman

I am qualified to give a talk on this subject because besides being born in England I am a Canadian citizen and was in Canada during the two votes on Quebec independence. I also wanted to reveal today that I grew up in Scotland and went to school there from the age of five to when I went to University. I was at Dumfries Academy most of that time. I wanted to point out the referendum question on the ballot only asks should Scotland be an independent country? This is not like the two ballots in Canada in 1980 and 1995. These referendums centred on sovereignty for Quebec and a negotiated association with the rest of Canada. The question is simply should Scotland be an independent country and my analysis is that the issues of association have been deliberately held off in the referendum question. The UK Government has agreed in the Edinburgh Declaration to a referendum. The UK Prime Minster David Cameron and the Scottish leader Alex Salmon issued a statement that states that if a majority of those who vote want Scotland to be independent, then Scotland will become an independent country after process of negotiations. There is therefore recognition that there will have to be negotiations in order to continue, some of the undoubted institutional benefits of being part of the UK in terms of international law especially. Following negotiations Scotland would leave the UK and become a new and separate state. Let me give you a short history of the two votes in Quebec. These were stand-up knockout fights, Pierre Elliot Trudeau was the Canadian Prime Minister, *René Lévesque* won a vote for a referendum in 1976, held in 1980. The referendum question centred on Quebec becoming a separate country, with its own laws and taxes and so on, but also that it would remain in association with Canada. This was to secure economic benefits such as, continue to use the Canadian currency, be in the Canadian Dollar Union, and use the same passports, and so on. Charismatic leaders on both sides debated the key issues, but the referendum was lost 60/40. The federal side kept pointing out that the negotiations would be difficult, pointing out that it would be difficult to have a Currency Union, certainly could not have a Canadian passport if Quebec were a separate country. In effect, the debate had many similarities to the issues debated in the Scottish referendum. I think the referendum was lost because of the perception of the costs of separation and the loss of the economic benefits. Jacques Parizeau, an International Business Professor from HEC, was the Premiere in 1995 for the second referendum and to his credit the referendum focused on, should Quebec become sovereign after having made a formal offer on a new economic and political partnership with the rest of Canada within the scope of the Bill? The Bill is about 500 pages long with key issues raised in detail; it was a kind of wish list of the Québécois to carry on the Currency Union, the common passport, and so on. Again, a prolonged debate provided the public with reasonable information on key issues about the association post-independence. This referendum was 50/50 only narrowly defeated mainly because the Prime Minister Jean Chrétien was not as charismatic as Trudeau and it was a kind of one-way fight. Parizeau was very clever, much like the current leader Alex Salmon in Scotland. In any event, the case for independence was lost, and now the issue is dead. There will not be another vote in Canada because Quebec has obtained most of what it wanted through what we would call devolution max. Quebec even has control over its immigration policy and pretty much has its own Consulates around the world. The key issue for Quebec is a desire for a distinct society that encompasses the benefits of association with the larger economy and society of Canada. This outcome displays a kind of angry emotional response to Canada's denying French-speaking people the rights they desired.

The point of this history for the current Scottish referendum is about the need for clarity about a post-independence association with the rest of the UK. Currently, I think the First Minster of Scotland is incredibly clever. He knows all about the Quebec–Canada story. I have colleagues who told me back in the 1990s that he was following things. The First Minster of Scotland expects negotiations to give them 10 per cent of the tax revenues as their share of UK tax, and about 80 per cent of the oil revenues. They would retain control over all sorts of infrastructure that currently Westminster owns; they would get rid of the nuclear base for Trident, and they wanted to have a Currency Union with the pound. The government in Westminster has said through the Treasury that a Currency Union is not possible, because Scotland would not be able as an independent country to operate its macroeconomic policies. Westminster would have to control those, and they are not willing to do this. There are therefore questions about key characteristics of an independent Scotland's association with the rest of the UK.

If we think about the key things that foreign investors need to know remembering that on the day of independence all firms in Scotland will become foreign firms, unless they are Scottish owned firms. On the day of independence, Scotland will not be in the WTO or the EU or part of the UK. Once we start looking at these things, we see the problems that Scotland faces in order to retain FDI and to avoid high political risk for foreign firms. Scotland hopes it can continue as a member of both the EU and WTO, but it would have to apply to both organizations. It looks like Spain would veto an application to the EU, at least once. It could apply to be in the World Trade Organization; it might well get in, but Russia did not get in for about 20 years. Scotland will also not be a member of the IMF: will it get IMF bailouts once it becomes a member, and so on? All of these issues will take time to resolve, so there is more than 18 months of problem solving for an independent Scotland. By definition, it would not be in the OECD, because these are the 35 largest economies; it would not be in the G7. These are all tricky areas, and it is therefore understandable why the pro-independence movement does not want to focus on these issues.

By law, the HQ of big banks would have to leave Scotland, the Royal Bank of Scotland and Lloyds have most of their assets not in Scotland, and they have to be headquartered in the regime where they have most of their assets. They would therefore have to leave Edinburgh. The insurance firms have been saying the same thing. Now you have had people from oil multinationals, which is the trump card that Scotland is supposed to have, saying they may also have to leave. If I were running a multinational oil firm, why would I be making more investments in this more risky environment? It seems that Scotland loses at least some the benefits of economic integration with the rest of the UK and with the EU. Scotland may eventually get some sort of miraculous Chinese-type benefits of owning its location country-specific advantages (CSA's), leading to firm-specific advantages (FSA), thus enabling it to attract and keep the sort of foreign firms that would promote economic development. Use can be made of the international production theory and the CSA/FSA model to analyse these issues, but I do not know how Scottish independence might generate production location advantages or CSA/FSA that would attract FDI and more importantly retain existing foreign investments.

What I am saying is that in International Business we should start using analysis such as international production theory and CSA/FSA models to examine the possible effects of Scottish independence. This is a rather different approach from what the UK Treasurer is putting out in terms of simple macroeconomics. Until, however, there is public discussion of the cost of losing at least some of the benefits of economic association it looks to me as if, if I were living in Scotland I would not have much difficulty voting yes. I would have great difficulty voting yes, if I knew the true economic costs. Thank you.

Frank Barry

I gave a paper last year on the topic looking at the broad aspects of Ireland's experience since independence but in thinking about this issue, I realise that independence both involves and necessitates a paradigm shift. Political independence has always been associated with an attempt to reduce economic dependency on the former colonial power or hegemonic power. That is the main feature of this talk. Initially in the postcolonial period, countries when they achieved independence – the US in 1776, Ireland in 1922, India in the 1940s and sub-Sahara Africa in the 1960s – tried to reduce economic dependency by turning protectionist. Obviously, protectionism ran out of stream everywhere. We live in a different world now. Globalisation is the name of the game that countries seeking independence face. Indigenous industries are typically restricted in terms of their ability to diversify export destinations because of transport and other distribution costs, so countries seek to develop export markets by inward investment. All countries around the world are clearly engaged in this, and I would like to talk about how the parameters of this game might change if Scotland did become independent.

An official policy statement from Ireland makes explicit the desire to reduce economic dependency on our former encompassing power: 'One of the central thrusts of Irish economic policy has been to reduce the country's trade dependence on the UK'. This statement is talking about Ireland's history within the EU: EU membership, support for the single market, for the single currency and so on. Nevertheless, right back to independence one can see that the whole thrust of Irish economic policy was to reduce dependence on Britain. For the paper of mine presented at the recent conference on Scottish independence, I toyed for a while with the idea of naming it 'From Act of Union to European Economic and Monetary Union'. I thought of this title because the Act of Union of 1800 drew Ireland into the United Kingdom, then Ireland broke from the Union with independence. We now see ourselves as a region of the broader European economy, which is, I think, the paradigm shift that independence entails.

The benefits of independence can be leveraged and need leveraging differently in the FDI-plentiful world of today. This was just coming into being in the 1950s when Ireland first adopted its FDI strategy. The paradigm shift necessitated by independence has not yet, I think, been sufficiently recognised. One aspect is that Scotland would be a small open economy in a way that the UK is not. In Ireland when we teach macroeconomics, we use small open economy models where fiscal policies are ineffective because demand leaks out through the balance of payments. We know that trade as a share of Scottish GDP would be much higher than is the case for the UK overall. The UK is a large open economy, in which fiscal policies are more powerful. For an independent

Scotland, the focus of attention would be much more on the supply side, or on what we call in Ireland industrial policy – particularly policies to try to attract FDI. A notable aspect of the current Irish crisis is that it is the export-oriented FDI sectors that have held the economy together: the rest of the economy was much flatter or experienced more substantial decline. The FDI sectors provided the macroeconomic stability that demand management tools can provide in large open economies. That is a point that I have not heard in the Scottish debate: industrial policy, or FDI policy, is more important in small open economies because it is one of the few tools at your disposal by which to adjust to macroeconomic shocks.

British economists did not recognise this different small open economy paradigm in the 1950s. The Nobel Prize winner James Meade was very pessimistic about Mauritius in a report to the Mauritius Government in 1961. Subsequently, Mauritius has been one of the two successful sub-Saharan African economies. Mauritius followed an Irish-type strategy. In Ireland, we turned to American consultants, whose experience in different parts of the world helped us to develop our FDI strategy. As you are probably aware, Ireland is one of the most FDI-intensive economies in the world (in employment terms, which is the best way to measure it). The American consultants recommended a strategy based on Puerto Rico's experience, and the Irish Industrial Development Agency made trips to America in the 1950s, where the American business community advised them to introduce tax concessions like those available in Puerto Rico. The Shannon Airport development area, which also came to prominence in the late 1950s, referred to as the first export-processing zone in the world. In fact, though, Panama came before Shannon, and American consultants – though with substantial Irish buy-in and ownership – were influential in this matter also.

So let me talk now about corporation tax. What is the optimum corporation tax rate for Scotland? Scotland is different from the UK. Scotland is a smaller economy and is more peripheral on two counts: first since the centre of gravity in the UK economy is the South East, and second since the centre of gravity of the European economy is Netherlands, Belgium, Germany, and eastern France down to northern Italy. What are the implications of this? Large economies and economies at the core of economic activity are by their very nature more attractive to FDI. A lot of market-seeking FDI goes to large economies, and centrality to economic activity is also important. Scotland does not have these advantages, implying that its optimum corporation tax is going to be lower than for the UK. The question is, how low? Scotland may have a higher GDP per head because of oil and gas revenues. Scotland industrialised early, and this may translate into a greater ability to spin off successful firms, but it is not clear that Scotland does have this ability. If it did, these factors would moderate the case for a lower rate of corporation tax. The UK in 2013 introduced the so-called Patent Box. This is essentially a back door way of having a low rate of corporation tax of 10 per cent. Scotland benefitted. Gallo SmithKline, the pharmaceutical company, made a huge investment in R&D in Scotland that Ireland had really hoped for. These arguments suggest that Scotland's optimal rate of corporation tax is lower than that for the UK.

Does this mean that if Scotland adopted Ireland's low rate it could replicate Ireland's experience? Here, the answer is no. Firstly, of course there would be big deadweight losses from the taxes paid by existing industry. Ireland had very few industries when it introduced low corporation tax in the 1950s, so there were no deadweight losses to begin with. Secondly, there is the role of the Industrial Development Agency (as it is now known) in Ireland. It has always had a huge degree of influence within the bureaucracy. Replicating that degree of influence within the bureaucracy would take a long time and may not be possible in other countries. These are, however, minor compared to the final point that I want to make, which connects to work I have been engaged on in recent times, connected to the aggressive tax planning strategies of US multinationals.

You may be familiar with the investigations conducted by the UK House of Commons and the US Senate sub-committee into the tax affairs of certain US multinationals, which hit the public domain in the summer of 2013. The British looked at Google and Starbucks and others; the Americans looked primarily at Apple. This work found that these multinational corporations have developed new strategies to minimise their global tax obligations. It is complicated of course (as it is mostly written by lawyers). Under US tax rules, introduced in 1997, two subsidiaries of the same parent with two subsidiaries operating in Ireland can submit a single tax return to the American tax authorities, the IRS. The IRS immediately tried to withdraw the new rules once they saw that lawyers for multinational corporations could drive a coach and horses through the loopholes that arose. Politics, however, got in the way, and the new rules instead got incorporated into US legislation. Of the two subsidiary companies in Ireland, an operating company and a holding company that owns all the Intellectual Property, the holding company subsidiary in Ireland can submit a single tax return for both companies to the IRS. All the income is active income and therefore can be held offshore, and there is no need to make an upfront tax payment to the US tax authorities. Previously, the profits associated with Intellectual Property were subject to immediate US taxes. Now under these new rules by sophisticated management of structures multinational corporations can avoid immediate payments to the IRS, and profits can be kept offshore to – more or less permanently – residual tax liabilities to the US authorities. According to US law, the holding company and the operating company are both incorporated in Ireland, so US law regards them are Irish companies. Irish law is different because it uses management and control as deciding factors on tax matters. This was derived from British legal tradition. American companies, under British legal precedence from the 1920s, can be incorporated in Ireland but begin tax resident there if they have no substantial activities in Ireland. The holding company is in effect an artificial company. It holds the intellectual property, it is incorporated in Ireland, but it does not employ anybody there, so it is not an Irish tax resident. British precedent establishes this for all Commonwealth countries and Ireland was in the Commonwealth at the time of adoption of this tax procedure. This was not something that the Irish did on purpose; it is just the basis of the law inherited from Britain. The holding company then will typically declare its tax residency in Bermuda where corporation tax is zero. That is in general how aggressive tax planning works.

What is the relevance of this for Scotland? In 1988, British tax rules changed substantially. If a company is incorporated in Britain that typically means that it is now tax resident in Britain. The previous precedent is no longer in operation. Ireland and most of the Caribbean tax havens still use the old British precedent. An independent Scotland would find it impossible to replicate the Irish experience because there would be an international outcry if Scotland tried to revert to the pre-1988 British system simply in order to facilitate aggressive tax planning by multinationals. The OECD, the EU, and the USA would not accept this. Ireland has been able to get away with it because this was Irish legal tradition arising from long-term use of a British precedent. I think there is no way that Scotland could revert to pre-1988 UK law. Even, therefore, if Scotland had a corporation tax rate of 12.5 per cent as in Ireland, it would not be able to replicate Ireland's success with FDI, because Scotland's tax system could not enable aggressive tax planning. This attribute of the Irish tax system has been advantageous to Ireland over recent decades (though it is currently under scrutiny), but is not likely to be available to an independent Scotland.

Nigel Driffield

What I want to do first is to talk a little bit about what I am going to label regional policy because I cannot think of anything else to call it. If at any point I inadvertently suggest that Scotland is a region of the UK, I apologise. It is very difficult to talk about regional policy and then talk about countries as well. So the focus of this really is sort of regionalism within the UK as it were. The source of my talk is largely from a report we did for Business Innovation and Skill (BIS) Foresight Report into the future of manufacturing done last year. Jim Love was involved as well. We wrote the inward investment bit of that, and what we were basically expected to do was a mixture if you like of speculation and data, so that is what I am going to talk about. The way these things work as ever were there were 50 or so underlying reports that fed into the BIS Foresight Report that then generated something that was about 1.5 inches thick, that then generated something that was about 17 pages, that then generated the one page that Vince Cable is actually going to read. I am intrigued by the idea of there being lots of FDI that Frank Barry talked about because certainly once one thinks about regions, whether it is regions of the UK or regions of Europe, the common view is that the inward investment climate is getting far more competitive in terms of regions being able to attract FDI. How far this connects to the Heseltine localism agenda is going to go that I do not want to get into now, because it is not about Heseltine and localism, but about regions of the UK and how they really have to sell their value proposition to firms. Firms come along, and they want to know about supply chains. They want to know what locations they are going to specialise in; it is interesting that most locations of the UK all seem to want to specialise in the same. Firms are very aggressive in terms of what they can get from locating in a region compared to other regions. I am talking about the physical location of firms. English regions or English locations recognise that this space is far more competitive than it has ever been before, and Scotland whether as an independent country or as part of the UK is going to have to compete in that increasingly localised competitive space.

I am not going to go into these issues in much detail because I know that the other people will focus on many of these topics. In the Scottish context, there is a lot of discussion about essentially the oil and gas sectors, and yet overall most of it is about other things. The figure below (Figure 2.1) is from the Foresight Report and is essentially a survey that somebody did of why firms said they

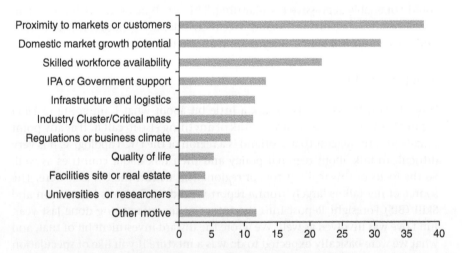

Figure 2.1   Top location determinants for greenfield investments: percentage of projects citing investment motives

Source: The authors, based on Financial Times Ltd, fDi Markets (www.fDimarkets.com).

located where they did. I am not going to get into the whole science of these things, because we all do international business and we all know you can show anything you like from these sorts of graphs, but we were told to make something of it. In this context, what I then did was I thought if you look at data such as in Figure 2.1, where could Scottish independence improve things? Well there are several where probably independence for Scotland would make things worse, you know, you look at those, we can speculate on the state of Scottish universities post-independence, but in general I would suggest it is probably not looking all that great. Clusters, critical masses, Scotland is going to be a smaller place, proximity to customers and markets that is again not going to be any better under independence. They are rather certain things where the potential is there to generate certain games or to be more attractive. We have talked about Scotland's GDP per head is higher than the UK, so maybe there is some market growth possibilities. Equally, you know it is clear if you read any of the policy documents that are coming out of the Scottish Parliament that they probably can be ahead of the UK on things like generating skills. In certain things, an independent Scotland will probably be better off than the Scotland is now in terms of things like generating support for inward investors because they can play by their own rules rather than those of UK regional policy. The same thing may be true with generating facilities attractive for FDI. So in terms of Scotland's ability as an independent place to attract inward investment as opposed to Scotland's position now, it is sort of about the same; you can sort of put your own weightings on those things and take your choice, but that is my thoughts.

In work for the Business Report we identified some key factors affecting attracting of inward FDI in the UK compared to other EU countries and emerging countries. Using this I did some thinking about how an independent Scotland might compare as an attractive location for FDI. There are several areas were my comments mirror the comments of Frank Barry (see above). Scotland is unlikely to gain in terms of corporation tax rates. There are all sorts of suggestions that Scotland as an independent country wants to spend more money; they have to raise that from somewhere. Equally, it is likely to be based on the policies that the Scottish Parliament associated that are likely to mean that Scotland's Labour markets will be less flexible than the UK's labour markets, and obviously market size is smaller the UK. There are some areas where probably there are again potentials for gain, such as host sector performance, as Scotland could have its own industrial policy tailored to Scotland's needs rather than being a sort of an add-on to the UK. Scotland can also have its own policy in terms of generating supply linkages, again linked to the sort of sectors that it wants to target, but that is an opportunity rather than an obvious benefit. There are certain things were Scotland would probably be the most open economy in the world if it does get independence and can do its own thing in terms of things like FDI incentives and after care and would probably be in a better position as an independent country than it would as a region of the UK.

In conclusion, one of the things that I put as a question is, can Scotland afford to have Edinburgh's financial district? Can Scotland afford to have something that is significantly bigger than the GDP of Scotland? Would the leader of an independent Scotland be looking at an Iceland situation if there were a meltdown in banking? I do not know, but it is an interesting question. One of the things that I think, certainly in the short term, which mirrors some of the comments of Alan Rugman (see above), is that there is an awful lot of uncertainty in this space in terms of firms making decisions; there is a huge chunk of uncertainty over which we do not really know what Scotland is going to do.

I am doing some work now on 50 years of data of inward investment into the UK, so you can think of it as being a time series of quarterly data. A time series econometrician has done usual stuff on the data looking for structural breaks, regime shifts, what policy instruments have an effect, etc. and basically the only things that make a difference in the long run to the amount of inward investment that the UK attracts are the big stories. Everything else simply shifts the existing pool around. We can all think of regional policies that have been successful in attracting inward investment to a given place, but what they do is they move it about. The things that really explain big regime shifts are things like the devaluation of the pound in 1967, the oil crisis where the pound changed against the dollar, the debate concerning the Euro and the Norman Lamont extravaganza with the ERM. In other words, they all connect to currency issues. The only things in the long run explaining changes in inward investment that comes into the UK are currency things and that seems to be the one thing that at the moment for which we do not know the answer.

Brad Mackay

Introduction

On 18 September 2014, Scottish citizens will go to the polls to vote on whether to become independent from the United Kingdom, a union they have shared since 1707. The vote has wide-spread implications, particularly for business. This chapter gives an overview into a nine-month study into business attitudes towards Scottish independence. It is part of a wider Economic and Social Research Council (ESRC) programme of research into the *Future of the UK and Scotland*. The ESRC is the UK's largest funding body for economic and social research. The study commissioned to produce some 'shovel-ready findings' on how business leaders of companies with significant operations in Scotland might actually be looking at the Independence debate. This chapter, therefore, reports on some of the preliminary data that has emerged from the study.

The sample

In terms of the sample, in the phase of the study covered here, there were 60 semi-structured interviews with senior business leaders in firms across five different industries, including energy (both hydro and oil and gas companies), and depending on how you define them, electronics and technology, engineering, financial services (including banking, insurance and wealth management) and life sciences. Half the sample was with business leaders in medium-sized firms (50 to 249 employees) and large firms (250+ employees), and most of the large firms were very large indeed, with 500+ employees. A characteristic of the Scottish economy is that, as of March 2013, Scottish Government statistics show that for both the national income and also for employment, large firms specifically, but also medium firms are very important. Large firms account for about 46 per cent of private-sector employment (compared to 41 per cent for England), and over 60 per cent of private sector turnover.

Business attitudes towards independence

During interviews, participants were asked a number of different questions around what uncertainties, if any, the debate posed for their business operations and strategies, whether it presented opportunities or risks for their businesses, whether there was any contingency planning being done around the issue, and finally, whether or not it was having any sort of material impact on their businesses. Responses, particularly when identifying uncertainties and risks, across the five industries were relatively consistent. What currency Scotland would use came across as being the most important, or the one that was most cited by business leaders, followed by regulatory changes (although what regulatory changes differed depending on the industry – e.g. for energy, it was who the regulator is going to be, and in financial services it was the possibility of facing double regulation). Personal taxes came across as being much stronger than corporate taxes. In addition, the EU was not as strong as one would have expected, but whether Scotland would remain in the EU as a continuing member, or have to exit and reapply, still came across as being a significant risk. Following the four uncertainties listed above, other risks varied depending on the specific circumstances of both companies and sectors. In life sciences, for example, where medical research is dependent on innovative science, university funding for basic science and access to funding from research councils is cited as a risk. Several business leaders mentioned uncertainties around pensions, while others cited barriers to and costs of cross-border trade.

The indicative view, to quote one business leader was:

> 'It's perceived risk around stability. And I guess there's a number of subsets of that, so one of them is fiscal ... issues around currency ... concerns around who the regulators will be, where they'll be based, what the influence of Europe

may or may not be on that...EU safety regulation...there's questions about Scotland's EU membership, our infrastructure will cross boundaries...So there's a whole host of issues but they all really come down to this question of stability or uncertainty around what these things might look like.'

However, there was also a minority view. To quote another business leader,

'I think the simple answer to that is no, because sometimes I think the people who are raising the uncertainty issues are not sure they get out enough. You know we are all in the EU transacting cross-border; we are dealing with a multitude of currencies, different nationalities, so for the life of me if Scotland chooses independence, I don't see necessarily why that is going to overcomplicate things; I just can't see it.'

When pressed about the potential opportunities presented by independence, what was interesting is that 23 in the sample said there would be no opportunity whatsoever in an independent Scotland for them. Seven business leaders in the sample said, well yes there would be opportunities, but they would be very marginal. Half the sample, or 30 business leaders, argued that there would be opportunities for their businesses in an independent Scotland. What is really quite interesting is that when they cited opportunities, only eight were actually able to cite opportunities that were specific to products or services, as opposed to when they were referring to the uncertainties and risks for their business operations and strategies, which were much more specific. Moreover, in only about four answered that such opportunities would lead to new investment or business growth. For the other 22 cases where opportunities were cited, they referred to more abstract possibilities germane to the wider economic and political debate, such as more tailored government policy for Scottish circumstances, tax decreases, targeted government export support or government accessibility for business. In the sample, only 10 per cent, or six business leaders, said that they did not see any risk and that the opportunities of independence outweigh the risks. In each of these cases, the business leaders were from privately owned companies, and with one exception, they tended to be on the smaller side of medium-size (70–90 employees) and in the electronics, engineering and life science industries.

The majority view from the sample can be summarised in the following comment by one business leader:

'I think if Scotland went Independent, it would make the most of it, and it would rise to the challenge, and everybody would do the best they could. ...Nevertheless, I think certainly initially in the short term, it would be a net loss and would not bring any benefits in the short term at all, other than to generate perhaps a bit more national pride and the will to overcome the difficulties. But it's not just about Scotland; it's about Scotland's place in the larger world.'

Then you had another minority view that emphasised some of the wider opportunities that might materialise with independence:

'[Reducing] import/export legislation. Taxation associated with cross-border trade. Regulation of the business in Scotland, and risk, and fear, and all these other things, plus opportunity, catalyse action in a way that doesn't happen if it's just the status quo. ... I think there would be a sense of immediacy in terms of what one could do that would really affect prosperity, in a way that's maybe different in a larger country.'

In terms of contingency planning, the interviews began in November right before the Scottish Government White Paper on independence was released, and since then, contingency planning has very much been evolving. When interviews began, the vast majority felt that independence was not likely, and what is interesting is, particularly since January when the polls began to narrow and the referendum is being discussed more in the media, views on the likelihood of independence have also begun to shift, as has contingency planning. Interviews indicated that contingency planning ranged from informal discussion to scenario planning, monitoring, relying on business continuity plans, setting up registered companies in England to 'restructure the business' if business interests are threatened and deferring investment decisions. As one business leader commented:

'There has been no contingency planning, though I am being asked more and more what "would you do if Scotland were to go independent?" Well, you know I can't afford to move my business, nor would I want to, but if there are problems by way of labour immigration or customers not wanting to necessarily trade as easily or suddenly I am a Scottish supplier not a UK supplier, then I am building a supply chain, a near-shore supply chain as a contingency.'

Other business leaders argued that there were too many uncertainties to plan a contingency for:

'If there is a yes vote, you do not know what the environment will be.'

Yet others were dismissive of contingency planning entirely:

'None at all; as I say, I can only see positives if Scotland were to gain its independence. And I think a lot of the debate up here around issues going across the border is just overheated nonsense, frankly.'

Conclusion

So what conclusions arise from the data? A number of clear patterns emerged from the data. If interview participants represented companies that were large PLCs with headquarters in Scotland, but their trade was primarily with the rest of the UK (i.e. England, Northern Ireland, Wales), they were universally concerned about the risks of independence, and were more likely to have contingency plans in place to migrate operations out of Scotland if necessary. The reasons for this were simple; Scotland's population is 5.3 million, and the rest of the UK has a population of 58 million people. Large companies had grown so in the market, policy and regulatory institutional context of the UK. Trade tended to follow a 90/10 rule, where 90 per cent of their trade was in the rest of the UK, and only 10 per cent in Scotland (roughly proportional to the population differences). Around 70 per cent of Scottish exports also go to England.

Companies who were supplying to, for instance, the Ministry of Defence, were also concerned about their ability to continue supplying following independence. EU law gives defence-related companies an exemption from EU procurement policies, and the UK Government has a long tradition of supporting domestic firms for defence-related needs. If participants represented large companies based in Scotland, but with most of their trade diversified globally, responses to interview questions indicated less concern with the uncertainties and risks of independence. Global companies that registered abroad, but with operations in Scotland, were also more likely to say 'look we do business all over the world; yes, it would be an event, but we have business continuity plans that can handle these sorts of things.' Finally, privately owned companies with exposure to the rest of the UK through their supply chains, labour mobility, customer location, etc. might express concern over the uncertainties and risks posed by independence, but they were also more willing to absorb downside risk than were PLC companies who also have an obligation to protect shareholder value.

Very few participants could identify opportunities for their companies, and of those who could, they tended to be smaller medium-sized companies with a specific issue, such as a licencing fee, which they were hopeful would be resolved by independence or companies looking for more government support. The main opportunities were, therefore, the possibility of tax decreases, more tailored government policy to Scottish needs, export support or easier access to government. The majority of business leaders, however, argued that they currently have the 'best of both worlds' in being able to leverage both the British and Scottish brands and British and Scottish institutions such as various economic development agencies or the network of foreign missions. Around 10 per cent of firms indicated they could scale down their business activity in

Scotland or move their head offices, depending on what materialised in negotiations following the referendum vote. One business leader concluded:

> 'But this is not a complex or complicated debate for us; it is really very
> straightforward. We have three categories of stakeholder whose interests we
> need to bear in mind: our customers, our shareholders and our employees.
> In addition, we are a PLC, so our shareholders' interests are obviously of
> paramount importance. So, does the economic environment in which we
> operate, does it support the continued sustainability of the business and
> the future prosperity of those three groups, and if it does not, what do we
> do about it? It is not a political debate for us; it is not complicated, but it is
> trying to take the politics out of it that is the difficult thing. If you take any
> of those three stakeholder groups, employees for example, it is very difficult
> in their minds to differentiate between the political statement and the state-
> ment protecting stakeholder interests, so it is quite difficult, but in terms of
> understanding, what the right thing to do is, that is not difficult at all. That
> is not difficult. We have got to protect the interests of those three groups.'

In summary, the key uncertainties for companies were the currency (with a
clear preference for the pound sterling, regulation (with a clear preference for
a common regulatory framework with England), taxes (with more concern
expressed for personal taxation then the relatively low corporate taxation in
the UK) and the EU (with a clear preference for remaining part of the EU).
Responses to the interview questions posed also reflected a clear pattern, determined by the location of customers for companies, the headquarters location
of the companies and the ownership structure of companies.

Stephen Young and Duncan Ross

I should declare my own interest, my own nationality. I am English, and I come
from a small town called Berwick-upon-Tweed, which has changed hands 13
times between England and Scotland and which at one point was the largest
town in Scotland. I should also say that I am working with Duncan Ross as a
conscious decision in order to ensure a balance in our work. Given the time
constraint, I am going to condense the material Duncan and I have worked on
to focus upon a limited number of issues.

The first of these highlights *Scotland's GDP per head* (Figure 2.2), and it
presents both the onshore and the geographic share. The geographic share is
the calculation used by the Scottish Government. It assumes that Scotland's
share of oil and gas revenues is about 90 per cent for oil and 50 per cent for gas,
but this is not uncontested. What the slide shows is that the UK is a true single

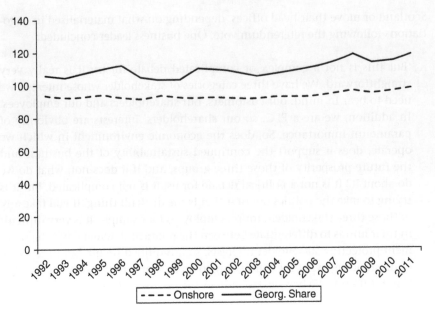

Figure 2.2   Scotland's GDP per head as proportion of the UK's, 1992–2011
Source: SNAP; ONS.

market because the two economies are highly integrated. Generally, in the recent past the performance of the Scottish economy has been very similar to that of the UK. This was not the case in the past, which is also interesting from an integrated market perspective, because the United Kingdom Government provided the poorer regions of the UK with a block grant, the Barnett formula, to remedy regional imbalances. Nowadays, Scotland is no longer a poor part of the UK but still receives funding through the Barnett formula. The consequence of this is that public expenditure in Scotland is 10 per cent higher than it is in the rest of the UK. Scotland's position in terms of *productivity levels* is very similar to the UK, both being middle-income countries within the OECD (Scottish Government, 2013).

My basic point when considering international business and independence is that we need to take a holistic, whole-economy perspective because cross-border flows within a single market become international trade, international investment, and international migration. I am only going to talk here about FDI. I should say a little about the organisational issues for international business in Scotland: currently, we do not have a single agency for attracting investment. Of course, Scotland as you know was a strong competitor for FDI, but the agency Land Information Search (*LiS*) was essentially wound up and replaced by *Scottish Development International* which is responsible for all international business activities in Scotland – namely, inward and outward investment and inward and outward internationalisation. But if we look only at FDI, Scotland has really had a high level of policy independence for many years in both industrial and economic development; and so, therefore, when you come to look at the opportunities for the country in an independent Scotland, it is somewhat difficult to identify them very clearly because many of these opportunities exist already.

Scotland's performance regarding inward investment has been very good over the past 10 or 15 years, and the country has been ranked second or third in terms of inward investment attraction in the UK, after London and the South-East (all data quoted is from a study conducted by Young and Ross, University of Glasgow). This success is in part due to the growth of renewables in Scotland. The economy is highly dependent upon inward FDI for investment for jobs and especially for R&D: 70 per cent of manufacturing R&D expenditure and 68 per cent of R&D employment is in foreign companies in Scotland. There are questions now, as there have been for a long time, about whether R&D is embedded in the local economy – and more generally whether or not Scotland is still a branch plant economy with a predominance of competence-exploiting subsidiaries. We have few headquarters of multinationals and very few decision-making functions. The positive factor is that FDI has been quite diverse as compared with the past; and I suppose the second point is that quite a significant part of FDI is now natural resource-seeking investment, which is location bound and to some extent immobile by definition. So 34 per cent of jobs and 62 per cent of FDI expenditure is in natural resource sectors which are oil and gas, renewables, tourism and food and drink. The Scottish Government strategic plan going forward for international business focuses upon a series of priority sectors, and the bulk of these are in natural resources. In a sense, this mirrors the Irish situation because the emphasis has for the last few years been less on inward investment and much more focused on outward trade – especially in these natural resource sectors, including tourism and food & drink.

A challenge for Scotland, as it has been for quite a long time, is that maximising the benefits from inward FDI requires a strong domestic sector for positive linkages and spillover effects, and generally these have been limited in the past; and this is still the case when one looks at innovation. Innovativeness in Scotland is weak in all innovation measures: the level of entrepreneurship, the business birth rate and research and development. This poses real difficulties for any government in Scotland, going forward.

I now want to highlight the challenges and the opportunities for an independent Scotland derived from this analysis. The perspective I am taking is that I view the costs as being largely *transition costs* and largely therefore short to medium term, although some of them run into the long-term as well. First, we have the institutional costs to build the infrastructure and the legal and regulatory framework, and managing both formal and informal institutional factors. The government's White Paper has identified 300 institutions in Scotland which are currently UK institutions and which therefore need to be replicated or re-created under a new regime. Work undertaken by the LSE and the National Audit Office suggests a cost of about £15 million to set up a new or reorganise an existing policy department. There is a lot of work and a lot of money that is going to be associated with this institutional reorganisation. The transactional costs include the obvious ones: negotiating costs, new administrative systems and human resource constraints. My question is, where are the people coming from in order to be able to manage this transitional change? Finally, there are political costs associated with transition, represented by the costs of unfulfilled promises, by whichever political party is in power. The third area concerns fiscal monetary and exchange rate policy, including the currency union issue that has been talked about already (see discussion on this issue above in pieces by Rugman, Barry, and Driffield). The fourth area is that of the border costs. These concern trade barriers related to potential immigration controls and more generally to the liabilities of foreignness. Finally, we have the risks and uncertainties for business and all the stakeholders, incorporating political risk, default risk (and people talk about a risk premium which varies between half a per cent and 1.7 per cent) and currency risk. The important factor from my perspective is that these costs might be short run or long run in nature; fixed and variable; national, regional and global (as indeed Alan Rugman was talking about); and they are economic and political. On top of this there are specifically sectoral dimensions in energy and renewables; defence, including shipbuilding (and the Trident nuclear deterrent); and banking and financial services.

On the other side are the *opportunities* that I have problems with since some of them exist already. There are opportunities such developing airport policy, competition policy, patents, and R&D support. The Scottish Government itself and the first minister talk about reindustrialisation through strategic coupling in renewable technologies. There is R&D going on in renewables, but we really need some new academic research to study this in-depth. Some opportunities are requirements – for example, new market opportunities as businesses in Scotland redirect their trade away from the rest of the UK. An enhanced role for Edinburgh as the capital city of an independent Scotland is a real possibility. A recent report, covering 2010–2012, showed that 23,000 new private sector jobs were created in Edinburgh (making it the second city in the UK); however, the equivalent for London was 216,000, so you have to put this in perspective. There is potential for an expanded role for the Scottish universities, although there are potential difficulties associated with the likely loss of Research Council funding, the treatment of English students under EU law, and so forth. In addition, there are requirements and opportunities for improved branding of Scotland in food and drink as well as tourism – but also promoting a weak Scottish brand for FDI.

In conclusion, I would like to comment on the types of companies likely to be affected by independence (not necessarily inward investors).The first group are those firms that operate across the border with the rest of the UK, either selling or sourcing. At Brad McKay's ESRC launch a few weeks ago, there was a really good example from one small businessman who was importing through Southampton in the South of England; then bringing product up through England; and re-processing it in Scotland, before 'exporting' back to the English market. One can see the problems for such businesses if they are faced with border controls. The second group of firms are those with firms with headquarters in Scotland, especially banking and financial services. You will have read in the papers that a number have already decided to set up new companies in England in order to move their asset base to reduce their risks. Scottish-based banking assets (including the Royal Bank of Scotland and Lloyds, both of which were set up by an Act of Parliament in 1695) represent 12.5 times the size of GDP in Scotland. The third group are those with political characteristics that will require negotiations between the UK Government and the Scottish Government. They are in the same sectors as I have talked about already. In defence, these negotiations could be very lengthy: I have seen a figure of 18 years being quoted for the removal of Trident nuclear missiles from the Clyde. As you know, the Scottish National Party has a policy of 'no nuclear' in Scotland. Then the final group (and maybe this is a little controversial) are global firms which are managing global and regional supply chains and where Scotland is integrated within these 'global factory' systems. Such MNEs will likely be considering alternative options because of the risks and uncertainties associated with a Scotland location.

So that is all I had to say except by concluding with the title of a Bob Dylan song from 1962: 'A hard rain's a-gonna fall'!

Summary of the views

All the speakers expressed opinions that indicated that independence would not lead to economic disaster for Scotland in terms of FDI and trade. Some of them, however, expressed concerns about the adjustment costs of creating new institutions and about the uncertainties and possible costs arising from the largely unknown post-independence association with the rest of the UK and bodies such as WTO and the EU (Alan Rugman, Stephen Young). All of them highlighted the uncertainties that exist over economic and political structures post-independence. Brad MacKay presented evidence that these uncertainties may be located most strongly in large PLCs with significant business links with the England and rest of the world. Most of the speakers referred to significant uncertainties over currency arrangements, and Nigel Driffield suggested that changes and uncertainty in currency systems were the major source of significant changes in long-run FDI flows. This view indicates that policies to attract FDI to particular countries or regions simply change the distribution of FDI location, with the size and patterns being driven by large-scale currency changes, new technologies and other major economic factors. This indicates that industrial policies and other policies to attract FDI can only succeed if they are able to generate advantages to multinational corporations that cannot be generate elsewhere in the world. This implies that Scotland, and other countries where separatists win independence, can achieve more FDI than their current position only if they are able to generate new and very effective policies. This connects to Frank Barry's point that Irish industrial policy succeeded because of the powerful influence that the Irish institutional system conferred on these policies. Frank Barry and Nigel Driffield expressed views that an independent Scotland would probably have very limited room to use taxation policy to attract FDI. An independent Scotland according to Rugman would have to generate policies and conditions that developed new CSAs to enable the creation of new FSAs, helped by more and higher quality FDI and trade. Most of the speakers also referred to the possible loss of some firms, notably large banks and insurance firms, and defence firms. Indeed some of the large banks and insurance firms have already stated that they will move their headquarters from Scotland in the event of a yes victory in the referendum. The low numbers of headquarters and small volumes of high level activities by multinational corporations in many of Scotland's industries (highlighted by Stephen Young) indicates Scotland has much to do to develop the type of CSAs compatible with multinational strategies aimed at high valued-added activities. Independence may be able to help with this if Scotland can replicate the Irish experience related by Frank Barry.

Most of the speakers thought opportunities exist as a result of independence. Frank Barry, using Irish experience, argued that independence could reduce Scotland's economic linkages to England and thereby promote an economy more open to the rest of the world, and hence potentially help to develop a more dynamic economy. Nigel Driffield hinted that there might be some opportunities if Scotland becomes more economically independent from England, thus enabling it to develop FDI policies that are more effective. The surveys overseen by Brad Mackay found evidence that some firms, especially medium-sized privately owned firms, thought that independence offered prospects for better relationships with government that could help to develop a more dynamic economy. Stephen Young argued that the embedding of Scotland's FDI and trade in natural resources (especially renewable energy), tourism, and food and drink, made it likely that they would not lose FDI and trade in these areas – and indeed were likely to be able to develop these sectors. This would suggest that

CSA and FSA of Scotland will rest in these areas, and they will be the centres of FDI and trade. An independent Scotland may be able to pursue policies compatible with developing these sectors.

In general, the speakers argued that uncertainties about Scotland's post-independence association with international bodies and the rest of the UK and the costs of setting up new institutional structures were the main dangers from independence. These are in effect medium term problems, which should be resolved quickly and thereby need not present long-term obstacles to successful independence. If, however, an independent Scotland faced extensive delay and costs in arranging relationships with rest of the UK, the EU and the WTO, and if the currency issue was not resolved quickly, the costs of independence for FDI and trade could be very substantial. It is possible that independence could result in the development of policies and a new business environment more embedded into the global economy that would move Scotland to become a more dynamic economy. Some of speakers, however, raise serious questions about the importance of industrial and FDI policies to attract high-quality foreign investment. A focus on natural resources is compatible with high income per head, but it is difficult to sustain a country with high income per head in the absence of the development of new knowledge-intensive industries. Moreover, Stephen Young hints at possible problems from reliance on new industries such as renewable energy that may not fulfil the hopes placed on them. These issues relate to how Scotland can use independence to develop CSAs from which FSA will flow, thereby generating inward and outward FDI and high engagement with foreign trade, especially trade embedded in high knowledge-intensive activities. Alan Rugman argues that the desire of Quebec for independence has dissipated because Canada has devolved many economic and social policies to the Quebec Government. Scotland already has devolved powers over much of FDI and industrial policy and more devolution seems likely if the referendum's proposal fails to secure a majority. It is therefore possible that Scotland could secure more benefits for FDI and trade by extending the existing autonomy that Scotland already has and/or using more effectively the powers already held in Scotland. This would grant the opportunity to reap the possible benefits of enhanced integration into the global economy to develop a more dynamic economy without the uncertainties and possible costs of independence. If the main driver of independence is to loosen economic and political linkages to England to gain greater and more effective integration into the global economy, it is not clear how independence will help to achieve this objective. Independence could help with this only if somehow it enabled Scotland to develop new CSAs that lead to new FSAs that were less reliant on links to the rest of UK.

Scottish independence, and possible independence for other separatist movements, would seem to deliver greater and more effective FDI and trade only if the restructuring of institutional systems and arranging post-independence association with the rest of the world are quickly achieved at low cost. More importantly, an independent Scotland would have to be capable of creating policies and structures that generate and sustain new CSAs and FSAs.

References

Barry, F., Kearney, C. (2006) 'MNEs and Industrial Structure in Host Countries: A Portfolio Analysis of Irish Manufacturing'. *Journal of International Business Studies*, 37(4), 392–406.

Buckley, P., Clegg, J., Forsan, N., Reilly, K. (2001) 'Increasing the Size of the "Country": Regional Integration and Foreign Investment in a Globalised World'. *Management International Review*, 41(3), 251–274.

Gammelgaard, J., McDonald. F., Tuselmann, H.-J., Dorrenbacher, C., Stephan, A. (2009) 'Subsidiary Role and Skilled Labour Effects in Small Developed Economies'. *Management International Review*, 49(1), 1–27

Hooley, G., Cox, T., Shipley, D., Fahy, J., Beracs, J., Kolos, K. (1996) 'Foreign Direct Investment in Hungary: Resource Acquisition and Domestic Competitive Advantage'. *Journal of International Business Studies*, 27(4), 683–695.

Scottish Government (2013) Productivity Purpose Target, available at http://www.scotland.gov.uk/About/Performance/scotPerforms/purpose/productivity

Scottish Government (2013) Scotland's Future: Your Guide to an Independent Scotland. http://www.scotland.gov.uk/Publications/2013/11/9348/downloads

Young, S., Ross, D., MacKay, B. (2014) 'Inward foreign direct investment and constitutional change in Scotland'. *Multinational Business Review*, 22(2), 118–138.

3

Geography and History Matter: International Business and Economic Geography Perspectives on the Spatial and Historical Development of Multinational Enterprises

Jennifer Johns, Peter Buckley, Liam Campling, Gary Cook, Martin Hess, and Rudolf R. Sinkovics

Situated within the broader conference theme of historical change, this panel session brought together international business and economic geography perspectives on multinational enterprise (MNE) evolutionary trajectories. The panel session follows a series of past conference sessions aimed to increase dialogue and interaction between economic geographers and international business scholars. These included several sessions at the Royal Geographical Society and Institute of Geographer's Annual Conference in 2010 and the Association of International Business in 2012. The aim for this conference panel session was for panellists to offer a range of empirical and conceptual observations to interrogate our existing understandings of the spatial and historical development of MNEs. While space and time often provide distinct lenses on the operations of MNEs, the panel discussed the ways in which the two can be combined to provide more nuanced conceptualisations and frameworks for analysis, which can powerfully complement existing conceptual frameworks and methodological approaches in international business. This chapter is a record of the panel session and, as such, offers a direct representation of the speakers' presentations, their discussions and their question and answer session. The chapter begins with Martin Hess' discussion of continuity and change in MNEs and global production networks, followed by Rudolf Sinkovics' analysis of the uptake of economic geography work on global sourcing by international business. Liam Campling then introduces us to commodity chains and commodity frontiers before Peter Buckley offers a summary and discussion of the key debates and issues raised. The chapter includes the questions posed to the panel and the answers and discussion offered in response.

Continuity and change: MNE and global production networks (GPN), by Martin Hess

Continuity and change with regard to MNEs and GPNs is something I have been working on for the last ten years with colleagues. I hope this will be useful as we look at the evolution of multinational enterprises in a world of fragmented value chains and the new geographies of MNEs that we see emerging especially in the Global South and as we look at what this means for the challenges facing international business and economic geography. I would argue the challenge is to explain the spatial and temporal fix of capital in contemporary capitalism.

Just as a quick reminder, and it will be brief as it is very familiar, MNEs are obviously still very important in the world economy, and according to statistics from UNCTAD (2011), there were 37,000 in the 1990s, and this has gone to a population of more than 100,000 MNEs in 2010. There was also a shift in where these parent companies originate. In the early 1990s, 90 per cent originated from the developed world, and this has gone down to 70 per cent (UNCTAD, 2011). So there has been an increase in MNEs originating from developing economies and emerging markets.

What I want to argue is that this is only part of the wider picture. Firms are part of wider global production networks. Global production networks, as we define them in economic geography, describe the nexus of interconnected functions and operations through which goods and services are produced and also distributed and consumed. These GPNS over the last decades have become both organisationally much more complex but also increasingly global in their reach and extent. What these networks do: they not only integrate firms and parts within firms into structures that tend to blur traditional organisational boundaries but also integrate national economies and parts of such economies in various ways that have enormous implications for the well-being and development of places. In a nut shell, they cut through state boundaries in various differentiated ways, and this is influenced in part by regulatory and non-regulatory barriers but also, and importantly, social and cultural conditions which create structures which are discontinuously territorial. This is important in the context of economic geography and international business dialogue because this goes way beyond methodological nationalism which often we find in both disciplines. It emphasises that place, rather than just the nation-state boundary, matters for MNEs and the GPNS they connect. What we want to do, within this GPN approach, is to understand the social and developmental dynamics of contemporary capitalism at the global-local nexus across different scales. This is an approach developed mostly within economic geography, and it is a development of a large project we worked on. What this GPN heuristic framework does is operate though three analytical lenses or registers. I'm not going into detail here; I just want to use these three analytical categories as a structuring element for the next few pointers.

So, GPNs look at processes of value creation, enhancement and, importantly, who captures value in these value production systems; the related governance and power structure – power as corporate power, exercised by firms, but also non-firm institutions, and ultimately it looks at global production networks and multinationals as embedded organisations, embedded in particular territories and places, but also creating embedded networks and embedded in society. I want to mobilise these three registers and think a little bit about them in relation to recent trends in MNE and GPN development.

Basically, the classic focus maybe of international business, if I can simplify, is mostly on the firm and maybe also on some sectors created by these firms. Whereas traditionally economic geography has focused more on territorial development and often left the firm as a black box. At the end I will argue that there is a fruitful interface for both our disciplines to explore. OK. Let me start with the first of these registers – value generation and capture. Again, I can address only one or two issues that I think are interesting and might be important for our discussion.

Over the last decade, we have seen quite a substantial process of financialisation, of changing sources and uses of profit by multinational enterprises, driven by financial markets and by shareholder capitalism. As a consequence, we have evermore finely sliced value chains emerging in many sectors. So FDI

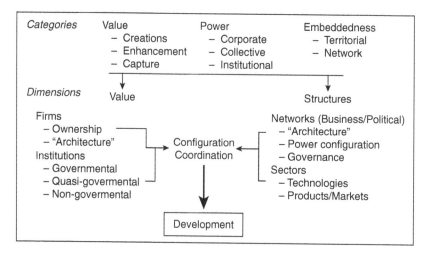

Figure 3.1 A framework for global value chain analysis
Source: Henderson *et al.* (2002: Figure 1).

is still important, but there are many other forms now, in terms of subcontracting and task segmentation in these systems. This slicing of the value chain has created new geographies of outsourcing and offshoring to keep costs down. This is a prerequisite for many firms in the process of financialisation. As a result, we also have seen, over the last couple of decades or so, a change in multinational enterprises towards fabless firms – a lot of companies that don't produce anymore but rather rely on brand-rents. One example for that – a very famous example – is Apple (See Figure 3.2).

Apple doesn't produce anything at all – at least it didn't until very recently when it brought back a production facility to the United States – but this is a classic example of a company relying on financialisation as a business strategy. As you can see (in Figure 3.2), brand-rents play an important part here. The gross margin for Apple is about 70 per cent of the whole production system. How an Apple 4G phone is produced involves multiple geographies, multiple global production networks. Each of these components creates GPNs in its own right and is often driven by multinational enterprises. Assembly takes place in China, which makes up only a small part of this whole system. Foxconn, the Taiwanese multinational, produces the Apple iPhone in various places in China and, unlike Apple, captures a lot of the value through this model. Foxconn has 70 per cent labour share of the value added. A very different kind of setting for this MNE, and the value-added to sales ratio for Foxcomm in this system is only 12 per cent. So that has certain implications for MNE strategy for companies like Foxconn.

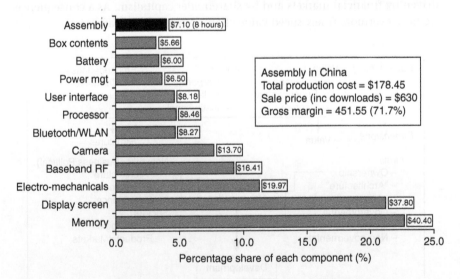

Figure 3.2   Share of production cost of an Apple 4G iPhone assembled in China

Notes: Excludes software, licensing, royalties.

Source: Froud *et al.* (2012: Figure 5).

The second register, and I guess this will feature more prominently throughout our discussion, features questions around power and governance in MNEs and their wider global production networks. I would argue that MNEs have become over time more and more 'networks within networks'. They have often become temporary coalitions of activities and value-added activities that break up and reassemble in new configurations to the boundaries of the firm. They have always been to some extent blurred but have become arguably more blurred over the last few years. So there arise questions about changing forms of governance of these wider production and value-added systems within and beyond firms. It also arguably creates some kinds of new breeds of multinational enterprises. Again, I want to use just a brief example to illustrate this. The global garment manufacturing industry has been discussed for a long time under the new international division of labour model, but there are companies now emerging that have very new and different characteristics. Li and Fung from Hong Kong is a classic example of that. Again, it is an intermediary company, a logistics company. It orchestrates 15,000 or so suppliers across a huge number of countries. It doesn't own a single one of them. It doesn't own any production facilities. It is a multinational enterprise, yes, because it has offices in 40 countries, but there is little foreign direct investment involved. The rationale of the OLI paradigm and FDI is much less relevant here given what they do in terms of orchestrating these massive production systems. They also apply particular strategies to divide and conquer these vast networks. What they try to achieve is ensuring that the lead supplier has at least 30 per cent of their capacity but no more than 70 per cent of the factory output in order to have enough share to be influential and important for the supplier, but not to be too dominant and be the single buyer from these suppliers. So it is a very intriguing strategy. They also increasingly try to branch out into the upper end of the value chain, into retail. They have their own brand, Fishman and Tobin, and they orchestrate supply chains for large multinationals like Walmart. Walmart is said to be potentially the eighth or ninth largest trade partner with China, if it were a country, so it is massive. Li and Fung moves into this system and orchestrates around 200 billion dollars' worth of sourcing for Walmart and operates all the global sourcing and US distribution of the brand Liz Claiborne.

Finally, the third register is the analytical category of embeddedness. In economic geography, I think the fundamental thing that we look into is the social-cultural context, and geographical context matters. It is about the territorial embeddedness of multinationals as well as the wider GPNs they connect. It also matters, of course, where MNEs come from, and that echoes discussions in the literature on national business systems, like Richard Whitley's work, but also the varieties of capitalism literature that came out as part of institutional economics. So, firms are embedded in particular territories, in particular wider networks and societies. Retail is a good example. Retail internationalisation is a phenomenon that took place over only the last 10–20 years really and wasn't discussed before that. It clearly emphasises the importance of the socio-polit-ical and cultural context as companies like Tesco expanded and also retracted, retreating from California, for instance, which is in part to do with the misun-derstanding of the frameworks within which they operate – the institutional and regulatory frameworks in the particular countries, but also arguably more importantly, consumer culture and the societies into which they expanded. At the same time, it is not only about expanding their sales floor space into coun-tries, but also about orchestrating a huge number of suppliers across the globe and hence have a dual influence in this regard.

Just to wrap-up, based on these brief pointers, bringing international business studies and economic geography together is an intriguing prospect, and coming back to issues around global production networks, the strategic coupling process between global production networks which are made up of focus firms, multinationals, but also their subsidiaries and suppliers, the strength of international business research, how this couples with regional assets in terms of technology, organisation and territory, that could be an interface that could be useful to explore further in an economic geography/ international business dialogue.

Global value chains (GVCS), global production networks (GPN) and international business (IB), by Rudolf R. Sinkovics

The presentation title is 'Global value chains, global production networks and international business', and I believe the invitation is a function of my involvement in an ESRC project dealing with firms from 'Rising Powers', which are increasingly taking on critical roles in GPNs and GVCs. This an interdisciplinary project where I am looking particularly at the firm aspect, while my colleagues in other departments in Manchester are looking at other dimensional outcomes – for example, labour, social responsibility issues. For me, when I first got involved in this network around 2010, it was a very sig-nificant, steep learning curve which I don't think I have quite completed as yet. What you will experience here is some of my own thinking around what has happened in the literature around GVCs and GPNs, which at some stage in their history became separated from what was originally, I would argue, an IB topic or a topic very much at the core of IB. So, we are working in an interdis-ciplinary context in this research project, and I wanted to look at the drivers and outcomes of emerging power and the players – not only firms but also state actors, governments, NGOs and so on – in the context of what is called 'rising power' countries, if using the Economic and Social Research Council (ESRC) terminology, otherwise also called the BRIC countries

In my presentation I essentially offer a bibliographic analysis, starting my search on the notion of 'value chain' within the domain of IB. Interestingly, there is a paper by Kogut (1985) that carries 'value chains' in the title, but after this 1985 paper, there was no single IB paper for quite some time that actually utilised the term in a similar way to how it is used in the sense of GVCs, in the more sociologically inspired literature, or how it is picked up and used by economic geographers. I would argue that, with the emergence of the resource-based view, there is less consideration of the orchestration and structuring of the value chain in the original Porterian way. It has fallen out of use in the literature. I proceed by exploring what the global value chain is, and when it was that GVCs as a term re-entered the landscape of IB. When was it taken up again? Is there a take up? If so, how is this being done? Ultimately, what I want to look at is which dimensions are being used very prominently in the GPN and GVC literature, but not in IB. I would like to finish with a question mark around the degree to which IB scholars can learn from this literature and – if useful – perhaps implement some of the concepts in their own work.

In the first step, I utilise the Social Sciences Citation Index (SSCI) database and look at the corpus of GVC research. The analysis that I am presenting is also narrowed down by the ability to scroll through the literature in SSCI, but what you see here is that I was looking comprehensively and very broadly around the issues of GVCs and GPNs, confined to all the articles published between 1970 and

Field: Authors	Record count	percentage of 549	Bar chart
NADVI K	10	1.821 %	I
BARRIENTOS S	8	1.457 %	I
COE NM	8	1.457 %	I
GEREFFI G	8	1.457 %	I
WEI YHD	8	1.457 %	I
FRANZ M	7	1.275 %	I
PONTE S	7	1.275 %	I
YEUNG HWC	7	1.275 %	I
HESS M	6	1.093 %	I
GRIMES S	5	0.911 %	I
HASSLER M	5	0.911 %	I
PAVLINEK P	5	0.911 %	I
PICKLES J	5	0.911 %	I
RABELLOTTI R	5	0.911 %	I
RIISGAARD L	5	0.911 %	I
Field: Authors	Record count	percentage of 549	Bar chart

Figure 3.3 Authors in the GVC/GPN domain

2014. A total of 549 papers came to light that had, in their abstract or title, some notion of GNCs or GPNs. When we look at the authors in this domain that are possibly being used and cited in IB, then we see quite an interesting ranking (3).

We see Khalid Nadvi, who is the lead author on this ESRC grant in Manchester; Stefanie Barrientos, at Manchester; Neil Coe who previously was in Manchester, now Singapore; Gary Gereffi, Duke University; and further down we have Henry Yeung and Martin Hess. Moving on beyond authors, I further looked at the papers and the titles, abstracts, and key words that gave any indication of GVCs or GPNs. If you look further down in terms of disciplinary utilisation of these 549 papers that we have here, where do they occur? Quite rightly, most of the members of this panel are economic geographers because most of the work is coming out of geography (232 papers) (see Figure 3.4). In total, there are 75 IB papers that either cite a GVC/GPN paper (as defined earlier) or mention the term GVC/GNP. There are three papers that mention the term but don't cite any of the GVC/GNP literature. There are some strategic citations in there as

Field: Web of science categories	Record count	percentage of 549	Bar chart
GEOGRAPHY	232	42.259 %	
ECONOMICS	175	31.876 %	
PLANNING DEVELOPMENT	120	21.858 %	
ENVIRONMENTAL STUDIES	96	17.486 %	
MANAGEMENT	62	11.293 %	
BUSSINESS	50	9.107 %	
SOCIOLOGY	45	8.197 %	
URBAN STUDIES	37	6.740 %	
AREA STUDIES	27	4.918 %	
POLITICAL SCIENCE	21	3.825 %	
ANTHROPOLOGY	18	3.279 %	
INTERNATIONAL RELATIONS	18	3.279 %	
ENVIRONMENTAL SCIENCES	11	2.004 %	
INDUSTRIAL RELATIONS LABOR	11	2.004 %	
OPERATIONS RESEARCH MANAGEMENT SCIENCE	11	2.004 %	
ETHICS	8	1.457 %	
GEOGRAPHY PHYSICAL	8	1.457 %	
AGRICULTURE MULTIDISCIPLINARY	7	1.275 %	
SOCIAL SCIENCES INTERDISCIPLINARY	7	1.275 %	
TRANSPORATION	7	1.275 %	
ENGINEERING INDUSTRIAL	6	1.093 %	
HISTORY PHILOSOPHY OF SCIENCE	6	1.093 %	
AGRICULTURAL ECONOMICS POLICY	5	0.911 %	
LAW	5	0.911 %	

Figure 3.4 Web of Science categories and published work

well. What I am trying to allude to here is, yes, the business and management literature is becoming more conscious of its origins. The Porterian value chain has been fed into the GVC discussion around Gereffi and other people, and recent publications over the last ten years are looking at issues like governance and notions of power, which have some interesting connotations for the agenda of IB. So, in a sense, there is increasing recognition of these topics within IB.

For further background, England is quite prominent in the origins of the papers (130 papers compared to 134 coming from the US). This is comforting from an AIB-UKI perspective as it is very closely behind the US in terms of the authors. Again, pleasing from the University of Manchester's point of view, we are apparently ranked number 1 in this particular analysis with respect to contributions to the topic of GVCs/GPNs. The 549 papers in the sample that carry GVC/GPN in their title and abstracts, have been cited 6,261 times. Around 2,000 citations would be self-citations, but there are more than 3,500 genuine citations, signifying the impact of these articles. The Hirsch index, an indication of the impact of these papers over time, is also quite significant, at 34. What is nice to see here is that, on the whole, the literature on GPNs and GVCs has taken off quite significantly over the last decade – in the specialist areas of economic geography and development studies, and before that there were some notable publications. But over the last few years the citations have increased substantially.

The next figure is a 3D diagram (Figure 3.5), illustrating how IB has taken up this topic.

The Gereffi, Humphrey and Sturgeon (2005) paper on the governance of GVCs in the Review of International Political Economy is the one that has been most widely utilised. In terms of IB citations it leads the crowd, with 16 papers utilising this particular contribution. If we go through the figure, we can see that Henderson et al. (2002) has been cited only once. The work by Humphrey and Schmitz (2002), who also showcased some of their work at the recent EIBA (European International Business Association) conference in Sussex, has been cited five times. We can see that Giuliani, Pietrobelli and Rabellotti (2005) on upgrading in GVCs has received some attention in IB, which is indicative of the fact that the notion of upgrading can be useful in the firm context. I believe Martin Hess is hidden in this chart somewhere as well, which in a way indicates how the work of economic geographers is frequently overlooked in IB. So, what you see here is that the zero citations are mostly coming from authors with an economic geography background.

In the next step I was interested in which concepts are most widely used in the most cited GVC papers. I extracted the most widely cited GVC/GPN papers here and examined their density to identify 'hot' and 'cold' terms. The hot zones are basically GVCs and, on the other side, GPNs, so there are two strands of literature. I guess Martin Hess would be exhibiting the GPN perspective.

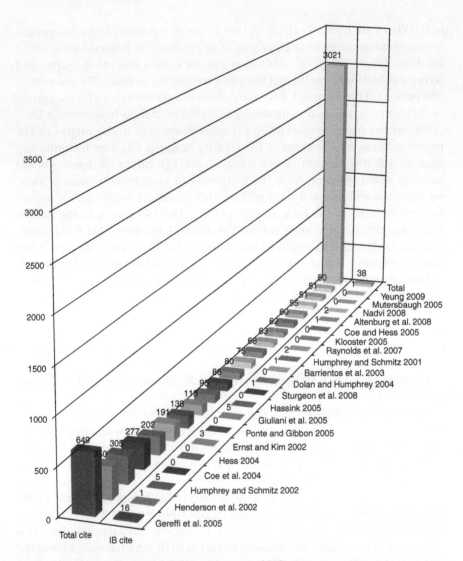

Figure 3.5   Twenty most cited GVC articles (out of 549)

And there are other people representing the GVC perspective, interested in the governance of firms, and issues such as the role of institutional actors. I also analyse the data using a cluster-density view, which – building on the most widely cited themes – in these literatures. In the 20 most cited papers, there is a red area which is GPNs, about upgrading, about implications for development, and then we have a green cluster around capabilities in terms of how deeply tacit knowledge is being absorbed – for instance, how much innovation is taking place. The central node is GVCs, and there we also have a lot of work using and drawing on the GVC literature related to issues of standards. So this is looking at the governance of production networks, including considerations of product and labour standards.

The next step before I conclude is to ask, really, where is it that the 20 most cited publications are used in IB? Here we see a shrinking of the space of IB, towards four or five papers, from the Journal of International Business Studies, the International Business Review, the Journal of International Management, the Journal of World Business and the Management International Review. You can see which types of papers are used most widely in which journal. There has been, interestingly enough, in JIBS recently, an increasing awareness of GVCs/GPNs, largely in the work of Ram Mudambi and the special issue around economic geography (Beugelsdijk and Mudambi 2013), so there are a couple of citations. This goes back to the sources which are really the foundational papers around GVC and GPN. There is an increasing level of awareness in IBR, but the rest of the journals are receiving fewer citations, or the authors who are publishing in them are not necessarily drawing that frequently on GVC/GPN papers.

So, in which context are these 20 most cited GVC/GPN papers used in IB? Mostly it is when we are talking about firm strategy. I use a term density map so, mostly, any type of GVC/GPN work that has implications for firms, or firms' strategic development, issues of improvements on certain strategic issues, such as in BRIC countries, these would be the central themes. The density view shows us the number of clusters in this context (Figure 3.6). Very briefly, I am not yet completely done with this study. I was only just getting started when I received the invitation to speak here, so I am not really fully finished with it and this is kind of an exploratory look so far. But now I go into a thematic analysis, looking

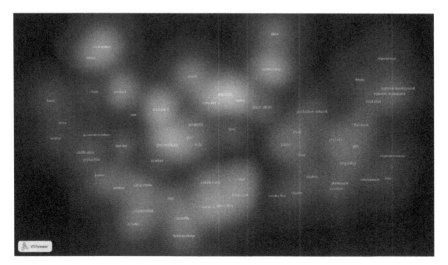

Figure 3.6   Cluster-density view of 20 most cited GVC/GPN papers (themes)

Note: The brightest areas on the figure are the 'hot' zones where terms occur most frequently.

at the 20 most used GVC/GPN papers and the themes that come out of them, so categorising the themes more widely and identifying those themes that are not necessarily directly linked to the issues we normally deal with in IB. So if we look at that, it is mostly to do with economic and social upgrading. I would like to point out the Giuliani paper in 2005 (Giuliani, Pietrobelli and Rabellotti 2005), for instance, an interesting paper that helps us to theorise around the notion of upgrading, which is something that was certainly alien, previously, to the IB literature. Supplier compliance – this is around standards and how suppliers are compliant with the ethical or production processes as scheduled by key lead firms. Issues of distributive outcomes, impacts: we are, in IB, less concerned with other distributional outcomes than with the performance outcomes for the key actor, the lead actor. So, as a function of this, there is more concern with impact and distributive outcomes in the GVC/GPN literature. There are also issues of poverty, asymmetry, some things which in the context of IB are lesser concerns, to date anyway. Issues of vulnerability, smaller suppliers who are at a power asymmetry disadvantage. A number of people in economic geography and economic development address issues of small suppliers and their marginalisation, labour skills development, sustainability issues, value capture at the periphery.

These are the kinds of themes, when looking very broadly into the most widely cited works, that I believe could be triggers for conversations around whether there is room for IB scholars to, kind of, get a bit out of the box of the firm focus and outcomes, which I believe would be very beneficial. I have to say, however, that there are of course many limitations to my work so far, as well. I didn't look at book chapters at all. I took this first step, which is just to look at papers mentioning GVC or GPN in the title, keywords or abstract. So there may be significant work which is basically not using those terms in the title but do cover these ideas in the body of the work. There is more work that I have to do in terms of fruitfully connecting IB writing with the work of the GVC/GPN literature. Mo Yamin has made a significant contribution in this respect (Yamin 2011). The next steps will entail going back over some of the IB literature and categorising the keywords in context ('KWIC' analysis). This is to say, in which contexts do specific citations take place? What are the implications that IB scholars are drawing from adopting specific literature? So, in a nut shell, this is a preview of what I believe could be a fruitful agenda, drawing on evidence of what has been published so far. Looking at different use of the terminology of GVC and GPN in IB and looking at ways in which the adoption of some of these concepts and their consequences can potentially invigorate new research avenues.

Commodity chains and commodity frontiers: ecology and the state in natural resource industries, by Liam Campling

Good morning all, and thanks again to Jennifer and Gary for the invite. I teach international business at the School of Business and Management at

Queen Mary, but I also publish in economic geography journals and have been working for some years on the global value chain/global commodity chain/ global production network frameworks, what I call a political economy variant of 'commodity studies' (Bernstein and Campling 2006). All of them, broadly, have a similar concern, although there are debates around the particularities and the ways in analytically, and so on. So, this all comes together under the idea of commodity chains, but that is just shorthand to capture this entire range of material. I want to talk to the theme of spatial/historical development of multinational enterprises. But I am not going to talk about specific firms. The case that I am going to be talking about is the global tuna industry. Here you have fairly major players like Mitsubishi, Heinz, Lehman Brothers, and private equity involved. There are lots of big players, but they are going to be in the background for the discussion here because instead I want to talk about some steps to try to understand the natural resource industries – in particular the role of multinational enterprises and their attempts to coordinate and control natural resource value chains, which of course, incorporates almost everything around us in the end. This is a little bit theoretical to start with. What I am trying to do here is synthesise the literature on 'commodity studies' (GVC, GPN, and so on), with a framework called the 'commodity frontier'. This is trying to bring in a more political ecology angle, which is another major concern of geography.

The first step is that I'm going to talk through this theoretically, and then I am going to illustrate it through the particular case of tuna. The first step is to identify the particular characteristics of any natural resource which are consti- tuted through the biological and geophysical specificities of that resource, in concert with the social priorities of any commodity sector at any particular moment in time. So, in other words, natural resources aren't natural, nat- urally resources as they depend on the social and cultural context, effective demand, appropriate technology and different priorities in political choice. So, for example, the insuring of property rights over particular areas at a par- ticular moment in time reflects different priorities of political choice. We can all think about the sub-soil but also the oceans, forests, and so on. So that is the first step.

The second step is the question of distance and durability. Any industry involved in extracting any natural resource or producing natural resources, including agriculture, faces the problem of how to synthesise the organic, and of course, this is a fundamental problem and a historical problem. Enterprises are attempting to overcome, and profit from, the tension between the organic – so organic matter deteriorates, it is perishable – and the syn- thetic; they are engaging directly in attempting to transform organic matter and face the risk therefore of its deteriorating before final exchange. This is a fairly obvious point but is a starting point to think through more care- fully about how these factors influence foreign direct investment decisions, the location of investment, and so on. So the point I am trying to focus on in terms of historical change over time is that enterprises deploy a range of business strategies and technological innovations to partially synthesise the organic, to maximise the potential for profitable accumulation. Again, this is fairly obvious and nothing revelatory.

The next step is slightly more of a jump. This is using a guy called Jason Moore (2010a; 2010b) who works on theorising the history of capitalism and is very grounded in lots of the literatures we are talking about today. He tries to see capitalism as an ecological regime that reproduces itself through new commodity frontiers rather than more commonly deployed notions of a 'resource' frontier in which economic activity simply impacts *on* nature. So what he is trying to argue is that we have to see the development of human society in concert with the development or our interactions with the natural world. In other words, we don't impact on nature; we function *through* it. He wants to see a more dialectical relationship...a more dialectical understanding of the relationship between human society and the natural world.

Enterprises engaged in the movement into new commodity frontiers – new forests, new arable land, new fisheries, and so on – have enhanced the possibilities for accumulation because they are entering zones of minimal or zero commodification *at first*. So this is a commodity *widening* strategy or a strategy of extensive development, geographically extensive development. This connects time and space. This offers the possibility, for a certain period of time at least, for a high ecological surplus. You can think of this in relation to ground rent and natural resource rents, if you prefer, but of course over time the underlying socio-ecological conditions of the reproduction of this system stagnate or they decline, and production costs tend to converge. So you lose out on the high ecological surplus the initial very high natural resource rent. A typical response – coming back to the point about distance and durability – is socio-technological innovations, capitalisation, to engage in commodity *deepening* strategies. So we can think of ever-deeper mines, increased intensification of agriculture, and so on, to try and extract ever more through capitalisation and socio-technological innovation and to appropriate nature from existing commodity frontiers. The way to think of this, in short, is the geographical extent and productive intensity of natural resource industries. This connects back to the first point on property rights which is that, of course, this isn't done in a frictionless environment. It depends entirely on the relationship of access and how you access the natural resources themselves. Because natural resources are very often found, at least in the contemporary context, in biologically or geophysically specific geographical ranges, and very often in the developing world, or Global South, foreign direct investment in natural resource industries often takes place in areas that are more difficult to invest in. Now, this often means that the extent of multinational enterprise territorial embeddedness becomes more deeply rooted because of the necessity of engaging in

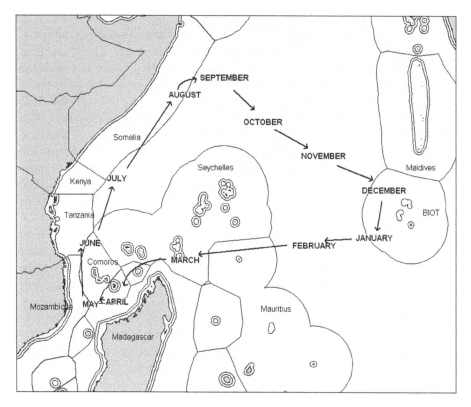

Figure 3.7   Schematic of the migratory flows of tuna
Source: Campling (2012).

a relationship with the state. For example, a concession arrangement with a government to establish a plantation, access rights to the sub-soil for mining or access rights in a fishery which is state property very often. So access to natural resources by multinational enterprises is politically contingent upon historical time and geographical space. In other words, different states demand different conditions of access at different times.

That is my opening gambit, and hopefully I am going to show how this works with one particular case which I have been working on for the last ten years, which is the global tuna industry. I am sure that while I am doing so we can recognise how this would connect to other natural resource sectors. The first thing when looking at the biological and geographical, geophysical characteristics of the resource itself, we can see the migration flows of tuna in the Western Indian Ocean (Figure 3.7).

They traverse millions of miles, cutting across all different kinds of state territories. You can see the outer lines here (Figure 3.7), these are the limits of exclusive economic zones – I'll come back to this later on. Another thing to note is the huge distances the tuna are travelling – their population movements. In the past, this created an industrial limit to extraction, previous to industrial fisheries. The other thing to note is the Seychelles, where I lived for three years and where I got into tuna in the first place, because the island is dependent on tuna and tourism. The key thing here from a business strategy perspective is that boats use the Seychelles as their home port in order to maximise their day's fishing, so they are following the fish around and minimise their day's 'steaming' – going to and from the fishing zone to offload. So you have a spatial-temporal fix by using the specific place of the Seychelles as the base for the operations themselves. The other thing to note is the different species of tuna. For example, we have the Skipjack which is what Northern Europeans eat in the cans, and the Yellowfin which is generally eaten in Southern Europe – Spain and Italy. Big industrial vessels are used to scoop these fish from the sea – damaging their flesh, but this deterioration in quality doesn't matter because they are put in a can. But if we take a different species like Bluefin, which you have all probably heard of in relation to Japan and sashimi, here each fish is caught with an individual hook, and great care is taken with the fish post-harvest and buyers select individual fish – one fish sometimes sells for a million dollars. Putting a price on the fish is connected to cultures of consumption, but it is also about the biology of the species. For Bluefin, you have an incredibly highly priced species, which can be understood in part by the biological characteristics of the resource itself. Skipjack reproduce very quickly (after 1.5 years), they are constantly reproducing all year round, and they grow to quite a small size – whereas Bluefin, which are even bigger than I am, reproduce for only a few months of the year, and it takes them up to eight years to reach sexual maturity. So species differentiation plays a massive role in understanding the strategies of businesses engaged in the particular commodity chains.

Now, on making the organic synthetic, this fairly abstract point that I was trying to make earlier, it is a simple point of canning a fish. The technology was developed by a commission by Napoleon during the Napoleonic Wars, the intellectual property for which was then stolen by a British firm to develop canning as a mass commodity. The other thing that is connected is that before the rise of freezer technology, boats had to offload their catch quickly. For the first canned tuna fisheries around the Bay of Biscay, there would be lots of little canneries dotted around all the coastline of France and Spain and Portugal and the boats would have to go back constantly to these small little canneries because they couldn't freeze the fish. So they would follow the fish around the coast when it was migrating, catch it, bring it back, catch it, bring it back. As a result, the economic geography of the production system until the 1950s was that these tiny little canneries dotted around the coastline which creates massive limitations on the economies of scale in the plants, and so on. With the advent of freezer technology, cold stores and especially recently the use of freezer containers, it doesn't matter where you are for processing. The largest processor, which owns the brand John West, is in Thailand. Thailand doesn't have any tuna fisheries of any significance near its coastline. So the role of freezer technology played a fundamental role in the shaping of the international division of labour in this commodity chain.

The other point, more outside of economic geography and international business, is the notion of capitalism as an ecological regime. I mentioned about the commodity widening strategy, and in tuna fisheries you can observe this with the geographical expansion and intensification of catch in the 1970s onwards around Central America and West Africa. Over time these areas became less productive as the initial ecological surplus declines, so you then see the expansion further out, to the Western Indian Ocean and Western and Central Pacific in the 1980s onwards. The commodity frontier is simultaneously widening but also deepening with the introduction of more effective techniques of extraction. Now the geographical expansion has reached across the entire latitude of the fish population movement.

To illustrate the notion of high ecological surplus: for the Yellowfin stocks in the Western Indian Ocean we can see the point in the late 1980s when the catch of Yellowfin declined relative to the catch of Skipjack. So, in other words, the population of the longer living fish that was there began to decline. In order to catch the same number of fish, the boats had to engage in more extensive methods of extraction. An obvious way of understanding a commodity deepening strategy is a shift in basic technology, from pole and line boats, which is what supermarkets like Waitrose and Sainsburys are pitching their sustainability criteria around today, to enormous purse seine boats which catch a whole shoal of fish in one go. So these bigger boats are able to extract more and more resource. They also use a thing called fish aggregating devises, which is a big thing in the UK environmental movement recently, where all the fish aggregate under a floating object, it uses sonar to tell the captain where the fish are. It is the intensification of the technology involved in trying to extract ever more from this resource.

Finally, I want to talk briefly about the question of property. It is a summary of work by a guy called C. B. MacPherson (1983) around property. He conceptualises property as a bundle of rights implemented and conferred by social relations and reflected in juridical practices, which of course change over time. This depends upon political context, and so on. The main thing to talk about in the oceans is that there is a doctrine of the freedom of the seas developed by Hugo Grotius in the 16th century. It was only in the 1980s that you really see the institutionalisation of property in the sea. You had the largest enclosure in human history in the 1980s when the United Nations declared, or UN members, declared the creation of exclusive economic zones. These introduced a new political struggle between coastal states, very often developing coastal states, and multinational enterprises including firms like Mitsubishi, Heinz, and so on. You can see here where the exclusive economic zones are. The way I am conceptualising these are as state property (Campling and Havice 2014). You can see the expansion of the world: suddenly overnight it became the property of particular states. So the question here is, how do you access it as a foreign fishing fleet? This is the debate around the competition between states and firms and around access to natural resources. The Pacific Islands' exclusive economic zones are grouped together which allows them to engage in a form of South-South cooperation where they collectively bargain with foreign fleets. This deepens the politicisation of accessing the resource. This is a particular story because the fish happen to flow through all these exclusive economic zones, and if you want to get access to fish anywhere, commercially, profitably, then you have to be able to follow the fish. So you have to engage in direct negotiation with this collectivity of states.

So to conclude, what I am trying to argue for here is to understand the role of multinational enterprise strategy in the context of relationships between nature and states, specifically in relation to the natural resource industries. The idea of a commodity frontier I hope helps to introduce a way of thinking through how these strategies develop over time, both intensive and extensive development. The big weakness in this approach so far, which is where I draw on international business literature, is to look at the specific firm-level strategies, the differential strategies of firms, in this sector. It is worth emphasising that the competitive conditions that create the intense race to fish are undermining the very conditions for this competition to exist. In other words, firms are fishing out the fish. Partly, this can be explained through the need for firms to intensify their extraction.

Review and discussion by Peter Buckley

Thank you. When I was asked to do this, I said I would play the role of 'sweeper' on the Kaiser Franz Beckenbauer model of picking up everything that is neglected by everyone else. But, in fact, I think this boils down to three sets of comments. The first set of comments is about the concepts that cut across international business and economic geography, which I think we have heard quite a bit about. Second, is the focus on global value chains and, related to that, the statistical and data issues which I think nobody has mentioned but that I think are incredibly important.

I think the first point is that as we can see, geography is one of the key comparators that we have in international business. We have historical comparisons; we have geographic comparisons. As we have alternative position comparisons, what would have happened if an event hadn't happened? My starting point with geographical elements is that the multinational enterprise is a really good testing point for this because you are holding the firm, the institution, constant and looking at different geographical manifestations of that firm. Clearly, we have gone quite a bit further here. I think one of the worries I have, and possibly the only worry I have, about this is that we might get hung up on terminology. I think the concepts that we have in common are strong and powerful and useful. But if we get hung up on whether we call something a global value chain, a global production network, a global commodity chain, I think that will set us back. I use the term 'global factory' (Buckley, 2009, 2011) and this panel that shows that there are three different people using 'global factory' in different ways. Rudolf did an excellent job there of showing, actually showing, some of the possible dangers of this, that it is not just about using those terms.

If we get hung up on terms and we worry too much about terms, it might detract from something that could be really intellectually important. This is that a whole set of groups of academics are working on very similar projects, and we have a lot to learn from each other. One of the 'buzz phrases' I use is that multinationals are increasingly internalising knowledge and externalising operations. If you think about a lot of what was said, that fits right across the board of all these concepts that we are using. The greater international division of labour, the finer and finer breakdown of international division labour. These are concepts that have a lot of life in them and are looked at from different angles. It is interesting when you use the term 'black box' your black boxes might be different from my black boxes. Your black box might be the multinational enterprise; my black box might be the geographical and environmental surroundings of it. That is very encouraging because we can put our black boxes together and hopefully make transparent boxes. I do think there are massive opportunities here. I think the other thing, we have been doing work on regional cities in China and looking at both place and space which is a paper we have given at this conference highlights. One of the things that economic geography has highlighted is a phrase that I think Martin used which is the assumption of 'methodological nationalism'. I think this is gradually breaking down in international business. We tended to think of the nation, we tended to think of FDI, going from country A to country B and now we really need to think of it as going from different places and spaces. There are loads of really interesting issues. My only concern is that the danger of this is that we get stuck on the terminology and that we forget the underlying concepts. I think this is really potentially really exciting.

The central issue is global value chains and how we conceive of that, and, again, we have the role of how far the creation and power of multinational enterprises running these is, and how far its external factors are. What are the geographical and locational factors, and how do we put that together? The way we conceive of that, I think, we are going to have to have debates about how best to conceive of this and how best to put the role of the multinational enterprise into this.

That leads to the third thing, which hasn't been mentioned, which is when we start to look at this, the statistics that we have are incredibly inadequate.

Statistics are either based on national trade flows, based on industries, which is a really dated concept because all global value chains, all global factories, go across conventional industries. The good news is that the people who work on this and put the statistics together and produce things like the World Investment Report are very aware of this. When I was principle consultant for the World Investment Report in 2011, we looked at non-equity modes, and that was the first time that the United Nations Conference on Trade and Development (UNCTAD) had got away from its fixation on FDI. Now as we all know, FDI is one way of doing international business. It is an iconic way, and in many senses it may be the most important way: it conveys control, blah, blah, blah. But non-equity modes are very important in global value chains. I think the 2011 World Investment Report (UNCTAD, 2011) was the start of UNCTAD looking more at what they are set up to do, which is transnational corporations, all the activities of transnational firms. That I think was a start. Now they are starting to look at value-added trade. This isn't going to go in the final report, but there is an incredible competition among international institutions to be the first to produce statistics that we can all really use. I was at Organisation for Economic Co-operation and Development (OECD) a couple of weeks ago in Paris, which it was one of the best days I've had. They were all statisticians and it was fantastic because they are really trying to get a handle on what is really happening in the world economy.

What is really happening in the world economy is not encapsulated by national income statistics. It is not encapsulated by industry-level statistics. It is encapsulated by dynamic changes in global value chains and all the ramifications that has for where activity takes place, who owns it, who appropriates the benefits from it, and so on. So I think that not only are we at a really exciting time with regard to the concepts; we are also at a really exciting time in terms of policy and measurement because if we can get proper measurement in this, then policies can become a lot more rational. Instead of countries going out and saying they want to attract more FDI, and it doesn't matter what it is, let's just get more in, we can be much more nuanced about exactly what type of FDI individual countries are more able to attract and get more benefit from. So, in a sense, watch this space for OECD, UNCTAD and the rest who are desperately trying to get value-added trade and then move on to ways we can get a handle on global value chains. I think this is a really worthwhile operation, and I think it might be the start of something big.

Questions

Question 1, Jean-Francois Hennart: Martin, if we look at the data you showed us on Apple, when we consider this, how does this impact on trade statistics? Because in terms of trade statistics, the full value of the Apple product, if it is a Chinese export...when in fact the value added is miniscule. We have people talking about bi-lateral trade balances...

Martin Hess: That is a major issue, and Apple produces all of its iPads, iPhones, etc. in China. This distorts the China/US trade balance because the value added in China is the labour cost within the Foxconn factories plus some other stuff that is produced in China by other multinationals in terms of components. It is compared to the sales price and the import price. Yes, it is minuscule. I think there is a reaction on the political side now, and Peter alluded to that in the context of the OECD about trade organisations trying to find new ways to get to terms with the value added and measuring global value chains. They have produced a recent report, a literature review on value chains on GPNs by the WTO and the Li and Fung Institute of all places (Elms & Low, 2013). They are critically aware of these issues, and for the US it is a massive debate about trade imbalances and what they reflect and what they hide. If you took this into consideration the trade data for the US/China would be very different.

Jean-Francois Hennart: And by the way, there is the equivalent when you look at this global value chain and products with value added being in one place and financial flows in terms of export and import being very different from the value added. You have the same thing in terms of financial flows because through tax havens basically what you have is a geography of accumulation of profits which is quite different from the physical value added of multinationals, which makes FDI data useless. We have the same problem in terms of the geography of profit accumulation versus the geography of profit generation. For example, the Netherlands, which is for everything but a name, a tax haven, you have got...and if you look at the profitability of multinationals in the US since most of the profits aren't declared in the US, because they are kept in offshore locations, this affects all the literature about multinationals and their performance because their reported profits aren't necessarily where the profits are. So there are tremendous issues.

Peter Buckley: The statisticians are on to that. One of the things that the OECD was talking about was looking at pass-through foreign investment where an American company invests in the Netherlands but the intention is to go somewhere else. They are working on techniques with tax authorities and others to be able to do that. This means that in a few years we could have a revolution in terms of the statistics that we are dealing with. It could be much more accurate, and then with the value-added trade I think there is a table in a recent World Investment Report (2013: Figure IV:32). Singapore is a classic one where it is an entrepôt, so you take the exports minus the imports and the value-added element is much smaller than the massive trade. It is a massive trading location, but not a massive value-added location. So I think there is awareness of these issues. I think that is to the credit of us as a community who have started to show that what we are working with are really very imperfect data to measure what is really going on in the world economy.

Question 2, Mohammad Yamin: I think this critical notion of methodological nationalism, it is mistaken. I would like to reflect on that. I think that the role of the state deserves more specific attention, and it doesn't seem to get that. I think the issues that Jean-Francois referred to about transfer pricing and tax havens means that regulation is very important. One of the issues that bothers me, and I don't know the solution, is really economic development is a national issue, fundamentally. Not exclusively, but I think fundamentally it is the role of the state. In emerging markets especially, if you ignore the role of the state, you misunderstand what is happening. When we look at global factories or global value chains, I think this notion of the nation state is under represented. I understand why, but I have issues with it.

Martin Hess: Can I answer that? Thanks, Mo. You are addressing an important point and there are recent papers, one just out by Adrian Smith (Smith, 2014) and another one in the pipeline by others, conceptualising the state with a GPN/global value chains framework because it has been neglected to some extent. Arguably, it has been seen in international business and much of economic geography as something external to all these value creation processes. I think it is important to recognise the state and the various roles the state has, and often contradictory roles. It's not just a regulator; the state is also a massive buyer. If you think of the emergence of companies like Samsung in South Korea that was much to do with military spending by the US, conflicts in Asia, the Cold War. The state is a massive buyer. The National Health Service (NHS) buys clothes to the tune of goodness knows how many billion pounds over the years. The state is a facilitator in terms of trade negotiations. Often it is a producer. We still have an incredibly large number of state-owned multinationals, part or fully state-owned in various parts of the world, even under neo-liberalism. The second issue that you raised about the importance of the nation-state and the scale of the nation-state as opposed to other scales like the local, again I agree we mustn't neglect it, but it must not be the single focus of our attention. Development within a nation-state is again contested. The state has a dual role: it is a supporter of accumulation of capital; at the same time, the state should implement and enforce labour laws, etc. Again, going back to the garment industry, countries like Bangladesh or Cambodia, at the same time they want to keep and maintain FDI by Korean garment multinationals and neglect labour rights to some extent to keep them happy; at the same time, they have a developmental role to play in securing labour rights and working conditions. So it is contradictory. You also have the politics of accumulation. In the UK we talk about the North-South divide – there was this BBC documentary *'Mind the Gap'*. Often state policies focus on developing particular clusters, whether it is London or Silicon Valley. Again, Silicon Valley also came out of military spending and government activities. The role of the state is clearly crucial. The nation-state as an arena of political activity is still important, but not at the expense of other scales, be they supranational or below the nation-state level. That is what I would argue.

Peter Buckley: I agree Mo, I think that is possibly something that has been neglected. I saw some figures recently that were really surprising about the size of the Chinese state. It is tiny. The Chinese state bodies are a fraction of government bodies in Western Europe as a proportion of the population, and by proportion of other things. That is really an interesting take on Chinese development, the unregulated nature of Chinese development. I think you are right, and the point is well taken.

Liam Campling: I would agree as well. That is what I was trying to do in my presentation. If you look at the national oil companies, they are emerging as major players, either as resource-seeking national oil companies or more national developmental oil companies using their own state property as it were. There is a dual model that is displacing the old oil majors and transforming the global oil economy.

Peter Buckley: I think the straw man that is being broken down is taking the nation as a homogenous thing. So, having moved away from that and saying it is much more differentiated by province, by city, particularly by city. Perhaps we have lost something in that.

Question 3, Jennifer Johns: I would like to ask a question about the use of these concepts and frameworks in relation to impact. Do we as a community have a sense of the degree to which these frameworks, such as GVC and GPN are understood by firms themselves? Is there a feedback mechanism in the sense that our concepts are impacting the empirics we seek to understand?

Peter Buckley: Yes. One of our impact studies was on the work we have been doing on regional cities in China. We did that for the UKTI (UK Trade and Investment) with CBBC (China-Britain Business Council) and how they used that as a locational choice for deciding exactly which city to locate in China. That is interesting because it is very much theory driven. The decision about where to put the most recent British Consulate was based on our model. I think they had their answer beforehand, but the model justified it, so next time you are in the British Consulate in Wuhan, you know why it is there!

Liam Campling: In my own work I use a global value chain analysis to understand the industrial structure and trade regimes, and that work has fed directly into developing country government policy on trade negotiation and outcomes. This had the result of creating a new trade rule, which provided a condition for considerable foreign investment in isolated places like Papua New Guinea. I think that it is useful and can be deployed very practically as well as theoretically. I think that is why it has been taken up so much by the World Bank, and so on. If you do the same exercise as Rudolf did for policy documents, what you see is a massive explosion around 2010 when the World Bank, ILO and other big international agencies, UNCTAD, etc., are using the global value chain framework precisely because it can be deployed in a very practical way to understand how industry works beyond the nation-state. The downside, which is where I think Peter is right to say that we need to avoid a semantic debate around whether you use the GVC/GPN/GCC frameworks the one thing that is important is the substantive debates across the literatures, within GVC or within GPN, and there is no agreement. For example, one of the biggest areas where there is contestation is around the question of whether we are using the framework as a policy mechanism or as a tool of analysis. Are we trying to design global value chains, or are we trying to understand how they work? That is a major area of debate.

Peter Buckley: I think there are also some unanswered questions. I say unanswered because I don't have the answer – which is the role of the satellite firms in the constellation of the global factory. OK, we know a lot about the strategy of the focal firm. But what about the strategies of all the companies that are linked in? And, if all that is true, can we really talk about the strategy of the global factory? We can talk about the strategy of the focal firm, but is that subsuming? Are we subsuming all the suppliers and customers, technology suppliers, alliance partners, etc. into one thing? How far can you do that? I don't have the answer to that. That is a really interesting area of research: to look at how far you can do that and how far the strategies of the individual firms work out. There is stuff being done on that now that looks interesting.

Question 4, Mohammad Yamin: Just on that point, I have just been reading a few papers and the message I got was that global value chains are actually restructuring, in some sectors anyway, and the restructuring is mostly in terms of consolidation. The number of suppliers is significantly less by factors of more than a hundred. That would speak to the fact that the strategy of the core firm is important as it is more concentrated. I know that it is a semantic issue, but geographically a lot of these suppliers are in China, in South East Asia, and we talk about global value chains. So in that sense they aren't really global – in the literal geographic sense. We shouldn't lose sight of this.

Peter Buckley: Yes, well Alan [Rugman] would talk about regional value chains.

Liam Campling: There is a neat trick around that, you would say a global value chain for automobiles as a whole and then a 'value chain' for automobiles that was specific to a particular region. That has been widely recognised in the literature as a problem and a trap to avoid. There are quite simple ways around it. Also, Peter Nolan's work on the cascade effect, and Peter Gibbon's on the role of first tier suppliers becoming ever more concentrated, which is what you are talking about. This concentration moving back into first tier suppliers, creating what Nolan calls the 'external firm' – talking about the externalisation of operations – they are externalised but still controlled by the lead firm, and it becomes that the firm is able to shape through procurement the way that the supply chains function.

Peter Buckley: I don't know if it is the same article, but the article I read had exactly the problem you were mentioning. It was almost using the word 'should'. It was saying the focal firm 'should' reduce the number of suppliers, 'should' consolidate. So we have gone towards strategy advice.

Mohammad Yamin: The paper with Gereffi for Review of International Political Economy did say what was happening, not that it should.

Peter Buckley: The one I read almost elided into advice about consolidation.

Question 5, Gary Cook: Going back some years ago to when the research I was doing was going out to talk to oil companies and asking them about their subcontracting relationships. This was at the kind of time when the view of firms was as a nexus of treaties or common practices was popular and there was talk of fuzzy boundaries. What really struck me was that when I talked to those oil executives, they saw the world in a very black and white way. They had no fuzziness at all about what they viewed as being in the firm and what they viewed as being outside the firm. They also had a very clear view about why they used particular kinds of subcontracting relationships with particular types of subcontractors. The methodological point that this gives us is that somewhere along the line, if we are going to understand these value chains, we need so spend some time getting inside the companies' heads if you like and understanding how they view the world because the danger with this is that social scientists can construct a view of what is happening which can be divorced from the way firms see themselves.

Peter Buckley: Yes, I had a similar experience when I was doing work on joint ventures and alliances from actually looking at contracts, which is what Coase recommended that we do. We should look at contracts, not theorise in the abstract.

Liam Campling: Yes, well economic geographers do tend to do applied empirical work. I have interviewed over 700 people in 20 countries and literally followed the fish and move away from blueprint theorising which is a real problem across the social sciences.

Jennifer Johns: When I've interviewed firms and explained the conceptual frameworks for projects. I have found that interviewees are often familiar with the notion of value chains, Porterian value chains, but are not aware of more complex concepts. I wonder how far the managers are aware of the interconnection between actors in the GVCs/GPNs and how few people have a genuine strategic overview of the network.

Liam Campling: I suppose it depends how high up you go.

Peter Buckley: I think it just depends on who you talk to. Whether senior managers have the overview is a difficult question.

Jennifer Johns: Yes, well sometimes it can go back to what you were saying yesterday in your keynote speech, Peter, about the power of the individual as well. We are educating some of these managers as well.

Peter Buckley: Indeed. It is rather like the story of the product cycle. It went out of being because we all taught it, and then everyone could anticipate what it was going to happen.

Liam Campling: It also comes to the political power of the corporation; the senior level technocrats in firms are very aware of what is happening in the WTO, lobbying their own governments, for example. Much depends upon whether a firm has more or less political interests. Some firms would benefit more from what some people would call policy rents than others would.

Question 6, Roseline Wanjiru: An observation on global production networks and as they touch down in particular places, I think that the geographical peripheries, those on the extreme margins of the global economy, countries such as those in sub-Saharan Africa, for example, where a lot of debate around lead firms and a lot of the theories that we present are based on particular assumptions. Possibly because there is a lack of information. One of the challenges of doing research on the margins is the lack of official, or reliable, empirical data on which to publish. The realities of global business are that these firms have real impacts on people, on families, on societies, so it is a limitation of the method that the literature is interesting and the theories are relevant, but if you look at some contexts where there is either no data or few researchers working, you have major challenges trying to get into the debate or show why that particular context is different. I see that we are giving firms privilege that comes from a Western context. I am trying to say that there is a world beyond what is reported in the articles.

Rolf Sinkovics: From my perspective, I think that there is some value in conceptualising academia as a global production network in itself. There are various actors producing work, and we are all driven towards some types of outputs. This is something that has quite significant implications now. PhD students are encouraged now, well no, they are required, to work towards their PhD within three years. That funnels the whole process towards something that is much more readily available. We have heard today about statistical challenges that need to be dealt with senior individuals in supra-regional organisations. We are not yet there that we cannot guide our students to doing research on the margins very frequently – because that will not produce the tangible output that is required by the PhD student and for the supervisor to report back that their through-put rate is appropriate. When we conceptualise what is happening in academia, we are seeing that we talk about outputs. There is some value in going through concepts, but when we review them, we will see that there are also some unique concepts that we are also ignoring. Some in economic geography and developmental literature have not resounded well in the international business literature for exactly these particular reasons, because they are more cumbersome.

Liam Campling: On Roseline's question I would look at the literature in development studies and development geography. People have been grappling with the problems you are talking about there since the 1960s. There are huge literatures on the relationship between multinationals and places in the periphery. But still, often the data aren't there for specific issues. For example, I was in Madagascar in December working on a particular value chain. There is no data. My research is all based on interviews. You are lucky to get bits and pieces of data here and there. Otherwise you rely on interviews. Talking of PhD students (Rudolf's point), I have one working on the global value chains of iron and rubber in Liberia, and another on e-waste in Malaysia. They are all based on the combination of descriptive statistics and very substantial semi-structured interviews. So I think it is possible in the timeframe.

Martin Hess: I would agree. Formal data is hard to come by for places on the periphery. There is a growing body of work done on GVC and GPN analysis of sub-Saharan Africa and elsewhere. It also includes research by people from these parts of the world, not just us parachuting in from the West and spreading the message of integrating into value chains. More nuanced analyses are on their way, which is encouraging.

Peter Buckley: What is important is to put it in a concrete and delimited context – to try to look at everything is difficult. To focus on one particular country, on one particular area, then you have a real chance of making a contribution.

Summary

This chapter has presented a record of the panel session aiming to illuminate and interrogate the shared – and occasionally divergent – perspectives on the spatial and historical development of MNEs by international business and economic geography. It is clear from this panel session that many of the key questions posed by each discipline in this specialist area are shared. However, each discipline has developed different (but not necessarily uncomplimentary) frameworks for collecting and analysing data on global sourcing and firm activities in general. The panel session revealed that there is much interest in, and excitement around, increased interaction between the two disciplines. Several barriers to greater communication – such as issues around the labelling of terms and frameworks, the low degree of cross-referencing between the two disciplines in this field and the availability and applicability of data – were identified by panellists and discussants. These barriers were not considered to be insurmountable, and the panel session highlighted a possibility of future fruitful collaboration with an aim to increasing our understandings of the spatial and historical evolution of MNEs and current change dynamics in the global economic environment.

References

Altenburg, T., Schmitz, H. & Stamm, A. (2008) 'Breakthrough China's and India's Transition from Production to Innovation'. *World Development*, 36(2)' 325–344

Barrientos, S., Dolan, C. & Tallontire, A. (2003) 'A Gendered Value Chain Approach to Codes of Conduct in African Horticulture'. *World Development*, 31 (9), 1511–1526.

Bernstein, Henry and Liam Campling (2006) 'Commodity Studies and Commodity Fetishism I: *Trading Down*'. *Journal of Agrarian Change*, 6(2), 239–264

Beugelsdijk, S. and Mudambi, R. (2013) 'MNEs as border-crossing multi-location enterprises: The role of discontinuities in geographic space'. *Journal of International Business Studies*, 44(5), 413–426

Beugelsdijk, S., Mudambi, R. & Andersson, U. (2013) 'Special Issue: The Multinational in Geographic Space'. *Journal of International Business Studies*, 44(5), 413–544.

Buckley, P. J. (2009) 'The impact of the global factory on economic development'. *Journal of World Business*, 44(2), 131–143.

Buckley, P. J. (2011) 'International integration and coordination in the global factory'. *Management International Review* 51(2), 269–283.

Campling, Liam (2012) '"The Tuna 'Commodity Frontier": Business Strategies and Environment in the Industrial Tuna Fisheries of the Western Indian Ocean'. *Journal of Agrarian Change*, 12(2–3), 252–278

Campling, Liam and Elizabeth Havice (2014) 'The problem of property in industrial fisheries'. *Journal of Peasant Studies*, 41, 1–21.

Coe, N.M., Hess, M., Yeung, H. W-C., Dicken, P & Hess, M. (2004) '"Globalizing" regional development: a global productions network perspective'. *Transactions of the Institute of British Geographers*, 29, 468–484.

Coe, N. & Hess, M. (2005) 'The Internationalization of Retailing: Implications for Supply Network Restructuring in East Asia and Eastern Europe'. *Journal of Economic Geography*, 5(4), 449–473.

Dolan C. & Humphrey J. (2004) 'Changing governance patterns in the trade in fresh vegetables between Africa and the United Kingdom'. *Environment and Planning A*, 36(3), 491 – 509

Elms, D. K. & Low, P. (2013) *Global value chains in a changing world*. Geneva: World Trade Organization.

Ernst, D. & Kim, L. (2002) 'Global production networks, knowledge diffusion and local capabilities formation'. *Research Policy*, 31, 1417–1429.

Froud, J., Johal, S., Leaver, A. & Williams, K. (2012) 'Apple business model: Financialisation across the Pacific'. University of Manchester: CRESC Working Paper 111. Available from: http://www.cresc.ac.uk/publications/apple-business-model-financialization-across-the-pacific

Gereffi, G., Humphrey, J. & Sturgeon, T. (2005) 'The governance of global value chains'. *Review of International Political Economy*, 12(1), 78–104.

Giuliani, E., Pietrobelli, C. & Rabellotti, R. (2005) 'Upgrading in Global Value Chains: Lessons from Latin American Clusters'. *World Development*, 33(4), 549–573

Hassink, R. (2005) 'How to Unlock Regional Economies from Path Dependency? From Learning Region to Learning Cluster'. *European Planning Studies*, 13, 521–535.

Henderson, J., Dicken, P., Hess, M., Coe, N. & Yeung, H. W-C. (2002) 'Global Production Networks and an analysis of economic development'. *Review of International Political Economy*, 9(3), 436–464.

Hess, M. (2004) 'Spatial Relationships? Towards a reconceptualization of embeddedness'. *Progress in Human Geography*, 28(2),165–186.

Humphrey, J. & Schmitz, H. (2001) 'Governance in Global Value Chains'. *IDS Bulletin*, 32(3), 19–29.

Humphrey J. & Schmitz H. (2002) 'How does insertion in global value chains affect upgrading in industrial clusters?'. *Regional Studies*, 36, 1017–1027.

Klooster, D. (2005) 'Environmental certification of forests: the evolution of environmental governance in a commodity network'. *Journal of Rural Studies*, 21, 403–417.

Kogut, B. (1985) 'Designing Global Strategies: Comparative and Competitive Value-added Chains'. *Sloan Management Review*, 26, 15–28.

MacPherson, C. B. (1983) *Burke*. Oxford: Oxford University Press.

Moore, J.W. (2010a) '"Amsterdam is Standing on Norway" Part I: The Alchemy of Capital, Empire and Nature in the Diaspora of Silver, 1545–1648'. *Journal of Agrarian Change*, 10(1), 33–68.

Moore, J.W. (2010b) '"Amsterdam is Standing on Norway" Part II: The Global North Atlantic in the Ecological Revolution of the Long Seventeenth Century'. *Journal of Agrarian Change*, 10(2), 188–227.

Mutersbaugh T. (2005) 'Fighting standards with standards: Harmonization, rents, and social accountability in certified agrofood networks'. *Environment and Planning A*, 37(11), 2033–2051

Nadvi, K. (2008) 'Global standards, global governance and the organization of global value chains'. *Journal of Economic Geography*, 8(3), 323–343.

Ponte, S. & Gibbon, P. (2005) 'Quality Standards, Conventions and the Governance of Global Value Chains'. *Economy and Society*, 34(1), 1–31.

Raynolds, L. T., Murray, D. & Heller, A. (2007) 'Regulating Sustainability in the Coffee Sector: A Comparative Analysis of Third-Party Environmental and Social Certification Initiatives'. *Agriculture and Human Values*, 24(2), 147–163.

Smith, A. (2014) 'The state, institutional frameworks and the dynamics of capital in global production networks'. *Progress in Human Geography*. Advanced online access DOI: 10.1177/0309132513518292

Sturgeon, T., van Biesebroeck, J. & Gereffi, G. (2008) 'Value chains, networks and clusters: reframing the global automotive industry'. *Journal of Economic Geography*, 8, 297–321.

UNCTAD (2011) *World Investment Report: Non-equity modes of international production and investment*. Geneva: United Nations.

UNCTAD (2013) *World Investment Report: Global Value Chains, Investment and Trade for Development*. Geneva: United Nations.

Yamin, M. (2011) 'A commentary on Peter Buckley's writings on the global factory'. *Management International Review*, 51, 285–293.

Yeung, H. W-C. (2009) 'Regional development and the competitive dynamics of global production networks: an East Asian perspective'. *Regional Studies*, 43(3), 325–351.

Part II
Rise of EMNEs

4
Institutions and Investments by Emerging-Economy Multinationals in Developed Economies: Solar PV Firms and the Role of Political Authorities in Germany

Matthew M.C. Allen and Maria L. Allen

Introduction

Foreign investments by emerging-economy multinational enterprises (EMNEs) have recently generated much scholarly interest (Buckley et al., 2008; Mathews, 2006; Williamson and Raman, 2011). Key theoretical debates have focused on how this investment differs, if at all, from that by developed-economy multinationals. This work has revealed key insights into the nature of EMNEs and the implications of their activities for international business theory (e.g. Annushkina and Colonel, 2013; Gameltoft et al., 2012; Mathews, 2006; Ramamurti, 2012; Sinkovics et al., 2014). In particular, research has highlighted two key factors that distinguish outward foreign direct investment (OFDI) by emerging-economy firms compared to their developed-economy counterparts. First, home-country governments play a relatively prominent role in pro-moting foreign investments by EMNEs, especially mergers and acquisitions (Buckley et al., 2007; Child and Marinova, 2014; Ramamurti, 2012; Sauvant, 2009; Zhang et al., 2011). Second, EMNEs often acquire firms abroad for their superior capabilities (Mathews, 2006).

However, this emphasis tends to downplay the importance of host-country governments in two key areas. First, host-country governments can play an active role in supporting firms and industries, either directly or indirectly. They, therefore, shape the type and strength of domestic firms' organisational capabilities. Second, host-country governments can influence which firms are for sale and to whom; thus, host-country governments shape foreign investors' opportunities to acquire domestic firms, including their assets and capabilities. As the recent examples of the bid by USA-based Pfizer to acquire the UK's AstraZeneca and the desire by GE (US) to own Alstom (France) demonstrate, proposed acquisitions by developed-economy companies by other developed-economy firms are not free from political influence. Proposed acquisitions of developed-economy firms by those from emerging economies, such as the attempted acquisition of 3Leaf Systems (USA) by Huawei (China), have added political piquancy, however, especially if these are in sensitive technological or economic areas (Child and Marinova, 2014; Zhang et al., 2011).

By incorporating the role of host governments in both promoting the formation and growth of companies in certain industries and determining which companies (would-be) EMNEs can (or cannot) buy into future analysis, a more nuanced understanding of the nature and scope of EMNEs' overseas activities will be developed. In short, not all firms – even those seeking an investor – may be for sale to companies from all countries. Even if (potential) EMNEs wish to acquire more advanced technological capabilities that are available in developed economies (Deng, 2009; Mathews, 2006; Ramamurti, 2012; Williamson and Raman, 2011), the 'supply' of those capabilities can be restricted by foreign governments. At a more fundamental level, the very existence and location of those assets will be shaped by foreign governments' economic policies (Allen, 2013; Whitley, 2007). This chapter, consequently, calls for research on (potential) EMNEs to be extended by assessing the interplay between the institutions and policies of home and host countries and its effect on the (non-) investments by firms from emerging economies in developed economies, especially when advanced organisational or technical capabilities are at stake. By doing so, it draws on key insights from the literature on comparative institutional analysis, the resource-based view of the firm and policy studies.

Studying the fate of solar photovoltaic (PV) firms in Germany is appropriate for three main reasons. First, various political authorities in Germany have provided substantial support to the industry. The industry is, in other words, a politically salient one. Second, the support has been provided on the basis of the current and future economic, employment, environmental and technological benefits that the sector can generate. Various political authorities in Germany view the industry and the firms within it as strategically important. Third and consequently, German political authorities can be expected to be reluctant to cede control of domestic firms that have indirectly and/or directly received significant financial support from political authorities to overseas rivals who are 'unfairly' supported by their own political authorities. In effect, the sale of German solar PV firms as well their associated intellectual property to foreign competitors represents a subsidy by German taxpayers and electricity consumers to foreign firms (Spiegel, 2011).

As will be seen, however, many German solar PV firms that have fallen into financial difficulties have been sold to overseas rivals, including those from emerging economies. This suggests that, despite its political and strategic salience and despite the millions of euros that political authorities have spent supporting firms in the industry, its relative importance is less than that of other sectors. Consequently, firms are not prevented by political authorities from going bankrupt and/or being sold to overseas companies from both developed and emerging economies, including China and the United Arab Emirates (UAE). These Chinese and UAE firms may well emerge as dominant players. Consequently, this research reveals that sectors and firms that are supported by governments are not always seen as being of sufficient economic and strategic importance to warrant protection. This apparent tension amongst political authorities that provide significant financial support to domestic firms and the willingness of those same authorities to sell firms to overseas rivals requires greater scrutiny.

In addition, this research reveals how EMNEs become established by, in part, acquiring overseas assets that owe much of their creation to German state support. The internationalisation process of emerging-economy firms is, therefore, influenced not just by home-country institutions but by host-country ones, too. Without general subsidies to the sector and without financial support to some firms in the industry, it is unlikely that German solar PV firms would have become important players (Bryant, 2012). Not all organisational capabilities are, therefore, equally distributed in developed economies; institutions shape where different types of organisational capabilities emerge and are reproduced (Allen and Aldred, 2013; Becker-Ritterspach et al., 2010; Hotho, 2014; Whitley, 2007). The existing literature neglects both the issue of where capabilities emerge and their potential acquisition by emerging-economy firms (cf. Child and Marinova, 2014; Sauvant, 2009).

This chapter is structured as follows. The next section sets out the theoretical framework and reviews the relevant literature. This is followed by a discussion of the nature of competition in the solar PV industry. The research design and methodology are then set out. Subsequent sections examine the support that German political authorities have provided to the solar PV industry, in general, and to some firms, in particular. The chapter then examines the acquisition of some German solar PV firms by their emerging-economy rivals; it focuses on the importance of organisational capabilities in German firms as well as the role played by institutions in 1) shaping the creation and development of those capabilities and 2) enabling emerging-economy firms to acquire those capabilities. Finally, conclusions are drawn.

Theoretical framework and literature review

States play a central role establishing regulations that help to constitute firms as well as shape their behaviour (Allen, 2013; Brewster et al., 2007; Hotho, 2014; Tüselmann et al., 2008; Whitley and Morgan, 2012). States also influence economic development; the degree to which they actively do so varies (Whitley, 2005).

While some states play a direct role in fostering the growth of particular firms or sectors, others adopt a more arm's-length approach (Evans, 1995; Hollingsworth and Boyer, 1997; Hollingsworth and Streeck, 1994; Johnson, 1982; Whitley, 2005). The latter type of *regulatory* state, in general, seeks to set regulations that create a 'level playing field' for all companies. As long as firms do not infringe legislation, they can act as they wish, free from direct political influence.

By contrast, developmental or promotional states adopt a more active approach to economic growth (Evans, 1995). Such states may provide financial support to particular firms or sectors, create incentives for firms to invest in certain technologies or markets, encourage individual firms to collaborate on specific projects and use publicly funded research to help boost firms' competitiveness in favoured markets or technologies (Amable, 2003; Johnson, 1982; Whitley, 2005). Developmental states encourage coordination between different economic actors in order to attain specific economic goals, such as the development or maintenance of targeted industries and, in some cases, firms.

Developmental states differ significantly in the extent to which business and labour are included in efforts to coordinate economic activities (Whitley, 2005). *Dominant developmental states* discourage the formation of both business and labour associations. Such intermediary associations may represent a rival source of power to that of the state. Consequently, they may impede the state's ability to guide the economy and the growth of particular firms or sectors. By contrast, *business corporatist states* actively encourage business associations to form, especially those that represent large businesses. By doing so, states can delegate some aspects of economic policy, such as training and investment, to large employers and their representatives. *Inclusive corporatist states* encourage union as well as business association involvement in managing certain policies to promote economic growth in particular industries (Whitley, 2005).

It is the role of the state in economic policy making that helps to differentiate emerging economies from developed ones (Buckley et al., 2007; Seyoum and Manyak, 2009). In the above framework, emerging economies fit the 'dominant developmental state' model. China, for instance, lacks independent business and labour organisations, and Chinese political authorities actively encourage the growth of certain firms rather than others. Germany, with its heritage of *Ordnungspolitk*, or the application of ordo-liberal economic ideas (Funk and Allen, 2012), conforms most closely to the regulatory state.

This does not, of course, mean that states in developed economies never play an active role in encouraging the growth of specific economic sectors. Even the 'pro-market' US Government has, for instance, helped to develop the biotechnology, defence and information technology sectors domestically (Allen, 2013; Block and Keller, 2009; Keller and Block, 2013). Indeed, as will be shown below, political authorities in Germany have actively encouraged the development of the solar PV industry. This encouragement has extended from indirect support, in the form of various types of subsidies, to direct aid, in the form of equity stakes by political authorities in particular firms. However, the links between political entities and firms are not as great in Germany as they are, say, in China.

In emerging economies, there is frequently a greater willingness by political authorities to become actively involved in the development of specific sectors and/or firms compared to those in developed economies (Child and Marinova, 2014; Ramamurti, 2012; Sauvant, 2009; Seyoum and Manyak, 2009; Wood and Frynas, 2006; Zhang and Whitley, 2013). Of course, not all firms and sectors in emerging economies are equally favoured (Buckley et al., 2007; Liu and Tylecote, 2009). It is, however, this general involvement in economic and company matters by political authorities in emerging economies that has made developed-economy governments chary of investments by firms from the former in the latter (Sauvant, 2009).

Solar PV technology: no dominant design

The solar PV industry covers firms that enable solar radiation to be converted into electricity using semi-conductors. It includes firms that currently focus primarily on research directly related to PV cells and modules as well as those that research, manufacture, sell, install and provide finance to customers. It extends to those that make important equipment for solar PV module manufacturers. For instance, components, such as inverters that convert the direct current that is generated in the PV modules into alternating current for the grid, play a key role in the efficiency of the PV system as a whole (BMU, 2011). The more efficient the solar PV system, the more electricity is generated and sold, and the higher the return on investment. This chapter focuses on the mass manufacturers, as some of them that have fallen into financial difficulties and have been put up for sale. Component suppliers have, by and large, not.

The strategies of solar PV firms in Germany reflect, in part, the nature of the solar PV market, technology, and degree of 'market readiness' of the technology that individual firms are developing (Allen, 2013; Casper 2009; Casper and Whitley, 2004; Tylecote and Visintin, 2008). The development of solar PV products is characterised by high levels of technological uncertainty. To be sure, solar PV modules based on one technology (poly-crystalline) currently lead the market; however, competing technologies threaten to disrupt the strengths of companies using poly-crystalline products. These competing technologies (mono-crystalline; concentrator photovoltaic (CPV); thin-film, including copper indium gallium selenide (CIGS), copper, indium, gallium, sulphur and selenium (CIS or CIGSSe), cadmium telluride (CdTe) products; dye-sensitised solar cells; and organic PV) are similar, yet distinct (BMU, 2012a). They require researchers with related but different areas of expertise. At present, no dominant design exists.

For those German companies that already manufacture large volumes of solar PV cells and/or modules, this technological uncertainty is a disadvantage as they must be aware of developments in related fields and may have to be prepared to reconfigure their organisations quickly if a serious threat emerges. Such producers face three other, related pressures. Firstly, competition from Asian large-volume manufacturers, in general, and Chinese ones, in particular, has increased over the last five years (BMU, 2012a; European Commission, 2009). Compared to German firms, Chinese companies enjoy better financing options, lower energy costs and reduced labour outlays (BMU, 2012a; Otto Brenner Foundation, 2013). Indeed, some in the industry argue that Chinese firms are 'dumping' their products on European markets (Meyer, former head of Soltecture, cited in Schwarzburger, 2013). Secondly, solar PV modules have become increasingly commoditised (BMU, 2012a; European Commission, 2009). Significant falls in solar module prices reflect this: since 2006, retail prices have fallen by 60 per cent or more (BMU, 2012a; BMWi, 2011; European Commission, 2013; Otto Brenner Foundation, 2013). Finally, the rapid growth of the industry has led to overcapacity (BMU, 2012a). This, too, has placed pressures on mass manufacturers to reduce costs. In short, for many solar PV firms in Germany, conditions are tough. This is true, despite the substantial support that, as will be shown, various political authorities in Germany have provided to the industry and, in some cases, individual firms.

Research design and methodology

The financial support that firms in the solar PV industry in Germany have received suggests that they are politically important. The industry is likely to be a source of employment, economic growth and technological advances in the future. It is one that can help countries to achieve energy independence and security. It is, therefore, a strategically important sector. Consequently, political authorities in Germany are likely to be reluctant to allowing foreign firms, especially those from emerging economies with a dominant developmental state, to buy German firms and their associated intellectual property. In short, German solar PV firms' very existence owes much to the policies of the political authorities in Germany. Their current travails create opportunities for foreign firms to acquire them and their assets. Yet, German political authorities are likely to prefer to see such firms remain in German ownership.

In order to analyse the role of German political authorities on, first, the creation of solar PV firms as well as the industry more generally and, second, the potential for emerging-economy firms to acquire capabilities in those firms and industries, numerous sources of information have been used. The analysis is based on an extensive examination of company documents, government reports and policies, analysts' reports and newspaper articles. German

Government sources provide a wealth of data on publically funded technological investments. They, along with reports by the European Commission,
provide details of the direct and indirect support that firms in the sectors
have received from political authorities. As a result of this support, newspaper
coverage of the industry and individual firms within it has been extensive. In
addition, financial analysts have provided coverage of the industry and several
solar PV companies as many of them have been listed on stock exchanges.
Analysts' reports provide key insights into the strategies and financial situations of individual firms.

The role of German political authorities in supporting solar PV firms in Germany

The dynamic nature of the technologies that underpin the solar PV industry,
outlined above, has led to significant difficulties for once important solar PV
manufacturers in Germany (BMU, 2012a, 2013; European Commission, 2009,
2013; Handelsblatt, 2012). Indeed, the list of major German solar PV companies that have been or are insolvent is long; it includes Calyxo, Conergy,
Odersun, Q-Cells, Solibro, Solon and Soltecture. Other firms or establishments
in Germany are either being sold off or have closed as a result of poor financial
results. This latter category includes Aleo solar, Bosch CIS-Technology and
First Solar Manufacturing GmbH. Some of these firms were once the largest
in their respective market segments and were technological leaders (European
Commission, 2013). The industry is, therefore, a volatile one. To survive, solar
PV mass manufacturers in Germany need to cut production costs and be able
to respond quickly to market demands (BMBF, 2009; BMU, 2012a, 2013; Silicon
Valley Bank, 2012).

German political authorities have provided various types of financial
support, both direct and indirect, to firms in the sector in order to help them
overcome these challenges as well as to reduce greenhouse-gas emissions;
to stimulate higher levels of economic growth, especially in less prosperous
eastern Germany; to support job creation; and to increase energy security (e.g.
BMU, 2012a; TMWAT, 2012).

Federal German governments have set a favourable regulatory framework to
promote the industry. Despite this, the German Federal Government remains
a regulatory one, as will be shown. The focus of Federal Government support
has tended to be on supporting the technologies that underpin the solar PV
industry or on fostering the growth of the sector as a whole rather than on
aiding individual firms. The eastern *Länder* governments have gone further
and have provided subsidies to firms and, in some instances, have participated
directly in the ownership of firms. Ultimately, they too, however, adopt more
of a regulatory role than a dominant developmental one. In short, political

authorities' significant direct and indirect support of firms in the sector has not prevented the bankruptcy of several firms and their acquisition by foreign rivals.

The Federal Government's decision to introduce feed-in-tariffs (FiTs) for renewable energies has supported the market for solar PV modules in Germany. Indeed, it is the largest in the world (European Commission, 2013). These subsidies have not just been a boon to German firms. The payment of FiTs does not depend upon where the solar PV modules are made. Chinese solar PV firms, among others, have also been able to take advantage of the subsidies. As the former Federal Environment Minister Peter Altmaier has stated:

> The Renewable Energy Sources Act (EEG) [which sets out FiT levels] is not a suitable tool for securing the survival of the [German] solar industry in particular. Yet in terms of industrial policy, Germany has an interest in the viability of its high-performance and competitive solar industry on the global market. (BMU, 2012b: 15)

FiTs are one of the main ways in which subsidies are paid to firms in the sector by the Federal Government. Yet, the Federal Government does not see them as benefitting German firms directly. These subsidies have helped to expand the market for solar PV modules in Germany, but their role is not to directly develop firms in the sector. FiTs are, consequently, a mechanism of a regulatory rather than a developmental state: a favourable legislative framework is set for the industry, but individual firms are not favoured, even if they are German. As a result, the money that Germany electricity consumers pay to support the FiTs flows not only to German firms, but to foreign ones as well.

The Federal Government also finances applied research in an attempt to promote the use of solar PV devices (BMU, 2013). In 2012, federal expenditure on all renewable-energy-related research amounted to over €154 million. Of that total, 41.7 per cent went to research institutes; 27.6 per cent to research projects involving public and private-sector partners; and 28 per cent funded activities carried out by firms alone. While the funds going solely to firms are significant, the amount that is channelled towards research institutes is greater. This implies that many of the projects funded by the Federal Government are likely to be of a technological nature rather than being solely process or manufacturing related. Once again, the German Government tends to favour the growth of renewable-energy sectors as a whole rather than the expansion of particular firms within them.

Out of all the renewable-energy technologies funded by the Federal Government, research related to solar PV technology received the greatest amount. In 2012, over €51 million was spent on developing the technology; that figure amounted to more than a third of all federal expenditures on research related to renewable-energy technologies (BMU, 2013: 12–14). Although the gravity of the situation facing many German solar PV firms is acknowledged by the BMU (2013: 14), it also stresses the importance of cutting-edge research projects that may have practical implications only in five years or more. The ability of German firms to take advantage of such projects is debatable, as many of them are unlikely to last that long. The government's emphasis appears, then, to lie in promoting the technology rather than firms directly.

The BMU stresses the importance of firms developing highly efficient products and having the most advanced production equipment as ways to respond to falling prices (BMU, 2013: 33). For instance, solar PV cells and modules with greater efficiencies will enable the same amount of solar radiation to be converted into more electricity. Similarly, technical improvements to inverters can increase the conversion rates of solar PV systems and, hence, the amount of electricity and income generated. This shows that the Federal German Government provides support for the various technologies involved in solar PV systems rather than a desire to foster the growth of particular firms within the industry directly. Indeed, an analysis of various government reports supports the view that the focus of the Federal Government's policy to promote the industry is on research and development (BMBF, 2009, 2010; BMU, 2012a; BMWi, 2011; cf., BMBF, 2007; BMU, 2012c).

The *Länder* governments in eastern Germany have been more actively involved in supporting individual firms than the Federal Government has. Indirect financial support has, for instance, been provided to many solar PV firms in eastern Germany. Soltecture, now bankrupt, received subsidies of approximately €20 million from the *Land* of Berlin. Before its recent insolvency, Solon was provided with loan guarantees by the *Länder* of Berlin and Mecklenburg-Western Pomerania; Berlin's amounted to €38 million (Evert, 2011, 2012). This means that the governments of Berlin and Mecklenburg-Western Pomerania guaranteed the loans that commercial banks had made to Solon. Consequently, Solon's bankruptcy means that the *Land* of Berlin is €38 million out of pocket. Before its bankruptcy, Q-Cells obtained approximately €200 million in state subsidies from Saxony-Anhalt between 2007 and 2012. Conergy received state aid of €76 million between 2006 and 2009 to support production in Frankfurt (Oder) in Brandenburg (European Commission, 2013). Far fewer jobs than were initially envisaged were created by Conergy, and many of those have since been lost. Solarworld received approximately €137 million to support production near Chemnitz in Saxony between 2003 and 2011 (European Commission, 2013).

Other firms that have received state aid from eastern *Länder* governments include Ersol (€55 million), which is now part of Bosch that is seeking to divest all of its solar PV activities; Masdar (€29 million); and Wacker Chemie (€98 million). For these three latter investments, the amount of state aid granted to the companies was either the maximum that is permitted under EU regulations or was very close to it (European Commission, 2013: 55). In return for these subsidies, firms invested and created jobs.

In addition, some *Länder* have provided financial support to firms by owning stakes in them. Through state-backed venture-capital funds, the *Land* of Berlin invested directly in the now bankrupt Soltecture (Evert, 2012) and the Regional Government of Thuringia has bought equity in Heliatek (Heliatek, 2013). The remit of the regional funds supporting these start-ups is to promote economic growth and employment creation in the regions where they are based. In some respects, then, the eastern *Länder* adhere closely to the model of a development state: they have provided financial support both directly and indirectly to promote economic growth in chosen sectors of the economy. When stakes have been bought in firms, the *Länder* governments are likely to be committed owners who take an active role via their venture-capital funds in the companies that they co-own. They potentially have a say in how the businesses are run and can be expected to be interested in long-term outcomes rather than short-term financial ones.

The German institutional environment and investments by EMNEs

However, there are important elements of the dominant developmental state model that the eastern *Länder* do not adhere to. Most importantly, politicians did not seek to protect the firms from takeover when the companies ran into financial difficulties. This occurs despite the firms' economic and technological importance and despite the large subsidies that some have received. Although foreign firms' acquisitions of local firms can ensure the survival of some domestic jobs, they can also lead to the transfer of the companies' intellectual property and organisational capabilities – competencies that direct and indirect financial support from political authorities helped to create (Steitz, 2014). The change in ownership is, therefore, tantamount to a subsidy from German taxpayers to the new overseas owners.

Several solar PV firms that were once major companies in the industry have been sold to foreign rivals, including those from emerging economies. For instance, Hanergy (China) bought Solibro's asset after Solibro's parent firm, Q-Cells, went bust. The purchase gave Hanergy control over key capabilities in thin-film solar PV, capabilities that it previously lacked (Hook, 2012). To facilitate foreign acquisitions, Hanergy received a Rmb 30 billion (approximately £2.8 billion) credit line from the China Development Bank in 2011 (Hook, 2012). The China Development Bank is one of three 'policy' banks in China. Its remit is to provide medium- to long-term funding to support the country's industrial policy, including help to promote new industries (China

Development Bank, 2014). As reported in the official government portal site to China, China.org.cn, Chairman of the Hanergy Board Li Hejun has said that the China Development Bank has played an important role in promoting the development of the company (China.org.cn, 2011). Hanergy's acquisition of Solibro illustrates how home- and host-country institutions shape the development of EMNEs. Solibro's growth is attributable, in part, to Germany's industrial policies at both the Federal and *Land* levels; China's economic policies and institutional structures, including its banks and financial system, facilitated Hanergy's purchase of Solibro.

Conergy's manufacturing facility in eastern Germany was bought by Astronergy, which is part of the Chint Group from China. The Conergy factory was built in 2007 for €250 million, of which €40 million came from state subsidies (Handelsblatt, 2013). Public-sector funding helped, therefore, to establish the facility in eastern Germany. When announcing the purchase of the manufacturing facility, Dr Chuan Lu, Vice President of Astronergy, said 'We are convinced of the high quality and profound know-how at the manufacturing site' (Astronergy, 2013). This demonstrates the importance of manufacturing capabilities, or know-how, at the site in Astronergy decision making. In an interview with EuPD Research, a market research company that specialises in the renewable-energy sector, Dr Liyou Yang, president and chief executive officer of Astronergy, noted that 'In the domestic market the Chint Group is already well positioned based on its long history, high brand awareness and its connections throughout China, *especially with the government and financial institutions*' (EuPD, 2012, emphasis added). When asked how Astronergy differed to other Chinese solar PV manufacturers, Dr Yang emphasised, *inter alia*, 'strong government relations' (EuPD, 2012). These two quotations illustrate how government links enable some firms in China to grow. While connections to governments are often important to firms in other countries, they would appear to be particularly significant in China.

Microsol International LL FZE, which is owned and controlled by a group of India businessmen, but is registered as a Free Zone Establishment in the United Arab Emirates (UAE), acquired Solon, whose head office and main manufacturing facility was in eastern Berlin. Microsol purchased Solon's key assets, including intellectual property, research and development capabilities and marketing skills (Solon, 2012). As noted above, Solon received significant loan guarantees from Berlin and Mecklenburg-Western Pomerania. This support helped the company to grow. According to Anjan Turlapati, CEO of Microsol International, an important advantage of carrying out solar PV manufacturing in the UAE is that manufacturing is the ease of regulatory compliance. Far fewer employees are needed to deal with legal requirements than are needed in many other countries (Knowledge@Wharton, 2011). The ability to take advantage of the UAE's institutions is underlined by the fact that the UAE is not a major market for the company. Most of what it manufactures is exported. However, there are also disadvantages to manufacturing in the region. There is a lack of advanced research organisations in the area to collaborate with, and certain types of employees are in short supply. The company is able to overcome these difficulties by, in part, engaging in 'institutional outsourcing' (Allen, 2013). For instance, some workers are flown in from India on a short-term basis to tackle immediate problems (Knowledge@Wharton, 2011).

Conclusions

Existing studies of the increasing role of EMNEs in international business have focused largely on the characteristics of their home countries. These studies have helped to explain the rise of EMNEs and how they differ to multinationals from developed economies. However, extant research tends to downplay the role of potential host countries in explaining EMNEs' creation and growth. In particular, existing studies neglect the importance of host-country institutions and their influences on investment patterns by (potential) EMNEs.

This chapter has three main findings. First, it has demonstrated how the opportunities for emerging-economy firms to invest overseas, especially if acquiring strategic assets, are shaped by the host country's institutional setting. Germany's devolved economic policy-making framework and financial support from the Federal and *Land* levels helped to foster the rapid growth of German solar PV firms with important capabilities. Second, it has illustrated how the host country's political and economic objectives allow foreign firms to acquire key assets whose existence, in part at least, is attributable to public subsidies. In Germany, political authorities have, in general, supported the solar PV industry as a whole, but not individual firms within it. Those authorities have not prevented firms with important capabilities being sold to foreign rivals. If politicians had blocked their acquisition, there probably would have been detrimental consequences for other, even more important, sectors. Finally, it has shown how the ability of EMNEs to buy those German assets is enhanced by home-country institutions. This institutional support ranges from funding from state-guided banks for Chinese firms to a favourable manufacturing environment in the case of UAE-based Microsol International.

This suggests that existing theory on EMNEs, in particular, and multinationals, more generally, should take into consideration both home- and host-country institutions to explain where, why and how firms from emerging economies invest overseas. Organisational capabilities, both at home and abroad, are shaped by institutions. Capabilities are often location specific and institutionally contingent. Institutions – in the shape of strategic considerations by politicians – influence which firms are for sale and to whom. Institutions can, therefore, help to explain where (potential) EMNEs may wish to invest overseas and whether or not they can do so. If the capabilities that EMNEs need to compete are either not available or difficult to create within the firm's home-country institutional setting, then firms may invest overseas to gain access to them. Institutions, hence, help to explain why firms invest overseas. The need for subsidiaries to be embedded abroad will also influence how they are managed (e.g. McDonald et al., 2008). Finally, home-country institutions affect how EMNEs expand overseas. In the case of Chinese firms, good political links and access to funding enable companies to take advantage of investment opportunities in developed countries.

References

Allen, M.M.C. (2013) 'Comparative capitalisms and the institutional embeddedness of innovative capabilities'. *Socio-Economic Review*, 11(4), 771–794.

Allen, M.M.C. and Aldred, M.L. (2013) 'Business regulation, inward foreign direct investment, and economic growth in the new European Union Member States'. *Critical Perspectives on International Business*, 9(3), 301–321.

Amable, B. (2003) *The Diversity of Modern Capitalism*. Oxford: Oxford University Press.

Annushkina, O.E. and Colonel, R.T. (2013) 'Foreign market selection by Russian MNEs – beyond a binary approach?'. *Critical Perspectives on International Business*, 9(1/2), 58–87.

Astronergy (2013) 'Astronergy intends to acquire Conergy's module factory in Germany'. Astronergy Press Release, 11/29/2013, available at: http://www.astronergy.com/press_detail.php?news_id=97 [Accessed 1 July 2014].

Becker-Ritterspach, F., Saka-Helmhout, A. and Hotho, J.J. (2010) 'Learning in multi-national enterprises as the socially embedded translation of practices'. *Critical Perspectives on International Business*, 6(1), 8–37.

Block, F. and Keller, M.R. (2009) 'Where do innovations come from? Changes in the U.S. economy, 1970–2006'. *Socio-Economic Review*, 7(3), 459–483.

BMBF (Federal Ministry for Education and Research) (2007) *Duale Berufsausbildung im Bereich erneuerbarer Energien: Ein expandierender Wirtschaftsbereich braucht qualifizierten Nachwuchs*. Berlin: BMBF.

BMBF (2009) *Research and innovation for Germany: Results and outlook*. Berlin: BMBF.

BMBF (2010) *Bundesbericht Forschung und Innovation 2010*. Berlin: BMBF.

BMU (Federal Ministry for the Environment, Nature Conservation and Nuclear Safety). (2011) *Renewable energies: perspectives for a sustainable energy future*. Berlin: BMU.

BMU (2012a) *GreenTech made in Germany 3.0: Environmental technology atlas for Germany*. Berlin: BMU.

BMU (2012b) *10-point programme for ambitious and judicious energy and environmental policy: Proposals and projects for the remainder of the legislative period by Federal Environment Minister Peter Altmaier*. Berlin: BMU.

BMU (2012c) *Renewably employed: Short and long-term impacts of the expansion of renewable energy on the German labour market*. Berlin: BMU.

BMWi (Federal Ministry of Economics and Technology) (2011) Research for an environmentally sound, reliable and affordable energy supply: 6th Energy Research Programme of the Federal Government. Berlin, Federal Ministry of Economics and Technology.

Brewster, C., Croucher, R., Wood, G. and Brookes, M. (2007) 'Collective and individual voice: convergence in Europe?'. *The International Journal of Human Resource Management*, 18(7), 1246–1262.

Bryant, C. (2012) 'Chinese solar company to buy Germany's Sunways'. *Financial Times*, 2 January 2012, available at: http://www.ft.com/cms/s/0/02ab3978–354c-11e1–84b9–00144feabdc0.html#axzz1wd8TALar.

Buckley, P.J., Clegg, J., Cross, A.R., Liu, X. Voss, H. and Zheng, P. (2007) 'The determinants of Chinese outward foreign direct investment'. *Journal of International Business Studies*, 38(4), 499–518.

Buckley, P., Cross, A.R., Tan, H., Voss, H. and Liu, X. (2008) 'Historic and emergent trends in Chinese outward direct investment'. *Management International Review*, 48(6), 715–748.

Casper, S. (2009) 'Can new technology firms succeed in coordinated market economies? A response to Herrmann and Lange'. *Socio-Economic Review*, 7(2), 209–215.

Casper, S. and Whitley, R. (2004) 'Managing competences in entrepreneurial technology firms: a comparative institutional analysis of Germany, Sweden and the UK'. *Research Policy*, 33(1), 89–106.

Child, J. and Marinova, S.T. (2014) 'The role of contextual combinations in the globalization of Chinese firms'. *Management and Organization Review*, 10(3), 347–371.

China.org.cn (2011) 'Hanergy secures 30 billion yuan credit line, 03/11/2011', available at: http://www.china.org.cn/business/2011–11/03/content_23805765.htm [Accessed 1 July 2014].

China Development Bank (2014) Mission statement, available at: http://www.cdb.com.cn/english/Column.asp?ColumnId=99 [Accessed 1 July 2014].

Deng, P. (2009) 'Why do Chinese firms tend to acquire strategic assets in international expansion?'. *Journal of World Business*, 44(1), 74–84.

EuPD (2012) Interview: Chint Solar (Zhejiang) Co. Ltd – Astronergy, 15/05/2012, available at: http://eupd-research.com/fileadmin/templates/pdf/Interview_Astronergy.pdf [Accessed 1 July 2014].

European Commission (2009) PV status report 2009: Research, solar cell production and market implementation of photovoltaics. Luxembourg: Office for Official Publications of the European Union.

European Commission (2013) *Ex-post evaluation of the Regional Aid Guidelines 2007–2013: Final report December 2012*. Luxembourg: Publications Office of the European Union.

Evans, P. (1995) Embedded autonomy: States and industrial transformation. Princeton: Princeton University Press.

Evert, H. (2011) 'Solon-Pleite wäre schwerer Schlag für Berlin, Beliner Morgenpost', 21/07/11, available at: http://www.morgenpost.de/wirtschaft/article1707765/Solon-Pleite-waere-schwerer-Schlag-fuer-Berlin.html.

Evert, H. (2012) Nach Solon droht auch Soltecture die Pleite, Berliner Morgenpost, 27/02/12, available at: http://www.morgenpost.de/wirtschaft/article1913870/Nach-Solon-droht-auch-Soltecture-die-Pleite.html.

Funk, L. and Allen, M.M.C. (2012) 'Germany: Economy'. In Europa Publications (ed.) *Western Europe 2013*. London: Routledge, pp. 308–322.

Gammeltoft, P., Filatotchev, I. and Hobdari, B. (2012) 'Emerging multinational companies and strategic fit: a contingency framework and future research agenda'. *European Management Journal*, 30(3), 175–188.

Handelsblatt (2013) Chinesen übernehmen Conergy-Fabrik, 12/12/2013, available at: http://www.handelsblatt.com/unternehmen/industrie/solarbranche-chinesen-uebernehmen-conergy-fabrik/v_detail_tab_print/9208360.html [Accessed 1 July 2014].

Heliatek (2013) 'A strong network of investors', available at: http://www.heliatek.com/uber-uns/investoren/?lang=en [Accessed 24 June 2014].

Hollingsworth, J.R. and Boyer, R. (1997) 'Coordination of economic actors and social systems of production'. In J.R. Hollingsworth and R. Boyer (Eds). *Contemporary Capitalism: The Eembeddedness of Institutions*. Cambridge: Cambridge University Press, pp. 1–47.

Hollingsworth, J.R. and Streeck, W. (1994) 'Countries and Sectors'. In J.R. Hollingsworth, P. Schmitter, and W. Streeck (Eds). *Governing Capitalist Economies: Performance and Control of Economic Sectors*. Oxford: Oxford University Press, pp. 270–300.

Hook, H. (2012) 'Chinese group to buy Q-Cells subsidiary'. *Financial Times*, 3 June 2012, available at: http://www.ft.com/cms/s/0/38cb10d2-ad7e-11e1-97f3-00144feabdc0.html#axzz368PAl22i.

Hotho, J.J. (2014) 'From typology to taxonomy: A configurational analysis of national business systems and their explanatory power'. *Organization Studies*, 35(5), 671–702

Johnson, C. (1982) *MITI and the Japanese miracle: The growth of industrial policy, 1925–1975*. Stanford: Stanford University Press.

Keller, M.R. and Block, F. (2013) 'Explaining the transformation of the U.S. innovation system: the role of a small government program'. *Socio-Economic Review*, 11(4), 629–656.

Knowledge@Wharton (2011) Microsol's Anjan Turlapati on the UAE's Free Trade Zones: 'The big bright point is the lack of bureaucracy', 11/01/2011, available at: https://knowledge.wharton.upenn.edu/article/microsols-anjan-turlapati-on-the-uaes-free-trade-zones-the-big-bright-point-is-the-lack-of-bureaucracy/ [Accessed 1 July 2014].

Liu, J. and Tylecote, A. (2009) 'Corporate governance and technological capability development: Three case studies in the Chinese auto industry'. *Industry and Innovation*, 16(4/5), 525–544.

McDonald, F., Warhurst, S. and Allen, M M.C. (2008) 'Autonomy, embeddedness and the performance of foreign-owned subsidiaries'. *Multinational Business Review*, 16(3), 73–92.

Otto Brenner Foundation (2013) *Solarindustrie: Pholtovoltaik Boom, Krise,Potentiale, Fallbeispiele. OBS-Arbeitspapier Nr. 4*. Frankfurt am Main: Otto-Brenner-Stiftung.

Mathews, J.A. (2006) 'Dragon multinationals: new players in 21st century globalization'. *Asia Pacific Journal of Management*, 23(1), 5–27.

Ramamurti, R. (2012) 'What is really different about emerging market multinationals?'. *Global Strategy Journal*, 2(1), 41–47.

Sauvant, K.P. (2009) 'Overview'. In K.P. Sauvant (Ed.). *Investing in the United States: Is the US Ready for FDI from China?* Cheltenham: Edward Elgar, pp. 1–21.

Seyoum, B. and Manyak, T. (2009) 'The impact of public and private sector transparency on foreign investment in developing countries'. *Critical Perspectives on International Business*, 5(3), 187–206.

Schwarzburger, H. (2014) 'Wir wurden vom schnellen Preisverfall überholt', 16/07/2013, available at: http://www.solarage.eu/wir-wurden-vom-schnellen-preisverfall-uberholt/ [Accessed 1 July 2014].

Silicon Valley Bank (2012) *The solar industry March 2012*. Santa Clara: SVB.

Sinkovics, R.R., Yamin, M., Nadvi, K., and Zhang, Y. (2014) 'Rising powers from emerging markets: The changing face of international business'. *International Business Review*, 23(4), 675–679.

Solon, (2012) 'Microsol acquires key assets of SOLON and forms SOLON Energy GmbH', 06/03/2012, available at: http://www.solon.com/global/press/detail.html?ID=715 [Accessed 1 July 2014].

Spiegel, (2011) 'The sun rises in the east: German solar firms eclipsed by Chinese rivals', 07/09/2011, available at: http://www.spiegel.de/international/business/the-sun-rises-in-the-east-german-solar-firms-eclipsed-by-chinese-rivals-a-784653.html [Accessed 1 July 2014].

Steitz, C. (2014) 'Germany's solar sell-off: picking up the remaining pieces', 06/03/2014, available at: http://www.reuters.com/article/2014/03/06/germany-solar-id-USL6N0M01ZQ20140306 [Accessed 1 July 2014].

TMWAT (Thuringian Ministry for Economy, Labour and Technology) (2012) *Wealth + Innovation + Natural Resources: Abstract of the 2020 Thuringia Trend Atlas*. Erfurt: TMWAT.

Tüselmann, H.-J., Allen, M.M.C., Barrett, S. and McDonald, F. (2008) 'Varieties and variability of employee relations approaches in US subsidiaries: country-of-origin effects and the level and type of industry internationalisation'. *The International Journal of Human Resource Management*, 19(9), 1622–1635.

Tylecote, A. and Visintin, F. (2008) *Corporate Governance, Finance and the Technological Advantage of Nations*. London: Routledge.

Whitley, R. (2005) 'How national are business systems? The role of states and complementary institutions in standardizing systems of economic coordination and control at the national level'. In G. Morgan, R. Whitley, and E. Moen (Eds). *Changing capitalisms? Internationalization, institutional change and systems of economic organization*. Oxford: Oxford University Press, pp. 190–231.

Whitley, R. (2007) *Business systems and organisational capabilities: The institutional structuring of competitive competences*. Oxford: Oxford University Press.

Whitley, R. and Morgan, G. (2012) 'Introduction'. In G. Morgan and R. Whitley (Eds). *Capitalisms and capitalism in the twenty-first century*. Oxford: Oxford University Press, pp. 1–10.

Williamson, P.J. and Raman, A.P. (2011) 'How China reset its global acquisition agenda'. *Harvard Business Review*, 89(4), 109–114.

Witt, M.A. and Redding, G. (2013) 'Asian business systems: institutional comparison, clusters and implications for Varieties of Capitalism and Business Systems theory'. *Socio-Economic Review*, 11(2), 265–300.

Wood, G. and Frynas, J.G. (2006) 'The institutional basis of economic failure: anatomy of the segmented business system'. *Socio-Economic Review*, 4(2), 239–277.

Zhang, J., Chaohong, Z. and Ebbers, H. (2010) 'Completion of Chinese overseas acquisitions: Institutional perspectives and evidence'. *International Business Review*, 20(2), 226–238.

Zhang, X. and Whitley, R. (2013) 'Changing macro-structural varieties of East Asian capitalism'. *Socio-Economic Review*, 11(2), 301–336.

5
Neither Western Nor Indian: HRM Policy in an Indian Multinational

Vijay Pereira and Peter Scott

The spotlight is increasingly on the human resource management (HRM) strategies of Indian-owned multinational enterprises (MNEs), including those that operate within the country's fast-growing business process offshoring (BPO) sector. Brewster et al. (2007: 206) argue that there exists a 'need for a broader geographical base to our understanding of' international human resource management. One of the important reasons for studying HRM strategies in diverse geographical locations is to examine the trajectories of policies in new multinational companies in emerging economies to assess if they mirror Western-derived models such as the life cycle schemes of Adler and Ghadar (1990) or Heenan and Perlmutter (1979). Until relatively recently (e.g. Kumar et al., 2009; Sauvant et al., 2010), there has been little discussion about how distinctive the HRM practices of Indian multinationals are and whether they are exportable or imitable. Cappelli et al. (2010: 4–5) claim there is a concept of an 'India Way' that encapsulates a national business philosophy, constructed on four pillars, including HRM dimensions such as holistic engagement with employees, improvisation and adaptability (*jugaad* in Hindi), creation of innovative value propositions and recognition of businesses' wider societal role. This book also claims international transferability of some practices, such as establishing a sense of social mission and employee engagement (Cappelli et al., 2010: 197–207).

This chapter utilises a longitudinal investigation of a major Indian-owned human resource outsourcing (HRO) firm to investigate the conflicting influences on the evolution of HRM in this emerging economy. The chapter examines the extent of forward diffusion to foreign operations of an indigenous Indian 'model' and where Indian firms are taking on outsourced human resources (HR) work from overseas the evidence for the adoption of Western-style 'high performance' practices, such as sophisticated recruitment and selection, extensive employee training and development and performance-contingent pay. Emerging market multinational enterprises' HRM policies and practices may also play crucial roles in helping facilitate reverse knowledge transfer to such MNEs' other subsidiaries and in the success of the firm in diverse cultural environments. The research uses qualitative fieldwork over five years and finds that developments can best be characterised by the emergence of a hybrid HRM model, incorporating an evolving mix of 'Indian' and 'Western' HRM practices. The data, drawn from a broader study of HRO companies operating in India, includes other firms headquartered outside of India.

The study focuses on three research questions. First, what HRM practices are characteristic of major indigenous Indian-owned HRO firms that operate across a broad range of HR services to international clients? Second, to what extent are internal HRM practices in HRO firms characterised by a desire to emulate or adopt what are sometimes regarded as global 'best practice' HRM at the expense of 'indigenous' practice? Third, following on from the first and second questions, what have been the principal internal and external drivers of these changes in HRM practices, and what main aspects of HRM have they transformed?

Influences on HRM in Indian HRO

A major academic debate in international and comparative HRM concerns the relative weights of various levels of influences upon the practice of HRM in firms. This connects to the sway exerted on employment practices by 'systemic' global pressures compared to those of national employment systems and sectoral, company or 'local' variations (Geppart and Meyer, 2006). The idea that high performance work systems (HPWS) embracing sophisticated voice, recruitment and training systems and performance-related pay (Pfeffer, 1994) are transferable is disputed area when outside of a Western context (Kramar and Syed, 2012; Marchington and Grugulis, 2000). In culturally distant, emerging markets it is more likely that a 'cross-vergence' perspective is adopted. This perspective incorporates 'both national culture influences and economic ideology influences synergistically to form a unique value system that is different from the value set supported by either national culture or economic ideology' is (Ralston et al., 1997: 183).

India represents an important case to assess the relative influences of 'indigenous' and 'international' employment practices. Although Indian HRM systems and practices are diffuse (Chatterjee, 2007: 98), they have distinctive Indian characteristics (Bhattacherjee and Ackers, 2010; Budhwar and Varma, 2010). Bhattacherjee and Ackers (2010: 106–107) identify three coexisting models of employment relations: an unsystematised form characteristic of the informal economy; a more formal model of domestic employment relations associated with traditional 'old' industries; and those of the new, outward-facing service industries that have emerged in the past two decades and will be discussed in greater detail below. The social and economic context of India comprises numerous cultural norms, beliefs and values. These include respect for seniority, status and group affiliation (Biswas and Varma, 2007); concomitant employment relations attributes typically consist of strong mutual bonds between employer and employee, welfarism and a form of paternalism – although not necessarily of an authoritarian and unitarist type (Mariappanadar, 2005; Cappelli et al., 2010; Saini and Budhwar, 2008).

The liberalisation of markets during the past two decades and the creation of global linkages have refashioned the context of HRM policies and practices in India (Budhwar and Bhatnagar, 2009). Changes to the business environment, including unionisation and technological development, ownership structures and a more benevolent atmosphere for organisational restructuring, have combined to influence the adoption of strategic HRM approaches (Som, 2007). These developments have enabled the adoption of practices linked to globalisation, including work quality, customer service and innovation (Chatterjee and Pearson, 2000). There is dispute about whether these developments are evidence of Westernisation of HRM. The growth of foreign direct investment and increasing numbers of Western-trained managers is seen as promoting the adoption of international HRM practices relating to recruitment and retention, training and development, reward systems and the management of the employment relationship (Budhwar and Baruch, 2003). On the other hand, Mariappanadar (2005) distinguishes between multinational firms operating in India that use predominantly Western HRM practices and others that amalgamate local and Western HRM traditions.

In Indian BPO organisations HRM is often distinctive from more traditional parts of the economy, with more emphasis on formal, structured and rationalised HRM systems that reflect the importation of practices from the call-centre industry in other countries (Budhwar et al., 2006). The workforce regard themselves as 'professional' rather than proletarian, as do the BPO firms that hire them, although this may not reflect the actual nature of much of the work (Noronha and D'Cruz, 2009). Part of the reason for the formalisation of this HRM strategy is the double-edged nature of the BPO industry's expansion. The rapid growth of the outsourcing industry resulted in high turnover, poaching and skill shortages, particularly in large cities, as employers fish within the same relatively small pool for a restricted segment of the graduate labour force (Chatterjee, 2009: 276–277; Kuruvilla and Ranganathan, 2010). Numerous sources, including the BPO industry body Nasscom (2010), suggest that relatively few new graduates are employable without further training. Bayadi (2008: 24) claims that HR managers within Indian MNEs consider 'only 10 to 25 percent' of India's two and a half million annual graduate output as immediately employable. One survey finds that in the sector the majority opinion is that use of better HRM practices is the main key to future success (Rajeev and Vani, 2009: 59). In the face of such conditions, companies have been forced to consider new types of HRM responses (Kuruvilla and Ranganathan, 2010). Some evidence exists of more innovative HRM practices in 'high end' knowledge processing services intended to recruit, retain and manage the performance of the relatively scarce group of graduates deemed to possess the right skills (Raman et al., 2007). Longitudinal data with Indian BPO firms suggests a degree of movement in their governance and organisational features from an initial transactional orientation to one more focused on achieving resource complementarity through the development of trust and a longer-term orientation to the provision and delivery of the offshore services (Vivek et al., 2009).

Employment and HR practices within the 'niche' market of Indian third-party providers of HRM services are somewhat distinct from the BPO mainstream, for various reasons that contribute to its appropriateness for study. Internationally, India is one of the main destinations for HRO work. Within India, HRO is a rather diffuse subsector that forms a small, but significant, part of the BPO market with modest growth potential (Rajeev and Vani, 2009: 56–57). The HRO subsector is varied in terms of activities and skill levels compared to much of the BPO sector. While it does include typical BPO transactional tasks, such as payroll, compensation, welfare and personnel administration, significant parts of the HRO 'menu', such as planning of workforce, succession, recruitment or reward, involve transformational work and processes that require a high level of skills (Sparrow and Braun, 2008). The Indian HRO subsector also reflects the HRO industry globally in comprising a diverse array of firms in terms of size and nationality of ownership but interestingly includes a small number of indigenous operators as major players.

The characteristics of the Indian business environment, especially in the HRO sector, imply that a number of different HRM 'paths' are plausible. First, as transaction cost economics might suggest, because of higher transaction costs, organisations offering transactional BPO services may be unlikely to engage and develop staff, as seen elsewhere in the call-centre sector. Second, development towards service provision that embraces 'transformational' services, more in line with the 'resource-based' approach, such as knowledge process outsourcing is more likely to suggest a more sophisticated HRM strategy (Raman et al., 2007). Third, HR offshoring in an emerging economy raises interesting questions about the nature of, and influences on, HRM practices in HRO firms. To some extent, Indian organisations that explicitly offer HRM services might be more likely to exhibit more sophisticated HRM practices than other firms in the BPO sector, not least because they may wish to use the quality of their internal practices as an exemplar to potential customers. Fourth, given the increasing international dominance of Indian firms in this sector, the logic of Cappelli et al.'s (2010) argument would suggest an export of some paternalist 'Indian' HRM practices. Fifth, it might be possible to find at least some iterative mutual cross-fertilisation, as embodied in the concept of cross-vergence (Ralston, 2008). The next section turns to explaining how we use a longitudinal case study of a major Indian-owned multinational HRO organisation to trace the actual pattern of developments within this emerging economy.

Methodology

Longitudinal, qualitative studies have the power to uncover the richness of evolving policies and sense-making processes, despite being time and resource intensive. They have an established track record in processual organisational studies (Pettigrew, 1990, 1997), and a number of influential authors propose their deployment to deepen our knowledge of the topics considered in this chapter. Ralston (2008: 37) argues for the value of such research techniques in understanding any unfolding processes of cross-vergence. Even authors better known for quantitative studies of HRM strategy have recently acknowledged the potential future role of longitudinal, qualitative studies in tracing the complex interrelationships between different permutations of HRM practice in combined application (Huselid and Becker, 2011: 427).

Thus, we use a major Indian-owned multinational HRO firm as a 'crucial' (Gerring, 2007: 115–122) or 'unusual' longitudinal single case (Yin, 2014: 51–53) because of the wider lessons that can be derived from its changing circumstances. Its appropriateness as a source for wider generalisation derives from several features. The firm code-named IndiaCo has a disproportionate weight and influence within the Indian HRO industry as a whole, having commenced as a BPO in 1968. It has been a major recruiter yet experiences relatively low attrition by industry standards. Its role as part of a larger Indian conglomerate (IndiaCo Group), employing some 350,000 persons worldwide, which has historical roots in influencing HRM in India for many years, makes IndiaCo a significant case study to investigate cross-vergence. Furthermore, its influence transcends national borders as its operations increasingly have global reach and are internationally significant in scale. The company employed approximately 166,000 persons from over 30 nationalities as of mid-2010 and has offices in 42 countries. IndiaCo is among the leading global IT consulting, services and BPO, offering services to clients across 55 countries, and it is headquartered in Mumbai. Most revenues derive from the United Kingdom and United States, with the banking, financial and insurance services providing the largest sources of clients. IndiaCo focuses on delivering technology-led business solutions to its international customers across varied industries. At the time of the study, it offered a range of information and communication technology (ICT) services to seven of the top ten Fortune 500 companies and provided services to many other firms. It offers a gamut of HRO services ranging from the transactional, such as payroll processing and answering employees' queries on employment matters, through to more skill- and knowledge-intensive services such as employee resourcing and talent management. The study includes two sites in large but contrasting Indian cities. These cities are IndiaCo's headquarters in Mumbai, India's financial capital, and Bangalore, the world's back office and ICT capital. These locations offer a range of HRO services. In Mumbai the work centres on transactional HR activities because the workers' qualifications are conducive to work of an administrative nature, whereas Bangalore, where employees have a higher level of technical qualification on average, concentrates more on HR planning and strategic issues.

The fieldwork involved over ten visits covers a period of nearly five years, from August 2006 to April 2010. These encompassed visits during the period of growth to the end of 2007, the recession affecting the Indian economy mid-2008–2009 and the recovery after August 2009. The research used two main qualitative primary data gathering techniques at each of the two sites: interviews with key HR managers and with focus groups. Wherever schedules allowed, interviews and focus groups involved participation of the same groups of individuals over time in order to facilitate real-time comparison of respondents' changing views, although some additional personnel were necessarily also drawn in. The in-depth interviews involved three separate rounds with chief human resource officers in the two locations and 13 interviews with HR managers in Mumbai and nine in Bangalore. The two focus groups in Mumbai and Bangalore probed the participants' views and experiences of implementing HRM practices and policies in the changing organisational and market context in which they operated. The focus group method was chosen to generate group interaction to produce data and insights that might otherwise have been less accessible, particularly to facilitate a discussion on participants' views and also why they held those views (Fern, 2001). The researcher also observed some in-house training sessions and the recruitment interview processes at all locations. Secondary data was used, including company reports, HR policies, company brochures and information from the web site. These various means permitted an assessment of the thought processes of the key actors and how these changed over time. These methods also enable a considerable degree of triangulation.

Findings

The findings indicate that changing business strategies and conditions over the course of the fieldwork is associated with the main HRM policies pursued by the company. These include policies on recruitment and selection; staff retention; training, learning and development; reward and performance management; and staff welfare. The results indicate which factors grow, diminish or remain constant over time (Saldaña, 2003: 78). The findings can be categorised into three broad phases, which correspond to the stages of the economic cycle experienced in this five year period. Discussion of the first phase sets the scene and thus is the lengthiest, with the following subsections highlighting the main contrasts and continuities experienced. Table 5.1 summarises the main organisational and HRM changes and stabilities discussed.

Broadly, three dominant longitudinal themes emerge: first, the evolution of HRM practices due to IndiaCo's phenomenal growth; second, a unique, innovative, and indigenous cross-vergent mix of HRM practices; and third, the pace of change that HRM at IndiaCo had to cope with, which gradually move the company towards strategic HRM. To put the findings in context, it is necessary to consider the growth experienced by IndiaCo before and during the period of the research. Table 5.2 shows that growth in employment numbers at IndiaCo in the period of 1996 to 2003, followed by much higher absolute and relative increases thereafter. Employment growth remained largely uninterrupted at IndiaCo even through the recession (phase 2: second quarter of 2008 – third quarter of 2009), although the recession punctuated the existing rhythms of HR development in ways discussed below.

In the first phase of the research, up until the first quarter of 2008, IndiaCo's practice was an uneasy mix of traditional Indian personnel values, but it was increasingly complemented and, in some cases, challenged by the need for more structured HRM practices as employment grew. The traditional values of paternalism and philanthropy derive, to some extent, from the culture of the IndiaCo Group more broadly, with employees, for example, being able to benefit from discounted access to the products and services offered by other parts of the IndiaCo Group. As has been found to be the case with other Indian BPO firms, however, more structured and Western-style HRM practices, including many of those associated with high-performance work systems, became more evident over time as IndiaCo grew and became more of a global company. There is evidence of the development of high-performance practices in, for example, the gradual implementation, after 2005–2006, of an economic value-added (EVA) performance management system. The EVA model is a basis for measuring individual and team performance and bonus at the enterprise and department levels. The system calculates profits after considering all costs, including that of capital. The EVA model linked to individual appraisal to the extent that low performance ratings for experienced employees two years running under this system could trigger dismissal. As we discuss below, this system developed and became linked to reward management.

The need to secure a supply of large numbers of new graduates was a continuing challenge, particularly during this first phase, and it lead to three main solutions. The company linked to a number of Indian universities and two other schemes developed from this. The first scheme was a faculty development programme to secure good quality graduates and involved IndiaCo accrediting approved higher education institutions, subject to their possession of certain minimum infrastructural requirements. The second scheme,

Table 5.1 Organisational and HRM change and continuity in IndiaCo, 2006–2010

Changes	Continuity	Phase 1: Aug 2006–Dec 2007	Phase 2: Sept 2008–July 2009	Phase 3: Aug 2009–April 2010
—	Budgetary spend on training, learning and development	10% (Mostly upgrading technical skills)	10% (Included soft skills)	10% (Included consulting and foreign language skills)
—	Attrition rates	~ 10–12%	~ 10%	~ 10–12%
Culture, values and tradition (organisation and national)	—	Influence of overall IndiaCo groups paternalistic and philanthropic philosophy.	Mix of Indian and Western best practices	A move to its own unique, innovative, strategic and indigenously cross-vergent model.
Diversity of employees Female (%)		~ 12	~ 17	~ 25
Non-Indian (%)		~ 7	~ 10	~ 12
Organisational structure	—	Entrepreneurial (centralised)	Entrepreneurial (move to semi-decentralisation)	Intrapreneurial (move to full decentralisation)
Performance and Compensation management		Introduction of EVA model (National level)	Spread of EVA model (Multi-country level)	A uniform global EVA model in place
Recruitment (Percentage increase)	—	~35% (>Laterals; Fair number recruited overseas; >Indian expatriates abroad)	~25% (<Laterals; recalled overseas Indian expatriates)	~30% (>Laterals; overseas recruitment returned to Phase 1 levels; >Indian expatriates abroad)
Welfare schemes	—	National level	Multinational level	Global level

Table 5.2 Employment growth at IndiaCo, 1996–2009

Year	Total headcount (rounded to nearest thousand)	Percentage increase (% rounded off)
1996	6,000	–
1999	12,100	102%
2000	14,300	18%
2001	16,800	17%
2002	19,000	13%
2003	22,000	16%
2004	30,000	36%
2005	46,000	53%
2006	66,000	43%
2007	89,000	35%
2008	111,000	25%
2009	144,000	30%

Source: IndiaCo.

known as the Academic Interface Programme, was to 'talent spot' to enable recruitment of high-flying graduates. Diversity was prioritised by increasing the proportion of female graduates recruited, doubling from a base of 12 per cent of all recruits over the three phases. The growth in employment led IndiaCo to develop the use of technology in the management of HR processes, including recruitment, training, induction and career development; this trend continues to the present. Technological systems were developed in conjunction with the company's software engineers, and they represent an example of reverse diffusion, where the kind of HR platforms offered to overseas customers wishing to outsource HRM have been utilised for internal purposes and became part of the curriculum design in certain approved institutions.

In this first phase of rapid expansion, IndiaCo adopted a strategy of extending its operations beyond India by opening offices abroad in regional centres closer to the growing customer base. It expanded into Latin America and China and opened offices in nearly three dozen countries. This internationalisation strategy underpinned a growing concern to recruit non-Indian nationals. Such recruits increased from approximately 7 per cent of all recruits in 2006 to about 12 per cent of the total workforce by 2010. This may appear to present some contradictions between internationalisation of work operations in practice and the cultivation of a 'brand India' image for marketing purposes. As with all Indian BPO firms, high rates of growth and recruitment in this phase were accompanied by high rates of attrition (approximately 10 per cent per annum), particularly noticeable in Tier 1 cities such as Mumbai and Bangalore, the two locations in this study. Attrition was attributable to the relative youth of the workforce, dissatisfaction with pay, poor relationships with clients or managers or opportunities for projects elsewhere. Nonetheless, managers considered IndiaCo's turnover rates to be relatively low by industry standards because of the company's brand name, the relative autonomy of the work and other reasons.

IndiaCo tried to minimise attrition by a number of strategies. Although managers who were interviewed conceded that IndiaCo paid less than some competitors, the company marketed the attractions of membership of a larger Indian parent organisation 'family' to counter this. The company also sought to turn the globalisation of projects and operating locations to a potential advantage, by permitting employees autonomy to choose the location in which they wished to work as part of career development package. All three of the chronological phases discussed here were also characterised by a heavy expenditure on training, learning and people development, with training expenditures at approximately 6 per cent of revenues and 'learning and development' a further 4 per cent. Within these totals, however, it is noticeable that as the company internationalised its operations the balance of training expenditures began to shift over time from technical skills towards cross-cultural, language and social skills, including such things as dining table manners and telephone skills. Certain policy development exemplifies the combining of 'traditional' and 'international' values. An example is the development of a subscription-based staff welfare association to assist the partners and families of IndiaCo's global workforce to adjust to different working environments and cultures. This policy also acted as a means for the company to contribute to the communities where the employees came from. The network of members spread across the world provided assistance in seeking housing, schooling, and so on for relocating families. The increasing globalisation of the workforce of IndiaCo induced the development of a tailored welfare system and conducted activities to help the social activities of families of company employees. Hence, the company formed a social platform for all members of the 'IndiaCo family' by extending its activities 'beyond the corporate'.

Between the second quarter of 2008 and the third quarter of 2009, the Indian BPO industry experienced the knock-on effects of the recession in its Western customer base, which caused a hiatus in growth. This cooler economic climate altered IndiaCo's unfolding HRM regime. The focus of recruitment changed from new graduates ('freshers') to individuals already skilled and experienced ('laterals'). In overseas operations, the changes to selection practices included withdrawal of written tests for 'lateral' recruits and of psychometric tests for all recruits. The poor economic climate in many locations led to a view that psychometric tests were time-consuming and unsuccessful in delivering the desired profile of recruit. IndiaCo also responded to the recession by partially reversing the former internationalisation strategy by repatriating some workers back to India. The other notable HRM consequence of the changed economic environment in this phase was the enhanced emphasis on employee performance in order to squeeze more out of the existing resource base. In this period, managers were able to extend the EVA model in the company to encompass reward management. Within the EVA system, the individual works towards the improvement of the benefit package, which essentially has three components – the corporate EVA, the business unit EVA, and the individual performance factor. Individual pay above a baseline amount now became contingent on the magnitudes of performance at corporate, team and employee levels.

The end of the recession in the final quarter of 2009 heralded the third phase of development. Continuity with previous periods was evident in matters such as training expenditures and performance management, but changes arose in other areas. First, the continuing growth of IndiaCo tended to lead to a reversal in the influence of HR techniques between the company and the IndiaCo Group. By the third phase, transfer of IndiaCo's increasingly Westernised HRM and personnel techniques to the wider group was more evident than in earlier periods. These transfers included sophisticated recruitment and selection systems, the spread of the EVA system and uniformity in global HRM practices. Second, a renewed surge of employee recruitment led to the adjustment of recruitment and internationalisation policies, notably a reversion to the emphasis on hiring 'freshers' rather than 'laterals' as large numbers of new contracts from overseas emerged connected to economic recovery the West. There was a reversal of the repatriation strategy evident in phase two as IndiaCo expanded its multinational operations in an attempt to become closer to the customer. The most novel feature since the end of the recession has been the instigation of an 'intrapreneurial' restructuring of the company into 23 separate decentralised business units, as the growth of the firm led to views that the company was unwieldy and stifled entrepreneurship at sub-management levels. During the periods covered in the study, there was an evolution of HRM at IndiaCo towards a more strategically orientated policy. As one HR manager in Mumbai phrased it: 'Determining what matters most to employees and aligning it to organisational goals is a strategic challenge for human resources here at [IndiaCo]' (Fieldwork interview, April 2010).

Discussion and conclusions

The first research question addressed the nature of the HRM practices adopted in a major Indian HRO firm. Discussion of the implications of the results is subject to the limitations imposed by the use of a single case study, albeit a case of a major player. The phenomenal employment growth experienced by such firms placed severe strain on the capacity of HR systems to keep up with HRM issues and led to a strong emphasis in the focus of HRM policy on fine-tuning and segmenting recruitment strategies, partly to counter the relatively high attrition rates that are characteristic of the BPO sector. There was also a considerable investment of effort and finance on increasing the sophistication of staff development and training strategies as part of a strategy to compete on quality service. The balance of recruitment alternated between new gradu- ates and older, experienced hands, depending upon the exigency of economic circumstances. Organisational innovations deployed to resolve the problems posed by expansion included decentralisation of business units and increased adoption, for in-house purposes, of HR systems originally marketed to resolve clients' HRM problems.

The second research question expanded the concerns of the first, enquiring into the relative significances of 'indigenous' and 'foreign' HRM influences. It is clear that a synergy exists between the business strategy of consciously inter- nationalising operations, projects and staff recruitment beyond India, which has a residual domestic orientation connected to exploiting the idea of 'brand India' – and the composite HRM strategy followed. This case study illustrates a dynamic effect whereby 'domestic' influences, partly resulting from the broader group-level views, become gradually less powerful by the adoption of some Western HRM practices. The adoption of Western HRM practices affected the HRM policies of IndiaCo and ultimately the group of which it is a part. Training and development expenditures were but one manifestation of a conscious shift by IndiaCo towards the adoption of HPWS. This was also visible in the gradual adoption of payment systems more contingent on business, team and indi- vidual performance. Such findings question the trajectory claimed by Cappelli et al. (2010). Here, a firm that would appear to be a major exemplar of the 'India Way' is selectively absorbing and adapting Western HRM techniques, the path to this smoothed through the transnational connections that HRO establishes.

In other respects, however, we do see a residual influence on HRM of indi- genous traditions of paternalism and adaptability (*jugaad*) in relation to pro- viding sources of welfare support for employees and their wider families, albeit that this is transformed, extended and intensified by the global expansion of locations of work within the firm. The development of a paternalist form of internal employee welfare and social network proved important to extending HR support beyond purely 'corporate' issues within such a multinational BPO firm. The influence of company reputation was also a tool to exploit recruitment and retention, given that pay levels were, on average, below those of rival com- panies. Broadly, a transition from an 'international' to a 'global' orientation (Adler and Ghadar, 1990) or from a 'polycentric', through a 'regiocentric', to a 'geocentric' multinational strategy (Heenan and Perlmutter, 1979) in the three successive phases was visible, although such life cycle models may oversimplify the pattern of developments observed in this case.

The third question was to identify the main drivers of change in IndiaCo's HRM strategies over time. There have been four main influences on the evo- lution of HRM practices, which we discuss in turn. The first and dominant factor is the growth of the company. The significance of this factor was the gradual systemisation of HRM, through such factors as the use of technology, the adoption of high-performance practices and a business partnering HRM model, the use of various strategies to match more closely recruitment, selection and training with required global skill sets and internal decentralisation of the firm. Second, the expansion of systemised HRM practices links closely to the deliberate globalisation and diversification of the workforce. The impact of this on HRM practices is evident in the cross-vergent hybrid of domestic cultural values overlaid by more international HRM practices with an increased emphasis on diversity and expatriation management, not least through training and welfare interventions. The third factor driving HRM change is the globalised nature of contracts, projects and clients over time. This is seen through such examples as the company's use of image branding and the exploitation of internationalisation in order to enhance staff retention through training opportunities and the autonomy for staff to choose where they wished to work. The fourth factor is the external economic context, which was influential in propelling HRM change during the Indian recession between second-quarter 2008 and third-quarter 2009. Growth slowed rather than reversed, but some distinct changes in HRM priorities were observable resulting from the recession. Here the results largely confirm those of existing literature. In the downturn, the new HRM challenges proved to be maintaining the motivation and morale of staff, employee engagement and a concern to enhance skills development in readiness for the upturn. Our results, however, project the effect of renewed growth on HRM. The end of the global recession saw a renewed influx of major international HRO contracts that, in turn, required large-scale recruitment drives. The end of the recession highlighted ongoing HRM concerns about the quality of recruits drawn in to meet this renewed expansion leading to a deliberate strategy to recruit a greater proportion of experienced subject specialists and to cast the recruitment net increasingly transnationally in order to broaden the firm's geographical base beyond India. Increased focus on organisational and staff performance and a 'harder', Western-style approach to HRM were characteristic of this period, notably through the integration of performance and reward management systems.

Overall, we contend that lead firms are enabling the emergence of a cross-vergent (Ralston et al., 1997) hybrid employment model in Indian BPOs, where an iterative cross-fertilisation of employment and business models between 'country of origin', 'host' country and offshore customer meets but in an unevenly way. The aspiration to operate internationally led to a multidirectional flow of employment practices, with a strategic and more implicit utilisation of domestic employment norms transformed by international business and employment pressures into something that is unique. Our longitudinal study captures this in a way not achieved by more time-bound research. Elements of HPWS have been imported into, and co-exist with, more traditional indigenous employment practices, but, as the study indicates, the emergent hybrid HRM system has been re-exported into IndiaCo's increasingly global operations, as work locations expand into intermediate 'third countries' between India and the offshore customer. The patterns of HRM influence from home and overseas locations have fluctuated markedly in the economic and business circumstances of recent years, and they continue to evolve.

This case study suggests that a more multidimensional and multidirectional set of international processes than some would suggest are at work, as Indian firms become increasingly global operators. The logic of our 'crucial case' method raises the likelihood that, if a relatively straightforward generalisation of 'Indianisation' cannot be observed in one of the major indigenous players in the HRO sector, then it is unlikely to be found elsewhere. In IndiaCo, we find increasing influence of some Western HRM techniques but also observe the export of some of its recruitment procedures and portfolio of staff in an attempt to relocate offshored services closer to the customer. Simultaneously, one sees the continuing attempt to retain at least some legacy of paternalism towards staff that, in the case of the development of a new staff welfare organisation, finds itself expressed in a transformed global context rather than a purely domestic one. The analysis demonstrates that a number of the 'innovative' practices highlighted are mediated by factors such as local indigenous traditions, the culture of the wider organisation and the aspiration to 'role-model' systematic HRM practices.

There are certain limits to this study. Not all will agree that the achievement of depth and length of study in one of India's prime HRO MNEs compensates for a more extensive, quantitative sample size. The respondents consisted primarily of HR managers in two of the firm's main Indian locations, and other grades of employee would not necessarily concur with their perspectives. Further research could certainly inquire into the representativeness of the experiences analysed here, although it would be hard to replicate the time-scale afforded to do so within this investigation.

References

Adler, N.J. and Ghadar, F. (1990) 'Strategic human resource management: a global perspective'. In R. Pieper (Ed.). *Human Resource Management in International Comparison*. Berlin: de Gruyter, pp. 235–260.

Aulakh, P.S. (Ed.) (2007) 'Special issue on emerging market multinationals from developing economies: motivations, paths, and performance'. *Journal of International Management*, 13(3), 235–402.

Bayadi, J. (2008) 'Will BPO remain as India's pride?'. *Siliconindia*. 5(5), 22–25.

Bhattacherjee, D. and Ackers, P. (2010) 'Introduction: employment relations in India – old narratives and new perspectives'. *Industrial Relations Journal*, 41(2), 104–121.

Biswas, S. and Varma, A. (2007) 'Psychological climate and individual performance in India: test of a mediated model'. *Employee Relations*, 29(6), 664–676.

Brewster, C., Sparrow, P. and Vernon, G. (2007) *International Human Resource Management*. London: Chartered Institute of Personnel and Development.

Budhwar, P. and Baruch, Y. (2003) 'Career management practices in India: an empirical study'. *International Journal of Manpower*, 24(6), 699–719.

Budhwar, P. and Bhatnagar, J. (2009) *The Changing Face of People Management in India*. London: Routledge.

Budhwar, P. and Varma, A. (2010) 'Emerging patterns of HRM in the new Indian economic environment'. *Human Resource Management*, 49(3), 345–351.

Budhwar, P., Luthar, H. and Bhatnagar, J. (2006a) 'The dynamics of HRM systems in Indian BPO firms'. *Journal of Labor Research*, 27(3), 339–360.

Cappelli, P., Singh, H., Singh, J. and Useem, M. (2010) *The India way: how India's top business leaders are revolutionizing management*. Boston, MA: Harvard Business Press.

Chatterjee, S. (2007) 'Human resource management in India: "where from" and "where to"?'. *Research and Practice in Human Resource Management*, 15(2), 92–103.

Chatterjee, S. (2009) 'From Sreni Dharma to global cross-vergence: journey of human resource practices in India'. *International Journal of Indian Culture and Business Management*, 2(3), 268–280.

Chatterjee, S. and Pearson, C. (2000) 'Indian managers in transition: orientations, work goals, values and ethics'. *Management International Review*, 40(1), 81–95.

Fern, E.F. (2001) *Advanced Focus Group Research*. London: Sage.

Geppart, M. and Meyer, M. (2006) *Global, National and Local Practices in Multinational Companies*. Basingstoke: Palgrave.

Gerring, J. (2007) *Case Study Research: Principles and Practices*. Cambridge: Cambridge University Press.

Heenan, D.A. and Perlmutter, H.V. (1979) *Multinational Organizational Development: a Social Architectural Approach*. Reading, MA: Addison-Wesley.

Huselid, M. and Becker, B. (2011) 'Bridging micro and macro domains: workforce differentiation and strategic human resource management'. *Journal of Management*, 37(2), 421–428.

Kramar, R. and Syed, J. (2012) *Human Resource Management in a Global Context: a Critical Approach*. Basingstoke: Palgrave Macmillan.

Kumar, N., Mohapatra P.K., and Chandrasekhar, S. (2009) *India's Global Powerhouses: how they are taking on the world*. Boston, MA: Harvard Business School Press.

Kuruvilla, S. and Ranganathan, A. (2010) 'Globalisation and outsourcing: confronting new human resource challenges in India's business process outsourcing industry'. *Industrial Relations Journal*, 41(2), 136–153.

Marchington, M. and Grugulis, I. (2000) '"Best practice" HRM: perfect opportunity or dangerous illusion?'. *International Journal of Human Resource Management*, 11(6), 1104–1124.

Mariappanadar, S. (2005) 'An emic approach to understand culturally indigenous and alien human resource management practices in global companies'. *Research and Practice in Human Resource Management*, 13(2), 31–48.

Nasscom (2010) *IT-BPO sector in India: strategic review 2010*. New Delhi: Nasscom.

Noronha, E. and D'Cruz, P. (2009) 'Engaging the professional: organising call centre agents in India'. *Industrial Relations Journal*, 40(3), 215–234.

Pettigrew, A. (1990) 'Longitudinal field research on change: theory and practice'. *Organization Science*, 1(3), 267–292.

Pettigrew, A. (1997) 'What is processual analysis?'. *Scandinavian Journal of Management*, 13(4), 337–348.

Pfeffer, J. (1994) *Competitive Advantage through People*. Boston, MA: Harvard Business School Press.

Rajeev, M. and Vani, B.P. (2009) 'India's export of BPO services: understanding strengths, weaknesses and competitors'. *Journal of Services Research*, 9(1), 51–67.

Ralston, D. (2008) 'The crossvergence perspective: reflections and projections'. *Journal of International Business Studies*, 39(1), 27–40.

Ralston, D.A., Holt, D.H., Terpstra, R.H. and Yu, K.C. (1997) 'The impact of national culture and economic ideology on managerial work values: a study of the United States, Russia, Japan and China'. *Journal of International Business Studies*, 28(1), 177–207.

Raman, S.R., Budhwar, P. and Balasubramanian, G. (2007) 'People management issues in Indian KPOs'. *Employee Relations*, 29(6), 696–710.

Saini, D.S. and Budhwar, P.S. (2008) 'Managing the human resource in Indian SMEs: the role of indigenous realities'. *Journal of World Business*, 43(4), 417–434.

Saldaña, J. (2003) *Longitudinal qualitative research: analyzing change through time*. Walnut Creek, CA: AltaMira Press.

Sauvant, K. and Pradhan, J. with Chatterjee, A. and Harley, B. (Eds) (2010) *The rise of Indian Multinationals: Perspectives on Indian Outward Foreign Direct Investment*. New York: Palgrave Macmillan.

Som, A. (2007)' What drives adoption of innovative SHRM practices in Indian organizations?'. *International Journal of Human Resource Management*, 18(5), 808–828.

Sparrow, P.R. and Braun, W. (2008) 'HR sourcing and shoring: strategies, drivers, success factors and implications for HR'. In M. Dickmann, C. Brewster and P. Sparrow (Eds). *International Human Resource Management: a European Perspective*. 2nd edition. Abingdon: Routledge, pp. 39–66.

Vivek, S.D., Richey, R.G. and Dalela, V. (2009) 'A longitudinal examination of partnership governance in offshoring: a moving target'. *Journal of World Business*, 44(1), 16–30.

Yin, R. (2014) *Case Study Research: Design and Methods*. 5th edition. London: Sage.

6
Against All Odds!: A Strategic Analysis of the Failures of Three State-Owned Firms

Joseph Amankwah-Amoah

Introduction

Over the past few decades, scholars have demonstrated that government policies and supports can foster innovation, help new firms to overcome liability of newness and provide conditions for local firms to thrive (Chu, 2011; Edquist, 2011). It has also been demonstrated that such supports can provide the basis for local firms' competitive advantage (Petersen and Pedersen, 2002). However, scholars have remained relatively silent on how government support for state-owned enterprises (SOEs) can become a source of liability and even lead to such firms' failure (Doganis, 2006). This dearth of scholarly work is puzzling given that such research has the potential to enrich our understanding of government policies, processes and factors that lead to business failure.

Although past studies have offered an array of rich explanations of the causes of organisational failure (Knott and Posen, 2005), this issue has been largely overlooked. Our purpose in this study is to fill this gap in our understanding by examining how state policy to support state-owned and local firms can become a source of liability precipitating in such firms' failure. In developing our arguments, we advance a novel concept of 'liability of domestic support' to elucidate the mechanisms through which state support can become a liability and precipitate the demise of SOEs.

To further shed light on our concept and the unanswered question, we examine a tale of three failed major airlines – namely Air Afrique (AA), Nigeria Airways (NA) and Ghana Airways (GA) over relatively short periods. These once-mighty airlines were owned by more than 12 countries and their histories are intertwined in the colonial history of the whole of sub-Sahara Africa. By employing these historical cases, we further enrich the ongoing scholarly discourse of the need to bring 'history' back into international business, industrial and government policy literature (Jones and Khanna, 2006). The rest of the chapter is organised as follows. The next section articulates the key features of our concept of 'liability of domestic support'. We then illustrate the theoretical analysis with the cases of AA, NA and GA. The chapter concludes by setting out the implications of the findings for theory and practice.

The 'liability of domestic support': a conceptual development

The study integrates insights from the concepts of the Icarus Paradox (Miller, 1990) and 'liability of foreignness' (Hymer, 1960; Zaheer, 1995) to help clarify the boundaries of the concept of 'liability of domestic support'. We contend that, by seeking to provide competitive advantages to SOEs through special measures such as subsidies, special privileges, preferential treatment and tax relief, governments unwittingly create conditions that allow inefficiencies, mediocrity and incompetence inherent in SOEs to thrive. Interestingly enough, the protection and privileges inherent in government supports, which sometimes discriminated against foreign and other firms, can often fool SOEs into believing that their past routines, processes and strategies which brought about success would guide them to future success even in the face of a changing competitive landscape.

Another notable feature is that SOEs are able to enjoy government subsidies and institutional support such as state aid, soft loans made on less than normal commercial terms, tax relief, debt forgiveness, discounts on charges for services, discounts on or exemptions from navigation and landing fees, privilege in the supply of fuel and debt forgiveness (see Amankwah-Amoah, 2010; Doganis, 2006). Indeed, government support has the potential to put off the need for reforms to improve efficiency and allow inefficacy to thrive (Doganis, 2006). Consequently, as the competitive landscape changes through market reforms and new competition, it becomes increasingly difficult for such firms to maintain the status quo and sustain their competitive advantages, which thereby precipitates their demise.

Another line of research has suggested that such preferential treatments and special privileges often lull SOEs into a false sense of security or robustness of their sources of competitive advantage and thereby become less attentive to changes in the external environment (Amason and Mooney, 2008; Miller, 1990). Because of such supports, the organisations may 'gradually slide so far out of touch with what is happening...that a potentially fatal disaster develops unseen' (Hedberg et al., 1976: 50). Such overconfidence rooted in the protections from the state can cause managers to delay or ignore rival firms' activities in their environment.

This line of thinking is similar to the notion of the Icarus Paradox concept (Miller, 1990), where past successes or supports seduce managers into a failing course of action, which ultimately led to the firm's demise. Past successes breed overconfidence such that managers begin to ignore the alternatives and the success becomes the imprint for the future even though the environmental conditions might have changed. The inability to take advantage of such special treatment to develop new sources of competitive advantage and improve processes can become liabilities in the face of a changing competitive environment (Amason and Mooney 2008). The unwillingness to deviate from the dogma and rituals eventually precipitates the firm's demise.

Government actions to provide protection and subsidies to help local firms might create conditions where they become overconfident about themselves and overlook their limited expertise. Indeed, such protection and preferential treatment may create conditions that foster inefficiencies, mediocrity and incompetence inherent in SOEs, which may ultimately precipitate the failure of the business (Amankwah-Amoah and Debrah, 2010).

The different treatments between insiders (SOEs) and outsiders (foreign firms or privately owned firms) put outsiders' firms at a competitive disadvantage relative to local firms (Miller and Richards, 2002; Miller and Parkhe, 2002). However, foreign and privately owned firms not party to such treatment can overcome some of the constraints in the business environment through resource commitment to understand the market. They can also develop new sources of competitive advantage, such as superior customer services, cheaper services, quality products and acquisition of market knowledge (Zaheer, 1995).

Government actions through discriminatory laws, rules and regulations may be overcome by developing superior attributes of an organisation, called competences or capabilities (Wernerfelt, 1984). As firms learn about the new market, the associated costs of doing business abroad falls over a period of time as they get acquainted with the new business environment (Nachum, 2003). Although effective management of foreign and privately owned firms can make a significant difference in overcoming their liabilities (Petersen and

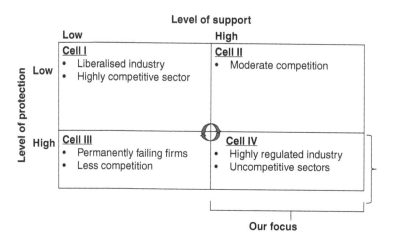

Figure 6.1   A four-cell typology of 'liability of domestic support'

Pedersen, 2002), it is extremely difficult for such firms to overcome government discriminatory actions to protect and aid SOEs (Nachum, 2003).

Although domestic firms are generally better informed about their country and its business environment (Hymer, 1976), the discriminatory and preferential treatments can become a sources of liability as they expand into new foreign markets. We contend that supports offered by governments in the forms of subsidies and tax relief can help new firms to find their feet in competitive industries. However, it can also create conditions for complacency, mediocrity, incompetence and inefficiency to flourish, which ultimately precipitate business failure.

The above discussion indicates that there are two main components of 'liability of domestic support': level of support (high/low) and level of protection (high/low). Crossing the two dimensions produces the 2x2 conceptual framework of the subject (see Figure 6.1). Although the importance of the domestic government support has fostered a steady stream of research, our understanding of the concept and how it can precipitate the failure of SOEs remains limited. We illustrate our theoretical analysis with the cases of the three state-owned airlines.

A tale of three failed airlines

It was against this backdrop in the 1950s and 1960s that the 'three Darlings' (i.e. NA, AA and GA) were established. Indeed, 'legend has it that when African states gained their political independence from Western countries, they were bequeathed three seemingly essential symbols of sovereignty – a national flag, a national anthem and a national airline' (Fadugba, 1991: nd). For decades, the governments took measures such as providing aid and subsidies to prevent the collapse of their symbolic firms. These airlines shared a number of characteristics and were considered the flag bearers of the 'New Africa'. Of their many similarities, such as being state-owned and recipients of government assistance for decades, there were repeated attempted to privatise by the nations. Despite that, decades have passed since the end of colonial rule and the lessons stemming from their formation and subsequent demise have not been learnt. Their collapse provides a background to the comparative analysis. Table 6.1 provides the background history of the three firms. Before we proceed to the cases, let us provide a historical backdrop of the industry.

Government interventions and the airline industry in Africa

Historically, the global airline industry has been governed through the system of bilateral air services agreements, which are effectively trade agreements between governments (Doganis, 2006). Since the late 1970s, when the United

Table 6.1 Features of the three state-owned airlines

Firms	Founded	Dominant logic at founding conditions	Exit	Exiting conditions
Ghana Airways	1958	• Political support following independence in 1957.	2004	• Dwindling circle of financial backers. • State involvement, over reliance on states' limited resources, global competition.
Air Afrique – formed by 11 Francophone countries in Africa	1961	• The firms focused fulfilling the political objectives of the founders.	2002	• Conflicting interests of contracting states, appalling service and over-employment, global competition. • Debt-ridden and corporate dysfunction.
Nigeria Airways	1958	• Strong political support	2003	• State involvement, over reliance on state's limited resources, global competition etc. • Cognitively constrained by decades of state subsidies which discouraged large-scale staff reductions.

Sources: synthesised by the authors from: African Development Bank, 1999; Akpoghomeh, 1999; Amankwah-Amoah and Debrah, 2010, 2011, 2014; Brooke, 1987, 1988; Tsamenyi et al., 2011; *Flight International*, 1960, 1961, 1962; 1988, World Bank, 1998, 2003.

States initiated the deregulation of its domestic freight and passenger markets, there has been a shift towards global liberalisation of air transportation markets (Button, 2002). In the face of increasing force of liberalisation in the US and elsewhere, African governments were forced to explore ways to help improve the competitiveness of African airlines. It was at the Yamoussoukro Convention on Market Access for Air Transport in Africa in 1988 where governments adopted the Yamoussoukro Declaration (YD) as Africa's blueprint for liberalisation (Amankwah-Amoah and Debrah, 2011). The adoption of the YD as Africa's blueprint to liberalisation ushered in a new era of competitive environment by seeking to remove all restrictions in intra-Africa routes by allowing free access of air traffic between member states in order to create a single African aviation market (UNECA, 1999).

African countries such as Ghana, Nigeria and founders of AA took initiatives to open their markets to regional and international competition. the end of the 1990s witnessed a little progress towards the implementation of the famous declaration, but many state-owned airlines became increasing resistant to the idea of opening the African market to major carriers from the developed economies that could drive them out of business. While the YD had not being fully implemented at this stage, the adoption of YD served as a catalyst and laid the foundations for countries to begin to open their markets to regional competition. In the industry, liability is likely to manifest through bilateral restrictions on market access, designations and frequency that have allowed nationality clauses to emerge, which puts foreign-owned airlines at a competitive disadvantage. In the case of Africa, the YD explicitly insists on states to designate an airline(s), which to some extent comes with a degree of nationality rules.

One of the main differences between foreign-owned and local or domestic airlines is the area of designation. Designation involves each country nominating one, two or more than two carriers, to operate any agreed international route(s) (Chang and Williams, 2001). This element helps to determine how many players there are in the market. In other words, it often limits the number of flights per foreign-owned airlines on a route which intentionally protects domestic or national carriers from fierce competition. For instance, the YD allows any airline, which has 'its headquarters, central administration and principal place of business physically located in the state concerned' to benefit fully from the advantages set forth (UNECA, 1999).

The requirement of states to designate an airline(s) in bilateral arrangements encouraged governments to set up or maintain an operation of an airline irrespective of its traffic potential (Doganis, 2006). This is partly because nationality clauses and ownership rules 'lie at the heart of bilaterals and without them the value of the agreements is questionable' (Baker, 2002: 26). This has provided grounds for bilaterals to be constructed in favour of domestic/local airlines or one owned by nationals. Since bilateral agreements are effectively 'trade agreements between governments, not between airlines' (Doganis, 2006: 28), they are often guided by strong political and national interest considerations. States guard the granting of traffic rights, and most rights issued by these treaties were based upon reciprocity.

In recent years, there has been a shift from single to multiple designations of airlines in most bilaterals (Knibb, 2007). This has eased restrictions on many airlines. The bilateral system is underpinned by the ownership rules, which limits foreigners to a minority stake. Indeed, most countries limit foreign ownership and control through bilateral agreements, which require airlines to be owned and controlled by nationals of the designating state (Knibb, 2007). This means that airlines are restricted from utilising alliances and mergers to consolidate their operations and achieve economies of scale. This anomaly has benefited airlines in operating in large domestic markets and regions such as the US and EU. Restrictions on ownership have dissuaded individuals and financial institutions from investing in airlines in other countries since it barred foreigners from exercising any effective controls on the management of the airlines. Consequently, there are little incentives for foreign investors to commit substantial resources into an airline.

Case 1: Ghana Airways (1958–2004)

Following decades of struggle and a concerted effort spearheaded by the United Gold Coast Convention and others to gain independence from colonial master Great Britain in 1957, Ghana, under the leadership of Kwame Nkrumah, decided that a national airline not controlled by former colonial powers would allow the country to take its rightful place in the world. Ghana Airways was formed following the disintegration of West African Airways Corporation (WAAC) which was a jointly owned airline operated by four nations, namely the Gold Coast (now Ghana), Nigeria, Sierra Leone and the Gambia (Amankwah-Amoah, 2010).

In 1958, this culminated in the formation of GA with national backing to train the indigenous population to manage and control the affairs of the airline. For President Nkrumah, who desired minimal foreign influence in the affairs of the nation, the new national airline was the major starting point in 'flying the flag' of a newly independent nation and a symbol of the emerging postcolonial Africa. In an editorial, *Flight International* (1962: 926) noted, 'GA have never made any secret of the fact that prestige comes first, economic considerations second.' These principles guided successive governments with unquenched thirst to protect the airline and maintain its operations through special privileges and access to abundant national resources.

Although the airline was formed with British Overseas Airways Corporation (BOAC) and companies holding 40 per cent (£400, 000 nominal capital), as part of the agreement at founding, 12 of the BOAC staff were seconded to GA, which included the general manager, station manager, reservations and sales superintendent, accountants and engineer (*Flight International*, 1961). One of the motives was to make a quick transition to moderate 'Ghanaisation' of the airline and the economy. The 'Ghanaisation' was aimed at diminishing the influence of former colonial powers in the affairs of the nation and thereby allowing the nation to find its feet in postcolonial Africa.

However, this quickly turned into an extreme 'Ghanaisation' process which extended beyond the airline industry into nationalisation of foreign-owned firms and the extending powers of the state. Consequently, the link with BOAC quickly became an obstacle to Nkrumah's ambitious projects of 'Ghanaisation' of the airline and the wider society and industries (*Flight International*, 1961). The agreement which was signed between the two airlines was revised in July 1958 to pave the way for Nkrumah to take full control and pursue his nationalistic goals. Earning the reputation as Osagyefo (the Redeemer) enabled the president to push ahead with these agendas with little social resistance.

Case 2: Nigeria Airways (1958–2003)

Following Ghana's exit from WAAC, the Nigerian government established NA, and it started operations in 1958. The formation paved the way for the airline to take over some of the services previously operated by the WAAC

(*Flight International*, 1969). By the late 1960s, most of the airline's route networks extended beyond Africa to European cities such as London, Rome and Frankfurt.

By March 1961, the government held 51 per cent of the shares and then acquired the 61 per cent of the shares from BOAC and 36 per cent from Elder Dempster (*Flight International*, 1969). Unsurprisingly, the acquisition of the stake of the two shareholders was followed by intense state involvement in the direction and processes adopted by the airline.

By the mid-1960s, the fortunes of the airline had turned dramatically. Indeed, a tribunal of inquiry into the affairs of the airline initiated by the Nigerian Federal Military Government uncovered factors such as incompetent management, inappropriate payment to unknown individuals and organisations, lack of financial control, mismanagement of funds and corruption as major factors in turning the profitable period from 1961 to 1962 into a loss of over £500,000 between 1963 and 1964 (*Flight International*, 1969b).

For decades the firm prospered under a regime of government subsidies to fund new routes and special tax regimes; it enjoyed the patronage of being a national airline and had a historical advantage over its rivals. Nevertheless, poor customer satisfaction records and the experience of firms dealing with them appears to have undermined its ability to sustain long-term operations. One of the sources of the airline's problems was the two decades of military rule and quest to use it as the main national symbol of independence. The military rule led to asset stripping, and revenues were diverted to private accounts of key individuals within the military rule. In many instances, planes were impounded at numerous airports due to unpaid bills and the poor safety track record of the airline. Following years of unresolved financial and political issues, the firm ceased operation in 2003.

From Nigeria Airways to 'Nigeria Air Waste'
This period was marked by a further shift from the founding principles to a new environment where corruption and mismanagement became major features of the airline. In 1984 the United States Civil Aeronautics Board threatened to impound NA aircraft found bringing drugs into their country. The events damaged the image of the airline, making it difficult to attract and retain customers, which forced the management to introduce new measures to identify and punish staff involved in and assisting trafficking of drugs to the US or any other country (Fadugba, 1985a).

'Our national airline is a disgrace. Lateness, delays, outright cancellation of flights and a nonchalant attitude of the staff toward customers are now part of your operational guide' Nigeria's Minister of Transport and Aviation, Brig. Jerry Useni, told airline employees in early April 1987 (Cited in Brooke, 1987).

In 1985, the company underwent sweeping administrative reorganisation in an attempt to arrest the shrinking resource base and address the debt-ridden and corporate dysfunction which had allowed corruption and mismanagement to thrive. The strategy adopted at this point entailed reduction in staff numbers (including the dismissing or retiring of more than 1,000 of the 10,000 workforce from January 1984 to April 1985) and to tighten up on malpractice and misallocation of the firm's resources to line the pockets of some individuals (Fadugba, 1985a, b). This was exemplified by the fact that in 1984, the airline's net revenue on its key European routes was 4.5 million Naira (£4.4 million pounds sterling) – a decline of around 21.6 per cent on 1983 data (Fadugba, 1985a).

In identifying the causes of the decline, scapegoating by the management was very evident, and they attributed the sharp decline to the then Military Government's austerity measures, which partly contributed to a 52.8 per cent fall in passenger traffic on the key London route in 1984 (Fadugba, 1985a; see also Figure 6.2). However, they ignored the fact that liberalisation of the air transport market was gathering momentum in Africa, and many customers switched to rival airlines due to the poor customer services offered by the airline. In addition to these, the strategy also sought to discontinue servicing of unprofitable routes, close some subsidiary offices around the world, eliminate excessive overseas travel by employees and their relatives paid from the airline's account and reduce wet-leased aircraft.

At this point in the firm's history, these expenses not only had become major obstacles to progress but had created an environment where anything goes. It is against these backdrops that the airlines came to be known as 'Nigeria Air Waste'. As far back as the late 1980s, the airline was dubbed 'Nigeria Air Waste' and 'Nigeria Errways' to reflect the rampant waste of the state's limited resources, its inefficiencies and looting by political appointees who ran the firm (Brooke, 1987).

High-level fraud among workers and management became very common. This took root with the emergence of military regimes which turned a blind eye to the corruption. Indeed, in many instances they were actually involved in the act. Between 1983 and 1999 more than US$400 million (£254 million) disappeared from the airline's account without trace. The company's abysmal record keeping and bad debts led to a decline in the number of fleets (BBC, 2002).

In the late 1980s Airbus A310s were among the most efficient aircraft at the time, and many airlines were eager to acquire them. However, in 1987, the Nigerian Transport and Aviation Minister, Major General Jerry Useni, declared that the airline was going to discontinue the use of Airbuses arguing that the aircraft were 'too technologically advanced' for the local engineers (*Flight International*, 1987). This was surprising given that additional training would have equipped the engineers to pave the way for the airline to use efficient planes at the time relative to the alternatives.

The growth of the airline and its increasingly appeal to travellers meant that, by 1986, it carried 2.1 million passengers to at least 22 international destinations and 16 domestic routes (Brooke 1987). At this point, the airline was seen as a symbol of black Africa's largest passenger carrier. In addition, some of the airline's employees were implicated in international drug trafficking, while others were seen selling boarding passes for $200 apiece.

> 'For every plane owned by the company, there are 500 employees, or about twice the international average. Yet domestic air fares, set by the Government, average 6 cents a mile – half the international average – and international fares are also kept artificially low. As a result, the airline is chronically short of cash and is the only carrier in the 125-member clearinghouse of the IATA that has been suspended for not paying debts' (Brooke, 1987: 3).

By mid-1987, the poor customer service, coupled with employees' counterproductive behaviour such as trading boarding passes for cash and general corruption, prompted many commentators to call for privatisation of the airline (Brooke 1987; Tsamenyi et al., 2011). This argument was further reinforced by the fact that the Government of General Ibrahim Babangida had imposed stringent austerity measures on the country to reduce its $20 billion foreign debt.

In addition, the government opposed any attempt to increase 'international air fares originating in its two international airports, in Lagos and Kano. Hence, a Lagos–London–Lagos first-class ticket costs $1,114 if it is purchased in Lagos, but $3,203 if bought in London' (Brooke, 1987: 3). Consequently, the air fares were considerably lower than those charged in other African and Western airlines for flights that covered a similar distance. Indeed, 'a one-way economy ticket to London or Paris – about 3,000 miles – costs $337. The same ticket for a flight from Abidjan, Ivory Coast, to London or Paris – also about 3,000 miles – costs $762' (Brooke, 1987: 3).

Furthermore, it was not uncommon for both reservations and scheduled flights to be 'ignored' by the airline (Brooke, 1987; Akpoghomeh, 1999). Such was the poor quality of service offered by the airline; even government workers, who were required to use the airline on overseas trips, often opted for other African and foreign airlines (Brooke, 1987). In 1993, economic progress in the country came to a halt when the military leader General Sani Abacha came to power, suspending privatisation and commercialisation of SOEs by a military decree (Tsamenyi et al., 2011). Indeed, the general's spending approach meant that the government was extremely reluctant to release any money for maintenance and other operational activities of the airline. The airline was able to sustain losses as well as sustain operations largely because of the support of the government to plug gaps in its finances.

In 1995, the government dismissed the entire top management team of the airline in an attempt to pave the way for fresh and innovative thinking to emerge (Endres, 1995). However, the major constraints on the airline's operations, such as political interference and continuous flow of financial resources to the firm, appeared to have made managers complacent to pursue any large-scale measures to improve efficiency. Historically, the government misidentified the causes of the airline's problems and the prescribed inappropriate solution. Despite frequent changes in the management team, the underlying problems remained for decades. At this point, it was clear that the protracted problems such as flight delays, corruption and mismanagement and looting had led to the loss of most fleets and international credibility (Endres, 1995).

Although both NA and GA emerged out of WAAC, there are similarities in their postcolonial trajectory and eventual collapse. Following decades of substandard performances, NA was liquidated in 2003, which was followed in 2004 with the collapse of GA. Tsamenyi et al. (2011: 3) noted that both airlines had deep-rooted 'political interference, poor accountability and mismanagement, inefficiency, saddled with excessive debt and eventual liquidation'.

Case 3: Air Afrique (1961–2002)

Although the creation of AA was not the first major attempt to establish a multi-flag world airline, it remains the most significant in postcolonial African history. The airline was formed in 1962 by 11 African countries with the support of France and Air France. It was the first major attempt by African countries to establish an airline which served the interests of multiple states. AA was a quintessential Pan-African airline, in which multiple countries held a stake. The sheer political weight and financial resources of the founding countries behind the airline provided the enabling environment for the firm to achieve global success as well as the ability to overcome the financial constraints that had served as an obstacle to other countries in establishing a global airline. Its strength lay in having more than 11 countries as owners, providing a wider pool of talent and resources to draw from.

Founder countries' expectation was that it would become not only Africa's largest airline but also one of the biggest on the globe. This to some extent was fulfilled during the heydays. However, the complex organisational structure became a source of confusion and periods of indecision (Amankwah-Amoah and Debrah, 2014). One of the problems encountered by all three firms was their inability to shake off their reputation of poor quality service once the reputation was acquired. This hampered numerous attempts to revitalise the airline due to low customer demands.

Cross-Case Analysis

Having identified the features of each firm, we now present the cross-case analysis. We tease out some the factors that led to the failure of GA, AA and NA.

National patriotism and patriotic purchasing

Consumer ethnocentrism played a major role in perpetuating mediocre services offered by the airlines and ensuring their survival for decades. Klein (2002: 346) defined consumer ethnocentrism as 'the belief that it is inappropriate, or even immoral, to purchase foreign products because to do so is damaging to the domestic economy, costs domestic jobs, and is unpatriotic.' For decades, the main marketing messages for AA and GA were to appeal to Africans in the diaspora that it was unpatriotic, harmful to the domestic economy or likely even to bring back colonial rule if they fail to fly with local airlines. For instance, GA vehemently pursued its 'Ghanaisation' strategy which appealed to local businessmen and women to fly with only its airline, while NA quickly pursued its 'decolonisation' strategy. The airlines made implicit use of national colours in packaging or labelling. These strategies were pursued to retain consumer loyalty and boost sales of the local airlines. Africa's past history of colonialism left many Africans, during the immediate postcolonial period, developing a negative attitude towards some of their colonial powers and firms connected to them. In many instances national affiliation was so strong that it superseded affordable and reliable services offered by rival airlines.

Patriotism was seen as a commitment and sacrifice to help protect the local economy and jobs. Against this backdrop, many consumers were willing to pay higher prices to contribute to their country and local economy. Despite the fact that decades had passed since colonial rule, patriotic Africans strongly opted for their national airline over a foreign airline (ARB, 2008). Indeed, many corrupt leaders have often invoked such sentiments to exempt themselves from any blame over their bad policies.

However, these strategies also made the airlines unattractive to Western European and North American travellers as well as consumers around the globe who sought quality services and affordable prices over national patriotism. For decades, the airlines could count on patriotic consumers. Discriminatory actions by consumers against foreign-owned airlines bred complacence and overconfidence among the top management teams of the firms. As liberalisation advanced in the late 1980s and 1990s, more local and international airlines emerged. It therefore became increasingly difficult for them to attract consumers due to the historical poor services offered by the airlines, characterised by long delays. They began to lose market share to private and foreign airlines which were able to offer competitive rates to consumers.

To illustrate this point further, we turn again to the case of NA. As new firms such as ADC (established in 1984), Concord Airlines (1986), Express Airways (1986), African Trans Air (1992) and Bellview Airlines (1992) emerged, it became increasingly difficult for the firm to attract new customers, and it also started losing customers to these rival firms (Akpoghomeh 1999). Consequently, the

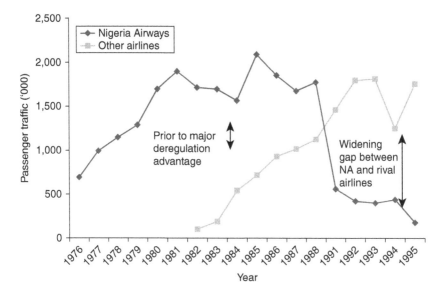

Figure 6.2 Domestic passenger traffic between Nigeria Airways and other airlines
Source: Akpoghomeh, 1999; Federal Office of Statistics, 1996.

competitive pressure on both domestic and international routes squeezed the revenue streams of the firm and precipitated a terminal decline.

Figure 6.2 provides details on the evolution of NA domestic passenger traffic and how it shrunk from 1985 to 1995, while at the same time the market share of autonomous carriers surged from 715,000 from 1,756,000. More importantly, the private airlines were able to overcome historical advantages of the SOEs to attract customers. On the other hand, multinational carriers such as British Airways and Air France have historically operated services across Africa and possess significant knowledge of the business environment. On intercontinental routes where the African carriers competed against European and American carriers, the number of customers began to dwindle, which led to loss of market share.

As new routes were opened up to allow more privately owned and non-African airlines to expand on its key routes to Europe, head-to-head competition advanced as Middle Eastern airlines also utilised their hub-and-spoke network to expand their geographical routes and compete indirectly with the airline. Consequently, their sources of revenue were further squeezed, culminating in loss of market share and shrinking customer base. It is worth noting that in the case of NA, the traffic decline on international routes is not as sharp as those experienced on domestic routes (see Figure 6.3). In the post-9/11 environment, it became increasingly difficult for them to make up for the loss in market

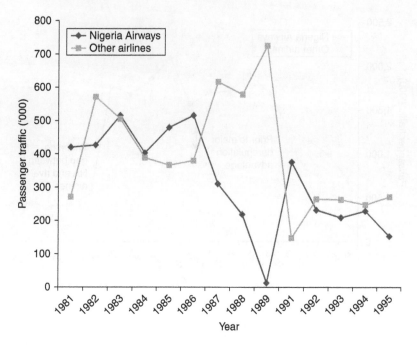

Figure 6.3 International passenger traffic between Nigeria Airways and other airlines
Source: Akpoghomeh, 1999; Federal Office of Statistics, 1995, 1996.

share while sustaining the decades of losses. AA exited from the industry in 2001, followed years later by the other airlines.

The dominant European airlines in Africa

Since the early 1980s, African countries increasingly signed favourable bilateral arrangements with European countries and thereby provided the conditions for major European airlines to open new routes across the continent. Given the poor quality of services that had been historically offered to African consumers by the three airlines, the emergence of more European airlines provided travellers opportunities to switch. It also enabled consumers to switch from traditional airlines such as GA and AA with historical track record of overbooking (Amankwah-Amoah and Debrah, 2014). In addition, several African airlines, including the three airlines, were noted for their poor safety records. In the case of AA, its passenger numbers declined as French airlines such as Air France saw significant growth in the market share which eventually sealed the fate of the firm.

Fadugba (1991: nd) identified the following symptoms associated with most African airlines at the time: they were 'handicapped by their small size, obsolete equipment, inadequate capital, insufficient traffic, weak national economy, strong international competition, lack of autonomy and transient management.

Separately, they lack the critical mass needed to benefit from economies of scale and to compete effectively in the tough international airline industry'.

Under these circumstances, no firm can afford to be oblivious to the needs of all its customers. However, the protection inherent in state ownership and fringe benefits made the airlines oblivious to changing consumer trends and often ignored numerous customers' complaints about poor quality in-flight and off-flight services. Despite the shift in the global airline industry towards privatisation of state-owned airlines (SOAs) in the 1980s, many African governments considered their flag carriers as a source of pride that needs to be protected (ARB, 2008). Due to their close cultural and national association, some countries, including Ghana and the owners of AA, saw privatising the unprofitable state-owned airlines as politically unwise and thus opted to maintain the current status quo.

By developing distinctive features, such as reputation for quality, reliable services, excellent safety record and extensive route networks, European airlines such as British Airways, KLM and Air France operating in Africa at the time were able to overcome the lack of local government support. By competing against EU and US carriers in Africa, excellent safety records that are associated with these carriers beaome a key selling point. The advantages associated with nationality appear to be minimal in the African airlines as many are largely uncompetitive and dwindling in numbers (Amankwah-Amoah and Debrah, 2011). By the 1990s, Fadugba (1990) observed that European airlines dwarfed African airlines on Europe–Africa routes and thereby weakened the competitive positions of African carriers in an era of global competition. This issue did not go away; rather, it accelerated and played a fundamental role in the demise of the three airlines.

Discussion and implications

This study set out to examine how government supports can become a source of liability in precipitating failures of SOEs. In so doing, the article develops the concept of 'liability of domestic support' to illustrate how government support can create conditions for complacency and inefficiency to abound and thereby precipitate the demise of SOEs. We illustrate our theoretical analysis with the cases of the 'three darlings' (i.e. AA, NA and GA) and demonstrated how governments' policies and supports created the conditions that led to their demises. The study uncovered that special measures such as subsidies, special privileges, preferential treatment and tax relief created conditions that allowed inefficiencies, mediocrity and incompetence inherent in SOEs to thrive, which eventually contributed to the demise of the business.

More importantly, protection and privileges bred overconfidence and inattentiveness in the face of changes in the environment, which pushed back necessary reforms in the face of increasing competition and the emergence of new firms. In addition, the firms 'indigenisation' approaches such as 'Africanisation' (at AA), 'Ghanaisation' (at GA) and 'de-colonialisation process' (at NA) made it difficult for them to attract foreign travellers to offset decline in their local consumer base, which contributed to their demise.

Contributions to theory and practice

The study makes two main contributions to the literature. First, it develops the concept of 'liability of domestic support' to demonstrate how government actions allowed SOEs to be lulled into a false sense of security or robustness of their sources of competitive advantage, which ultimately led to their demise. By charting the evolution and eventual demise of the three firms, our study adds to scholarly works that have argued that business failure may be best understood in historical phases, which entails the evolution of factors, interaction of firm-specific and external factors, firm response to early-warning signals of decline and eventual demise. In so doing, we further contribute to ongoing efforts to develop a theory of business failure pathways (Moulton et al., 1996) which take into consideration the evolution and interactions of firm-specific factors and general changes in the external environment. In addition, the study builds on Sutton's (1987) process of organisational death by introducing how governments' actions through policy formulation and directives can either slow or accelerate the process of organisational death, thereby providing further insights into why some organisations die more quickly than others.

From the public policy standpoint, firms can accumulate superior resources and capabilities to outwit their competitors to offset such liabilities and, in the process, precipitate the demise of rivals. By deploying these organisational strengths and cultivating inter-organisational relationships, firms would be able to circumvent regulatory constraints in their operating environments. The findings indicate that governments should seek to create a level playing field where competition flourishes and allow inefficient firms to fail rather than be propped up by limited financial resources of the state. A fertile area for future research would be to seek a wider sample of firms to determine whether our findings are borne out in other contexts. In closing, we hope that the chapter serves as a catalyst for more research on how 'liability of domestic support' precipitates business failure.

References

Africa Research Bulletin (ARB) (2008) 'Economic, financial and technical series'. *Africa Research Bulletin*, 44(12), 17171–171206.
African Development Bank (1999) *Multinational Company Air-Afrique Reinforcement Project: Project Completion Report*. Abidjan: ADB.
Akpoghomeh, O.S. (1999) 'The development of air transportation in Nigeria'. *Journal of Transport Geography*, 7(2), 135–146

Amankwah-Amoah, J. (2010) 'Organisational responses to liberalisation: Evidence from the airline industry in Africa.' Doctoral Dissertation, University of Wales Swansea.
Amankwah-Amoah, J. and Debrah, Y. (2010) 'The protracted collapse of Ghana Airways: Lessons in organizational failure'. *Group & Organization Management*, 35(5), 636–665.
Amankwah-Amoah, J. and Debrah, Y. (2011) 'The evolution of alliances in the global airline industry: A review of the Africa experience'. *Thunderbird International Business Review*, 53(1), 37–50.
Amankwah-Amoah, J. and Debrah, Y. (2014) 'Air Afrique: The demise of a continental icon'. *Business History*, 56(4), 517–546.
Amason, A.C. and Mooney, A.C. (2008) 'The Icarus paradox revisited: How strong performance sows the seeds of dysfunction in future strategic decision-making'. *Strategic Organization*, 6(4), 407–434.
Baker, C. (2002) 'Bilaterals in the dock'. *Airline Business*, 18(12), 26.
BBC (2002) 'Fresh fraud probe for Nigeria Airways', available at http://news.bbc.co.uk/1/hi/business/2569841.stm (accessed 19 June 2012).
Brooke, J. (1987) 'Nigeria's Flying Elephant'. August 03, *New York Times*, 3.
Brooke, J. (1988) 'In Lagos, economic dream is now nightmare'. *New York Times*, August, 14.
Button, K. (2002) 'Toward truly open skies'. *Regulation*, 25(3), 12–16.
Chang, Y.-C. and Williams, G. (2001) 'Changing the rules – Amending the nationality clauses in air services agreements'. *Journal of Air Transport Management*, 7, 207–216.
Chu, W.W. (2011) 'How the Chinese government promoted a global automobile industry'. *Industrial and Corporate Change*, 20(5), 1235–1276.
Doganis, R. (2006) *The Airline Business*. 2nd edition (London: Routledge).
Edquist, C. (2011) 'Design of innovation policy through diagnostic analysis: Identification of systemic problems (or failures)'. *Industrial and Corporate Change*, 20(6), 1725–1753.
Endres, G. (1995) 'New broom sweeps Nigeria Airways'. *Flight International*, October, 12.
Fadugba, N. (1985a) 'Nigeria Airways radically reorganises'. *Flight International*, April, 5.
Fadugba, N. (1985b) 'Prospects for a West African airline'. *Flight International*, September, 5.
Fadugba, N. (1990) 'European airlines dominate African sky', available at http://africanaviation.com/European_airlines_dominate_African_sky.html (Accessed 19 June 2012).
Fadugba, N. (1991) 'A national flag, national anthem and national airline', available at http://africanaviation.com/A_national_flag,_national_anthem_and_national_airline.html (Accessed 19 June 2007).
Federal Office of Statistics (1995) *Annual Abstract of Statistics*, (Lagos: FOS).
Federal Office of Statistics (1996) *Annual Abstract of Statistics*, (Lagos: FOS).
Flight International (1960) 'Ghana's status symbol,' January, 125.
Flight International (1961) 'Ghana's status symbol,' January, 65.
Flight International (1962) 'Pruning in Ghana,' June, 926.
Flight International (1969a) 'Nigeria Airways,' April, 584.
Flight International (1969b) 'Tribulations of Nigeria Airways,' February, 198.
Flight International (1987) 'No more Airbuses for Nigeria,' November, 11.
Flight International (1988) 'Nigeria Airways restructures,' July, 8.
Hedberg, B., Nystrom, P. and Starbuck, W. (1976) 'Camping on Seesaws: Prescriptions for a self-designing organization'. *Administrative Science Quarterly*, 21(1), 41–65.
Hymer, S.H. (1976) *The international operations of national firms: A study of direct foreign investment*. Cambridge, MA: The MIT Press.
Jones, G. and Khanna, T. (2006) 'Bringing history (back) into international business'. *Journal of International Business Studies*, 37(4), 453–468.

Klein, J.G. (2002) 'Us versus them, or us versus everyone? Delineating consumer aversion to foreign goods'. *Journal of International Business Studies*, 33(2), 345–363.

Knibb, D. (2007) 'Foreign rights'. *Airline Business*, 23(3), 28--29.

Knott, A.M. and Posen, H.E. (2005) 'Is failure good?'. *Strategic Management Journal*, 26(7), 617–641.

Miller, D. (1990) *The Icarus paradox: How exceptional companies bring about their own downfall*. New York: Harper Business.

Miller, S.R. and Parkhe, A. (2002) 'Is there a liability of foreignness in global banking? An empirical test of bank's x-efficiency'. *Strategic Management Journal*, 23(1), 55–76.

Miller, S.R. and Richards, M. (2002) 'Liability of foreignness and membership in a regional economic group: Analysis of the European Union'. *Journal of International Management*, 8(3), 323–337.

Moulton, W., Thomas, H. and Pruett, M. (1996) 'Business decline pathways: Environmental stress and organizational response'. *Journal of Management*, 22(4), 571–595.

Nachum, L. (2003) 'Liability of foreignness in global competition? Financial service affiliates in the City of London'. *Strategic Management Journal*, 24(12), 1187–1208.

Petersen, B. and Pedersen, T. (2002) 'Coping with liability of foreignness: Different learning engagements of entrant firms'. *Journal of International Management*, 8(3), 339–350.

Shimp, T. and Sharma, S. (1987) 'Consumer ethnocentrism: Construction and validation of the CETSCALE'. *Journal of Marketing Research*, 24(3), 280–289.

Sutton, R.I. (1987) 'The process of organizational death: Disbanding and reconnecting'. *Administrative Science Quarterly*, 32(4), 542–569.

Tsamenyi, T., Onumah, J.M. and Sa'id, H. (2011) 'Neopatrimonialism and the failure of control & accountability systems in state institutions in less developed countries: The case of Ghana and Nigerian Airlines'. *AOS Fraud conference*, London.

UNECA (1999) 'Decision relating to the implementation of the Yamoussoukro Declaration concerning the liberalization of access to air transport markets in Africa', available at http://www.uneca.org/itca/yamoussoukro (Accessed 19 June 2007).

Wernerfelt, B. (1984) 'A resource-based view of the firm'. *Strategic Management Journal*, 5, 171–180.

World Bank (1998) *Air Transport Trends and Economics in Western and Central Africa*. (Washington, D.C.: World Bank).

World Bank (2003) *Air Transport in Western and Central Africa: facts and Issues* (Washington, DC.: World Bank).

Zaheer, S. (1995) 'Overcoming the liability of foreignness'. *Academy of Management Journal*, 38(2), 341–363.

Part III
Performance/Survival in DMNEs in Emerging Economies

Part III

7
Subsidiary Survival of Multinational Enterprises in China: An Analysis of Nordic Firms

Yi Wang and Jorma Larimo

Introduction

Internationalisation of multinational enterprises (MNEs) has received considerable attention in the international business (IB) literature in the past decades. Survival of MNEs' subsidiaries is of great interest to both academicians and practitioners. Although there has been discussion whether foreign direct investments (FDIs) or subsidiary performance is positively correlated with subsidiary survival, several studies have found that subsidiary survival positively correlates with financial performance and investors' satisfaction (Geringer and Hebert, 1991; Vermeulen and Barkema, 2001). Further on, subsidiary survival provides good information related to dynamics of foreign subsidiaries, which is useful to policymakers in the host country (Dhanaraj and Beamish, 2009). In this study, the goal is to analyse firm-, industry- and institution-specific determinants of subsidiary survival of Nordic MNEs in China from 1982 to 2012.

China opened its door to foreign investments in late 1978. There has been a rapid growing on global FDI inflows into China in the past three decades (see figure 7.1). Although China has been an important FDI recipient in the world, several studies have reported relatively high divestment/exit rate for foreign subsidiaries in China (Papyrina, 2007; Kim, Delios and Xu, 2010). These studies focused their analysis on the influence that timing of entry, ownership structure and industry-specific experience have on subsidiary survival in China. While considerable China-based studies found that R&D intensity, international experience, host-country experience, degree of product diversification, firm size, government policies and investments locations are important determinants of foreign entry-mode strategy (Luo, 2001; Shi, Ho and Siu, 2001; Chen and Hu, 2002; Chiao, Lo and Yu, 2010), limited studies have linked these factors with subsidiary survival in China. We argue that by including above mentioned variables in the subsidiary survival analysis will enhance our

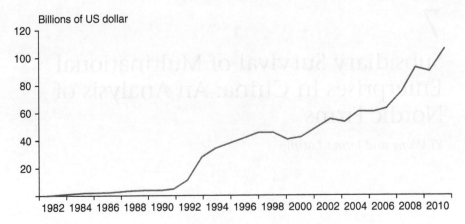

Figure 7.1   Growth in global FDIs in China from 1982 to 2010 (billions of US dollars)
Source: China Statistical Yearbook (1983–2011).

understanding of the determinants of both market entry mode strategy and post-entry survival/performance of subsidiaries in China.

In analysing firm-, industry- and institution-specific determinants of subsidiary survival in China, we combine arguments from three theories: transaction cost economics (TCE) (Williamson, 1975; 1985; Anderson and Gatignon, 1986), resource-based view (RBV) (Barney, 1991) and institution-based view (IBV) (Peng, 2002). TCE, RBV and IBV have been identified as the leading theoretical foundations underpinning research in IB strategy in emerging markets such as China and Central Eastern Europe (CEE) (Hoskisson, Eden, Lau and Wright, 2000; Meyer and Peng, 2005; Wright, Filatotchev, Hoskisson and Peng, 2005). The choice of the three theories is further justified that the core constructs of TCE, RBV and IBV have been operationalised with a similar range of variables (Claver and Quer, 2005; Dikova and Witteloostuijn, 2007; Dikova, Rao and Witteloostuijn, 2010; Demirbag, Apaydin and Tatoglu, 2011; Dikova, 2012). For example, asset specificity has been proxied by R&D intensity either at or industry level (Hennart, 1991; Larimo, 2003; Chiao et al., 2010), the same construct has also been used in RBV studies to proxy important intangible firm-specific resources (Erramilli, 1991; Park, Lee and Hong, 2011). Since the present study combines arguments from more than one of the three above mentioned theories, we argue that our study contributes to China-based FDI literature by analysing the factors influencing subsidiary survival in a more comprehensive way.

Earlier subsidiary survival research has for a great part based its analysis on FDIs made by Japanese MNEs around the globe (Delios and Beamish, 2001; Delios and Makino, 2003; Gaur and Lu, 2007; Danaraj and Beamish, 2009; Demirbag et al., 2011). Subsidiary survival studies on small and open

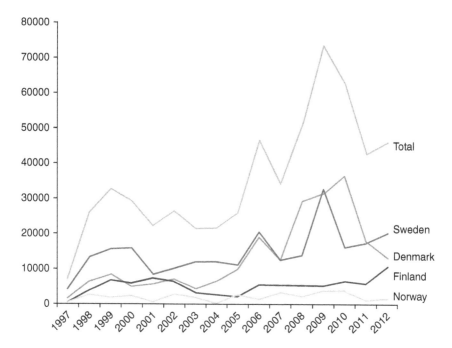

Figure 7.2   Nordic FDIs in China from 1997 to 2012 (10,000 US dollars)
Source: National Bureau of Statistics of China (www-site: data.stats.gov.cn).

economies (SMOPECs) are relatively limited (Vermeulen and Barkema, 2001), and research in Nordic economies (Denmark, Finland, Norway and Sweden) is especially scant. Nordic FDIs show a similar increasing trend compared to that of global FDIs. FDI stock by Nordic MNEs at the globe level increased from US$80.17 million in 1990 to US$994.72 million in 2012 (UNCTAD, 2013). China has been an important host country for Nordic MNEs. FDIs by Nordic firms in China increased from US$71.06 million in 1997 to US$735.46 million in 2009. Although the total number of FDIs dropped to 437.62 million in 2011, FDIs by Nordic firms in China started to grow again in 2012 (figure 7.2). Given the increasing trend of Nordic FDIs around the globe, it is of great importance to analyse the survival/performance of Nordic firms. It is therefore expected that this study will provide interesting findings as well as managerial implications to Nordic MNEs aspiring to enter the Chinese market.

Our paper starts with a brief theoretical discussion leading to the development of the study's hypotheses. The next section addresses methodology and data collection followed by discussion of study findings. The paper concludes with discussion concerning the study's limitations as well as managerial guidelines.

Theoretical background and the study's hypotheses

Subsidiary survival literature

Subsidiary survival has received increasing interest in the IB field. The conceptualisation of subsidiary survival has been inconsistent. This is particularly true for research on instability and/or survival of joint ventures (JVs) (Blodgett, 1992; Yan, 1998; Steensma and Lyles, 2000; Dhanaraj and Beamish, 2004; Gaur and Lu, 2007; Meschi and Riccio, 2008; Belderbos and Zou, 2009; Fang and Zhou, 2010). Existing studies have conceptualised and operationalised JVs instability in two ways: outcome-oriented approach and process-oriented approach. Yan and Zeng (1999) defined outcome-oriented instability as outright sales or liquidation and changes in ownership structure. This approach was adopted in several studies, such as Mata and Portugal (2000), Steensma and Lyles (2000), Dhanaraj and Beamish (2004), Meschi and Riccio (2008), Gaur and Lu (2007) and Belderbos and Zou (2009). On the other hand, a process-oriented approach conceptualises instability as reorganisation and contractual renegotiation (Yan and Zeng, 1999). A process-oriented approach to JV instability was adopted by Blodgett (1992) and Fang and Zou (2010). In this study both WOS and JVs are included in analysis, and thus, we follow an outcome-oriented approach and consider *sales or liquidation of JVs and WOS* as non-surviving subsidiaries. The rest of the subsidiaries are treated as surviving FDIs.

TCE, RBV and IBV have been the leading theoretical foundations to address various issues of MNEs in emerging markets (Hoskisson et al., 2000; Meyer and Peng, 2005; Wright et al., 2005). TCE argues that firms opt for a particular governance structure which would minimise the total transaction and production costs (Williamson, 1975; 1985). Since TCE has been frequently used to address market-entry strategy, TCE-based IB studies have linked various forms of market-entry modes with subsidiary survival (Pan and Chi, 1999; Mata and Portugal, 2000; Dhanaraj and Beamish, 2004). RBV argues that the performance of an MNE's subsidiary is attributable to firm-specific resources and capabilities. Valuable, rare, imperfectly inimitable and non-substitutable resources (VRIN framework) would provide a firm some types of sustainable competitive advantage, which in turn, would influence performance of an MNEs' subsidiary (Barney, 1991). In recent years, drawing on both economic (North, 1990; Williamson, 2000) and sociological versions of institutions (DiMaggio and Powell, 1983; Scott, 1995), IB scholars have started to apply IBV (Peng, 2002) to investigate the effects of institutional variables on the survival of MNEs' subsidiaries (Dhanaraj and Beamish, 2009; Demirbag et al., 2011). IBV tends to argue that a firm's strategy and performance are not only driven by a firm's resources, capabilities (Barney, 1991) and industry conditions (Porter, 1980); they are also shaped by the institutional environment of the host country (Peng, 2003; 2009).

Table 7.1 summarises the characteristics of early research on subsidiary survival. The percentage of survived subsidiaries included in reviewed studies has varied between 49 per cent to over 85 per cent. In two China-based studies (Papyrina, 2007; Kim et al., 2010), the percentage of subsidiary survival is 71.5 per cent and 76.7 per cent, respectively. Existing studies have analysed various determinants of subsidiary survival, and the results have been mixed. *One line of research* has linked various entry-mode strategies with subsidiary survival (Mata and Portugal, 2000; Vermeulen and Barkema, 2001; Dhanaraj and Beamish, 2004; Papyrina, 2007; Gaur and Lu, 2007). This line of research has provided mixed results regarding the relationships of various entry-mode strategy and subsidiary survival. *A second line of studies* has investigated the impacts of firm-specific determinants such as R&D/advertising intensity (Delios and Makino, 2003), firm experience (Delios and Beamish, 2001; Vermeulen and Barkema, 2001; Gaur and Lu, 2007) and timing of entry (Pan and Chi, 1999; Delios and Makino, 2003; Papyrina, 2007). *A third group of studies* has analysed institutional factors such as subsidiary density (Silverman, Nickerson and Freeman, 1997; Demirbag et al. 2011), regulative and normative institutional distance (Gaur and Lu, 2007), political and social openness (Dhanaraj and Beamish, 2009), economic distance, economic freedom distance and cultural clusters (Demirbag et al., 2011) on subsidiary survival. A limited number of studies have also analysed interaction effects. For example, Dhanaraj and Beamish (2009) found that political and social openness in the host country interacted with JV-ownership strategy to increase the mortality of Japanese subsidiaries.

The study's hypotheses

In this section, we discuss how firm-, industry- and institution-specific variables are expected to influence survival of Nordic MNEs in China.

International Experience: Both TCE and RBV theorists consider international experience to be an important determinant of firm strategy (Anderson and Gatignon, 1986; Erramilli, 1991; Hennart, 1991; Clark, Tamaschke and Liesch, 2013). International experience is one of the core constructs of the famous Uppsala Model (Johanson and Vahlne, 1977). It has been argued that MNEs with no or limited international experience usually lack the general skills and knowledge of setting up and managing subsidiaries in a foreign market (Dow and Larimo, 2009; Li and Meyer, 2009). This knowledge is primarily developed through foreign presence and therefore is tacit in nature (Johanson and Vahlne, 1977; Slangen and Hennart, 2007). TCE-based studies have emphasised the important role of international experience in lowering internal uncertainty (Anderson and Gatignon, 1986; Zhao, Luo and Suh, 2004). Early empirical studies have found that international experience is positively associated with subsidiary survival (Delios and Makino, 2003; Tsang and Yip, 2007). While Papyrina (2007) found that the international experience of MNEs increased the

Table 7.1 Characteristics of the studies reviewed

Study	Home country	Host country	Explanatory variables	MNE type	Time period	No. of investments	Divestments rate	Method of analysis
Silverman et al. (1997)	Multiple countries	U.S.	Subsidiary density, liability of newness, profitability	Manufacturing (motor carrier)	1977–1989	2669	42%	Event history analysis
Mata and Portugal (2000)	Multiple countries	Portugal	Establishment mode, ownership structure, ownership advantage	Manufacturing	1983–1989	1033	Divestiture (5.7%/year), disclosure (5.9%/year)	Cox regression analysis
Delios and Beamish (2001)	Japan	Asia, North America and Europe	Intangible asset, host-country experience, IJV experience	Manufacturing	1986–1996	3080	21.1%	Event history analysis
Vermeulen and Barkema (2001)	Netherlands	Multiple countries	Number of preceding greenfields or acquisitions, preceding greenfields in familiar/ unfamiliar markets, preceding acquisitions in related/unrelated domain	Manufacturing	1966–1994	1349	51%	Cox regression analysis
Delios and Makino (2003)	Japan	Asia, North America and Europe	Timing of entry, R&D/ advertising intensity expenditures to its sales	Manufacturing	1986–1999	6955	n.a.*	Event history model
Chuang and Beamish (2005)	Japan	Indonesia, Thailand, Korea, Malaysia and Philippines	Pre- and post-crisis institutional differences; ownership mode choice; level of equity, trading vs. manufacturing operations	Trading vs. Manufacturing operations	1986–2001	3515	22.8%	Cox regression analysis
Papyrina (2007)	Japan	China	Timing of entry, ownership structure	Manufacturing, whole sale and retail, finance, etc.	Pre- 2001	1733	28.5%	Cox regression analysis

Study	Home country	Host countries	Independent variables	Industry	Period	Sample size	Survival	Method
Delios et al. (2008)	Japan	120 countries in the globe	Host institutional environment, within country product diversification, corporate-level product diversification and corporate-level geographic diversification	Manufacturing	1988–2001	29,279	36%	Event history analysis
Gaur and Lu (2008)	Japan	52 countries	Ownership structure, regulative and normative institutional distance	Manufacturing, whole sale, retailing	Pre-2001	20,177	41%	Cox regression analysis
Dhanaraj and Beamish (2009)	Japan	25 countries	Political openness, social openness	Manufacturing	1986–1997	12,000	n.a.	Cox regression analysis
Kim et al. (2010)	Japan	China	A subsidiary's relative proximity to other Japanese subsidiaries, industry-specific experience	Manufacturing	1979–2001	3416	24.3%	Exponential transition rate analysis
Demirbag et al. (2011)	Japan	Middle east and North Africa	Economic distance, economic freedom distance, subsidiary density	Manufacturing	1956–2003	265	49%	Cox regression analysis
Park et al. (2011)	Korea (Chaebol)	51 countries in the globe	Order of entry (pioneers and latecomers)	Manufacturing	1999–2004	500	n.a.	Cox regression analysis

probability of foreign subsidiaries to survive in China, a non-significant relationship was found in the study by Kim et al. (2010). Therefore, we propose:

Hypothesis 1: International experience is positively associated with the probability of foreign subsidiaries to survive in China.

Host-Country Experience: In RBV-based studies, host country experience has been referred to as an important firm-specific resource for the success of foreign subsidiaries (Kim et al., 2010). Firms with no or only limited experience of operation in a particular host market usually lack the knowledge of local business and management practices (Hennart, 1991). Experiential knowledge about a particular country is more important for MNEs entering into emerging markets (Li and Meyer, 2009). MNEs need to develop new resources and capabilities in order to cope with the difficulties of doing business in a new environment. MNEs with more host-country experience obtained local knowledge – that is, how to deal with local governments (Li and Meyer, 2009; Kim et al., 2010). Early studies have provided mixed results. Delios and Beamish (2001) and Park et al. (2011) indicated that host-country experience was not a significant determinant of subsidiary survival. Delios and Makino (2003) found that host-country experience increased the likelihood of survival of Japanese subsidiaries. The positive impact of host-country experience on subsidiary survival was also found in the study by Papyrina (2007) and Kim et al. (2010), focusing on subsidiary survival in China. Based on theoretical argumentation and China-based empirical studies, we expect:

Hypothesis 2: Host country experience is positively associated with the probability of foreign subsidiaries to survive in China.

Degree of Product Diversification: While some firms concentrate on a single business or one main product line, diversified firms operate in multiple products markets. The degree of product diversification has been frequently proxied using three- or four-digit Standard Industrial Classification (SIC) codes (Mudambi and Mudambi, 2002; Larimo, 2003). Based on TCE, when the degree of product diversification of the MNEs increases, the lack of product-specific knowledge in all fields of industries becomes evident, which increases the failure rate of foreign subsidiaries. Early findings on the relationship of degree of product diversification and subsidiary survival have been mixed. While Delios, Xu and Beamish (2008) found that the degree of product diversification was positively associated with subsidiary survival, Vermeulen and Barkema (2001) and Tsang and Yip (2007) found the opposite relationship, and Delios and Makino (2003) found that the relationship of the degree of product diversification and subsidiary survival was not significant. The impact of the degree of product diversification has not been specifically analysed in China-based studies. Based on the theoretical arguments and non-China-based studies, we expect:

Hypothesis 3: Degree of product diversification is negatively associated with the probability of foreign subsidiaries to survive in China.

Parent Firm Size: Both TCE- and RBV-based studies consider parent firm size as an important determinant of MNEs' strategies (Larimo, 2003; Claver and Quer, 2005). Large MNEs are able to provide adequate resources (Padmanabhan and Cho, 1996; Dhanaraj and Beamish, 2009) and to absorb risk (Taylor, Zou and Osland, 1998); thus, a positive relationship between parent firm size and subsidiary survival could be expected. Interestingly, Vermeulen and Barkema (2001) and Demirbag et al. (2011) found that parent firm size decreased subsidiary survival of MNEs. However, Dhanaraj and Beamish (2009) and Park et al. (2011) found that firm size was positively related with subsidiary survival. Tsang and Yip (2007) found that the impact of firm size was not a significant determinant of subsidiary survival. In China-based studies, the findings have also been mixed. Firm size was found to increase the subsidiary survival of MNEs (Papyrina, 2007); however, Kim et al. (2010) found an insignificant relationship. Although the findings for both China-based and non-China-based studies have been somewhat mixed, we expect that subsidiaries located in China need adequate resources to absorb risks. Therefore, we expect:

Hypothesis 4: Parent firm size is positively associated with the probability of foreign subsidiaries to survive in China.

Industry Research and Development Intensity: R&D intensity is a frequently used proxy for asset specificity in TCE-based studies (see review studies by Zhao et al., 2004; Meyer and Wang, 2014 forthcoming). It has been argued that firms with a high level of R&D intensity are likely to exploit significant amount of technological knowledge in international markets (Slangen and Hennart, 2007). The possession of technological knowledge helps parent MNEs to develop competitive advantages in a host country (Delios and Makino, 2003). According to TCE, intangible assets possessed by MNEs can be an effective barrier against failure in the host country (Delios and Beamish, 1999; Delios and Henisz, 2000; Lu and Hebert, 2005). In the study by Papyrina (2007), R&D intensity was found to be non-significantly associated with subsidiary survival in China. However, Demirbag et al. (2011) found that R&D intensity increased the probability of Japanese parent MNEs to survive in the Middle East and North Africa. Therefore, we propose:

Hypothesis 5: Research and development intensity is positively associated with the probability of foreign subsidiaries to survive in China.

Industry Sales Growth: Industry sales growth has been used to proxy external uncertainty in TCE-based studies (Cui and Jiang, 2009). It has been argued that the high growth rate in a particular industry makes FDIs even more attractive, and hence, the probability to survive in a high-growth industry is likely to be high (Hollonsen, 2014: 411). However, firms in a high-growth industry are also likely to be the target firms in acquisitions. Hence, TCE arguments on the impacts of industry sales growth seem to be ambiguous. Li (1995) find that industry sales growth is positively associated with subsidiary survival. In accordance with both theoretical argument and empirical findings, we propose:

> *Hypothesis 6*: Industry sales growth is positively associated with the probability of foreign subsidiaries to survive in China.

Industry Growth in a Number of Firms: A typical TCE argument is that MNEs are less profitable when entering into highly competitive industries. As China started its economic and political reforms, such as decentralisation and privatisation, the number of firms actually increased to meet the huge market demand. It has been argued that the growth in the number of firms is a good proxy to the degree of competition in transition economies (Luo, 2001). It has also been argued that the growth in the number of firms in an industry is associated with greater business potential and market opportunities. Li (1995) used industry concentration ratio as a proxy to industry competition and found that it was not related with subsidiary survival. Since there are no studies that have specifically linked industry growth in the number of firms with subsidiary survival in China, we developed a hypothesis based on theoretical arguments and non-China-based studies. Thus, we expect:

> *Hypothesis 7*: Industry growth in number of firms is positively associated with the probability of foreign subsidiaries to survive in China.

Stages of Institutional Transitions: IBV-based studies claim that firm strategy is considerably influenced by the development and effectiveness of market economy institutions of their host countries (Peng, 2003; Child and Tsai, 2005; Meyer and Peng, 2005). An important issue to note while analysing various FDI issues in emerging economies like China is related to timing as a proxy to the levels of market economy institutional development (Peng, 2003, 2009). During the early stage of institutional transitions and development of market economy, China was characterised by government intervention for business operations, lack of reliable business information and weak intellectual property protection (Luo, 2001; Wei et al., 2005; Chung and Beamish, 2005). On the other hand, in later stages of institutional reforms, the market economy institutions were strengthened, and volatility in the institutional environment gradually started to decrease (Norton and Chao, 2001; Papyrina, 2007). The empirical results by

Papyrina (2007) indicated that foreign subsidiaries formed in the early stage of institutional reforms are less likely to survive in China. For non-China-based studies, Dhanaraj and Beamish (2009) found that transition periods were not significantly associated with subsidiary survival. Therefore, we expect:

Hypothesis 8: Later stages of institutional transitions are positively associated with the probability of foreign subsidiaries to survive in China.

Regional Institutional Differences: A key feature of institutional reforms and the development of a market economy in China has been the development of special economic zones (SEZs) and open coastal cities (OCCs), where the government restriction of foreign MNEs tended to be far lower than the interior part of China (Luo, 2000; He, Wei and Xie, 2008; Chan, Makino and Isobe, 2010). A World Bank survey of 120 Chinese cities (2006) has shown that both the overall investment climate and local government effectiveness and efficiency in SEZs and OCCs were ranked in the top quintile of all surveyed cities. On the other hand, the cities in the lowest-ranked quintile were all located within inland of China. In addition, parent MNEs operating in SEZs and open coastal cities received a preferential corporate tax rate, which was generally lower than tax rates were for other enterprises. Moreover, although laws and regulations were consistent at the nation level, the time spent on interactions with the Chinese local government differed across regions. MNEs conducting business in SEZs and OCCs generally spent less time with local government. In a China-based study, Kim et al. (2010) found non-significant relationship between SEZs and subsidiary survival. We followed the discussions presented above and expect:

Hypothesis 9: Regional institutional differences (SEZs and/or OCCs) are positively associated with the probability of foreign subsidiaries to survive in China.

Interaction Effect: The past IB and FDI studies have largely ignored potential interaction effects (Zhao et al. 2004; Slangen and Hennart 2007). We therefore propose to include some interaction terms in our analysis. The objective of including an interaction term is to detect joint effects of two variables pulling in opposite directions. The interaction term included in this study is R&D intensity and degree of product diversification. It has been hypothesised that R&D intensity is positively associated with subsidiary survival (H5), whereas the degree of product diversification would decrease the probability of subsidiary survival in China (H3). Certain industries (mostly technological and research intensive) have long been labelled as strategic industries where Chinese government wanted to develop local competencies via knowledge and technology transfer (He et al., 2008; Huang, 2008). MNEs transferring advanced technology receive financial incentives, such as tax exemptions or reductions (Huang, 2008). Hence, we would argue that the survival probability

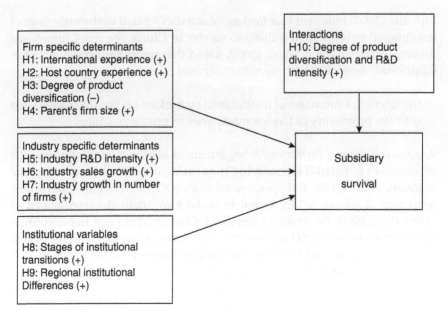

Firm specific determinants
H1: International experience (+)
H2: Host country experience (+)
H3: Degree of product
diversification (−)
H4: Parent's firm size (+)

Industry specific determinants
H5: Industry R&D intensity (+)
H6: Industry sales growth (+)
H7: Industry growth in number
of firms (+)

Institutional variables
H8: Stages of institutional
transitions (+)
H9: Regional institutional
Differences (+)

Interactions
H10: Degree of product
diversification and R&D
intensity (+)

Subsidiary
survival

Figure 7.3   Research model of FDI subsidiary survival in China

for firms operating in multiple product markets would increase when they transfer advanced technology in China.

> *Hypothesis 10:* Degree of product diversification positively interacts with R&D intensity to influence on the probability of foreign subsidiaries to survive in China.

The research model is shown in Figure 7.3. The model depicts the impacts of firm-, industry- and institution-specific variables on subsidiary survival. In line with the theoretical arguments and early empirical studies, we expect that while international experience, host country experience, firm size, R&D intensity, industry sales growth, industry growth in number of firms, later stages of institutional transitions and regional institutional differences (SEZs and/or OCCs) are positively associated with subsidiary survival, the degree of product diversification leads to divestments of foreign subsidiaries. Moreover, we hypothesise that the interaction between R&D intensity and degree of product diversification is positive.

Methodology, sample and operationalisation of variables

Statistical method

This study applies binary logistic regression to examine the impacts of explanatory variables on subsidiary survival. The regression coefficients estimate the impact of independent variables on the probability that the investment will be a survived subsidiary, with a positive coefficient indicating that an independent variable increases the probability of subsidiary survival. In general, the terms of the model can be expressed as

$$P(yi = 1) = 1/(1 + \exp(-a - XiB),$$

where yi is the dependent variable, Xi is the vector of the independent variables for the ith observation, a is the intercept parameter and B is the vector of regression coefficients (Amemiya, 1981). The recent version of PASW 21.0 is used to run binary logistic regression in this study.

Description of sample

In the empirical part of this paper, the developed hypotheses will be tested on a sample of FDIs made by Nordic parent MNEs in China from 1982 to 2012. The company information is obtained from a large internal data bank focusing on FDIs made by Nordic firms in the world collected during several years and based mainly from the annual reports and press releases of the investing firms, but the information is also supplemented with the data gathered from Thomson one databank, articles in leading local business magazines and direct contact with several of the investing companies. We identified 405 investments made by Nordic MNEs in China during the observed period (1982–2012). The target population includes manufacturing investments made in all two-digit manufacturing sectors (SIC 20–39), but almost half of the sample comprised investments made in SIC 26 (paper and allied products), SIC 28 (chemicals and allied products), SIC 35 (machinery) and SIC 36 (electronics).

Of the 405 FDIs, 97 (24.0 per cent) were divested in or prior to 2012. This rate is similar to the two China-based studies by Papyrina (2007) and Kim et al. (2010) – 28.5 per cent and 24.3 per cent, respectively. While 293 FDIs were established through greenfield investments, 112 investments were acquisition entries. In terms of ownership-mode choice, 210 investments were JVs, whereas 195 FDIs were WOS. For the country of origin, 277 investments were made by Finnish and Swedish firms, representing 68.4 per cent of all observations. The average number of investments by a single company in the sample was around two. High-tech and medium high-tech branches accounted for more than 70 per cent of all investments. Compared to other Nordic firms, Swedish firms on average were larger and had more international experience. Danish investors had greatest target country experience. More than half of the investments were made between 1982 and 2001. A larger proportion of the investments were located in the SEZs and OCCs.

Operationalisation of variables

The dependent variable is subsidiary survival, where survived subsidiaries are coded as 1 and divested subsidiaries are coded as 0. International experience was measured by the number of foreign manufacturing investments preceding a subsidiary's establishment. Host country experience was measured by the number of years since the first manufacturing investment of the parent firm in China. Degree of product diversification of was proxied by the number of four-digit SIC codes in which the company was operating. R&D intensity is a categorical variable, where 1 stands for low-tech branch, 2 for medium-tech branch and 3 for high-tech branch. Industry sales growth and growth in number of firms were calculated using the compound growth rate over three consecutive years prior to the divestment year or 2012. A categorical variable was created to proxy stages of institutional differences, where 1 stands for investments made in the period of 1982–1995, 2 for investments made in 1996–2001 and 3 for the period of 2002–2012. Regional institutional differences were operationalised by a dummy variable, where subsidiaries established in SEZs and/or OCCs were coded as 1, and investments made in other parts of China were coded as 0. The operationalisation of the independent variables, data sources and examples of earlier studies where similar operationalisation has been used are presented in table 7.2 in the below.

In addition to independent variables, we added several control variables that are also likely to influence subsidiary survival. First, we controlled for both FDI ownership-mode and establishment-mode strategy (Papyrina, 2007; Tsang and Yip, 2007; Kim et al., 2010). Second, we created a dummy variable which equals one if the subsidiary's main products are in a resource-intensity industry such as SIC 20 (food and beverage), 22 (textile), 24 (wood except furniture), 26 (paper and paper related products), 29 (petroleum), 30 (rubber), 32 (stone and glass) and 33 (primary metals) (Hennart, 1991). Third, we controlled for industry restrictions, a dummy variable where 1 stands for investments made in restricted and 0 for encouraged manufacturing industries. Fourth, we included subsidiary age to control for liability of foreignness and length of operations (Delios et al., 2008; Demirbag et al., 2011). Lastly, we controlled for cultural distance (Kogut and Singh, 1988) between Nordic countries and China (Delios et al., 2008; Demirbag et al., 2011).

Results

Before running logistic regression, a correlation analysis (see Table 7.3) was conducted to detect any multicollinearity between various variables. The bivariate correlation between international experience and degree of product diversification is above the cut-off point of 0.70, indicating a potential for multicollinearity. Following Pallant (2007), an additional multicollinearity diagnostic (variance inflation factor (VIF)) was also conducted. According to Wetherill (1986) and Allison (1999), the VIF values for independent and control variables used in regression analysis should not exceed 2.50. In our study, the VIF value for international experience is above the cut-off point; thus, the potential multicollinearity between international experience and

Table 7.2 Operationalisation of independent variables

Variables	Operationalisation
Firm specific determinants	
International experience	The number of foreign manufacturing investments made by the company before the reviewed investment (e.g. Padmanabhan and Cho 1999; Larimo 2003; Arslan and Larimo 2011, 2012) (Source: internal database).
Host country experience	The experience in years from the first manufacturing investment of the firm in the target country (e.g. Hennart and Park 1993; Padmanabhan and Cho 1999; Larimo 2003; Arslan and Larimo 2011, 2012) (Source: internal database).
Degree of product diversification	The number of 4-digit SIC codes in which the company was operating based on the annual reports and websites of the firms (e.g. Hennart and Larimo 1998; Vermeulen and Barkema 2001; Mudambi and Mudambi 2002) (Source: internal database).
Firm size	Worldwide annual sales of the company (in million euros) in the year preceding the investment (e.g. Hennart and Larimo 1998; Vermeulen and Barkema 2001; Larimo 2003) (Source: internal database).
Industry-specific determinants	
Industry R&D intensity	A classification of various 4-digit SIC industries into three categories based on their value added figures (e.g. Hennart and Park 1993; Larimo 2003; Dikova and Witteloostuijn 2007) (Source: internal database).
Industry sales growth	Compound sales growth rate over three consecutive years prior to the establishment year (e.g. Luo 2001) (Source: China statistical yearbook).
Industry growth in number of firms	Compound growth rate of number of firms over three consecutive years prior to the establishment year (e.g. Luo 2001) (Source: China statistical yearbook).
Institution-specific determinants	
Regional institutional differences	A dummy variable where 1 stands for subsidiaries located in SEZs and OCCs and 0 for otherwise (e.g. Pan and Tse 2000; Luo 2001) (Source: internal database, complemented with Thomson one databank and Orbis databank).
Stages of institutional transitions	A dummy variable where 1 stands for investments made from 1982 to 1995, 2 for investments made during 1996–2001 and 3 for investments after 2002 (e.g., Zhang, Zhang and Liu 2007) (Source: internal database).

degree of product diversification is expected to influence the results of binary logistic regression. Table 7.4 and 7.5 displays the results for subsidiary survival of Nordic MNEs in China. While model 1 and 2 presented in table 7.4 analysed the main effects of independent variables, interaction term was included in

Table 7.3 Correlation table

Variables	1	2	3	4	5	6	7	8	9	10	11	12	13	14
1. Ownership mode strategy	1.00													
2. Establishment mode strategy	−0.12*	1.00												
3. Resource intensive industry	−0.09	0.09	1.00											
4. Subsidiary age	−0.22**	−0.18**	−0.08	1.00										
5. Cultural distance	−0.03	−0.06	−0.06	−0.12*	1.00									
6. International experience	−0.20**	0.14**	0.04	−0.13*	−0.06	1.00								
7. Host country experience	0.01	0.27**	0.05	−0.32**	−0.11*	0.60**	1.00							
8. Degree of product diversification	−0.22**	0.09	0.12*	−0.03	−0.02	0.71**	0.28**	1.00						
9. Firm size	−0.08	−0.05	−0.06	−0.02	−0.13*	0.48**	0.29**	0.37**	1.00					
10. R&D intensity	−0.01	−0.08	−0.60**	0.05	−0.02	−0.04	0.05	−0.08	0.16**	1.00				
11. Industry sales growth	0.09	−0.06	−0.08	−0.09	−0.01	0.04	0.10*	−0.02	0.02	0.09	1.00			
12. Industry growth in number of firms	0.10*	0.02	−0.12*	−0.27**	0.03	0.06	0.28**	−0.06	0.05	0.11*	0.39**	1.00		
13. Stages of institutional transitions	0.27**	0.16**	0.09	−0.68**	0.11*	0.17**	0.43**	−0.06	0.06	−0.07	0.03	0.34**	1.00	
14. Regional institutional differences	0.18**	−0.26**	−0.12*	0.09	0.93	−0.28**	−0.22**	−0.21**	−0.15**	0.08	−0.08	−0.01	−0.12*	1.00

Table 7.4 Binary logistic regression analysis (main effects) (Subsidiary survival = 1)

Variables	Model 1 (with international experience)	Model 2 (without international experience)
Control variables		
WOS ownership mode strategy	1.51***	1.55***
Acquisitions establishment mode strategy	0.76	1.22**
Resource intensive industry	−0.70	−0.38
Industry restrictions	−0.78	−0.80
Subsidiary age	0.91***	0.86***
Cultural distance	0.38	0.01
Firm-specific factors		
International experience	0.01	
Host-country experience	0.28***	0.27***
Degree of product diversification	−0.09**	−0.06*
Parent firm size	0.01**	0.01**
Industry-specific factors		
Industry R&D intensity	−0.53	−0.52
Industry sales growth	0.56	0.32
Industry growth in number of firms	6.49**	6.34**
Institution-specific factors		
Stages of institutional transitions	3.77***	3.73***
Regional institutional differences	0.12	0.32
N = 405 (divested subsidiaries = 97)	405 (Divestments = 97)	405 (Divestments = 97)
Nagelkerke R^2	0.76***	0.73
Correctly classified (%)	92.6%	91.7%
Model Chi square (x^2)	257.779***	250.454***

Note: *** p≤0.01, ** p≤0.05, * p≤0.10.

model 3 and 7.4 in table 7.5. The explanatory power of all regression models is good, as the Chi square (x^2) value is good and highly significant.

The results of the study show that out of the *control* variables, three are significant. Both WOS ownership-mode and acquisitions establishment-mode strategy are positively and significantly associated with subsidiary survival (p≤0.01 and p≤0.05, respectively). The positive and significant relationship was found between subsidiary age and subsidiary survival (p≤0.01).

Five *independent* variables were found to directly influence subsidiary survival. The regression coefficient associated with international experience is not significant, suggesting that international experience provides no prediction to subsidiary survival in China. Hence, *hypothesis 1* is not supported. Our findings depict the host country experience increases the likelihood of subsidiary survival (p≤0.01), which is consistent with our expectation. *Hypothesis 2* is therefore supported. Further on, the impact of degree of product diversification is a significant (p≤0.05; p≤0.1) level, and the negative coefficient depicted that diversified Nordic MNEs are associated with subsidiary divestments. Thus, *hypothesis 3*

152 *Wang and Larimo*

Table 7.5 Binary logistic regression analysis (interaction effects) (Subsidiary survival = 1)

Variables	Model 3 (with international experience)	Model 4 (without international experience)
Control variables		
WOS ownership-mode strategy	1.59***	1.59***
Acquisitions establishment-mode strategy	0.85	1.27**
Resource intensive industry	−0.68	−0.33
Industry restrictions	−1.01	−1.06
Subsidiary age	0.92***	0.87***
Cultural distance	0.59	0.25
Firm-specific factors		
International experience	0.01	
Host–country experience	0.30***	0.29***
Degree of product diversification	−0.21**	−0.20***
Parent firm size	0.01**	0.01**
Industry-specific factors		
Industry R&D intensity	−1.10**	−1.17**
Industry sales growth	0.54	0.33
Industry growth in number of firms	6.91**	6.61**
Institution-specific factors		
Stages of institutional transitions	3.85***	3.80***
Regional institutional differences	0.23	0.44
Interaction term		
Industry R&D intensity and degree of product diversification	0.06*	
Industry R&D intensity and degree of product diversification		0.07**
N = 405 (divested subsidiaries = 97)	405 (Divestments = 97)	405 (Divestments = 97)
Nagelkerke R^2	0.76	0.74
Correctly classified (%)	92.9%	91.5%
Model Chi square (x^2)	260.69***	254.84***

Note: *** p≤0.01, ** p≤0.05, * p≤0.10.

is supported. The coefficient of firm size is significant at p≤0.05 level, and hence, larger Nordic MNEs are more likely to survive. Thus, *hypothesis 4* is supported. The regression coefficient of R&D intensity is not significant; thus, *hypothesis 5* is not supported. Industry sales growth is not significant, and hence, *hypothesis 6* is not supported. The impact of industry growth in the number of firms is positive and significant at p≤0.05 level. Thus, *hypothesis 7* is supported. Further on, later stages of institutional transitions is positively and highly significantly (p≤0.01) related with subsidiary survival. This result is consistent with our prediction, and thus, *hypothesis 8* is supported. Surprisingly, the coefficient associated with regional institutional differences is not significant, and thus, *hypothesis 9* is rejected.

Table 7.5 presents the results of interaction effects. The objective is to analyse the joint effects of two variables pulled in opposite directions. The interaction term

Table 7.6 Comparison of the findings of this study with Papyrina (2007) and Kim et al. (2010)

	This study	Papyrina (2007)	Kim et al. (2010)
Research design	Nordic firms in China 1982–2012	Japanese firms in China established before 2001	Japanese firms in China 1979–2001
International experience	Not significant	Positive	Not significant
Host-country experience	Positive	Positive	Positive
Degree of product diversification	Negative		
Parent firm size	Positive	Positive	Not significant
Industry R&D intensity	Not significant	Not significant	
Industry sales growth	Not significant		
Industry growth in number of firms	Positive		
Later stages of institutional transitions	Positive	Positive	
Regional institutional differences (SEZs and/or OCCs)	Not significant		Not significant

included in analysis is between R&D intensity and the degree of product diversification. We aim to answer the question, 'will R&D intensity increase the probability of subsidiary survival (H5), even when Nordic MNEs operate in multiple product markets (H3)?' As depicted in models 3 and 4 in Table 7.5, the regression coefficient of the interaction term is positive and significant at level $p \leq 0.1$ and $p \leq 0.05$, respectively. This result points out that although diversified Nordic firms are negatively associated with subsidiary survival, they are more likely to survive when they operate in an R&D intensive industry. Thus, *hypothesis 10* receives support.

Summary and conclusions

Our study analysed the determinants of the survival of Nordic subsidiaries operating in China from 1982 to 2012. Drawing on transaction cost economics, resource-based and institution-based view, ten hypotheses were developed. Our study contributes to China-based FDI literature in several ways. First, our study theoretically analysed the determinants of subsidiary survival by combining arguments from the three theories: TCE, RBV and IBV. Second, this study addresses potential interaction effect of variables when pulled in opposite directions. Third, in the empirical study we used a unique sample of Nordic investments, which received relatively limited attention in previous literature.

Several hypotheses were supported in our analysis. The positive relationship of host-country experience and subsidiary survival was confirmed by our study. Moreover, our results indicated that the degree of product diversification indeed decreased the probability of subsidiary survival in China. The logistic regression showed that larger Nordic MNEs are more likely to survive in China. Consistent with our expectation, later stages of institutional transitions were found to be positively and significantly associated with subsidiary survival. The joint effect of R&D intensity and the degree of product diversification on subsidiary survival is positive and highly significant.

There are several surprising results. Our study indicates that international experience was not significantly associated with subsidiary survival. It has been argued that transition economies differ widely from developed economies, and thus, Western MNEs may not be able to directly exploit their managerial and organizational capabilities in transition economies (Meyer and Peng, 2005; Li and Meyer, 2009). Surprisingly, our findings indicated that industry R&D intensity was not a significant determinant of subsidiary survival. This may be explained by the idea that technological knowledge developed in MNEs' home countries cannot be easily exploited in subsidiaries established in transition economies where the business environments are widely different from Western economies. The impact of industry sales growth was not significant. Luo (2001) argued that MNEs may benefit from industry sales growth at the expense of stability. Although the regression coefficient of regional institutional differences is positive, it is not a significant determinant of subsidiary survival.

It is interesting to compare these findings with two China-based studies by Papyrina (2007) and Kim et al. (2010), focusing on subsidiary survival of Japanese firms. Papyrina (2007) found that international experience is positively associated with subsidiary survival, whereas both Kim et al. (2010) and the present study found a non-significant relationship. All three studies empirically found that host-country experience is positively associated with subsidiary survival. Moreover, both Papyrina (2007) and the present study found a positive relationship between parent firm size and subsidiary survival, whereas Kim et al. (2010) found a non-significant relationship. Similar to the present study, Papyrina (2007) found that R&D intensity is not a significant determinant of subsidiary survival. Moreover, early stages of institutional transitions in China positively increase the probability of subsidiary survival. Thus, there are both similarities and differences in the determinants for Japanese and Nordic firms.

Since our study analysed determinants of subsidiary survival at multiple levels, it is expected that Nordic MNEs' managers are able to better evaluate the conditions under which their subsidiaries are more likely to survive in China. Our study has several limitations. First, subsidiary divestments mode has not been analysed. In our study, subsidiaries that are either liquidated or sold off are considered as divestments. Mata and Portugal (2000) found that the determinants for above mentioned divestment modes are different. Of great interest is analysing weather the influence of determinants for different divestment modes have been changed in China. Second, our study included a sample of manufacturing industries. Early studies pointed out that behaviours of service firms are different from behaviours of manufacturing firms (Brouthers and Brouthers, 2003). Future subsidiary survival studies are encouraged to include service firms in their empirical design.

References

Allison, P.D. (1999). *Logistic regression using the SAS system: theory and application*. Cary, N.C: SAS Institute, cop.

Amemiya, T. (1981). 'Qualitative response models: a survey', *Journal of Economic Literature*, 19(4), 1483–1536.

Anderson, E. and Gatignon, H. (1986). 'Modes of entry: a transaction cost analysis and propositions', *Journal of International Business Studies*, 17(1), 1–26.

Arslan, A. and Larimo, J. (2010). 'Ownership Strategy of Multinational Enterprises and the Impacts of Regulative and Normative Institutional Distance: Evidence from Finnish Foreign Direct Investments in Central and Eastern Europe', *Journal of East – West Business*, 16(3), 179–200.

Arslan, A., and Larimo, J. (2012). 'Partial or Full Acquisition: Influences of Institutional Pressures on Acquisition Entry Strategy of Multinational Enterprises'. In M. Demirbag and G. Wood (Eds), *Handbook of Institutional Approaches to International Business* United Kingdom: Edward Elgar, pp. 320–343.

Barney, J.B. (1991). 'Firms resources and sustained competitive advantage', *Journal of Management*, 17(01), 99–120.

Belderbos, R. and Zou, J. (2009). 'Real options and foreign affiliate divestment: A portfolio perspective', *Journal of International Business Studies*, 40(4), 600–620.

Blodgett, L.L. (1992). 'Factors in the instability of international joint ventures: An event history analysis', *Strategic Management Journal*, 13(6), 475–491.

Chen, H.Y. and Hu, M.Y. (2002). 'An analysis of determinants of entry mode and its impact on performance', *International Business Review*, 11(2), 193–210.

Chen, C.M., Makino, S, and Isobe, T. (2010). 'Does subnational region matter? Foreign affiliate performance in the United States and China', *Strategic Management Journal*, 31(11), 1226–1243.

Chiao, Y.C., Fang Y.L., and Chow, M.Y. (2010). 'Choosing between wholly-owned subsidiaries and joint ventures of MNCs from an emerging market', *International Marketing Review*, 27 (3), 338–365.

Child, J. and Tsai, T. (2005). 'The dynamic between firms environmental strategies and institutional constraints in emerging economies: Evidence from China and Taiwan', *Journal of Management Studies*, 42(1), 95–125.

Chung, J. and Beamish, P.W. (2005). 'The performance and survival of joint ventures with parents of asymmetric size', *International Management*, 10(1), 19–30.

Clarke, J.E., Tamaschke, R, and Liesch, P.W. (2013). 'International experience in international business research: a conceptualization and exploration of key themes', *International Journal of Management Review*, 15(3), 265–279.

Claver, E. and Quer, D. (2005). 'Choice of market entry mode in China: the influence of firm-specific factors', *Journal of Global Management*, 30(3), 51–70.

Cui, L. and Jiang, F.M. (2009). 'FDI entry mode choice of Chinese firms: a strategic behavior perspective', *Journal of World Business*, 44(4), 434–444.

Delios, A. and Beamish, P.W. (1999). 'Ownership strategy of Japanese firms: transactional, institutional, and experience influences', *Strategic Management Journal*, 20(10), 915–933.

Delios, A. and Beamish, P.W. (2001). 'Survival and profitability: the roles of experience and intangible assets in foreign subsidiary performance', *Academy of Management Journal*, 44(5), 1028–1038.

Delios, A. and Henisz, W.J. (2000). 'Japanese firms' investment strategies in emerging economies', *Academy of Management Journal*, 43(3), 305–323.

Delios, A. and Makino, S. (2003). 'Timing of entry and the foreign subsidiary performance of Japanese firms', *Journal of International Marketing*, 11(3), 83–105.

Delios, A., Xu, D., and Beamish, P.W. (2008). 'Within-country product diversification and foreign subsidiary performance', *Journal of International Business Studies*, 39(4), 706–724.

Demirbag, M., Apaydin, M., and Tatoglu, E. (2011). 'Survival of Japanese subsidiaries in the Middle East and North Africa', *Journal of World Business*, 46(4), 411–425.

Dhanaraj, C. and Beamish, P.W. (2004). 'Effect of equity ownership on the survival of international joint ventures', *Strategic Management Journal*, 25(3), 295–305.

Dhanaraj, C. and Beamish, P.W. (2009). 'Institutional environment and subsidiary survival', *Management International Review*, 49(3), 291–312.

Dikova, D. and Witteloostuijn, A.V. (2007). 'Foreign direct investment mode choice: entry and establishment modes in transition economies', *Journal of International Business Studies*, 38(6), 1013–1033.

Dikova, D., Rao, S.P., and Witteloostuijn, A.V. (2010). 'Cross-border acquisition abandonment and completion: the effect of institutional differences and organizational learning in the business service industry, 1981–2001', *Journal of International Business Studies*, 41(2), 223–245.

Dikova, D. (2012). 'Entry mode choices in emerging economies: the moderating effect of institutional distance on managers' personal experiences', *Journal of East–West Business*, 18(1), 1–27.

DiMaggio, P.J. and Powell, W.W. (1983). 'The iron cage revisited: institutional isomorphism and collective rationality in organizational fields', *American Sociological Review*, 48(2), 147–160.

Dow, D. and Larimo, J. (2009). 'Challenging the conceptualization and measurement of distance and international experience in entry mode choice research', *Journal of International Marketing*, 17(2), 74–98.

Erramilli, M.K. (1991). 'The experience factor in foreign market entry behavior of service firms', *Journal of International business Studies*, 22(3), 479–501.

Fang, E. and Zhou, S. (2010). 'The effects of absorptive and joint learning on the instability of international joint ventures in emerging economies', *Journal of International Business Studies*, 41(5), 906–924.

Gaur, A.S. and Lu, W. (2007). 'Ownership strategies and survival of foreign subsidiaries: Impacts of institutional distance and experience', *Journal of Management*, 33(1), 84–110.

Geringer, M.J. and Hebert, L. (1991). 'Measuring performance of international joint ventures', *Journal of International Business Studies*, 22(2), 249–263.

Hennart, J.F. (1991). 'The transaction costs theory of joint ventures: an empirical study of Japanese subsidiaries in the United States', *Management Science*, 37(4), 483–497.

Hennart, J.F. and Park, Y.R. (1993). 'Greenfield vs. acquisition: the strategy of Japanese investors in the United States', *Management Science*, 39(9), 1054–1070.

He, C., Wei, Y.H.D., and Xie, X.Z. (2008). 'Globalization, Institutional change, and industrial location: economic transition and industrial concentration in China', *Regional Studies*, 42(7), 923–945.

Hogenbirk, A. and Narula, R. (1999). 'Globalisation and the small economy. The case of the Netherlands'. In D. Van Den Bulcke and A. Verbeeke (Eds) *Globalisation and the small economy*, Edward Elgar: Cheltenham.

Hollensen, S. (2014). *Global Marketing*, United Kingdom: Pearson Education Limited.

Hoskisson, R.E., Eden, L., Lau, C.M., and Wright, M. (2000). 'Strategy in emerging economies', *Academy of Management Journal*, 43(3), 249–267.

Huang, Y. (2008). *Capitalism with Chinese characteristics: Entrepreneurship and state during the reform era*, New York: Cambridge University Press.

Johanson, J. and Vahlne, J.E. (1977). 'Internationalization process of the firm. A model of knowledge development and increasing foreign market commitment', *Journal of International Business Studies*, 8(1), 23–32.

Kim, T.Y., Delios, A., and Xu, D. (2010). 'Organizational geography, experiential learning and subsidiary exit: Japanese foreign expansions in China', 1979–2001, *Journal of Economic Geography*, 10(4), 579–597.

Larimo, J. (2003). 'Form of investment by Nordic firms in world markets', *Journal of Business Research*, 56(10), 791–803.

Li, J.T. (1995). 'Foreign entry and survival, the effects of strategic choices on performance in international markets', *Strategic Management Journal*, 16(5), 333–351.

Li, P.Y. and Meyer, K.E. (2009). 'Contextualizing experience effects in international business: A study of ownership strategies', *Journal of World Business*, 44(4), 370–382.

Lu, J.W. and Hebert, L. (2005). 'Equity control and the survival of IJVs: A contingency approach', *Journal of Business Research*, 58(6), 736–745.

Luo, Y. (2000). *How to Enter China: Choices and Lessons*, Michigan: University of Michigan Press.

Luo, Y. (2001). 'Determinants of entry in an emerging economy: A multilevel approach', *Journal of Management Studies*, 38(3), 443–472.

Mata, J. and Portugal, P. (2000). 'Closure and divestiture by foreign entrants: the impact of entry and post-entry strategies', *Strategic Management Journal*, 21(5), 549–562.

Meschi, P.X. and Riccio, E.L. (2008). 'Country risk, national cultural differences between partners and survival of international joint ventures in Brazil', *International Business Review*, 17(3), 250–266.

Meyer, K.E. and Peng, M. (2005). 'Probing theoretically into Central and Eastern Europe: Transactions, resources, and institutions', *Journal of International Business Studies*, 36(6), 600–621.

Meyer, K., Estrin, S., Bhaumik, S.K., and Peng, M. (2009). 'Institutions, resources, and entry strategies in emerging economies', *Strategic Management Journal*, 30(1), 61–80.

Mudambi, R and Mudambi, S.M. (2002). 'Diversification and market entry choices in the context of foreign direct investment', *International Business Review*, 11(1), 35–55.

North, D.C. (1990). *Institutions, Institutional Change and Economic Performance*, New York: Cambridge University Press.

Norton, P.M. & Chao, H. (2001). 'Mergers and acquisitions in China', *The China Business Review*, 28(5), 46–53.

Padmanabhan, P. and Cho, K.R. (1996). 'Ownership strategy for a foreign affiliate. An empirical investigation of Japanese firms', *Management International Review*, 36(1), 45–65.

Park, Y.R., Lee, J.Y., and Hong, S.H. (2011). 'Effects of international entry-order strategies on foreign subsidiary exit. The case of Koream Chaebols', *Management Decision*, 49(9), 1471–1488.

Pallant, J. (2007). *SPSS survival manual: a step by step guide to data analysis using SPSS for windows*, Buckingham: Open University Press.

Pan, Y.G. and Chi, P.S.K. (1999). 'Financial performance and survival of multinational corporations in China', *Strategic Management Journal*, 20(4), 359–374.

Pan, Y. and Tse, D.K. (2000). 'The hierarchical model of market entry modes', *Journal of International Business Studies*, 31(4), 535–554.

Papyrina, V. (2007). 'When, how, and with what success? The joint effect of timing and entry mode on survival of Japanese subsidiaries in China', *Journal of International Marketing*, 15(3), 73–95.

Peng, M. (2002). 'Toward an institution-based view of business strategy, Asia Pacific Journal of Management', 19(2), 251–267

Peng, M. (2003). 'Institutional transitions and strategic choices', *Academy of Management Review*, 28(2), 275–296

Peng, M. (2009). *Global strategy*, Mason: South-Western Cengage Learning.

Porter, M. (1980). *Competitive strategy*, New York: Free Press.

Scott, W.R. (1995). *Institutions and organizations*, Thousand Oaks, CA: Sage.

Shi, Y.Z., Ho, P.Y., and Siu, W.S. (2001). 'Market entry mode selection: the experience of small Hong Kong firms investing in China', *Asia Pacific Business Review*, 8(1), 19–41.

Silverman, B.S., Nickerson, J.A., and Freeman, J. (1997). 'Profitability, transactional alignment, and organizational mortality in the U.S. trucking industry', *Strategic Management Journal*, 18(Summer Special Issue), 31–52.

Slangen, A.H.L. and Hennart, J.F. (2007). 'Greenfield or Acquisition Entry: A Review of the Empirical Foreign Establishment Mode Literature', *Journal of International Management*, 13(4), 403–429.

Steensma, H.K. and Lyles, M.A. (2000). 'Explaining IJV survival in a transitional economy through social exchange and knowledge–based perspectives', *Strategic Management Journal*, 21(8), 831–851.

Taylor, C.R., Zou, S., and Osland, G.E. (1998). 'A transaction cost perspective on foreign market entry strategies of US and Japanese firms', *Thunderbird International Business Review*, 40(4), 389–412.

Tsang, E.W.K. and Yip, P.S.L. (2007). 'Economic distance and survival of foreign direct investments', *Academy of Management Journal*, 50(5), 1156–1168.

UNCTAD (2013). *World Investment Report. Global value chains: investment and trade for development*, Switzerland: United Nations Publications.

Vermeulen, F. and Barkema, H.G. (2001). 'Learning through Acquisitions', *Academy of Management Journal*, 44(3), 457–476.

Wei, Y.G., Liu, B, and Liu, X.M. (2005). 'Entry modes of foreign direct investment in China: a multinomial logit approach', *Journal of Business Research*, 58(11), 1495–1505.

Wetherill, G.B. (1986). *Regression analysis with applications*, London: Chapman and Hall.

Williamson, O.E. (1975). *Markets and hierarchies: Analysis and antitrust implications*, New York: Free Press.

Williamson, O.E. (1985). *The economic institutions of capitalism*, New York: Basic Books.

Williamson, O.E. (2000). 'The new institutional economics: taking stock, looking ahead', *Journal of Economic Literature*, 38(3), 595–613.

Wright, M., Filatotchev, I., Hoskisson, R.E., and Peng, M. (2005). 'Strategy research in emerging economies: Challenging the conventional wisdom', *Journal of Management Studies*, 42(1), 1–33.

Yan, A. (1998). 'Structural stability and reconfiguration of international joint ventures', *Journal of International Business Studies*, 29(4), 773–795.

Yan, Y. and Zeng, M. (1999). 'International joint venture instability: a critique of previous research, a conceptualization, and directions for future research', *Journal of International Business Studies*, 30(2), 397–414.

Zhang, Y., Zhang, Z., and Liu, Z. (2007). 'Choice of entry modes in sequential FDI in an emerging economy', *Management Decision*, 45(4), 749–772.

Zhao, H., Luo, Y., and Suh, T. (2004). 'Transactional cost determinants and ownership-based entry mode choice: A meta-analytical review', *Journal of International Business Studies*, 35(6), 524–544.

8
Control Position Strategy, Cultural Distance, Conflict Resolution Strategies and Performance of International Joint Ventures

Huu Le Nguyen, Jorma Larimo and Tahir Ali

Introduction

Facing fierce global competition, firms often establish international joint ventures (IJVs) with foreign firms (Kwon, 2013). However, researchers notice a high rate of IJV failure (e.g. Hennart, Kim and Zeng, 1998). One of the key reasons is that firms often have different goals and ways of communications. Another reason is that inter-partner conflicts often lead to dissolution of partnership (Fey and Beamish, 1999; Pajunen and Fang, 2013). Thus, understanding conflict is crucial to organisations (Boonsathorn, 2007, Das and Kumar, 2010; Krone and Steimel, 2013) since conflict resolution strategies of parent firms affect IJV performance (Fey and Bearmish, 1999; Lu, 2006; Yavas, et al., 1994). Lin and Germain, 1998) suggest that foreign parent firms differ in their choice of conflict resolution strategies (CRS). Wang, Lin, Chang and Shi (2005) notice that conflict handling styles of partner firms becomes an important topic in IJV research, and White III, Joplin and Salama (2007) maintain that conflict resolution strategy is an underexplored area in the international business and management literature.

Wang et al. (2005) maintain that understanding the way in which firms resolve conflict is very important. Nguyen (2009) and Krone and Steimel (2013) suggest that further studies need to investigate the effect of cultural distance on cooperative behaviours of partners in IJVs. About 20 years ago, Yavas et al. (1994) suggested that further study should investigate CRSs that take into account of influence of parent control. Recently, Ma, Lee and Yu (2008) still notice that conflict management literature has received little attention from researchers. They also propose that the future of conflict management studies should focus on conflict management styles and cultural differences. Furthermore, Lin and Germain (1998) and Nguyen and Larimo (2011) maintain that relative power between partners (e.g. control power) in IJVs seems also to be one of the key influencing factors on partners' choice of CRS needing further analysis.

To provide new insights on conflict management in IJVs, our study investigates the influence of the control position strategy of foreign partners and cultural distance between partners on their CRS used in IJVs, and the impact of CRS on IJV performance. More specifically, this study aims to answer the research questions: 'How do control position strategy and cultural distance between partners influence their choice of CRS?' and 'what are the relationships between CRS and IJV performance?' Besides the main research questions, we also examine the interaction effects between control position strategies, cultural distance and CRS.

A key feature of earlier CRS studies has been that they have focused on only one factor, such as culture or trust (e.g. Ding, 1996; Lin and Germain, 1998; Doucet et al., 2009), and at the general level. Our study aims to contribute to the research tradition both in IJV research and in conflict management literature by specifying how three different control position strategies (dominant, equal and minor control) and cultural distance between partners influence their choice of CRS. In addition, our study differs from previous studies in the three ways.

1. We analyse how both control position strategies of foreign firms and cultural distance between partners integrated with CRS.
2. We point out how different CRSs link to IJV performance.
3. We examine the interaction effects of control position strategies, cultural distance and the selections of CRS and performance.

In the next section, first we will make an overview of CRS studies. Then, we will discuss how different control position strategies will lead to foreign parent firms' choices of different CRSs. After that, we continue with analysing the influence of cultural distance on the selection of CRSs. We next discuss the interaction effects of control position strategy and cultural distance on the selection of CRSs. We then examine the relationship between CRS and IJV performance. After that, we discuss our methodology and the results of our data analysis. Finally, we conclude the paper by discussing the implications and limitations of our study and showing opportunities for further research.

Literature review

Conflict is a common characteristic of every organisation (De Dreu and Weingart, 2003). It is often regarded as a negative force, a harmful element (Boonsathorn, 2007) leading to discomfort, misunderstanding and disruption of relationships or even the collapse of organisations (Robbins, 2005) or unplanned terminations of IJV (Pajunen and Fang, 2013). The need to deal with conflict arises because it is inherent in relationships (Fey and Beamish,

1999). Thus, it is important to understand different CRSs in partnerships. Finally, we will explain different CRSs.

There are different strategies that firms can apply to handle conflicts, such as confronting, ignoring, avoiding, compromising, accommodating, problem solving and seeking mediation (Thomas, 1976; Rahim, 1983). The basis for a conflict management style is concern for the benefits of oneself and/or concern for the benefits of others. Using two dimensions – namely assertiveness (to satisfy one's own concern) and cooperativeness (to satisfy the concern of the other) – Thomas (1976) constructs five conflict handling strategies: competing, collaboration, compromising, accommodating and avoiding. According to Rahim and Bonoma (1979), CRSs include dominating, obliging, avoiding, compromising and integrating. Lin and Germain (1998) and Lu (2006) categorise CRSs into four main strategies: problem solving, compromising, forcing and legalistic strategy. Our study adopts conflict resolution strategy by Lin and Germain (1998) and Lu (2006). The reason is that, in their typology, each strategy is clearly different from the others. With problem solving strategy, partners aim to satisfy the needs of all parties involved. Exercising this strategy, partners attempt to provide new effective solutions that will increase stakes for all parties involved. With compromising strategy, partners aim to achieve a common solution from both sides by offering some concessions from all involved parties. Exercising forcing strategy, partners aim to dominate decision making. Legalistic strategy often involves solving conflict by using a written contract. This is a formal communication with partners in IJVs in order to get the desired target.

After carefully reviewing articles published in leading international business and management journals like Journal of International Business Studies, Journal of International Management, International Business Review, Management International Review, International Journal of Conflict Management, Journal of International Marketing and Academy of Management Review, we identified 24 of the key studies on CRSs. Most of the previous studies focused on analysing conflict management style of parties in one country (e.g. Ding, 1996; Fey and Beamish, 1999) or comparing two countries (e.g. Doucet et al., 2009; Boonsathorn, 2007; Yavas et al., 1994) or a number of countries (e.g. Kim et al., 2007; Lu, 2006; Onishi and Bliss, 2006). Other studies examine differences between Western style and Asian style (i.e. Wang et al., 2005) or use one single cultural dimension to analyse the preference for CRSs (e.g. Komarraju et al., 2008).

Previous studies also focused on providing strategies to avoid conflict (e.g. White III et al., 2007; Barden, 2005) or the effect of cultural similarity, age of relationship and general relative power of partners (e.g. Lin and Germain, 1998) on their preference for CRSs. Our study focuses on the most important factors that influence firms' preferences for CRSs, including control position and cultural distance of partners. We go further from previous studies by analysing three control power strategies, including dominant, equal and minority control (Killing, 1983; Chung and Beamish, 2010; Kwon, 2013). This study examines the importance of culture to the preference for CRSs by analysing cultural distance between partners and the selection of CRSs. This approach takes into consideration the foreign firm's point of view regarding their own culture and their local partner's culture rather than studying one cultural dimension or one country or some countries as in previous studies. Next, we discuss in detail the influence of three control position strategies, cultural distance between partners and the preference for CRSs.

Hypothesis development

Control position strategies and CRSs

The fit between subsidiary strategy and the subsidiary control mechanism is an important issue (O'Donnell, 2000) for performance of the units. Makino and Beamish (1999) and Nguyen and Larimo (2009) find a strong link between foreign control structure for their IJVs and the strategies that they carry out in the IJVs. This section aims to elaborate on how a control strategy in their IJVs will lead foreign parent firms to have different CRSs. IJV control strategies can be divided into three categories: dominant, equal and minority control (e.g. Killing, 1983; Chung and Beamish, 2010; Kwon, 2013).

Dominant Control

Foreign parent firms who have dominant control position in IJVs often have more negotiating power than do their local parent firms. Thus, foreign parent firms may have more alternative strategies in the way they deal with conflicts with local firms because foreign parent firms have dominant control position in IJVs. This enables them to use all four available strategies, namely forcing strategy, problem solving strategy, compromising strategy and legal strategy. However, firms with dominant control position may prefer the forcing strategy to resolve conflicts in order to avoid the long process of problem solving (Lin and Germain, 1998) or legal procedure. Similarly, White III et al. (2007) argue that partners with the dominant position often used their power to obtain their interests. Partners with the dominant control position are also likely not to use compromise strategy as they can easily realise their interests through their power (Schaan, 1983).

> *Hypothesis 1*: Foreign parent firms with the dominant control position in IJVs will use (a) the forcing strategy and will not use (b) problem solving, (c) compromising and (d) the legalistic strategy.

Equal Control

In cases where foreign and local firms have equal control position in IJVs, foreign parent firms may not be able to use the forcing strategy in solving conflicts with local firms (Nguyen and Larimo, 2011). An earlier study (e.g. Lin and Wang, 2002) suggests that when partners have equal power, they tend to use a more cooperative approach. As the stake is shared equally in IJVs, either partners may try to solve problems by increasing stake for both parties, or they may try to make a compromise with local firms so that the results of resolved conflicts will lead to smaller stakes for both parties. In cases where partners cannot reach a compromise on the disputed issue and where partners have the same decision power, they may need to solve the conflicts with legal support.

Hypothesis 2: Foreign parent firms with equal control position in IJVs will use (a) problem solving, (b) compromising (c) or the legalistic strategy and will not use d) the forcing strategy.

Minority Control

In cases of minor control position in IJVs, foreign parent firms will have the least power to force local firms on how to manage IJV activities, thus they have to solve problem related to conflicted issue in IJV operations. Thus, strategies that are available for only the dominant owner of IJVs, such as the forcing strategy, is difficult to apply in minority control position partners. White III et al. (2007) suggest that partners with minority position in IJVs often prefer the harmony strategy to resolve conflict in their IJVs. Thus, the only available strategies for minor ownership position firms are trying to get a compromise with local firms or solve problems. In the worst case scenario, they may need to take some legal actions to solve problems.

Hypothesis 3: Foreign parent firms with minority control position in IJVs will use (a) compromising, (b) problem solving and (c) the legalistic strategy and will not use (d) the forcing strategy.

Cultural distance

Cultural differences between firms in international markets will influence their strategies (Drogendijk and Slangen, 2006), and especially partner's strategies in their IJVs (Nguyen, 2009). Partners coming from very distant cultures to each other may have different purposes in entering IJVs as well as different ways of managing conflicts in their IJVs (Ding, 1996; Komarraju, et al., 2008; Doucet et al., 2009). In conflict situations, managers who perceive high cultural distance with their local partners tend to use forcing or compromising strategies to resolve conflicts as they believe that these strategies help their IJVs to get quickly back to their daily operations. These strategies save them a lot of problems in the long process of solving conflicts through problem solving and legalistic procedures. This is because when partners are from very different cultures, there is high chance of misunderstanding when they try to communicate with each other, or it may take long time for partners to understand each other (Weiss,

1990). Furthermore, when cultural distance between partners is high, partners may have different ways of thinking and different logics in their arguments. Therefore, the more partners try to solve the problem, the more they feel the differences from their partners, leading to more conflicts to occur. Therefore, a quick strategy, such as forcing, can help IJVs to get back to their daily operations. Thus, when conflicts arise, managers will use the forcing strategy to eliminate different opinions or to avoid a long procedure of problem solving because in the long process there is risk of the problem remaining unsolved or of a new problem arising when solving the old problem. Managers can also avoid a long process of problem solving of conflicts caused by such differences by getting quick solution with partners through the compromising strategy. As a result, we propose:

Hypothesis 4: Cultural distance between partners is positively related to a) the forcing strategy and b) the compromising strategy, while it is negatively related to c) problem solving and d) the legalistic strategy.

Interaction effects between cultural differences, the control position strategy and CRSs

Because operating IJVs requires team work with partners from different countries, possibly with very different cultures informing each decision, operations also require considerations of the behaviour and reactions of the other partners and how this will influence IJV operation as a whole. Partners making decisions related to CRS will be also likely taking into consideration their partners' cultures. However, availability of different strategies for resolving conflicts between partners is often subject to a firm's control position. The higher control position the firms have in their IJVs, the more options on different strategies the firms have to exercise. Therefore, in the case that ownership power position and cultural distance have different implications for strategies used to solve conflicts between partners, the control position of partners may have stronger influence on CRS choice than the impact of cultural distance between partners. As a result, we propose:

Hypothesis 5: The control position of foreign parent firms interacts with cultural distance between partners so that control position overrides cultural distance in the choice of CRS.

CRSs and IJV performance

Researchers (e.g. Lin and Germain, 1998) argue that CRSs have an impact on IJV performance. With more cooperative strategies, such as problem solving and compromising strategies, firms are concerned not only for themselves but also for their partners' interests and feelings. In these two strategies, firms tend to face conflicts and try to find solutions that can satisfy both partners (Lu, 2006), leading to more cooperative behaviours from partners. This will have a positive impact on the relationship between partners, and therefore, they will continue to contribute to and support IJV, resulting in a positive impact to IJV performance.

On the other hand, although assertive strategies, such as forcing and legalistic strategies, sometimes can solve problems quickly (forcing strategy) or may prevent future conflict (legalistic strategy) (Lu, 2006), they may hurt the feelings of the other partners, and if these kinds of strategies are repeatedly used by partners, it will deeply damage the relationship between partners. When partners are hurt, they will not be interested in continuing the IJV relationship (even though IJV can perform well). As a result, when forcing or legalistic strategies are used by one of the partners, the other partner(s) may gradually decrease their contribution and involvement to IJVs, leading to reduced IJV performance. Hence, we suggest:

Hypothesis 6: There are positive relationships between a) problem solving and b) compromising strategies and IJV performance while there are negative relationships between c) forcing strategies and legalistic strategies and IJV performance.

Methodology

Data collection

This study consists of Nordic (Denmark, Finland, Sweden and Norway) firms' IJVs operating in Asia, Europe and America. By reviewing the press releases and annual reports of the Nordic firms, we identified a target population of 464 equity IJVs made during 2000 and 2011. In order to increase the response rate, we identified respondents who were knowledgeable regarding their IJV operations. These respondents included regional directors, country-specific directors, product-specific directors, vice presidents and managing directors. These target respondents' names and their emails were identified from company websites, from annual reports, from press releases and by directly contacting the human resource management (HRM) directors of Nordic firms.

The questionnaire development and design follows the suggestions of Collis and Hussey (2009). Silva (2007) posits that web survey is useful compared to mail survey. This approach allows the researchers to access a large number of dispersed respondents faster, more easily and more cheaply. It also displays the data in numerical form in real time. Therefore, a web-based survey in spring 2012, followed by a second email to non-respondents three weeks later led to 928 possible respondents in 464 IJVs. In total, 89 responses were received, a response rate of 19.11% of the identified IJVs.

Krishnan, Martin and Noorderhaven (2006) suggests that survey research requires checking for non-response bias. Therefore, independent samples t-test was performed for comparing the early respondents (N=48) to the late respondents (N=41) in terms of firm sise and industry of Nordic parents. There were no significant differences between the early and late respondents in terms of firm size (p = .708) and industry (p = .548). Thus, non-response bias was not an issue.

The sample characteristics

The sample characteristics indicate that the 89 IJVs of Nordic firms formed from 2000 to 2011 were operating in three regions (49 in Asia, 27 in Europe and 13 America). Of the 89 IJVs, 24 (26.96 per cent) Nordic firms held minority ownership, 19 (21.36 per cent) had equal ownership and 46 (51.68 per cent) had dominant ownership. Of the IJVs, 24 were formed in 2000–2003, 40 in 2004–2007 and 25 in 2008–2011. In 13 cases, the Nordic parent firms had less than 500 employees; in 23 cases between 500 and 5000; and in 53 cases over 5000 employees.

Measures

Table 8.1 describes the operationalisation of the variables included in the model and a summary of the relationships between the independent and dependent variables. We operationalised IJV performance using four measures taken from prior empirical research (e.g. Geringer and Hebert, 1991; Lane, Salk and Lyles, 2001; Krishnan et al., 2006). These measures included overall performance, profitability, market share and achieving the goals set for IJV.

We asked the respondents to identify the level of their firm's satisfaction with these measures on a scale of 1–5, from 'very unsatisfied' to 'very satisfied'. We took the average of these performance measures and transformed to a dummy variable with '0' if the average score is ≤ 3, and '1' if it has higher score. The four dependent variables of CRS (i.e. problem solving, compromising, forcing and legalistic) were operationalised from the work of Lin and Germain (1998) and Lu (2006). For each conflict resolution strategy, the respondents stated if their firm used this strategy when there are disagreements between IJV partners regarding the operations and\or strategic decision of the IJV. We coded '1' if the foreign parent of the IJV used that strategy and '0' if they did not.

Control position of foreign firms over IJVs based on their ownership share. A foreign partner's ownership share was gauged by a single question adopted from Hsieh, Rodrigues and Child (2010) that asked the respondents to provide the percentage of their firm's ownership share in the IJV. Measurement of national cultural distance used a single question from the approach by Bener and Glaister (2010). In addition to the variables specified in our theoretical model, we included the IJV age, trust and business relatedness as control variables.

Related to control variables, consistent with Krishnan et al. (2006), IJV age was measured by using the number of years since the IJV had been set up.

Table 8.1 Measurement of variables and expected direction of signs

Variables	Measurement	Expected sign				
		Per	Pro	Com	For	Leg
Dependent variables						
IJV Performance (Per)	'1' if the foreign parent of IJV is satisfied with the performance of the IJV, and '0' if it was unsatisfied					
Problem solving (Pro)	Set to '1' if the foreign parent of IJV used problem solving strategy, and '0' if it did not use	+				
Compromising (Com)	'1' if the foreign parent of IJV used compromising strategy, and '0' if it did not use	+				
Forcing (For)	Set to '1' if the foreign parent of IJV used forcing strategy, and '0' if it did not use	−				
Legalistic (Leg)	'1' if the foreign parent of IJV used legalistic strategy, and '0' if it did not use	−				
Independent variables						
Minority control	Set to '1' if the foreign parent of IJV had minority control in IJV, and '0' otherwise		+	+	−	+
Equal control	'1' if the parents of IJV had equal control (50%) in IJV, and '0' otherwise		+	+	−	+
Dominant control	Set to '1' if the foreign parent of IJV had dominant control in IJV, and '0' otherwise		−	−	+	−
National culture distance	'1' if the national cultural difference between the partners' countries is high, and '0' if it is low		−	+	+	−
Control variables						
IJV age	Coded as '1'= ≤ 2 years, '2'= 3–4 years, '3'= 5–6 years, '4'= 7–8 years, '5'= ≥ 9 years					
Trust	Set to '1' if the foreign parent of IJV has high trust on counterpart, and '0' if it has low trust					
Business relatedness	'1' If both IJV partners operate in same business line, and '0' otherwise					

In order to measure the foreign firm's trust on counterpart, we adopted and modified the question from Lane et al. (2001) to measure the overall level of trust by asking the respondents whether their firm has high or low trust on IJV partner firm. The response was coded '0' if the foreign firm has low trust on counterpart and '1' if it has high trust. Finally, business relatedness received a code of '1' if both IJV partners operate in same business line and '0' otherwise.

Test methodology and results

The correlations between all variables in order to test for individual relationships (see Table 8.2) revealed a few problems of multicollinearity. Notably, dominant ownership was highly correlated with minority ownership (r > .60) and equal ownership (r > .50). Gulati (1995) suggests that separate binomial logistic regression models are necessary for variables having multicollinearity. Therefore, we ran two distinct binomial logistic regression models for each dependent variable of conflict resolution strategies to determine which factors predicted the CRS. Model 1 included the (a) constructs of ownership – that is, minority and equal ownerships – and the (b) national cultural distance. Model 2 included the dominant ownership and (c) control variables of trust, business relatedness, and IJV age.

The binomial logistic regression results with conflict resolution strategies as the dependent variables are provided in Table 8.3. The results indicate that dominant ownership is positively related to the forcing strategy (β = 2.31; $p < 0.01$) and inversely related to the problem solving (β = –2.61; $p < 0.01$) and compromising (β = –1.77; $p < 0.01$) strategies and not significantly related to the legalistic strategy. The results support hypotheses H1a, H1b, and H1c, but not H1d. The results for H2a (β = 3.84; $p < 0.01$) and H2d (β = –3.26; $p < 0.01$) supported the notion that equal ownership has a strong positive effect on the problem solving strategy and strong negative impact on the forcing strategy. There is, however, no significant relationship between equal ownership and the comprising strategy and the legalistic strategy. Hypotheses H2a and H2d are thus supported but not hypotheses H2b and H2c.

Supportive findings for H3a (β = 2.67; $p < 0.01$), H3b (β = 1.24; $p < 0.05$) and H3d (β = –1.12; $p < 0.05$) indicate that minority ownership has a positive effect on the compromising strategy and the problem solving strategy and a negative impact on the forcing strategy. However, the results suggest that minority ownership does not relate to the legalistic strategy, thus failing to support H3c. Hypotheses 4a, 4b, 4c and 4d respectively hypothesise that when cultural distance between IJV partners is high, foreign parents use forcing and compromising strategies and do not use problem solving and legalistic strategies. The results indicate that cultural distance is positively related to the compromising

Table 8.2 Means, standard deviations and correlations

Variables	Mean	s.d.	1	2	3	4	5	6	7	8	9	10	11	12
1. Minority control	0.27	0.45	1											
2. Equal control	0.20	0.40	-0.31	1										
3. Dominant ownership	0.52	0.50	-0.63	-0.52	1									
4. National Cultural Dis.	0.83	0.38	0.00	0.08	-0.08	1								
5. Trust	0.82	0.39	0.02	-0.06	0.02	-0.33	1							
6. Business relatedness	0.83	0.38	0.00	-0.07	0.05	0.20	-0.05	1						
7. IJV age	2.70	1.41	0.24	-0.01	-0.19	0.10	0.02	-0.08	1					
8. CRS-Legalism	0.22	0.42	0.02	0.04	-0.07	0.03	-0.31	0.04	0.03	1				
9. CRS-Forcing	0.55	0.50	-0.16	-0.45	0.44	0.08	-0.19	-0.03	0.01	0.22	1			
10. CRS-Compromising	0.29	0.46	0.50	0.03	-0.37	0.22	-0.18	0.17	-0.02	0.19	0.03	1		
11. CRS-Problem Solving	0.36	0.48	0.18	0.56	-0.49	-0.03	0.02	-0.23	-0.01	-0.18	-0.45	-0.12	1	
12. IJV performance	0.60	0.49	0.09	0.13	-0.20	-0.01	0.35	-0.08	-0.03	-0.38	-0.22	0.18	0.47	1

Table 8.3   Results of binomial logistic regression analysis – ownership, national culture and conflict resolution strategies

Variables	Problem solving strategy		Compromising strategy		Forcing strategy		Legalistic strategy	
	Model 1	Model 2	Model 1	Model 2	Model 1	Model 2	Model 1	Mode 2
Minority control	1.24**(.035)		2.67***(.000)		-1.12** (.038)		.206 (.728)	
Equal control	3.84*** (.000)		.034 (.964)		-3.26*** (.000)		.042 (.950)	
Dominant control		-2.61*** (.000)		-1.77*** (.002)		2.31*** (.000)		-.516 (.230)
National cultural distance	-.199 (.781)		2.52**(.031)		.782 (.219)		.173 (.807)	
National cultural distance * Dominant control				-1.18** (.032)				
Control variables								
Trust		.13 (.572)		-1.04* (.085)		-1.10** (.041)		-2.12*** (.002)
Business relatedness		-1.55** (.036)		1.30* (.092)		-.14 (.837)		.07 (.931)
IJV age		-.19 (.315)		-.027 (.880)			.19 (.300)		.245 (.223)
Model quality								
N	89 (32)	89 (32)	89 (26)	89 (26)	89 (49)	89 (49)	89 (20)	89 (20)
Model χ²	32.46*** (.000)	29.02*** (.000)	28.32*** (.000)	16.46*** (.002)	30.67*** (.000)	29.33*** (.000)	18.7 (.980)	22.52** (.017)
-2 Log likelihood	83.80	87.24	79.20	91.07	87.59	89.12	94.65	84.72
Nagelkerke R²	41.9%	38.2%	38.9%	24.1%	39.5%	37.6%	.3%	20.4%
Correctly classified (%)	79.8%	78.7%	82%	76.4%	73.3%	73.8%	77.5%	76.4%

Note: *** p ≤ 0.01, ** p ≤ 0.05, * p ≤ 0.10.

strategy (β = 2.52; p < 0.05) and not significantly related to the forcing, problem solving and legalistic strategies, thus providing support for hypotheses H4b but not H4a, H4c and H4d. Furthermore, in relation to H5, we found that the results did support our contention that control position overrides the cultural distance in the choice of CRS.

We found that in choosing the compromising strategy, dominant control significantly overrides cultural distance (β = –1.18; p < 0.05). Therefore, finding seems to support H5. Finally, concerning the control variables, the results show strongly the negative impact of trust on the forcing strategy (β = –1.10; p < 0.05) and the legalistic strategy (β = –2.12; p < 0.01). There is a negative impact of business relatedness on the problem solving strategy (β = –1.55; p < 0.05) and the compromising strategy (β = 1.30; p ≤ .1), and there is no significant impact from IJV age on the choice of CRS.

Table 8.4 shows the binomial logistic regression results for the impacts of conflict resolution strategies on IJV performance. The results indicate that problem solving (β = 2.30; p < 0.01) and compromising (β = 1.95; p < 0.01) strategies are positively related to IJV performance, and forcing (β = –1.03; p ≤ .1) and legalistic (β = –2.47; p < 0.01) strategies are inversely related to IJV performance. These results support hypotheses H6a, H6b, H6c and H6d.

Discussions and conclusions

Most previous studies focused on the question of why conflicts occur in IJVs and on the relationships between partners' conflicts and IJV performance. A few studies examined the strategies firms use to solve conflicts with their partners and how different CRS affect IJV performance. This study expands this sparse literature by investigating the links between control position

Table 8.4 Results of binomial logistic regression analysis – conflict resolution strategies and IJV performance

Conflict resolution strategies	IJV performance
Problem Solving Strategy	2.30*** (.003)
Compromising strategy	1.95*** (.009)
Forcing strategy	–1.03* (.095)
Legalistic strategy	–2.47*** (.003)
Model quality	
N	89 (53)
Model χ^2	45.13
–2 Log likelihood	74.98
Nagelkerke R^2	53.7
Correctly classified (%)	84.3

Note: *** p ≤ 0.01, ** p ≤ 0.05, * p ≤ 0.10.

strategies and cultural distance of firms and their strategies to solve conflicts with local partners. The study divided control position into dominant control, equal control and minor control positions and set cultural distance on the perceived cultural differences between foreign and local partners.

Implications

Our framework related to the influence of cultural distance and control positions in IJVs help further development of IJV literatures in the future. This study extends previous studies by Wang et al. (2005) where the authors focused on the influence of only one dimension of culture: individualistic vs. collectivist. In our study, we used cultural distance from the perception of mangers. In addition, previous studies on partners' choice of CRS in IJVs (e.g. Wang et al., 2005; Ding, 1996; Lin and Germain, 1998; Doucet et al., 2009) have ignored the influence of either cultural distance or ownership position of partners. As Lin and Germain (1998), Lin and Wang (2002) and White III et al. (2007) suggest, relative power of firms in IJVs influence their choice of strategy to solve conflict. This study extends these studies by further discussing one of the most important elements of relative power between partners: control positions. Our results are in line with Lin and German's (1998) view that relative power (the dominant ownership position) is inversely related to problem solving and compromising strategies and positively related to the forcing strategy.

In the case of the age of IJVs, opposing Lin and Germain (1998), we did not find any impact from age on the selection of CRS by foreign parent firms. Furthermore, White III et al. (2007) classified relative power of partners in IJVs to only two types: dominant and subservient. In our study, we have better classifications because we have three types: minority, equal and dominant positions. Finally, our study is one of the few studies that also tests interaction effect between relative power and cultural distance between partners in the relation to the choice of CRS. The result of the testing implicates that control position seems to override the impact of cultural distance in the selection of CRS, especially in the case of dominant control by foreign parent firms.

Our results on the role of cultural distance showed that cultural distance was positively related to the compromising strategy, which is in line with the results by White III et al. (2007) that indicate that in the case of high cultural distance between partners, harmony strategies will be preferred. The results partly support previous studies on the role of trust for the selection of CRS. Han and Harms (2010) proposed that trust plays an important role in an IJV relationship, and they maintained that trust plays a mediating role in conflict management. In our study, we clearly found that when there is high trust between partners, foreign firms would not prefer the forcing and legalistic strategies.

In the relationship between CRS and IJV performance, the results of our study are in line with Lin and Germain (1998) and Lu (2006), indicating that the legalistic strategy has a negative impact on IJV performance. Our results related to the positive impact of the problem solving strategy and IJV performance are in line with Lin and Germain (1998), whereas Lu (2006) did not find any significant relationship between the problem solving strategy and IJV performance. The results of our study also differ from those from Lin and Germain (1998) and Lu (2006) because we found a positive impact of the compromising strategy and a negative impact of the forcing strategy to IJV performance, whereas in their studies the findings did not support these relations.

As most IJV cases in the study are located in Asia, our findings can be applied to other Nordic firms that have IJVs especially located in that region. Our framework provides guidance for the relationships between three control positions including dominant, equal and minor positions and CRSs. Therefore, our further framework can help to predict the partner's choice of CRS in IJV relationship if conflicts arise. This study therefore helps managers to understand the selection of different alternatives of CRSs by their counterparts in IJVs and thus helps them to manage better relations with their partners.

Limitations and future research

The study did not consider types of conflicts (e.g. task conflict and relational conflict) and the role of local partners. Future research could use case method to investigate how different types of conflicts and local partners' role as well as their reaction can affect foreign firms' choices of conflict resolution strategy. Furthermore, in the study, we used data from Nordic MNEs; thus, the results may not be applicable to MNCs from other region of the world such as Latin America, Asia or even Eastern Europe. Moreover, as organisations evolve over time, future studies may apply a longitudinal approach to investigate changes of partner behaviour before and after partners' selections of CRS alternatives. If one CRS alternative is selected but it failed to solve the conflicts, then the question of how foreign parent firms will select a follow-up strategy is also worthy to investigate.

References

Barden, Q.J., Steensma, H.K. and Lyles, M.A. (2005). 'The influence of parent control structure on parent conflict in Vietnamese international joint ventures: an organizational justice-based contingency approach'. *Journal of International Business Studies*, 36(2), 156–174.

Bener, M. and Glaister, K.W. (2010). 'Determinants of performance in international joint ventures'. *Journal of Strategy and Management*, 3(3), 188–214.

Bisseling, D. and Sobral, F. (2011). 'A cross-cultural comparison of intragroup conflict in the Netherlands and Brazil'. *International Journal of Conflict Management*, 22(2), 151–169.

Boonsathorn, W. (2007). 'Understanding conflict management styles of Thais and Americans in multinational corporations in Thailand'. *International Journal of Conflict Management*, 18(2), 196–221.

Chung, C.C. and Beamish, P.W. (2010). 'The trap of continual ownership changes in international equity joint ventures'. *Organization Science* 21(5), 995–1015.

Collis, J. and Hussey, R. (2009). *Business research: A practical guide for undergraduate and postgraduate students*, 3rd edition. UK: Palgrave Macmillan.

Das, T.K. and Kumar, R. (2010). 'Interpretive schemes in cross-national alliances: Managing conflicts and discrepancies'. *Cross Cultural Management: An International Journal*, 17(2), 154–169.

De Dreu, C.K. and Weingart, L.R. (2003). 'Task versus Relationship Conflict, Team Performance, and Team Member Satisfaction: A Meta-Analysis'. *Journal of Applied Psychology*, 88(43), 741–749.

Ding, D.Z. (1996). 'Exploring Chinese conflict management styles in joint ventures in the People's Republic of China'. *Management Research News*, 19(9), 43–53.

Doucet, L., Jehn, K.A., Weldon, E., Chen, X. and Wang, Z. (2009). 'Cross-cultural differences in conflict management: An inductive study of Chinese and American managers'. *International Journal of Conflict Management*, 30(4), 355–376.

Drogendijk, R. and Slangen, A. (2006). 'Hofstede, Schwartz, or managerial perceptions? The effects of different cultural distance measures on establishment mode choices by multinational enterprises'. *International Business Review*, 15(4), 361–380.

Fey, C.F. and Beamish, P.W. (1999). 'Strategies for Managing Russian International Joint Venture Conflict'. *European Management Journal*, 17(1), 99–106.

Geringer, J.M., and Hebert, L. (1991). 'Measuring performance of international joint ventures'. *Journal of International Business Studies*, 22(2), 249–263

Gulati, R. (1995). 'Does familiarity breed trust? The implications of repeated ties for contractual choice in alliances'. *Academy of Management Journal*, 38(1), 85–112.

Han, G. and Harms, P.D. (2010). 'Team identification, trust, and conflict: a medication model'. *International Journal of Conflict Management*, 21(1), 20–43.

Hennart, J.M.A., Kim, D.J. and Zeng, M. (1998). 'The impact of joint venture status on the longevity of Japanese stakes in U.S. manufacturing affiliates'. *Organization Science*, 9(3), 382–395.

Hsieh, L.H.Y., Rodrigues, S.B. and Child, J. (2010). 'Risk perception and post-formation governance in international joint ventures in Taiwan: The perspective of the foreign partner'. *Journal of International Management*, 16(3), 288–303.

Killing J.P. (1983). *Strategies for Joint Ventures Success*. Praeger Publishers, New York.

Kim, T.Y., Wang, C., Kondo, M. and Kim, T.H. (2007). 'Conflict management styles: the differences among the Chinese, Japanese and Koreans'. *International Journal of Conflict Management*, 18(1), 23–40.

Komarraju, M., Dollinger, S.J. and Lovell, J.L. (2008). 'Individualism-collectivism in horizontal and vertical directions as predictors of conflict management styles'. *International Journal of Conflict Management*, 19(1), 20–35.

Krishnan, R., Martin, X. and Noorderhaven, N.G. (2006). 'When does trust matter to alliance performance?'. *Academy of Management Journal*, 49(5), 894–917.

Krone, K. and Steimel, S. (2013). 'Cooperative struggle: Re-framing intercultural conflict in the management of Sino-American joint ventures'. *Journal of international and intercultural communication*, 6(4), 259–279.

Kwon, Y.-C. (2013). 'Ownership decisions, resource-sharing and performance in international joint ventures'. *Advances in Management*, 6(10), 24–33.

Lane, P. Salk, J.E. and Lyles, M.A. (2001). 'Absorptive capacity, learning, and performance in international joint ventures'. *Strategic Management Journal*, 22(12), 1139–1161.

Lin, X. and Germain, R. (1998). 'Sustaining Satisfactory Joint Venture Relationships: The role of conflict resolution strategy'. *Journal of International Business Studies*, 29(1), 179–196.

Lin, X. and Wang, C.C.L. (2002). 'Relational contexts of conflict resolution strategies in international joint ventures: An intra-Asia case'. *Journal of Relationship Marketing,* 1(3/4), 23–35.

Lu, L-T. (2006). 'Conflict resolution strategy between foreign and local partners in joint ventures in China'. *Journal of American Academy of Business,* 8(1), 236–240.

Ma, Z. Lee Y. and Yu, K.-H. (2008). 'Ten years of conflict management studies: Themes, concepts and relationships'. *International Journal of Conflict Management,* 19(3), 234–248.

Makino, S. and Beamish, P.W. (1999). 'Matching strategy with ownership structure in Japanese joint ventures'. *The Academy of Management Executive,* 13(4), 17–28.

Nguyen, H.L. (2009). 'Do partners´ differences affect international joint venture control and performance?'. *Journal of International Business Research,* 8(2), 67–86.

Nguyen, H.L. and Larimo, J. (2009). 'Foreign Parent Strategies, Control and International Joint Venture Performance'. *International Business Research,* 2(1), 1–13.

Nguyen, H.L. and Larimo, J. (2011). 'Determinant of conflict resolution strategies in International Joint Ventures: An Integrative Theoretical Framework'. *Journal of Transnational Management,* 16(2), 116–132.

O'Donnell, S.W. (2000). 'Managing foreign subsidiaries: agents of headquarters, or an interdependent network?'. *Strategic Management Journal,* 21(5), 525–548.

Onishi, J. and Bliss, R.E. (2006). 'In search of Asia ways of managing conflict: a comparative study of Japan, Hong Kong, Thailand and Vietnam'. *International Journal of Conflict Management,* 17(3), 203–225.

Pajunen, K. and Fang, L. (2013). 'Dialectical tensions and path dependence in international joint venture evolution and termination'. *Asia Pacific Journal of Management,* 30(2), 577–600.

Rahim, M.A. (1983). 'A measure of styles of handling interpersonal conflict'. *Academy of Management Journal,* 26(2). 361–376.

Rahim, M.A. and Bonoma, T.V. (1979). 'Managing organizational conflict: a model for diagnosis and intervention'. *Psychological Reports,* 44(3), 1323–1344.

Robbins, S.P. (2005). *Organizational Behavior,* 11th edition. Upper Saddle River, NJ: Prentice-Hall.

Schaan, J.L. (1983). *Parent ownership and joint venture success: The case of Mexico.* Doctoral Dissertation, University of Western Ontario.

Silva, S.C.L.C. (2007). *The Impact of Trust and Relational Quality in the Performance of International Alliances.* Unpublished doctoral dissertation, University College Dublin.

Thomas, K.J. (1976). *Conflict and Conflict Management.* Chicago: Rand McNally.

Traavik, L.E.M. (2011). 'Is bigger better? Dyadic and multiparty integrative negotiations'. *International Journal of Conflict Management,* 22 (2), 190–210.

Wang, C.L., Lin, X., Chan, A.K.K. and Shi, Y. (2005). 'Conflict handling styles in international joint ventures: Across cultural and cross national comparison'. *Management International Review,* 45(1), 3–21.

Weiss, S.E. (1990). 'The long path to the IBM-Mexico agreement: an analysis of the microcomputer investment negotiations, 1983–1986'. *Journal of International Business Studies,* 21(4), 565–596.

White III, O.G., Joplin, J.R.W. and Salama, M.F. (2007). 'Contracts and CRS in foreign ventures: a transaction cost perspective'. *International Journal of Conflict Management,* 18(4), 376–389.

Yavas, U., Eroglu, D. and Eroglu, S. (1994). 'Sources and management of conflict: The case of Saudi-US joint ventures'. *Journal of International Marketing,* 2(3), 61–82.

9
Determinants of Foreign Firms' Collective Action in Emerging Economies: Evidence from India

Vikrant Shirodkar

Introduction

Emerging economies are increasingly becoming long-term investment locations for Multinational Enterprises (MNEs) from developed countries. An important facet of foreign firms' strategies in emerging economies is to engage in the policymaking process of these economies, as a means to reduce the negative impact of uncertain institutional environments and to shape host-government policy in a way that is conducive to their long-term business operations (Ahuja and Yayavaram, 2011; Li, Zhou and Shao, 2008; Luo, 2001, 2006; Sun, Mellahi and Thun, 2010; Zhou, Poppo and Yang, 2008). A key decision for firms in this regard is about their nature of participation in the policymaking process (Hillman and Hitt, 1999; Hillman, Keim and Schuler, 2004). While some firms may choose to participate in the policy process on an *individual* basis – that is, without co-acting with other firms, others may decide to participate *collectively*, or in a collaborative manner, such as through associations of firms belonging to the industry/sector or with those that collate the voices of firms across industry verticals (Astley and Fombrun, 1983). By engaging in collective action, foreign firms can influence policy and governance issues such as product quality standards, codes of conduct and environmental protection that are of collective interest (Boddewyn and Doh, 2011).

Despite differences in political environments across emerging economies, in general, the transition process of emerging economies from agriculture-based economies to market-based economies has given rise to a large number of business and non-business associations that allow for collective voices to be heard as part of the industrial policymaking process in these economies (Kochanek, 1996). These associations provide developed country MNEs with legitimate mechanisms to participate in the policymaking process of these economies. For example, in India, the Associated Chambers of Commerce (Assocham) represents the collective interests of foreign firms (Kochanek,

1996). Similarly in China, the All-China Federation of Trade Unions (ACTFU) and the Chinese People's Political Consultative Conference (CPPCC) have been important associations that have influenced industrial policymaking over decades (Chan, 1993). Yet, research on this *collective* aspect of business-government interface within the context of emerging economies has attracted limited attention. Most of the research on political activities of firms in emerging economies has been interested in mainly MNEs' *individual* political activities, such as the creation and management of ties to politicians (Li, Zhou et al., 2008; Luo, 2001; Peng and Luo, 2000; Sun et al., 2010; Zhou et al., 2008) and the creation and exploitation of family or other social networks (Dieleman and Boddewyn, 2012). While this focus on *individual* ties was due to lack of institutional support to participating in collective structures, recent developments in the institutional environment in emerging economies have increased the scope for foreign firms to pursue political action through *collective* means.

From a theoretical perspective, prior studies on the *determinants* of firms' collective action have suggested that firms in fragmented industries would be more likely to influence policy through collective means, whereas those in concentrated industries would be more likely to act individually (Grier, Munger and Roberts, 1994; Hillman and Hitt, 1999; Ozer and Lee, 2009). Studies have also highlighted the role of institutional factors such as the degree of corporatism vs. pluralism of a host country on the choices of individual vs. collective action (Hillman, 2003; Hillman and Wan, 2005). Although few studies have focused on firm-level determinants of this choice, such as firm size and age (Bennett, 1995, 1998; Hillman, 2003), there is a general lack of research on the underlying determinants of MNEs' choices of political action arising from their 'interdependencies' on the external environment (Pfeffer and Salancik, 1978), in particular on their interdependencies stemming from the criticality of locally available resources in host countries and due to path dependencies of learning from local business practices and networks (Pierson, 2000). Such dependencies could potentially be an important rationale for firms' collective action, particularly within the context of emerging economies in which MNEs depend on a variety of locally available resources, and on local business networks (Meyer, Estrin, Bhaumik and Peng, 2009). Reflecting on the importance of these issues, scholars have recently suggested resource dependence theory (RDT) as an important and underexploited lens in studying political activities of firms in an international context (Hillman, Withers and Collins, 2009).

This study aims to examine this perspective by focusing on subsidiaries of developed-country MNEs operating in India. Within this context the key research question is to explain the firm-level determinants of MNEs' collective action in emerging economies. More specifically, I aim to investigate the extent to which MNEs' criticality of host-country resources and MNEs' business ties in the host country determine the extent to which the subsidiary would be involved in collective action.

The remainder of the paper is structured as follows: The next section provides a brief review of literature relating to the concepts used in this study. Later, I use resource dependency theory and the notions of path dependence to develop the hypotheses. I then explain the research context, data basis and measures used in the study before presenting the findings. This is followed by the discussion of the findings and a conclusion that highlights the paper's contributions to research and practice.

Corporate political action in developed vs. emerging economies

Studies on the differences between developed and emerging economies with respect to firms' choices regarding political action have mainly emphasised upon two factors. *Firstly* with respect to the general rationale of pursuing political action, scholars have suggested that in developed countries, political action is most likely associated with gaining from opportunities from access to political stakeholders (Hillman, 2005; Hillman, Zardkoohi and Bierman, 1999; Lester, Hillman, Zardkoohi and Cannella, 2008), whereas in developing and emerging markets, due to the greater and unpredictable influence of host-country government on business operations, political action is considered important both for survival and to gain a competitive advantage (Getz, 1997). For instance, in the United States, firms employing ex-politicians on their boards were found to be associated with better performance outcomes (Hillman, 2005), and those adopting political strategies were able to raise costs for their rival firms (McWilliams, Fleet and Cory, 2002). Although firms in emerging economies have also gained an advantage from individual political connections (Fisman, 2001), these connections have also proven to be detrimental in the long term (Li, Poppo and Zhou, 2008) or due to specific political events such as when autocratic regimes collapsed (Dieleman and Boddewyn, 2012). *Secondly*, scholars have emphasised that differences between political and cultural systems between developed and emerging economies make corporate political action different in these contexts (Gao, 2006). Within this context the existence and effectiveness of supporting institutions and business-government interfaces make the adoption of various political strategies legitimate within the context of developed countries (Hillman and Hitt, 1999; Hillman et al., 2004), and the lack of such institutions, or the ineffectiveness of available interfaces, makes the adoption of these choices difficult within the context of emerging economies (Rizopoulos and Sergakis, 2010; Zhilong and Xinming, 2007). Due to such institutional 'voids' in emerging markets (Khanna, Palepu, and Sinha, 2005), firms' political activities have predominantly focused on the role of creating and managing informal and individual ties to political decision makers that would allow potential firms to gain individual benefits (Li, Zhou et al., 2008; Luo, 2001; Sheng, Zhou and Li, 2011). For example, Sun, Mellahi and Wright (2012) have highlighted the importance of guanxi-networks in China, and Sawant (2012) has underlined the importance of firms' building long-term relationships with government officials in India. However, at the same time, it is also suggested that recent institutional developments in emerging economies have started to increase the scope for foreign firms to adopt other/additional types of political strategies as described by Hillman and colleagues (Hillman and Hitt, 1999; Hillman et al., 2004). For instance, in India, several favourable outcomes associated with firms' individual political connections and the exploitation of family networks in gaining business opportunities are being linked to corruption (Economist, 2014). Reflecting on this change in the institutional environment in emerging economies, scholars have begun to test the evidence of potentially legitimate political strategies (such as through collective associations) to analyse the non-market activities adopted by foreign firms operating in emerging economies (e.g. Puck, Rogers and Mohr, 2013).

Insights on collective action

Seminal past studies on collective action (Olson, 1965) primarily suggest that common interests of a group of organisations are the basis of participating collectively in political action, and that in comparison to individuals, groups of people or organisations are more efficient in deriving economic incentives for all. Additionally, organisations may also be motivated to join groups in order to win prestige, respect, friendship and other 'social capital' (Tsai and Ghoshal, 1998). Scholars have also highlighted the importance of different types of collectives, such as agglomerate, confederate, conjugate and organic collectives, and that each of these forms is used to cater to the needs of a distinct species of firms (Astley and Fombrun, 1983). Overall, when the outcomes of government policy are applicable to a group of firms as a whole, certain firms may show greater activeness and take the 'lead' on issues, while others may prefer to enjoy the free-rider benefits through passive participation (Yoffie, 1987); yet 'followers' are also required to compromise their individual interests to achieve collective objectives (Lenway and Rehbein, 1991). Thus, a distinction exists between firms that participate actively in collective action and those that prefer to act individually (Hillman and Hitt, 1999; Hillman et al., 2004; Lenway and Rehbein, 1991). Studies have found several determinants of this choice. Most notably. it has been established that large firms in concentrated industries are likely to act individually, whereas small firms in fragmented industries would be politically active through collective means (Hillman et al., 2004; Lenway and Rehbein, 1991; Masters and Keim, 1985; Salamon and Siegfried, 1977). Based on the *resource dependence theory* (Pfeffer and Salancik, 1978), this difference is explained by the fact that firms in a concentrated industry would compete over the same set of critical resources and would be less likely to resolve uncertainties

over access to critical resources collectively. Yet scholars have argued that collective action may be pursued through informal leadership in concentrated
industries – for instance, to circumvent antitrust activities of the government
(Astley and Fombrun, 1983). Using insights from *resource-based views* (Wernerfelt,
1984), Hillman (2003) found that among US-based firms in Europe, larger firms
with greater slack resources pursued individual strategies, whereas smaller firms
with less resources participated more actively in collective action through associations of industry horizontals and across industry verticals. Scholars have also
identified *institutional* determinants of this choice – such as the degree of a host
country's corporatism, defined as the extent to which the policymaking process
is centralised and achieved through consensus between a few powerful groups
(Siaroff, 1999). Accordingly, US-based firms in Europe showed greater activeness
in collective associations when the degree of host-country corporatism was less
(e.g. in the UK), whereas in highly corporatist countries (e.g. Austria, Sweden,
Norway), firms were found to pursue political strategies individually (Hillman,
2003; Hillman and Wan, 2005). In emerging economies, due to various institutional voids and asymmetrical and unreliable information obtained from publicly available sources, scholars have emphasised the role of informal collectives
such as business groups (Dieleman and Boddewyn, 2012; Guillén, 2000; Kock
and Guillén, 2001) and business ties (Sheng et al., 2011) as alternative mechanisms to political action. Due to the large and diversified nature of business
groups in emerging markets (for example, the Tata Group in India) such groups
often act as conjugate collectives. For example, by engaging in collaborative
projects and interlocking directorates among firms within these groups, these
groups as a whole try to fill up the institutional voids created by imperfect
capital, labour and product markets in emerging economies (Kedia, Mukherjee
and Lahiri, 2006). Such groups also take up leadership in other types of collectives such as trade associations and cartels in emerging markets (Chan, 1993;
Kochanek, 1996).

Overall, despite vast insights into the industry-level, firm-level and institutional determinants of collective action, I suggest that empirical research on this
aspect of political activity has been limited to domestic firms' collective action
in their home countries. In addition to this general lack of international focus,
limited attempts have been made to investigate the determinants of foreign
firms' collective action within the context of emerging markets (Richards and
Gugiatti, 2003; Zhilong and Xinming, 2007).

Theoretical background and hypotheses

First, the resource dependence theory (Pfeffer and Salancik, 1978) suggests that
organisations depend on *resources* from their environment, which consists of
the society in general, other businesses, interest groups and the government.

Furthermore, the *criticality* of a resource to an organisation determines the dependence of an organisation on its external environment. Critical resources are essential for an organisation's survival, and a resource is less critical if the organisation can use alternative ways to survive or alternative ways to procure the essential resources for its survival (Malatesta and Smith, 2011). Pfeffer and Salancik's (1978) concept of the 'negotiated environment' emphasises how organisations can reduce uncertainty related to dependence on critical resources by establishing collective structures that facilitate negotiation between organisations. Based on the above notions, it can be argued that collective political action is a means to managing uncertainty of access to resources that developed-country MNEs depend on in emerging economies.

Second, firms operating in emerging economies are known to benefit from 'managerial ties' to or informal managerial linkages across organisations (Li, Zhou et al., 2008; Luo, 2001; Sheng et al., 2011). Not only are *ties* with related businesses such as suppliers, key customers, marketing collaborators and technological collaborators important to foreign firms in order for them to gain information that may not be publicly available in emerging markets, but closer informal interaction and communication between managers in business ties also promote learning and mutual adjustment, eventually facilitating knowledge transfer (Sheng et al., 2011). From a *path-dependence* perspective (Pierson, 2000) one could argue that developed-country MNEs with ties to related businesses and other groups will use their learning from the development of ties to participate actively in collective associations in order to express their interest to the host-country government in a similar way.

Local resource criticality and foreign firms' collective action in emerging economies

According to resource dependence theory (Pfeffer and Salancik, 1978), collective action mechanisms such as trade associations and cartels serve as centralised mechanisms of achieving inter-firm linkages. Trade associations and cartels are also helpful in order to reduce interdependence and uncertainty of resources particularly when '(1) there is asymmetrical distribution of power at a regional or national level, and (2) there is need to establish homogeneity through standardisation of value systems, costing and information' (Pfeffer and Salancik, 1978: 175). Trade associations explicitly share cost data and market information between interdependent organisations; and by acquiring this information, organisations can plan coordinated actions. Some trade associations also sponsor research activities and allow new developments to be disclosed to all member firms that would otherwise result in surprise and disrupt the competitive equilibrium. It is therefore suggested that participation in collective structures such as trade associations, cartels and cross-sector alliances is a mechanism by which firms can reduce their dependence on critical resources that they depend on for their survival and competitive advantage.

In emerging economies, developed-country MNEs depend on access to new markets, skilled/unskilled labour at low cost and natural resources in order to survive, and these resources are frequently controlled by the government and its regulatory agencies (Meyer et al., 2009; Peng, Wang and Jiang, 2008). At the same time, foreign firms' resources, such as modern technology and innovative management styles, are critical for emerging economies to advance local economic and human development. Due to such interdependence, it is important for such MNEs to understand the collective interests of the industry and other social groups in emerging economies and to align their strategies with the collective interest (Lawton, Doh and Rajwani, 2014). Resources such as land, machinery, less-skilled labour and natural resources that are critical for many developed-country MNEs operating in emerging economies are often tightly controlled by government policymakers in emerging economies. Such resources are often more easily accessible to local business groups and a few trustworthy entrepreneurs, as compared to foreign firms (Guillen, 2000). Through collective action, such MNEs can better align their interests with the interests of the industry and development initiatives pursued by government policymakers and other environmental groups. Likewise, resources such as skills embedded in knowledge-workers, intellectual property and reputation are 'socially constructed' (Rao, 1994), and foreign firms critically depending on these types of resources are less likely to know who their targeted policymakers are in order to be contacted directly through individual mechanisms. Active participation in collective structures allows foreign firms to gain access to a wider variety of policymakers and powerful businesses in emerging economies. Thus, by using collective action, resources critical to foreign firms can be better safeguarded. Overall it is suggested that:

> *Hypothesis 1*: Foreign firms that depend critically on local resources in emerging economies are more active in collective action than those that don't depend on local resources.

Local business ties and foreign firms' collective political action in emerging economies

Foreign firms depend on business ties in emerging economies as a critical resource for gaining market information, specialised knowledge and network legitimacy (Sheng et al., 2011). Several studies have highlighted the role of knowledge associated with developing effective business networks as a key resource to the firm (Scarbrough, 1998; Scarbrough and Swan, 2001; Tsai, 2001; Tsai and Ghoshal, 1998). The path-dependence logic (Pierson, 2000) suggests that the experiential knowledge gained from managing external dependence by socially integrating with other related businesses will become an important part of the firms' overall absorptive capacity and will increase the likelihood that foreign firms manage their relationships with political actors in a similar way (Todorova and Durisin, 2007). With greater business ties, foreign firms can use specialised information and knowledge obtained from their informal networks to discuss issues such as compliance to licenses, software piracy or use of child labour (Bennett, 1995, 1998). Therefore, firms that have developed extensive business ties will participate in the policymaking process through collective action while managing issues and influencing host-country governments. Conversely, foreign firms that have few ties with local businesses may lack the confidence of dealing with the government in a collective way. Such firms are therefore likely to contact political actors on an individual basis. Based on this, it is suggested:

Hypothesis 2: Foreign firms that have larger business ties in emerging economies are more active in collective action than those that have fewer business ties.

Methodology

Research context and sample

India was chosen as the setting for this study because business associations and groups have been an integral part of industrial policymaking in India when compared to other large emerging economies, such as China or Russia (Hardgrave and Kochanek, 2008; Kochanek, 1974, 1996). Although India attracts high levels of FDI, many resources critical to foreign firms in India remain under government control (WIR, 2012). India thus provides a very good setting to investigate our hypotheses because we expect a high level of variability with regard to foreign firms' collective political action as well as the factors that have been argued to affect foreign firms' choice of collective action.

Data was collected through a web-based questionnaire survey of the top managers (CEOs, managing directors or country managers) of foreign subsidiaries operating in India. We obtained the 'India MNC Directory 2011–2012' from *Amelia Publications*, which provided contacts of such top managers of over 3000 firms. The directory included contacts of both (1) partly or wholly foreign-owned companies in India and (2) Indian firms that have overseas operations. From this directory, foreign-owned companies headquartered in nine countries (USA, UK, Australia, Germany, Netherlands, Italy, Malaysia, Sweden and Switzerland) were filtered out. With the exception of Malaysia, all other companies belonged to developed-country contexts. Subsidiaries in which the foreign partner held less than 25 per cent of the equity were excluded because in such subsidiaries foreign partners are understood to act as only 'sleeping partners' and thus are unlikely to be interested in political action (Delios and Beamish, 2001). Subsidiaries with incomplete contact details were also excluded. This reduced the list to 1910 foreign firms, each of which in 2011 received a link to a web-based questionnaire via email. About 900 emails could not be delivered and 'bounced', indicating that only 1010 emails were successfully delivered. After email and telephone follow-ups over a three-month period, 120 responses were obtained. 15 responses were further excluded due to missing data, resulting in 105 usable responses (10.24 per cent). This is similar to the response rate reported in prior research on political strategies (Puck et al., 2013). Due to the sensitivity of the questions asked, surveys on firms' political strategies usually achieve low response rate. In addition, the survey was carried out at a time when the Anna Hazare–led anti-corruption movement had gained momentum in India (Sengupta, 2012), and this may have further reduced firms' willingness to provide information on their political strategies.

Measures

In order to measure firms' *collective action* as the dependent variable, the method and construct suggested by Hillman (2003) and Hillman and Wan (2005) was used. Accordingly, survey participants were asked to indicate their level of activeness in four types of collective structures – horizontal trade associations, vertical trade associations, alliances with non-governmental/environmental groups and business advisory groups to the government on a five-point *likert*-type scale (α .73), and the overall collective activeness was taken as the average activeness in these associations.

To measure *local resource criticality* as the first *independent* variable, survey participants were asked to indicate their level of importance on a set of seven resources (land, machinery, unskilled labour, raw materials, specific technological know-how, highly skilled employees and reputation) as suggested by Srivastava, Fahey and Christensen (2001). A five-point *likert*-type scale (α .79) was used, and it calculated the overall criticality by taking the average importance placed over the 11 resources.

In order to measure foreign firms' *local business ties*, items suggested in previous studies by Sheng et al. (2011) and Peng and Luo (2000) were used. Survey respondents were asked to assess their firm's connections with (1) supplier firms, (2) customer firms, (3) marketing based collaborators and (4) technological collaborators (alpha .64). One item (ties with competitors) with low item-to-total correlation was eliminated to improve overall internal consistency.

Several controlling factors were used that were previously investigated to have an effect of firms' collective action in an international context. These included *subsidiary size,* measured by the number of employees; *subsidiary age,* measured by the number of years the subsidiary has been operating in India

(Hillman, 2003; Hillman and Wan, 2005); *industry type*, coded into a dummy – manufacturing (0) and services (1); and *MNEs' international experience*, measured as the number of foreign countries in which the MNE is present (Hillman, 2003; Hillman and Wan, 2005).

To avoid a common method bias, several *ex ante* measures were used during the design of the questionnaire (Chang, van Witteloostuijn and Eden, 2010). Most importantly, questionnaire items were adjusted to use terms that were familiar to Indian managers in order to minimise ambiguity; and survey participants were assured of confidentiality and anonymity and were assured that there are no right and wrong answers. Two *ex post* approaches were also used to check for a potentially common method bias. First, Harman's single factor test (Podsakoff, Mackenzie and Lee, 2003) did not indicate a common method bias. Second, the partial correlation procedure using the *marker* technique (Lindell and Whitney, 2001) was used to test for a common method bias. A marker variable (managerial autonomy) that was not related to resource criticality; business ties and collective action were used. This variable was not significantly associated with any of variables, indicating the absence of a common method bias.

A potential non-response bias was also tested for by comparing the responses of early respondents (first 30 responses) and late respondents (last 30 responses), and this comparison is in line with past research that has used this test (e.g. Armstrong and Overton, 1977; Keillor and Hult, 2004). There were no significant differences between the responses of early and late respondents, thus indicating that there was no bias.

Results

Table 9.1 provides the industry-wide distribution of the firms (that participated in survey) that are active vs. inactive in collective action. Table 9.2 provides the means, standard deviations (SD) and correlations. Although there were some correlations among our independent variables (see Table 9.1), these were very low, and multicollinearity was thus not considered to be an issue. The means and SDs of predictor variables indicates a good representation of firms with both high and low levels of resource criticality, business ties and foreign firms' participation in collective political action.

Linear multiple regression was used to test the hypotheses. Table 9.3 shows the regression results.

Model 1 shows the baseline model with the control variables only. Only *subsidiary age* appears to have a weak but statistically significant and positive effect on foreign firms' collective action ($p < .1$). This result indicates that foreign firms that have stayed longer in India were more active in participating in collective action as compared to foreign firms that have recently entered. The model also shows that the MNEs' overall *international experience* also had a

Table 9.1 Distribution of foreign firms' activeness in collective action by industry

Industry	MNEs Participating in Survey	*Inactive* in Collective Action	*Active* in Collective Action
Agriculture, Forestry, Fishing and Hunting	1	0	1
Mining, Quarrying, and Oil and Gas Extraction	2	1	1
Energy or Utilities	4	3	1
Construction	2	2	0
Manufacturing	36	19	17
Wholesale Trade	3	1	2
Retail Trade or Merchandising	1	0	1
Logistics, Transportation or Warehousing	5	3	2
Information (Publishing, Motion Picture and Sound Recording, Broadcasting, Telecommunications and Data Processing)	6	1	5
Finance and Insurance	7	5	2
Real Estate and Rental and Leasing	3	1	2
Professional, Scientific and Technical Services	32	21	11
Management of Companies and Enterprises	1	0	1
Health Care or Social Assistance	1	0	1
Accommodation, Hotel and Food Services	1	0	1
Totals	105	57	48

significant and positive effect on foreign firms' activeness in collective participation ($p < .05$).

In model 2 the predictor variables have been added to the baseline model. The results show a highly significant positive relationship ($p < .001$) between criticality of local resources and foreign firms' collective action, thus supporting our

Table 9.2 Means and correlations

	Mean	SD	(1)	(2)	(3)	(4)	(5)	(6)	(7)
(1) Collective Action	3.07	.88	1						
(2) Local Resource Criticality	3.32	.85	.46**	1					
(3) Local Business Ties	3.85	.58	.39**	.13	1				
(4) Subsidiary Size	1969.06	6774.86	.19	.03	.21	1			
(5) Subsidiary Age	18.66	19.86	.28**	.05	.07	.17	1		
(6) Industry Dummy	0.61	.49	.02	−.23*	−.21*	.19	−.06	1	
(7) MNE International Experience	35.31	41.36	.33**	−.01	.23*	.09	.32**	−.02	1

Note: *p < .05; **p < 0.01; N=105.

Table 9.3 Linear regression results

	Model 1	Model 2
Independent Variables		
Local Resource Criticality		.42**
Local Business Ties		.50**
Control Variables		
Subsidiary Size	.00	.00
Subsidiary Age	.01+	.01*
Industry Dummy (1=services)	.12	.50**
MNE's International Experience	.01*	.01+
Adjusted R-square	.14	.40

Note: = 105; +p < 0.10; *p < .05; **p < 0.01.

first hypothesis. The model also provides support for our second hypothesis which suggested a positive association between business ties and foreign firms' collective action. There is significant association (p <. 01) between these variables and our second hypothesis is also supported. Among the control variables there is a significant association (p < .05) between industry and collective action, indicating that foreign firms belonging to the services sector are more active in collectives than firms belonging to the manufacturing sector.

Discussion and conclusion

Overall, this study emphasised the increasing importance of collective action among MNEs from developed countries operating in emerging economies as a result of institutional changes in these countries. Using resource dependence theory (RDT) (Pfeffer and Salancik, 1978), not only did this paper identify the role of external resource dependence, path dependence and prior learning (Pierson, 2000) in affecting this choice. The empirical results also provide support for both of the hypotheses regarding the role of resource criticality and business ties on foreign firms' collective action in emerging economies. *First*, the findings support the existence of a positive association between criticality of resources and foreign firms' adoption of a collective action in emerging economies in line with hypothesis 1. In line with resource dependence logic (Pfeffer and Salancik, 1978), this finding indicates that foreign firms that critically depend on local resources participate actively in collective structures so that they can align their interests with, and influence policies to ensure access to, critical local resources. *Second*, the study finds empirical support for the argument (hypothesis 2) that foreign firms' business ties in emerging economies increase the scope of their collective action towards political activities. While previous scholars have indicated that firms operating in emerging economies may use business ties as an alternative to political activities (Sheng et al., 2011), this paper argued that that due to the effects of path dependence and learning, business ties can lead to greater participation in collective political strategy. Thus, using the notions of path dependence and learning within the RDT framework, this paper sheds new light on the role of business ties as a determinant of foreign firms' political activities in emerging economies.

Overall, by using RDT as theoretical anchor, this paper also responds to the call for a better integration of the insights provided by this theory into the theory on corporate political action (Hillman et al., 2009). The study also extends previous research on political activities of firms anchored in RDT (e.g. Dieleman and Boddewyn, 2012; Meznar and Nigh, 1995) and contributes by extending the boundaries of Hillman and Hitt's (1999) typology of political strategies in the context of emerging economies, similar to recent studies that have done so (e.g. Puck et al., 2013). The paper's integration of the notions of path dependence (Pierson, 2000) and learning in the context of managing external dependence provides a starting point for theoretical extensions of resource dependence and institutional theory.

There are a number of limitations to this study which open new alleys for further research on the topic of foreign firms' political activities in emerging economies. First, future research could focus on comparative issues, such as differences between domestic and foreign firms' collective action in emerging economies; the role of institutional distance; and foreign firms' home-country imprinting, which could affect this choice. Second, a larger sample of firms would have helped to increase the robustness of the empirical results presented in this study. However, asking questions on political strategies is highly sensitive, particularly in emerging economies, where such information would not be publicly shared. Despite these limitations, I believe that this study enhances our general understanding of developed-country MNEs' strategies in emerging economies, and particularly that of foreign firms' choice of collective action in these economies.

References

Ahuja, G. and Yayavaram, S. (2011). 'Explaining Influence Rents: The Case for an Institutions-Based View of Strategy'. *Organization Science*, 22(6), 1631–1652.

Armstrong, J.S. and Overton, T.S. (1977). 'Estimating Nonresponse Bias in Mail Surveys'. *Journal of Marketing Research*, 14(3), 396–402.

Astley, W.G. and Fombrun, C.J. (1983). 'Collective Strategy: Social Ecology of Organizational Environments'. *Academy of Management Review*, 8(4), 576–587.

Bennett, R.J. (1995). 'The Logic of Local Business Associations: an Analysis of Voluntary Chambers of Commerce'. *Journal of Public Policy*, 15(03), 251–279.

Bennett, R.J. (1998). 'Explaining the Membership of Voluntary Local Business Associations: The Example of British Chambers of Commerce'. *Regional Studies*, 32(6), 503–514.

Boddewyn, J. and Doh, J. (2011). 'Global strategy and the collaboration of MNEs, NGOs, and governments for the provisioning of collective goods in emerging markets'. *Global Strategy Journal*, 1(3–4), 345–361. doi: 10.1002/gsj.26

Chan, A. (1993). 'Revolution or corporatism? Workers and trade unions in post-Mao China'. *The Australian Journal of Chinese Affairs*, 29, 31–61.

Chang, S.-J., van Witteloostuijn, A. and Eden, L. (2010). 'From the Editors: Common method variance in international business research'. *Journal of International Business Studies*, 41(2), 178–184.

Delios, A. and Beamish, P.W. (2001). 'Survival and Profitability: The Roles of Experience and Intangible Assets in Foreign Subsidiary Performance'. *Academy of Management Journal*, 44(5), 1028–1038.

Dieleman, M. and Boddewyn, J.J. (2012). 'Using Organization Structure to Buffer Political Ties in Emerging Markets: A Case Study'. *Organization Studies*, 33(1), 71–95.

Economist, T. (2014). 'Fighting corruption in India: A bad boom', available at http://www.economist.com/news/briefing/21598967–graft-india-damaging-economy-country-needs-get-serious-about-dealing-it

Fisman, R. (2001). 'Estimating the Value of Political Connections'. *The American Economic Review*, 91(4), 1095–1102.

Gao, Y. (2006). 'Corporate political action in China and America: a comparative perspective'. *Journal of Public Affairs*, 6(2), 111–121.

Getz, K.A. (1997). 'Research in Corporate Political Action'. *Business & Society*, 36(1), 32–72.

Grier, K.B., Munger, M.C. and Roberts, B.E. (1994). 'The Determinants of Industry Political Activity, 1978—1986'. *The American Political Science Review*, 88(4), 911–926.

Guillen, M.F. (2000). 'Business groups in emerging economies: A resource-based view'. [Article]. *Academy of Management Journal*, 43(3), 362–380.

Hardgrave, R.L. and Kochanek, S.A. (2008). *India : government and politics in a developing nation*. Boston: Thomson/Wadsworth.

Hillman, A.J. (2003). 'Determinants of Political Strategies in U.S. Multinationals'. *Business & Society*, 42(4), 455–484.

Hillman, A.J. (2005). 'Politicians on the Board of Directors: Do Connections Affect the Bottom Line?'. *Journal of Management*, 31(3), 464–481.

Hillman, A.J. and Hitt, M.A. (1999). 'Corporate Political Strategy Formulation: A Model of Approach, Participation, and Strategy Decisions'. *The Academy of Management Review*, 24(4), 825–842.

Hillman, A.J. Keim, G.D., and Schuler, D. (2004). 'Corporate Political Activity: A Review and Research Agenda'. *Journal of Management*, 30(6), 837–857.

Hillman, A.J. and Wan, W.P. (2005). 'The determinants of MNE subsidiaries' political strategies: evidence of institutional duality'. *Journal of International Business Studies*, 36(3), 322–340.

Hillman, A.J. Withers, M.C. and Collins, B J. (2009). 'Resource Dependence Theory: A Review'. *Journal of Management*, 35(6), 1404–1427.

Hillman, A.J., Zardkoohi, A. and Bierman, L. (1999). 'Corporate political strategies and firm performance: indications of firm-specific benefits from personal service in the U.S. government'. *Strategic Management Journal*, 20(1), 67–81.

Kedia, B.L., Mukherjee, D. and Lahiri, S. (2006). 'Indian business groups: Evolution and transformation'. *Asia Pacific Journal of Management*, 23(4), 559–577.

Keillor, B.D. and Hult, G. (2004). 'Predictors of firm-level political behavior in the global business environment: an investigation of specific activities employed by US firms'. *International Business Review*, 13(3), 309–329.

Khanna, T., Palepu, K.G. and Sinha, J. (2005). *Strategies that fit emerging markets* (Vol. 83). Boston: Harvard Business School Publishing Corporation.

Kochanek, S.A. (1974). *Business and politics in India*. Berkeley: University of California Press.

Kochanek, S.A. (1996). 'Liberalisation and business lobbying in India'. *The Journal of Commonwealth & Comparative Politics*, 34(3), 155–173.

Kock, C.J. and Guillén, M.F. (2001). 'Strategy and structure in developing countries: Business groups as an evolutionary response to opportunities for unrelated diversification'. *Industrial and Corporate Change*, 10(1), 77–113

Lawton, T.C., Doh, J.P. and Rajwani, T. (2014). 'Aligning for Advantage: Competitive Strategies for the Political and Social Arenas'. *OUP Catalogue*.

Lenway, S.A. and Rehbein, K. (1991). 'Leaders, Followers, and Free Riders: An Empirical Test of Variation in Corporate Political Involvement'. *The Academy of Management Journal*, 34(4), 893–905.

Lester, RH., Hillman, A., Zardkoohi, A. and Cannella, A.A. (2008). 'Former Government Officials as Outside Directors: The Role of Human and Social Capital'. *Academy of Management Journal*, 51(5), 999–1013.

Li, J.J., Poppo, L. and Zhou, K.Z. (2008). 'Do managerial ties in China always produce value? Competition, uncertainty, and domestic vs. foreign firms'. *Strategic Management Journal*, 29(4), 383–400.

Li, J.J., Zhou, K.Z. and Shao, A.T. (2008). 'Competitive position, managerial ties, and profitability of foreign firms in China: an interactive perspective'. *Journal of International Business Studies*, 40(2), 339–352.

Lindell, M.K. and Whitney, D.J. (2001).'Accounting for common method variance in cross-sectional research designs'. *Journal of Applied Psychology*, 86(1), 114–121.

Luo, Y. (2001). 'Toward a Cooperative View of MNC-Host Government Relations: Building Blocks and Performance Implications'. *Journal of International Business Studies*, 32(3), 401–419.

Luo, Y. (2006). 'Political behavior, social responsibility, and perceived corruption: a structuration perspective'. *Journal of International Business Studies*, 37(6), 747–766.

Malatesta, D. and Smith, C.R. (2011). 'Resource Dependence, Alternative Supply Sources, and the Design of Formal Contracts'. *Public Administration Review*, 71(4), 608–617.

Masters, M.F. and Keim, G.D. (1985). 'Determinants of PAC Participation Among Large Corporations'. *The Journal of Politics*, 47(04), 1158–1173. doi: 10.2307/2130811

McWilliams, A., Fleet, D.D.V. and Cory, K.D. (2002). 'Raising Rivals' Costs Through Political Strategy: An Extension of Resource-based Theory'. *Journal of Management Studies*, 39(5), 707–724.

Meyer, K.E., Estrin, S., Bhaumik, S.K. and Peng, M.W. (2009). 'Institutions, resources, and entry strategies in emerging economies'. *Strategic Management Journal*, 30(1), 61–80.

Olson, M. (1965). *The logic of collective action: Public goods and the theory of group.* Cambridge, MA: Harvard University Press.

Ozer, M. and Lee, S.-H. (2009). 'When Do Firms Prefer Individual Action to Collective Action in The Pursuit of Corporate Political Strategy? A New Perspective on Industry Concentration'. *Business & Politics*, 11(1), 1–21.

Peng, M. and Luo, Y. (2000). 'Managerial Ties and Firm Performance in a Transition Economy: The Nature of a Micro-Macro Link'. *Academy of Management Journal*, 43(3), 486–501.

Peng, M., Wang, D. and Jiang, Y. (2008). 'An institution-based view of international business strategy: a focus on emerging economies'. *Journal of International Business Studies*, 39(5), 920–936.

Pfeffer, J. and Salancik, G.R. (1978). *The external control of organizations: a resource dependence perspective.* Stanford: Stanford Business Books.

Pierson, P. (2000). 'Increasing Returns, Path Dependence, and the Study of Politics'. *The American Political Science Review*, 94(2), 251–267.

Podsakoff, P.M., Mackenzie, S.B. and Lee, J.-Y. (2003). 'Common Method Biases in Behavioral Research: A Critical Review of the Literature and Recommended Remedies'. *Journal of Applied Psychology*, 88(5), 879–903.

Puck, J., Rogers, H. and Mohr, A.T. (2013). 'Flying under the radar: Foreign firm visibility and the efficacy of political strategies in emerging economies'. *International Business Review*, 22(6), 1021–1033.

Rao, H. (1994). 'The Social Construction of Reputation: Certification Contests, Legitimation, and the Survival of Organizations in the American Automobile Industry: 1895–1912'. *Strategic Management Journal*, 15(S1), 29–44.

Richards, A. and Gugiatti, M. (2003). 'Do collective action clauses influence bond yields? New evidence from emerging markets'. *International Finance*, 6(3), 415–447.

Rizopoulos, Y.A. and Sergakis, D.E. (2010). 'MNEs and policy networks: Institutional embeddedness and strategic choice'. *Journal of World Business*, 45(3), 250–256.

Salamon, L.M. and Siegfried, J.J. (1977). 'Economic power and political influence: The impact of industry structure on public policy'. *The American Political Science Review*, 1026–1043

Sawant, R.J. (2012). 'Asset Specificity and Corporate Political Activity in Regulated Industries'. *Academy of Management Review*, 37(2), 194–210.

Scarbrough, H. (1998). 'Path(ological) Dependency? Core Competencies from an Organizational Perspective'. *British Journal of Management*, 9(3), 219–232.

Scarbrough, H. and Swan, J. (2001). 'Explaining the Diffusion of Knowledge Management: The Role of Fashion'. *British Journal of Management*, 12(1), 3–12.

Sengupta, M. (2012). 'Anna Hazare and the Idea of Gandhi'. *The Journal of Asian Studies*, 71(3), 593–601. doi: doi:10.1017/S0021911812000617

Sheng, S., Zhou, K.Z. and Li, J.J. (2011). 'The Effects of Business and Political Ties on Firm Performance: Evidence from China'. *Journal of Marketing*, 75(1), 1–15.

Siaroff, A. (1999). 'Corporatism in 24 industrial democracies: Meaning and measurement'. *European Journal of Political Research*, 36, 175–205.

Srivastava, R.K., Fahey, L. and Christensen, H.K. (2001). 'The resource-based view and marketing: The role of market-based assets in gaining competitive advantage'. *Journal of Management*, 27(6), 777–802.

Sun, P., Mellahi, K. and Thun, E. (2010). 'The dynamic value of MNE political embeddedness: The case of the Chinese automobile industry'. *Journal of International Business Studies*.

Sun, P., Mellahi, K. and Wright, M. (2012). 'The Contingent Value of Corporate Political Ties'. *Academy of Management Perspectives*, 26(3), 68–82.

Todorova, G. and Durisin, B. (2007). 'Absorptive capacity: Valuing a reconceptualization'. *Academy of Management Review*, 32(3), 774–786. doi: 10.5465/amr.2007.25275513

Tsai, W. (2001). 'Knowledge Transfer in Intraorganizational Networks: Effects of Network Position and Absorptive Capacity on Business Unit Innovation and Performance'. *Academy of Management Journal*, 44(5), 996–1004.

Tsai, W. and Ghoshal, S. (1998). 'Social Capital and Value Creation: The Role of Intrafirm Networks'. *The Academy of Management Journal*, 41(4), 464–476.

Wernerfelt, B. (1984). 'A resource based view of the firm'. *Strategic Management Journal*, 5(2), 171–180

WIR. (2012). *World Investment Report 2012: Towards a New Generation of Investment Policies*. New York and Geneva: UNCTAD.

Yoffie, D.B. (1987). 'Corporate strategies for political action: A rational model'. In A. Marcus, A. Kaufman and D. Beam (Eds), *Business Strategy and Public Policy*. New York: Quorum, pp. 43–60.

Zhilong, T. and Xinming, D. (2007). 'The determinants of corporate political strategy in Chinese transition'. *Journal of Public Affairs*, 7(4), 341–356.

Zhou, K.Z., Poppo, L. and Yang, Z. (2008). 'Relational ties or customized contracts? An examination of alternative governance choices in China'. *Journal of International Business Studies*, 39(3), 526–534.

Part IV

Coming In and Going Out: Dynamic Interaction between Foreign and Local Firms

10
Human Capital and Conflict Management in the Entrepreneur-Venture Capitalist Relationship: The Entrepreneurs' Perspective

Huan Zou, Grahame Boocock and Xiaohui Liu

Introduction

Modern venture capital is recognised as an important catalyst for fostering entrepreneurship, innovation and economic growth, especially in emerging economies (Lerner, 1999). Venture capital firms seek to support enterprises that progress within a relatively short space of time from start-ups or small beginnings to high growth firms (Shane, 2008). Value-adding activities by venture capitalists (VCs) can result in higher survival rates for investee firms compared to similar 'non-venture capital' ventures (Arthurs and Busenitz, 2006). Yet, the input of VCs does not always result in positive outcomes (Zacharakis and Meyer, 2000), and failure or weak performance in investee firms is frequently explained by conflict in the entrepreneur–venture capitalist (E-VC) relationship (Higashide and Birley, 2002; Yitshaki, 2008). Indeed, conflict is almost unavoidable in a relationship often defined by control rather than trust (Das and Teng, 2001) and where power asymmetry typically favours the investors (Pfeffer and Salancik, 2003). The root of much conflict is a failure to agree on the goals to be achieved by an investee firm or the strategy to be adopted in pursuit of those goals (Jehn and Mannix, 2001).

Although there is growing academic interest in the development of venture capital industries in emerging economies (Ahlstrom, Bruton and Yeh, 2007), the majority of these studies have been conducted from the perspective of VCs; very few studies have taken into account the views of entrepreneurs or CEOs in venture capital-backed firms (Ehrlich et al., 1994; Yitshaki, 2008). The causes and consequences of conflict still require greater academic scrutiny, (Manigart and Sapienza, 2000; Zacharakis et al., 2010), and we view the role of entrepreneurs' human capital as critical in this context. If entrepreneurs and VCs can build a productive relationship based on mutual respect and trust, this should enhance a portfolio firm's prospects of survival and/or success and, at the same time, increase the chance of a healthy return for the venture capital fund.

195

Conflict resolution thus benefits investee firms and their backers and generates wealth in the wider economy. Specifically, we contend that the human capital of entrepreneurs gives them the capacity to face the challenges of developing their firms under VCs' supervision. However, our knowledge of the interaction between human capital and conflict management is limited. To address this gap in the existing literature, we focus on two research questions:

1. What are the sources of conflict in the E-VC relationship, with particular reference to cultural factors?
2. How does the human capital of entrepreneurs affect their responses to managing conflict with VCs, especially foreign VCs?

China represents an interesting research setting. Its venture capital industry has been one of the fastest growing in the global venture capital market (Ahlstrom et al., 2007). Foreign VCs have played an increasingly important role in financing domestic new ventures, particularly in the high-technology sphere; foreign venture capital firms funded over 52 per cent of venture capital investments by number in China in 2010, representing 71 per cent of venture capital investment by value (Cai and Song, 2010). Our empirical research was conducted in Beijing and Shanghai, cities where large numbers of new ventures have been financed by venture capital (Cai and Song, 2010). Yet, this form of capital (whether from domestic or foreign sources) remains in short supply for many Chinese firms, and its impact on investee firms is underexplored (Xiao, 2011). It is therefore imperative that firms in receipt of venture capital are able to respond appropriately to conflict in the E-VC relationship.

This chapter makes a number of contributions to the literature. First, it adds a new dimension to existing studies by investigating how the human capital of entrepreneurs leads to the adoption of different strategies in the management of conflict with VCs. Second, our analysis is based upon in-depth interviews with nine entrepreneurs in receipt of venture capital funding and hence it complements previous studies conducted from the perspective of VCs. We offer new insights into how conflict stems from different cultural contexts of entrepreneurs and also their differing characteristics. Third, we put forward a series of propositions that enhance our understanding of the complexity of the E-VC relationship. Finally, our findings have important implications for all those seeking to maximise the positive impact of venture capital on entrepreneurial ventures.

Theoretical foundations

Conflict: sources and resolution

Conflict refers to a situation where the parties in a relationship are aware of, yet still seek to occupy, a position that is incompatible or irreconcilable with the wishes of others (Boulding, 1963; Jehn and Mannix, 2001). As stated earlier, conflict is almost unavoidable in the E-VC relationship (Higashide and Birley, 2002), commonly linked to a failure to agree on goals or the strategy to secure those goals (Jehn and Mannix, 2001; Zacharakis et al., 2010). However, Yitshaki (2008) argues that conflict in VC provision stems from three broad (and interlinked) *sources*: 'contractual' – covering a whole range of perceived contract violations, not just disputes over the best way to secure the goals laid down in the term sheet but also disagreements on the support provided by a venture fund, the imposition of a new management team, the timing of any VC exit, and so on (Parhankangas and Landström, 2004); 'contextual' – usually stemming from differences in perception over the competitive environment facing the investee firm or the firm's level of performance; and 'procedural' – largely relating to communication issues.

The role of different cultural contexts in creating conflict has been emphasised in both the general literature in this field (Tjsovold, Law and Sun, 2006) and also in VC-focused studies (Yitshaki, 2008). Cultural diversities can lead to procedural conflict between Chinese entrepreneurs and foreign VCs, for example, as Western VCs tend to concentrate on building relationships with the CEO, whereas their Chinese counterparts also maintain contact with senior and middle-ranked managers (Pukthuanthong and Walker, 2007). At the strategic level, contractual conflict might ensue in cases where indigenous entrepreneurs resent the imposition of short-term targets by Western VCs, rather than the longer-term, collectivist approach favoured by their Asian counterparts (Wright et al., 2005).

The literature in conflict management has proposed four approaches to *resolving* conflict – collaborating, competing, accommodating and avoiding (Deutsch, 1973; Thomas, 1976). The collaborative approach implies that one party attempts to work with the other in an effort to find a mutually acceptable solution; it requires the parties in conflict to be open, to share information and to be aware of their differences (Wang, Jing, and Klossek, 2007). This strategy creates shared understanding, and it usually results in positive and constructive outcomes (Yitshaki, 2008). The competing approach is employed when one party is resolute in what s/he believes and wants. This strategy implies that one party holds a position of power, expertise or strength and thus a high level of assertiveness; the needs and expectations of the other party are sometimes ignored (Rahim, 2002). The accommodating approach occurs where one party makes sacrifices to satisfy the requirements of the other; again, this may reflect a power-based relationship. Finally, the avoiding approach attempts to smooth over conflicts and minimise discussion of them (Chen, et al., 2005); this may involve turning away from conflict or even refusing to acknowledge its existence.

Human capital

Human capital gives entrepreneurs a reservoir of skills, knowledge and abilities to draw upon as they face ongoing challenges (Cooper, Estes and Allen, 2004;

Keong and Mei, 2010). Despite its importance, research on the relationship between human capital and conflict management has been limited (De Vries and Shields, 2006; Envick, 2005), especially in the E-VC relationship (Wright, Low and Davidson, 2001). Moreover, scholars have concentrated largely on establishing the psychological traits required by entrepreneurs in times of conflict (Cooper and Lucas, 2006) – for example, Timmons (1999) argues that successful entrepreneurs have the ability in their DNA to recover from adversity. However, we endorse the view of Morris (2002), who suggests that the sustainability of a venture depends more heavily on behavioural capabilities than psychological characteristics.

We view human capital as a spectrum of skills and knowledge with varying degrees of transferability. The acquisition of knowledge is a long-term process by which 'entrepreneurs transform experience into knowledge in disparate ways' (Politis, 2005: 408). As well as his/her formal education, an entrepreneur's previous start-up experience, knowledge of the industry and market, past employment experience, and technical knowledge can affect his/her behaviour and strategic decision making and, ultimately, firm performance (Bruderl, Preisendorfer and Ziegler, 1992; Bosma et al., 2004). We share the view that prior experience, education and personal background shape the perceptions and mindsets of entrepreneurs (Kor, Mahoney, and Michael, 2007), enabling them to make appropriate strategic responses in fast-changing external environments (Huff, 1990) or to develop early warning systems to visualise and anticipate future events (Cope, 2010).

Research methodology

While a positivist approach has dominated in entrepreneurship research, it is acknowledged (McDougall and Oviatt, 2000) that this stance may not have generated meaningful causal laws or principles in the context of entrepreneurial activities such as opportunity recognition or value creation – key goals of venture capital-backed firms (Shane, 2008). Coviello and Jones (2004) called for a more interpretive perspective. Our study answers this call. Drawing on the literature from the fields of conflict management and human capital, we utilised a number of in-depth case studies to examine how the characteristics of entrepreneurs affect their attitude and approach towards conflict and also their strategic responses to the resolution of conflict. Following established procedures for inductive research (Glaser, 1978; Miles and Huberman, 1994), we captured situated insights into the interaction of entrepreneurs and VCs as well as rich details and thematic descriptions of the E-VC relationship.

Sample selection

A common feature of interpretive studies is the use of small samples, yet a competent theoretical perspective can be developed as long as adequate contextualisation is preserved (Chapman and Smith, 2002). Researchers have to be pragmatic in choosing participants (Reid, Flowers and Larkin 2005), particularly where the topic under investigation is rare and issues of accessibility and willingness to participate are problematic (as was the case here).

We used the Thomson Financial Private Equity/Venture Capital Dataset to identify high-tech firms in China that had received VC investment. We emailed the research proposal to 200 firms, but only five firms indicated a willingness to participate. The very low response rate was not unexpected, mainly because of a reluctance to talk openly about conflict with VC investors. Nonetheless, five cases constituted an acceptable number for the initial round of interviews; the data were collected and analysed almost simultaneously, and it was evident that it was necessary to gather more data. We asked the initial interviewees to recommend other firms that had received VC investment. This snowball or chain sampling strategy (Hartley, 1994) secured an additional four participants. We called a halt to the interview programme only when we were satisfied that sufficient data had been collected on each of the issues of relevance to our research questions.

In total, nine interviews were completed, with entrepreneurs representing venture capital-backed firms in Beijing and Shanghai. Table 10.1 provides an anonymised profile of the participants as well as basic information on the firms and their venture capital investors. Table 10.2 captures the previous experience of the interviewees and summarises the networks available to them.

Findings

Sources of conflict in the E-VC relationship

We classify our findings by reference to Yitshaki's (2008) three sources of conflict (contractual, contextual and procedural), although the boundaries between these categories are somewhat blurred. Quotes from the interview transcripts are used sparingly to emphasise key issues or common themes.

Contractual conflict

This type of conflict emanated from disputes over the goals to be pursued by investee firms or the level of support provided by VCs. The analysis below shows that some of our sample firms avoided this type of conflict, whereas other firms had very different experiences.

In *Firms H and R*, both funded by Japanese and domestic VCs, there was a mutual acceptance of the goals to be pursued; for example, the CEO of *Firm H* stressed that 'We *[entrepreneur and VC Fund]* take decisions that achieve reliable and sustainable operations. The VCs have to immerse themselves in the firm for the long haul; they could not succeed if they just wanted to gamble and pursue short-term interests.' On similar lines, *Firm D* held fruitful discussions with its

Table 10.1 Basic information about the participants and the firms

Firm	Industry	Founding Year	Participant	VC	Interview Location
D	Internet audio video	2005	CEO	U.S. VC	Beijing
H	Internet 3D	2005	CEO	Japanese VC; Domestic Group Firm	Beijing
K	Internet search	2006	CTO	U.S. VC; Domestic Private Firm	Beijing
I	Mobile search	2005	CEO	U.S. VC	Shanghai
E	Internet service	2004	CEO	U.S. VC	Shanghai
R	DM service	2001	CFO	Japanese VC; Domestic Private Firm	Shanghai
V	Software	1995	CEO	U.S. VC; HK Public Firm	Beijing
N	Software	1994	CFO	Singaporean VC; Domestic Public Firm; Domestic State-owned Firm	Shanghai
Y	Robots	2007	Deputy GM	Domestic Private Firm	Beijing

VC-backer (the Asian arm of the venture capital unit formed by IDG – a global data company) to secure future growth by moving from a funding structure appropriate for angel investors into one which complied with NASDAQ listing requirements.

This level of agreement was not present in *Firms K, E and Y. Firms K and E* were funded partly or wholly by U.S. VC Funds, whereas *Firm Y* was backed by domestic venture capital. The CTO of *Firm K* pointed to fundamental differences in outlook ('We stood on different planets'), sentiments that were echoed by the CEO of *Firm E* (These guys *[VCs]* do not position themselves as value-added investors') and the deputy general manager (DGM) in *Firm Y* ('We have tried to meet the investors' short-term targets even though we knew that this would damage our long-term objectives').

In relation to the support provided, *Firm R* applauded its Japanese investors for promising (and then delivering) introductions to potential customers and suppliers, while *Firm D* praised its VCs for playing to the strengths of both parties: 'We are technically-proficient in the internet industry, but IDG have much greater expertise on commercial issues.' By contrast, *Firms K, E and Y* were disappointed with the support offered by their VCs – for example, the CEO of *Firm E* complained about the investors' failure to provide contacts: 'companies that we might acquire or who might partner with us'.

Table 10.2 Human capital of the entrepreneurs interviewed

Firm	Experience	Network
D	First-time entrepreneur	Former classmates form the founding team; limited networks
H	'90s: Manager of an Internet firm; '00s: Started an online book firm	Well-known in Internet sector; connections with VC community; friends from previous Internet ventures form the founding team;
K	First-time entrepreneur	Classmates form the founding team; limited network involvement
I	Over 15 years management experience in high-tech industry, including nine years in Great China region; Worked for a large MNE in '90s when it established a subsidiary in Shanghai; Started two firms in U.S. in '00s	Previous colleague at the MNEs form the founding team; good connections with U.S. VC community
E	First-time entrepreneur	Some connections with U.S. VC community
R	Worked for a large domestic firm in '90s in message servicing sector Started up business in customer databases in late '90s	Previous contact with VCs; Leading firm position in the industry
V	Worked for a large domestic firm in '90s in software industry; Started up two businesses in '90s	Well-known in software industry; good connections with VC community; contacts with previous colleagues, classmates and other players in the industry, both in China and the US
N	'90s: started up first business in IT equipment '00s: started up firm in software industry	Leading firm position in the market; previous contacts with VCs

Firms H, R, N and D could agree on the goals to be pursued with their VC backers, whereas *Firms K, E and Y* could not. There was a similar split of opinion concerning VCs' support. These outcomes cannot be explained solely by 'East versus West' disputes, as *Firm D* dealt with the local arm of a U.S.-based VC group while *Firm Y* was funded by a domestic venture capital. However, it was noticeable that first-time entrepreneurs *(K, E and Y)* tended to be involved in contractual conflict; *Firm D* was an exception – inexperienced entrepreneurs acknowledged the superior skills that the VCs could supply.

Contextual conflict

At the root of contextual conflict are differences in perceptions, attitudes and values between entrepreneurs and VCs (Yitshaki 2008). The impact of cultural differences was also a major factor under this heading. Contextual conflict was averted in cases where the firm and its VC investors shared the same time perspective or business orientation. For example, the CFO of *Firm R* conceded that he and his colleagues sometimes wanted to grasp opportunities immediately, whereas their Japanese investors might take a more cautious line: '*[Yet, overall]*... our VCs respect our experience and judgment, and we are lucky to have investors who are quite patient in relation to firm growth. The growth demands of U.S. investors would have had a serious impact on the confidence of our top management team.' *Firm H* said likewise: 'Our Japanese investors share similar ideas and philosophies with us, and they do not push us aggressively in a certain direction.'

These positive views can be contrasted with a range of complaints from other interviewees. In *Firm K*, for instance, U.S. VCs challenged the entrepreneurs on both operational issues and corporate strategies: 'The investors kept telling us how much profit we should generate, what we should do daily, what business model we should follow etc. To be honest, I am not happy with that.' In *Firm Y* the management team was prepared initially to work with the investors, but this situation deteriorated rapidly: 'We accept that the investor can give advice on strategies, such as the R&D to be undertaken, yet it is down to us to manage the company.' Disputes also arose when the entrepreneurs believed that VC appointees were not familiar with the Chinese environment. *Firm E* complained: '*[a female American-Chinese board member]* was supposed to guide us, but all her suggestions ended up as being irrelevant or inappropriate for the local market.'

Procedural conflict

In relation to procedural issues, various aspects of communication created difficulties for investee firms, but we also found several instances of positive interaction in the E-VC relationship. By way of illustration, *Firm H* stressed that 'communication is critical', and explained how the founder built up trust with investors by establishing monthly, face-to-face meetings, backed up by email or phone contact in the interim. Similarly, the CEO of *Firm V* stated that informal contacts with VCs beforehand ensure that: 'board meetings are productive and efficient in delivering decisions'.

The experiences of *Firms E and D* in communicating with their U.S. investors were very different. *Firm E* viewed the VCs' contribution as lacking empathy, and communications with investors were seen as a burden rather than as a support mechanism. The CEO of *Firm D* stated that the two IDG board members (both overseas Chinese) commute regularly between different continents: 'the VC appointees have too many projects, and they have limited time to take care of us or to communicate frequently with us.' Such problems were not confined to U.S. venture capitalists, as the experience of *Firm Y* illustrates. Contractual agreements with its domestic VC Fund were not supported by procedural guidelines; this created a situation of uncertainty and potential future conflict.

The experiences of five entrepreneurs *(Firms I, V, R, H and N)* were broadly positive in communicating with their investors. The other four participants *(Firms K, E, D and Y)* had all experienced communication problems or other procedural disputes – for example, *K and E* had severe difficulties in communicating with their US VCs, even though both firms had secured second-round VC funding, and *Firm D* felt that the investors did not provide enough dedicated local support. The range of discord cited by study's participants suggests that communication problems are often associated with other, deep-rooted sources of conflict.

Conflict resolution – the role of human capital

In the 'contractual' category, the human capital of the CEO in *Firm H* enabled him not only to obtain VC funding but also to secure a long-term collaboration that enabled this firm to thrive in a very competitive market (Internet 3D). In this (and other) instances, the entrepreneurs' stock of human capital had enabled them to anticipate and thus prevent conflict. Positive intentions to establish the motivations of VC investors and to explore collaboration and/ or compromise had improved the quality of decision making and generated benefits for all parties. By contrast, contractual conflict was prevalent when such flexibility and adaptability was absent, notably in *Firms K and E*; both firms were convinced that their VCs had consistently imposed unrealistic goals and provided inadequate support.

In relation to contextual factors, *Firm H* stressed that communication with their Japanese VCs was not just about 'procedure' but an important mechanism for maximising the potential of the business: 'We always prepare for the worst scenario then do our best to solve problems together; for instance, in the face of technical problems affecting the firm, we worked together to tackle this threat by recruiting specialist employees and seeking technology partners.' This willingness to accept help or advice, based on mutual respect, was also seen in *Firm R*. The CFO explained that the founder's experience and ability to judge market trends persuaded the VCs to allow the firm to dictate its overall growth strategy, yet the CFO admitted that VC expertise helped *Firm R* to improve budget control and investment appraisal. The representatives of *Firms N, I and V* also stressed the importance of accepting advice, albeit with limits on their willingness to accede to the demands of VCs.

Where conflict from contextual sources did arise, it usually stemmed from disagreements on the most appropriate strategy to be pursued in the face of rapidly changing competitive environments. This was most evident in *Firms K and E* (Internet-based firms) and *Y* (robotics). The U.S. investors in *Firm K* imposed their decisions on management: 'We had arguments over critical strategic decisions, but they had the final call. This definitely harmed the mental state of some of the key founders; they have left or are about to leave the firm. The more the investors got involved, the more damage they did to the firm'. Likewise, the CEO of *Firm E* accepted that he had lost control to the VCs, and he concluded, with an air of resignation, that, 'I don't see any possibility of resolving disputes with the investors. I have officially given up, although I am still on the board.'

The first-time entrepreneurs in *Firms K and E* (and *Firm Y* where similar issues were evident) did not have the capacity to leverage personal skills and experience to prevent or resolve conflict. They maintained a negative attitude towards the VCs and pursued a strategy of passive accommodation or outright avoidance towards conflict, and the firms' prospects were seriously compromised. However, not every first-time entrepreneur experienced contextual conflict – for example, *Firm D* pursued a collaborative approach that maximised the complementary skills of the two parties: 'We are technically very sound, but we lack an understanding of the wider business environment; *[by contrast]* our VCs have thorough insight into inter- and intra-industry competition, potential markets, legal issues, etc.'

For procedural disputes, effective communication proved to be a powerful mechanism for resolving such conflict. A majority of sample firms (*H, I, N, R and V*) had benefited from frequent and effective exchanges of information; the examples below demonstrate how the prior experience of key individuals helped VC-backed firms to lay the foundation for sound communications and collaboration with investors.

The CEO of *Firm H* argued that his prior entrepreneurial experience and his credibility within the VC community had been critical in forging a partnership with the firm's Japanese investors; he had the confidence to share risks as well as opportunities with the VCs: 'We know that VCs get quite concerned about technical, market and even business model risks; *[hence]* we are very frank with them'. The CEO of *Firm V* also stressed the value of informal meetings and contact with VCs in avoiding conflict and building trust; a key part of this process (also cited by *Firm H*) was to confront any problems quickly.

By contrast, the firms led by first-time founders had all experienced communication problems. For example, *Firms K and E* had enjoyed some degree of success but had encountered severe communication difficulties and faced an uncertain future; and the CEO of *Firm D* felt that communication was hindered by an absence of dedicated local support. These cases confirm that communication problems were often associated with other sources of conflict, but we propose that a lack of experience and adaptability were the underlying reasons for procedural conflict.

The evidence indicates that, whatever the source of conflict, experienced entrepreneurs can anticipate potential challenges by adopting collaborative (and proactive) strategies that enhance trust; this trust facilitates effective communication and reduces the incidence of misunderstanding. First-time entrepreneurs lack the requisite experience and personal skills to deal with challenges and conflict in the E-VC relationship; they find it very difficult to develop a productive relationship with VCs.

Discussion

In addressing our first research question, we verified that there are different sources of conflict in the E-VC relationship, yet our study extends our understanding of those sources to the Chinese (and wider) VC environment by taking cultural contexts into account. Specifically, we found that when entrepreneurs and VCs share the same goals or when they can negotiate mutually-agreed targets, the relationship tends to be productive and healthy. In contrast, goal divergence between the two parties leads to conflict. Likewise, when entrepreneurs value the support received from their VCs, the relationship was generally sound, especially in cases where the entrepreneurs and VCs had complementary skills. When entrepreneurs perceived that VCs had not fulfilled expectations or supplied anticipated benefits, conflict was present. Some VCs were viewed as unwanted external monitors rather than as valuable resources; there was also resentment when VCs were closely involved in the day-to-day management of firms. Hence, we propose:

> Proposition 1: Goal divergence and perceived deficiencies in the support from VCs are likely to lead to contractual conflict in the E-VC relationship.

Contextual conflict in our study stemmed from differing cultural strategic orientations, and this encompassed differing attitudes towards investee firm performance. Our interviewees confirmed that Asian VCs adopt a longer-term strategic orientation (Wright et al., 2005); a number of interviewees were able to build strategic relationships on this basis. Conversely, U.S. investors were generally perceived to pay greater attention to short-term sales and profit figures, as when *Firm E* complained of a 'lack of empathy' from its investors and intervention in day-to-day operations that was 'irrelevant or inappropriate for the local market'. In such cases, frustrated and demotivated entrepreneurs can lack the capacity to think decisively and hence fail to grasp opportunities as they arise. Therefore, we propose:

> Proposition 2: Differences in cultural strategic orientations and in attitudes towards business performance are likely to cause contextual conflict in the E-VC relationship.

The principal source of procedural conflict in our study was difficulties in communications between entrepreneurs and VCs (usually, but not exclusively, foreign VCs). We found that entrepreneurs who had established a close working relationship with their investors adopt a variety of communication strategies, with open discussion and frequent contacts bringing mutual, long-term benefits. Entrepreneurs in the latter category were able to create and then maintain effective communication systems with their VCs; they were also more prepared to embrace a flexible approach towards communication – to make adjustments where necessary, to admit past failings and so on. This leads to the following proposition:

Proposition 3: The failure to utilise a variety of communication mechanisms is likely to result in procedural conflict in the E-VC relationship.

In tackling the second research question – that is, the role of human capital in responding to conflict with VCs – we found that first-time entrepreneurs, especially those with limited experience and knowledge in managing conflict with foreign VCs, tended to lack flexibility and adaptability compared to their more experienced counterparts. First-time entrepreneurs generally held negative views towards their VC investors, and this led to conflict. Moreover, whatever the source of that conflict, it tended to escalate over time.

In relation to contractual conflict, the prior experience of management proved vital in aligning the goals of VCs and investee firms. In addition, when the two parties had different perceptions of the strategy to be pursued in achieving those goals, accumulated human capital gave experienced entrepreneurs the confidence and credibility to insist upon taking and then implementing crucial decisions. In support of this assertion, we suggest that *Firms H and N* adopted a proactive 'competing' approach to conflict resolution; we contend that this approach, rather than collaboration, allowed these entrepreneurs to make positive decisions in the best interests of the firm, VC investors and the wider economy. We thus take issue with the view of Rahim (2002) that a competing/dominating strategy is always a win/lose game in which one party pursues his/her own concerns at the other's expense.

Another important finding was that, in the event of VCs challenging their strategic goals and/or firm performance, both experienced entrepreneurs and start-up players tended to employ the competing approach initially. This contention is tempered with two caveats. First, experienced entrepreneurs were prepared to seek collaboration with their VCs by establishing those areas where skills sets were complementary. Second, and perhaps more significantly, the competing method when pursued by first-time entrepreneurs was not as productive as the same approach adopted by experienced entrepreneurs. For example, in the face of conflict over growth aspirations and performance, the entrepreneurs in *Firms K and Y* had relatively weak bargaining power; this weakness probably stemmed from a combination of factors, including the entrepreneurs' lack of experience, skill deficiencies in certain areas and their perceptions (possibly misplaced) that the VC investors had superior knowledge or power. Nonetheless, these individuals tried to resist the wishes of the VCs until the founder members eventually concluded that they had no option but to comply with their investors' demands and to leave the firm (i.e. conflict avoidance). We therefore propose:

> Proposition 4a: Entrepreneurs with start-up experience are likely to be effective in managing contractual conflict by adopting a collaborative or an assertive competing approach.

> Proposition 4b: Inexperienced entrepreneurs are likely to have relatively weak bargaining power in the E-VC relationship and hence pursue a passive accommodating or an avoiding approach to contractual conflict.

The role of human capital in managing contextual conflict was again critical. In sample firms where conflict was avoided, the entrepreneurs established the abilities and motivations of VC investors, discussed potential problem areas in advance and then worked together to neutralise potential disagreements. These entrepreneurs were prepared to acknowledge that VCs offer generic strategic skills that cross continents. We propose that a key component of human capital in China is the ability to accept and act upon external advice, although some firms insisted on retaining control over certain decisions. These approaches to countering contextual conflict helped the sample firms to formulate an appropriate strategic framework, while maximising their ability to survive and prosper in the Chinese market.

Where contextual conflict did occur, it usually involved disputes between VC investors and first-time entrepreneurs over both strategic and operational issues. These firms were forced to accept advice perceived as culturally misguided and/or inappropriate for the Chinese market. Inexperienced entrepreneurs lacked the capacity to respond to contextual conflict in a positive manner by offering a strong entrepreneurial vision or displaying effective negotiation skills. Hence, we propose:

> Proposition 5a: Entrepreneurs with start-up experience are likely to be effective in managing contextual conflict by adopting a collaborative or an assertive competing approach.

> Proposition 5b: Inexperienced entrepreneurs are likely to pursue strategies of passive accommodation or open avoidance in managing contextual conflict.

In considering the resolution of procedural disputes, it was difficult for the authors to isolate actions undertaken solely in response to procedural conflict; nevertheless, the analysis below sheds important new light on this source of discord. By and large, the greater the human capital possessed by an entrepreneur, the greater the capacity to develop effective communications with VCs. Experienced entrepreneurs recognised the importance of frequent communication with investors (through formal and informal channels) not only to reduce the prospect of misunderstandings but also to increase the scope for the fruitful exchange of ideas. It was also critical to confront any problems quickly. Communication problems were minimised through cooperation and the creation of ample opportunities to explain, exchange, share and discuss operational and strategic issues with the investors.

In contrast, first-time entrepreneurs struggled to establish effective communication systems with their VC investors. Despite the existence of standard communication channels (such as quarterly board meetings), these mechanisms served only to generate negativity and mistrust. It is thus no surprise that inexperienced entrepreneurs found it very difficult to resolve procedural conflict. Our study revealed that avoidance tended to be employed more frequently in response to procedural conflict. There was some evidence of accommodation strategies being implemented, but avoidance was the more prevalent reaction, especially where there was acceptance of the *status quo* and little desire to tackle procedural conflict. Hence, we propose:

> Proposition 6a: Entrepreneurs with start-up experience are likely to be effective in managing procedural conflict by adopting collaborative and proactive strategies.
>
> Proposition 6b: Inexperienced entrepreneurs are likely to be ineffective in managing procedural conflict by pursuing an avoiding approach.

By conducting a systematic and detailed analysis of the E-VC relationship from the perspective of the entrepreneurs, our study contributes to the existing literature in several ways. First, this study complements previous studies conducted from the perspective of VCs. We offer new insights into how the sources of conflict are influenced by the different cultural contexts of entrepreneurs and also by their differing characteristics. Second, by adopting a combined conceptual perspective which embraces the literature on human capital and conflict management, we extend previous studies by providing fresh evidence that the human capital of entrepreneurs plays a vital role in shaping the E-VC relationship. By investigating how human capital acquired over time affects entrepreneurial responses to conflict with their VCs, we add a new dimension to studies of entrepreneurial experience.

The findings from the study also have important managerial implications. First, entrepreneurs need to be sensitive towards differences in value systems and in ways of communicating. While some studies have found evidence of cultural convergence between the West and China (House et al., 2002), we contend that entrepreneurs need to be equipped with appropriate skills to manage cultural differences in the E-VC relationship and hence to respond to conflict in an effective manner. Second, the findings should raise awareness among entrepreneurs that they can employ a variety of approaches in handling conflict with VCs. Entrepreneurs should be encouraged to adopt a collaborative strategy in the management of procedural conflict; if inexperienced entrepreneurs received training in, for example, communication and negotiation skills, this should enable them to utilise the expertise of the VCs more effectively and increase their chances of securing VC in future.

Conclusion

Adopting a qualitative analysis, this study examines the sources of conflict between entrepreneurs and VCs as well as factors affecting conflict resolution. Communication barriers and different value systems are the main sources of conflict between Chinese entrepreneurs and VCs, especially foreign VCs. Our findings show that entrepreneurs with start-up experience are able to manage conflict more constructively in an assertive and cooperative manner, whereas inexperienced entrepreneurs tend to be rather passive, resorting to accommodating and/or avoiding approaches to resolving conflict. Our results show that the approach and attitude of an entrepreneur, mainly shaped by human capital, affect the investee firm's strategic responses to managing conflict; the implication is that individuals with broader pools of human capital and experience should demonstrate greater flexibility and adaptability when managing and resolving conflict. We conclude that a synthesis of the literature in the fields of conflict and human capital offers new insights into the E-VC relationship.

References

Ahlstrom, D., Bruton, G. and Yeh, K. (2007). 'Venture Capital in China: Past, Present, and Future'. *Asia Pacific Journal of Management*, 24(3), 247–268.

Arthurs, J.D. and Busenitz, L.W. (2006). 'Dynamic Capabilities and Venture Performance: The Effects of Venture Capitalists'. *Journal of Business Venturing*, 21(2), 195–215.

Bosma, N., van Praag, M., Thurik, R. and de Wit, G. (2004). 'The Value of Human and Social Capital Investments for the Business Performance of Start-Ups'. *Small Business Economics*, 23(3), 227–236.

Boulding, K. (1963). *Conflict and defense: A general theory*, NY: Harper and Brothers.

Bruderl, J., Preisendorfer, P. and Ziegler, R. (1992). 'Survival Chances of Newly Founded Business Organizations'. *American Sociological Review*, 57(2), 227–242.

Cai, M. and Song, C. (2010). 'Chinese VC/PE Industry to Show Modest Growth, Targeting Emerging Industries' (Zhong Guo Feng Tou Hang Ye Mu Zi Hui Nuan, Xin Xing Chan Ye Shou Guan Zhu Chinahightech.com, Retrieved: August 2, 2010, available at http://paper.chinahightech.com.cn/html/2010–11/15/content_20245.htm.)

Chapman, E. and Smith, J.A. (2002). 'Interpretative Phenomenological Analysis and the New Genetics'. *Journal of Health Psychology*, 7(2), 125–130.

Chen, G., Liu, C. and Tjosvold, D. (2005). 'Conflict Management for Effective Top Management Teams and Innovation in China'. *Journal of Management Studies*, 42(2), 277–300.

Cooper, N., Estes, C.A. and Allen, L. (2004). 'Bouncing Back'. *Parks and Recreation*, April (28–35).

Cooper, S.Y. and Lucas, W.A. (2006). 'Developing Self-Efficacy for Innovation and Entrepreneurship: An Educational Approach'. *International Journal of Entrepreneurship Education*, 4, 141–162.

Cope, J. (2010). 'Entrepreneurial Learning from Failure: An Interpretative Phenomenological Analysis'. *Journal of Business Venturing*, In Press, Corrected Proof.

Coviello, N.E. and Jones, M.V. (2004). 'Methodological Issues in International Entrepreneurship Research'. *Journal of Business Venturing*, 19(4), 485–508.

Das, T.L. and Teng, B.S. (1998). 'Between trust and control: Developing confidence in partner cooperation in alliances'. *Academy of Management Review*, 23(3), 491–512.

De Vries, H. and Shields, M. (2006). 'Towards a Theory of Entrepreneurial Resilience: An Analysis of New Zealand Sme Owner-Operators'. *The New Zealand Journal of Applied Business*, 5(1), 33–44.

Deutsch, M. (1973). *The Resolution of Conflict*. New Haven, CT: Yale University Press.

Ehrlich, S.B., De Noble, A.F., Moore, T. and Weaver, R.R. (1994). 'After the Cash Arrives: A Comparative Study of Venture Capital and Private Investor Involvement in Entrepreneurial Firms'. *Journal of Business Venturing*, 9(1), 67–82.

Envick, B.R. (2005). 'Beyond Human and Social Capital: The Importance of Positive Psychological Capital for Entrepreneurial Success'. *The Entrepreneurial Executive*, 10, 41–52.

Glaser, B. (1978). *Theoretical Sensitivity*. Sociology Press, Mill Valley: CA.

Hartley, J.F. (1994). 'Case Studies in Organisational Research'. In Cassell, C. and Symon, G. (Eds). *Qualiative Methods in Organisational Research*. London: Sage Publications.

Higashide, H. and Birley, S. (2002). 'The Consequences of Conflict between the Venture Capitalist and the Entrepreneurial Team in the United Kingdom from the Perspective of the Venture Capitalist'. *Journal of Business Venturing*, 17(1), 59–81.

House, R., Javidan, M., Hanges, P. and Dorfman, P. (2002). 'Understanding Cultures and Implicit Leadership Theories across the Globe: An Introduction to Project Globe'. *Journal of World Business*, 37(1), 3–10.

Huff, A.S. (1990). *Mapping Strategic Thought* Chichester: Wiley.

Jehn, K. and Mannix, E. (2001). 'The dynamic nature of conflict: A longitudinal study of intragroup conflict and group performance'. *Academy of Management Journal*, 44(2), 238–251.

Keong, F.W.F. and Mei, L.Y. (2010). 'Sustainable Development: The Effect of Adopting Green Technology on Small and Medium Enterprises' (SMEs) Business Resilience and Competitiveness'. *International Conference on Business and Economic Research (ICBER 2010)*. Kuching Sarawak, Malaysia.

Kor, Y.Y., Mahoney, J.T., and Michael, S. (2007). 'Resources, Capabilities, and Entrepreneurial Perceptions'. *Journal of Management Studies*, 44(7), 1185–1210.

Lerner, J. (1999). 'The Government as Venture Capitalist: The Long-Run Impact of the SBIR Program'. *Journal of Business*, 72(3), 285–318.

McDougall, P.P. and Oviatt, B.M. (2000). 'International Entrepreneurship: The Intersection of Two Research Paths'. *Academy of Management Journal*, 43(5), 902–908.

Manigart, S. and Sapienza, H. (2000). 'Venture Capital and Growth'. In Sexton, D.L. and Landström, H. (Eds). *The Blackwell Handbook of Entrepreneurship*. Oxford: Blackwell Publishers Limited, pp. 240–258.

Miles, M.B. and Huberman, A.M. (1994). *Qualitative Data Analysis*, Sage Publications, Thousand Oaks: CA.

Morris, M.H. (2002). 'Revisiting "Who" Is the Entrepreneur'. *Journal of Developmental Entrepreneurship Theory and Practice*, 7(7), 5–7.

Parhankangas, A. and Landström, H. (2004). 'Responses to psychological contract violations in the entrepreneur–venture capitalist relationship: An exploratory study'. *Venture Capital*, 6(4), 217–242.

Pffefer, J. and Salancik, G. (2003). *The external control of organizations: A resource dependence perspective*. Stanford, CA: Stanford University Press.

Politis, D. (2005). 'The Process of Entrepreneurial Learning: A Conceptual Framework'. *Entrepreneurship Theory and Practice*, 29(4), 399–424.

Pukthuanthong, K and Walker, T. (2007). 'Venture Capital in China: a culture shock for Western Investors'. *Management Decision*, 45(4), 708–731.

Rahim, M. (2002). 'Toward a Theory of Managing Organizational Conflict'. *International Journal of Conflict Management*, 13, 206–235.

Reid, K., Flowers, P. and Larkin, M. (2005). 'Exploring Lived Experience'. *The Psychologist*, 18(20–23).

Shane, S.A. (2008). *The Illusions of Entrepreneurship: The Costly Myths That Entrepreneurs, Investors and Policy Makers Live By*. New Haven, CT: Yale University Press.

Thomas, K. (1976). 'Conflict and Conflict Management'. In Dunnette, M. (Ed.). *Handbook of Industrial and Organisational Psychology*. Chicago: Rand McNally.

Timmons, J.A. (1999). *New Venture Creation: Entrepreneurship for the 21st Century (5th Ed)*. Boston: Irwin.

Tjsovold, D., Law, K. and Sun, H. (2006). 'Effectiveness of Chinese Teams: The Role of Conflict Types and Conflict Management Approaches'. *Management and Organization Review* 2(2), 231–252.

Wang, G., Jing, R. and Klossek, A. (2007). 'Antecedents and Management of Conflict: Resolution Styles of Chinese Top Managers in Multiple Rounds of Cognitive and Affective Conflict'. *International Journal of Conflict Management*, 18(1), 74–97.

Wright, M., Low, M. and Davidson, P. (2001). 'Entrepreneurship Research, Progress and Prospects'. *Entrepreneurship, Theory and Practice*, 25(4), 5–15.

Wright, M., Pruthi, S. and Lockett, A. (2005). 'International Venture Capital: From Cross-Country Comparisons to Crossing Countries'. *International Journal of Management Reviews*, 7(3), 135–166.

Xiao, L. (2011). 'Financing High-Tech Smes in China: A Three Stage Model of Business Development'. *Entrepreneurship and Regional Development*, 23(3–4), 217–234.

Yitshaki, R. (2008). 'Venture Capitalist-Entrepreneur Conflicts: An Exploratory Study of Determinants and Possible Resolutions'. *International Journal of Conflict Management*, 19(3), 262–292.

Zacharakis, A.L. and Meyer, G.D. (2000). 'The Potential of Actuarial Decision Models: Can They Improve the Venture Capital Investment Decision?'. *Journal of Business Venturing*, 15(4), 323–346.

Zacharakis, A., Erikson, T. and George, B. (2010). 'Conflict between the VC and entrepreneur: the entrepreneurs' perspective'. *Venture Capital*, 12(2), 109–126.

11
International Joint Ventures and Dynamic Co-learning between MNEs and Local Firms

Jeong-Yang Park, Yoo Jung Ha and Yong Kyu Lew

Introduction

Forming an international joint venture (IJV) is a strategically important step that shapes a firm's internationalisation process (Park and Ungson, 1997) and is a strategy intended to quickly achieve geographical diversification or organisational growth. Many IJVs have been created for partners to comply with local restrictions on foreign ownership in host economies. Although there are many other reasons, one agreed upon point regarding IJV creation is that IJV learning is essential for a firm's sustainable growth in highly heterogeneous and competitive international markets (Bresman, Birkinshaw and Nobel, 1999; Hamel, 1991; Lane, Salk and Lyles, 2001).

This chapter focuses on IJVs as vehicles for dynamic co-learning between foreign and local IJV partners. Previous studies have proposed that IJV partners' shared learning objectives drive IJV formulation (Lane et al., 2001). Learning is critical for both foreign and local firms. In emerging economies, for instance, foreign entrants are exposed to intense competition with other foreign and local rivals over new market opportunities, while experiencing difficulties due to institutional voids and liabilities of foreignness (Hoskisson, Eden, Lau and Right, 2000). Local firms in emerging economies experience difficulties in acquiring resources due to underdeveloped institutions in local factor markets, such as financial and labour markets, and this raises barriers to pre-internationalisation learning (Hennart, 2012; Hitt, Li, and Worthington IV, 2005; Lu, Liu, Filatotchev and Wright, 2014; Prahalad and Lieberthal, 2003). Thus, foreign and local firms have shared needs and objectives to learn about emerging markets and use knowledge and experience to shape their present or future internationalisation. This is why the issue of dynamic co-learning is essential in order to understand the formation and performance of successful IJVs (Fang and Zou, 2010).

Previous studies on IJV learning have focused on independent learning at the single IJV parent's level (Lane et al., 2001; McCann and Mudambi, 2005;

Noorderhaven and Harzing, 2009). In single-party organisational learning, each parent passes its existing knowledge to the IJV and acquires the other partner's knowledge through the IJV (Hitt et al., 2005; Johanson and Vahlne, 1977, 1990). This research stream has undermined attention to inter-organisational learning across IJV parents and co-learning within IJVs (Beamish and Berdrow, 2003; Fang and Zou, 2010; Hitt et al., 2005). Furthermore, IJV learning has been described as a static process. Learning effectiveness has been understood in relation to the existing knowledge bases of parent firms rather than in the context of a dynamic process in IJV learning or co-evolutionary path of partners' knowledge bases (Evangelista and Hau, 2009).

To close these gaps, this chapter explores processes through which IJVs achieve dynamic co-learning, and it addresses IJV learning from a broader evolutionary perspective. Building on organisational learning theories, we propose a conceptual framework of inter-organisational processes for co-learning, a single and double-loop feedback system for dynamic learning and joint absorptive capacity-building within IJVs as an IJV outcome. The framework extends existing IJV learning research and generates implications for IJV effectiveness, IJVs' own evolutionary processes and the role of IJV strategy in a firm's internationalisation.

Literature and research constructs

IJV learning

Internationalisation process research has documented how foreign knowledge acquisition and experiential learning shape the internationalisation process in MNEs. MNEs obtain knowledge resources by interacting with local and international networks that can share learning experiences (Child and Czegledy, 1996; Freeman and Cavusgil, 2007; Laanti, Gabrielsson and Gabrielsson, 2007). MNEs gain experiential knowledge through learning by doing, either independently or jointly with local partners (Johanson and Vahlne, 1977, 1990, 2006; Lyle, 1994). Interplay between knowledge development, sensing and seizing opportunities and the degree of foreign commitment is considered to be essential for the internationalisation process (Johanson and Vahlne, 2006).

MNEs often move into emerging economies by creating IJVs in partnership with local firms (Luo, Shenkar and Nyaw, 2002; Prahalad and Lieberthal, 2003). Task environments in emerging economies are highly volatile due to inconsistent regulation, institutional voids and unfamiliar organisational structures (Boisot and Child, 1996; Khanna and Palepu, 1997; Peng and Heath, 1996). Thus, in emerging economies organisational learning is more critical in foreign entrants' operations than it is in other locations (Luo and Peng,

1999; Kogut and Zander, 1992; Hitt et al., 2005). Using IJV strategy, MNEs acquire knowledge to facilitate local operations in emerging economies. In IJVs, learning also occurs through experiences shared between the partners in their finding solutions to problems in complex foreign markets (Bresman et al., 1999; Child and Czegledy, 1996; Hamel, 1991; Kogut, 1988; Lane et al., 2001; Lyles, 1988). In doing so, foreign entrants innovate from current business models to survive competition with other foreign entrants and local firms (Prahalad and Lieberthal, 2003).

Most internationalisation and IJV learning research has investigated learning by individual IJV parents (Tsang, 2002). In IJVs there is an intrinsic imbalance in learning capabilities between foreign and local partners, and the literature focusing on single-partner learning emphasises instability and early termination and dissolution of IJVs. A foreign IJV partner with greater learning ability can be in a stronger bargaining position with regard to demanding changes in IJV structure and organisation (Fang and Zou, 2010). The tendency towards management conflicts between foreign and local partners can be high, which may interrupt organisational learning by the weaker IJV partner in the competitive learning race within IJVs (Hamel, 1991; Kumar, 2005). The likely result is a partnership suffering loss of stability and unplanned termination (Beamish and Lupton, 2009; Fang and Zou, 2010; Hyder and Ghauri, 2000; Park and Ungson, 1997).

However, the many counterexamples of successful IJVs surviving for a long time raise unanswered questions. In China, for instance, many foreign and local IJV partners have successfully undertaken co-learning and jointly generated new knowledge useful for their future internationalisation processes (Fang and Zou, 2010). Using IJVs, emerging-economy firms can successfully learn about international markets, foreign institutions and managerial practices acquired or jointly conceived through collaboration with foreign firms in their home country (Lu et al., 2014).

To complement the imbalanced learning-race view and replace the current focus on static and independent learning at a single parent's level, the inter-organisational and dynamic dimensions of learning undertaken by both IJV parents should be taken into consideration. This chapter explores which processes can be used in IJVs for inter-organisational and dynamic learning and how IJVs facilitate co-learning and co-evolution in IJV partners. The following section will unpack inter-organisational learning, focusing on multidimensionality and plurality of learning types. We will then document dynamic feedback systems within IJVs.

Co-learning processes within IJVs

Internationalisation process research has focused on the importance of learning from experience of IJV operations (Johanson and Vahlne, 1977, 1990, 2006).

From the organisational learning perspective, organisational learning occurs through multiple processes (Huber, 1991; Hyder and Ghauri, 2000; Yli-Renko, Autio and Sapienza, 2001). Furthermore, IJV learning involves both intra- and inter-organisational learning.

Huber (1991) suggests five processes of organisational learning which can be implemented within IJVs. *Searching* refers to intentional scanning through search and performance monitoring. *Noticing* is accidental acquisition of such information. *Congenital learning* refers to the acquisition of knowledge available at the organisation's birth, which can impact on the future path of organisational learning. In the IJV context, IJV formulation is followed by transfer of knowledge from the IJV parents to the IJV as part of congenital learning (Reuer, 2000). Such knowledge transfer is organised through training and technological and managerial assistance from IJV parents (Lane et al, 2001; Lyle and Salk, 1994). *Grafting* refers to knowledge acquisition from external new members who possess knowledge not formerly obtainable within the organisation. It is coordinated through strong organisational commitment, teamwork and inter-partner relationship within IJVs (Evangelista and Hau, 2007). Grafting may require a knowledge-assimilation mechanism to integrate knowledge acquired from different sources and ensure that it is embedded firmly within the IJV organisational structure (Drucker, 1988). In the IJV context, experiential learning refers to learning from shared experiences in operating an IJV. Partners learn from building micro-foundations to communicate and operate inter-partner learning, integrate differential knowledge and store new organisational memory within the IJV organisation (Fang and Zou, 2010). Finally, *vicarious learning* involves organisations acquiring knowledge through second-hand experience by observing their IJV partner (Huber, 1991). Experiences of technology sharing, interaction with the partner, personal exchanges and strategic integration strengthen knowledge connection between partners as a channel of vicarious learning (Inkpen and Dinur, 1998).

Tsang (2002) divides the objectives of IJV learning into intra- and inter-organisational learning. Intra-organisational learning is operated by single IJV parents and involves implementing each parent's knowledge to the IJV and the reverse acquisition of the partner's knowledge through the IJV (Lane et al., 2001; Tsang, 2002). In this view, the IJV serves each parent as an instrument to configure learning from the partner's knowledge. Searching and noticing as well as congenital learning and grafting are associated with independent intra-organisational learning by each IJV partner. Inter-organisational learning is operated within IJVs, and it combines both parents' knowledge and shared experiences of operating IJV learning (Beamish and Berdrow, 2003; Fang and Zou, 2010). In this view, IJV learning incorporates assimilation to connect multiple parents' knowledge bases, exploitation of the combined set of knowledge and harvesting of new IJV-specific knowledge. Thus, the IJV is used for joint problem solving and the co-creation of knowledge between IJV parents. Part of grafting, vicarious and experiential learning is associated with inter-organisational learning (Tsang, 2002).

IJV parents' absorptive capacity is an essential step towards operationalising IJV learning. Absorptive capacity is related to prior related knowledge – that is, the basic skills and general knowledge available within the organisation (Zahara and George, 2002). Due to the cumulative nature of learning, absorptive capacity-building is both an outcome and a source of dynamic capabilities in an organisation (Todorova and Durisin, 2007). Previous research has focused on how IJV parents' performance and their absorptive capacity determine an IJV's absorptive capacity and performance (Inkpen and Dinur, 1998; Reuer, 2000; Tsang, 2002). Parental absorptive capacity influences, first, the formulation of a knowledge base for the IJV through knowledge transfer from each parent and supports knowledge searching, congenital learning and grafting; and it influences, second, the reverse knowledge transfer from IJVs to parents (Lane et al., 2001; Tsang, 2002).

The process perspective shows that IJV learning involves inter-organisational learning between IJV parents as well as intra-organisational learning involving each single parent. The next section extends the discussion to the conditions under which IJV learning is directed towards a dynamic process.

Dynamic learning system within IJVs

In the knowledge-based view of the firm, the ability to continuously generate and exploit knowledge is the main source of a firm's sustainable competitive advantage (Nelson, 1993; Nonaka, Toyama and Konno, 2000; Teece, Pisano and Shuen, 1997). In this view, the firm is a 'dynamic body of knowledge in action' (Spender, 1994: 355). As a setting for dynamic learning within an organisation, we consider trial-and-error experimentation within IJVs. In this view, organisational learning can be facilitated by an iterative feedback system of trialling actions, detecting errors and correcting actions or objectives linked with the action (Argyris and Schön 1978, 1996; Sosna, Trevinyo-Rodríguez and Velamuri, 2010).

Dynamic learning within IJVs can be undertaken through single- and double-loop processes. A single-loop process is aimed at convergence between action and objective. In single-loop learning, an organisation focuses on detecting and correcting errors in an action, based on deviations from the initial objective (Argyris and Schön, 1978, 1996; Sosna et al., 2010). Thus, single-loop learning focuses on incremental improvements of knowledge while retaining current organisational structure and values. A double-loop process allows learning from divergence between actions and objectives. Instead of retaining objectives, an organisation using double-loop learning detects and corrects errors in fundamental objectives within the organisation (Argyris and Schön, 1978: 96;

Sosna et al., 2010). Through a recursive backward feedback system correcting both action and objective, double-loop learning favours fundamental innovation in the organisation (Mattes, 2014).

Double-loop, rather than single-loop, learning is critical to organisations needing to learn turbulent task environments and actively implement change management. As a result of double-loop learning, both actions and objectives are constantly reviewed, and routines, processes and practices are refined. In a dynamic feedback system, IJVs constantly innovate micro-foundation in a way that fits into strategy and action in changing task environments (Lewin, Massini and Peeters, 2011; Zahra and George, 2002). The key difference between single-loop and double-loop learning is between being adaptive and containing adaptability. Being adaptive is about adjusting current paradigms (Senge, 1990), whereas containing and sustaining adaptability requires firms to model themselves as 'experimenting' or 'self-designing' firms in the course of an evolutionary process of learning (Hedberg, Nystrom and Starbuck, 1976; Starbuck, 1983). Thus, double-loop learning is a key characteristic of successful IJVs.

Dynamic learning reinforces joint absorptive capacity-building. Joint absorptive capacity is a main outcome of knowledge connection between the differential knowledge bases of parents (Glaister, Husan and Buckley, 2003; Reuer, 2000). Through intra-organisational and inter-organisational learning, the initial absorptive capacities rooted in the separate parental knowledge bases converge. More newly identified and acquired knowledge by IJVs from elsewhere can be utilised to further enrich transformation and exploitation at the IJV level. The single and double-loop process monitors and constantly improves co-learning and knowledge co-creation in IJVs by detecting and correcting errors in terms of action type, learning objective and fundamental structural deficiencies. Thus, IJVs with dynamic co-learning processes contribute to the generation of joint absorptive capacity across parents.

Overall, IJVs can implement dynamic learning by means of a single and double-loop process of recursive feedback and generate joint absorptive capacity. In the next section, we develop a framework that integrates absorptive capacity at the single parent's level, processes of intra- and inter-organisational learning, feedback systems and the generation of joint absorptive capacity at the IJV level.

Conceptual framework

We propose an exploratory dynamic research framework to examine dynamic co-learning processes within IJVs (see Figure 11.1). Although absorptive capacity-building and learning processes in IJVs are dynamic in nature, current research on IJV learning has focused on a static learning process and assumes a rather passive role for IJVs in parents' intra-organisational learning rather

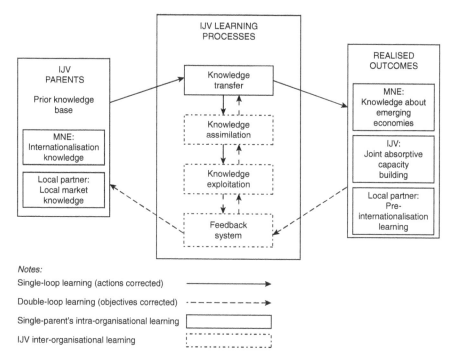

Figure 11.1 Dynamic co-learning process in an IJV

than an active role in inter-organisational learning (Hyder and Ghauri, 2000). Furthermore, IJV learning effectiveness has been evaluated in terms of successful knowledge transfer between IJVs and their parents rather than knowledge connection and creation at the IJV level.

The dynamic processes of IJV learning renew competences and are essential in a turbulent environment like emerging economies. The meaning of 'dynamic' in this chapter refers to 'the capacity to renew competences so as to achieve congruence with the changing business environment' (Teece et al., 1997: 515). Through dynamic learning processes, IJVs are engaged in an extensive sensing of the organisation's external condition, which is needed to ensure fit between strategy, organisation and task environments (Miller and Friesen, 1980). The framework reflects successful IJVs in emerging economies, incorporating processes for dynamic co-learning and achieving joint absorptive capacity-building between IJV partners and their IJVs.

The conceptual framework includes six process variables within three different levels, as illustrated in Figure 11.1: (1) prior knowledge base of IJV partners (parents), (2) knowledge transfer from parents to the IJV, (3) knowledge assimilation within the IJV, (4) knowledge exploitation within the IJV, (5) feedback system within the IJV through both single- and double-loop processes and (6) joint absorptive capacity-building within the IJV. These variables are placed within three levels: IJV parents' absorptive capacity (Level 1), IJV learning process (single parent's intra-organisational or inter-organisational) in the IJV (Level 2), and realised outcomes (Level 3).

Level 1 includes IJV parents' prior knowledge base and parental absorptive capacity. A firm's prior knowledge comprises market, product and technological knowledge. In the framework, a firm's prior knowledge base for internationalisation to realise and identify new learning and knowledge acquisition is an antecedent to the IJV's learning capacity (Autio, Sapienza and Almeida, 2000; Cohen and Levinthal, 1990). At inception, the two partners are involved in knowledge acquisition and learning through separate processes.

Level 2 reflects learning processes and feedback within the IJV itself. Initial learning in an IJV depends on the partners' prior knowledge base, but the IJV's own knowledge bases are gradually created. This level comprises four interlinked process variables: knowledge transfer, knowledge assimilation, knowledge exploitation and a feedback system with recursive loops. Knowledge transfer is linked to a single partner's intra-organisational learning. The rest of the process is inter-organisational within an IJV, leading to shared experiential learning and generation of new knowledge between the parents. In IJV inter-organisational learning, knowledge assimilation and exploitation is based on the combined knowledge assets inherited from the parents, but successful assimilation and exploitation results in the co-creation of new knowledge and co-learning across the parents. A single parent's intra-organisational learning and IJV inter-organisational learning are undertaken by various modes of learning. Contrary to assumptions in the internationalisation process model, IJV learning is not limited to experiential learning and can be understood in a broader context. Thus, what is embedded in the framework are various learning modes encompassing processes of internal and external knowledge transfer, assimilation and exploitation – learning with regard to searching, noticing, congenital learning, grafting, vicarious learning and experiential learning (Huber, 1991).

The last process at Level 2 is a dynamic feedback system within the IJV. Single-loop and double-loop processes within the system detect and recursively correct errors in knowledge assimilation and exploitation processes, and they determine whether to modify actions, objectives of the action or fundamental organisational structure. This single and double-loop feedback system leads to dynamic learning. IJVs' experience of operating a feedback system leads to subsequent development of experiential knowledge beyond the IJV parents' prior knowledge bases and to advanced opportunities for vicarious learning (Cohen and Levinthal, 1990; Fang and Zou, 2010; Huber, 1991; Zahara and George, 2002).

On Level 3 are the realised outcomes from the IJV – joint absorptive capacity-building. Joint absorptive capacity is affected by the levels of prior knowledge: learning processes start from the link with IJV partners' prior knowledge

(Level 1) but end with joint absorptive capacity-building (Level 3). Furthermore, capacity-building is affected by inter-organisational processes of knowledge assimilation and exploitation. Through inter-organisational learning and single-/ double-loop feedback, this type of IJV learning engages in exploration as well as exploitation (Cohen and Levinthal, 1990; Tsai, 2001). Renewal of action, strategy and structure is challenging but surmountable, and the impact on the development of a new product or service on the level of resource commitment by each parent, on ownership and governance mode and on co-evolution across IJV parents is crucial. Overall, dynamic co-learning allows the IJV to conduct business innovatively beyond the exploitation of parents' existing knowledge.

Overall, the conceptual framework presents flows encompassing three-level processes that affect the formulation of IJVs, inter-organisational learning, co-learning and knowledge co-creation, dynamic learning and joint absorptive capacity-building within IJVs. With dynamic co-learning processes, IJVs can not only passively serve the integration of different knowledge bases and organisational structures but also act as a vehicle for learning and new knowledge generation. New IJV knowledge and experiences are reversely transferred from IJVs to parents and to the parents' internationalisation process. Dynamic learning shapes the IJV's evolutionary path, and the IJV may self-determine its own future prospects.

Drawing on the above discussion, we suggest the following propositions regarding joint absorptive capacity-building in the course of organisational learning and single- and double-loop learning processes in the IJV boundary.

Proposition 1. IJV parents' absorptive capacity contributes to knowledge transfer between IJV parents and the IJV and to inter-organisational learning in the IJV.

Proposition 2. Inter-organisational learning processes in the IJV are related to co-creation of knowledge and joint absorptive capacity in the IJV.

Proposition 3. Dynamic learning in the IJV, as operated through single- and double-loop feedback systems, affects joint absorptive capacity in the IJV.

Proposition 4. Joint absorptive capacity in the IJV determines the stability and evolutionary path of the IJV in the first place and the internationalisation process of foreign and local parents of the IJV in the second place.

Concluding remarks

Research in the internationalisation process and IJV learning has recognised the importance of learning in IJV formulation and operation. To explain the wide variance in IJV stability and survival, this chapter has identified processes through which IJVs operate inter-organisational and dynamic learning.

We have discussed under what conditions IJVs may build joint absorptive capacity across foreign and local parents by conceptually documenting dynamic co-learning processes within IJVs. The paucity of studies concerning knowledge creation and inter-organisational learning processes within IJVs has been noted as a research gap (Beamish and Berdrow, 2003; Fang and Zou, 2010).

Our conceptual framework complements current IJV learning research and reinforces understanding of IJVs' management of learning and its outcomes. More specifically, we have identified an inter-organisational learning process for co-learning and an iterative feedback system for dynamic learning, and we have shown how both can lead to joint absorptive capacity-building. Fine-grained documentation of processes predicting dynamic co-learning within IJVs establishes how IJVs may survive, avoid unplanned premature termination, co-create knowledge on a sustainable basis and perhaps shape their internationalisation process. Furthermore, we show that IJVs that implement dynamic co-learning can be a vehicle for co-evolution of foreign and local firms in emerging economies before competing in broader global markets.

Based on the conceptual framework, a managerial implication is that the survival and stability of IJVs are endogenously determined by the willingness of IJV parents to conduct dynamic co-learning and also their capabilities in engineering an organisational process and system in a way that provides matching micro-foundations to implement IJV learning. IJVs where partners encompass different but complementary abilities are difficult to manage. A co-learning process and single-/double-loop iterative feedback system can ensure IJV-level learning willingness and the autonomy of IJV managers. The system promotes a sense of system ownership within the IJV, the IJV's awareness and motivation to learn and manage change and continual joint absorptive capacity-building. As a result, the learning capability gap is closed, and both IJV partners benefit in terms of knowledge acquisition and experiences for their future internationalisation.

This chapter has some limitations. It has not considered potential critical events that may influence the ongoing evolutionary path of an IJV partnership and direct the organisation towards unplanned serendipitous learning. Another limitation is that we have assumed both foreign and local IJV partners to be willing to learn through the IJV operation and that intended learning activities are mutually complementary. Furthermore, our model omits relational factors such as trust, conflict management and cross-cultural or cross-organisational differences.

In future research, we urge empirical studies to test our propositions. To establish generalisability, the conceptual framework could be empirically tested across different emerging economies, in emerging economies compared with developed economies or across different levels of environmental turbulence. Future research may also test dynamic learning processes in IJVs using longitudinal analysis.

References

Argyris, C. and Schön, D.A. (1978). *Organizational learning: A theory of action perspective.* Reading, MA: Addison-Wesley.

Argyris, C. and Schön, D.A. (1996). *Organizational learning II: Theory, method and practice.* Reading, MA: Addison-Wesley.

Autio, E., Sapienza, H.J. and Almeida, J.G. (2000). 'Effects of age at entry, knowledge intensity, and imitability on international growth'. *Academy of Management Journal,* 43(5), 909–924.

Beamish, P.W. and Lupton, N.C. (2009). 'Managing joint ventures'. *Academy of Management Perspectives,* 23(2), 75–94.

Beamish, P. and Berdrow, I. (2003). 'Learning from IJVs: The unintended outcome'. *Long Range Planning,* 36(3), 285–303.

Boisot, M. and Child, J. (1996). 'From fiefs to clans and network capitalism: Explaining China's emerging economic order'. *Administrative Science Quarterly,* 41(4), 600–628.

Bresman, H., Birkinshaw, J. and Nobel, R. (1999). 'Knowledge transfer in international acquisitions'. *Journal of International Business Studies,* 30(3), 439–462.

Child, J. and Czegledy, A.P. (1996). 'Managerial learning in the transformation of Eastern Europe: Some key issues'. *Organization Studies,* 17(2), 167–179.

Cohen, W.M. and Levinthal, D.A. (1990). 'Absorptive capacity: A new perspective on learning and innovation'. *Administrative Science Quarterly,* 35(1), 128–152.

Drucker, P. (1988). 'The coming of the new organization'. *Harvard Business Review,* 66(1), 45–53.

Evangelista, F. and Hau, L.N. (2009). 'Organizational context and knowledge acquisition in IJVs: An empirical study'. *Journal of World Business,* 44, 63–73.

Fang, E. and Zou, S. (2010). 'The effects of absorptive and joint learning on the instability of international joint ventures in emerging economies'. *Journal of International Business Studies,* 41(5), 906–924.

Ferraro, G. (2002). *Knowledge and competencies for the 21st century.* New York: Intercultural Associates Inc.

Freeman, S. and Cavusgil, T. (2007). 'Towards a typology of commitment states among managers of born-global firms: A study of accelerated internationalisation'. *Journal of International Marketing,* 15(4), 1–40.

Glaister, K.W., Husan, R. and Buckley, P. (2003). 'Learning to manage international joint ventures'. *International Business Review,* 12(1), 83–108.

Hamel, G. (1991). 'Competition for competence and interpartner learning within international strategic alliances'. *Strategic Management Journal,* 12(S1), 83–103.

Hedberg, B., Nystrom, P.C. and Starbuck, W.H. (1976). 'Camping on seesaws: Prescriptions for a self-designing organization'. *Administrative Science Quarterly,* 21(1), 41–65.

Hennart, J.F. (1988). 'A transaction costs theory of equity joint ventures'. *Strategic Management Journal,* 9(4), 361–374.

Hennart, J.F. (2012). 'Emerging market multinationals and the theory of the multinational enterprise'. *Global Strategy Journal,* 2, 168–187.

Hitt, M.A., Li, H. and Worthington IV, W.J. (2005). 'Emerging markets as learning laboratories: Learning behaviours of local firms and foreign entrants in different institutional contexts'. *Management and Organization Review,* 1(3), 353–380.

Hoskisson, R.E., Eden, L., Lau, C.M. and Wright, M. (2000). 'Strategy in Emerging Economies'. *The Academy of Management Journal,* 43(3), 249–267.

Huber, G.P. (1991). 'Organizational learning: The contributing processes and the literatures'. *Organizational Science,* 2(1), 88–115.

Hyder, A.S. and Ghauri, P.N. (2000). 'Managing international joint venture relationships: A longitudinal perspective'. *Industrial Marketing Management*, 29(3), 205–218.

Inkpen, A.C. and Dinur, A. (1998). 'Knowledge Management Processes and International Joint Ventures'. *Organization Science*, 9(4), 454–468.

Johanson, J. and Vahlne, J.E. (1977). 'The Internationalization Process of the Firm: A Model of Knowledge Development and Increasing Foreign Market Commitments'. *Journal of International Business Studies*, 8(1), 23–32.

Johanson, J. and Vahlne, J.E. (1990). 'The Mechanism of Internationalization'. *International Marketing Review*, 7(4), 11–24.

Johanson, J. and Vahlne, J.E. (2006). 'Commitment and opportunity development- A note on the internationalization process (IP) model'. *Management International Review*, 46(2), 165–178.

Khanna, T. and Palepu, K.G. (1997). 'Why focused strategies may be wrong for emerging markets'. *Harvard Business Review*, 41–51.

Kogut, B. (1988). 'Joint ventures: Theoretical and empirical perspectives'. *Strategic Management Journal*, 9(4), 319–332.

Kogut, B. and Zander, U. (1992). 'Knowledge of the firm, combinative capabilities, and the replication of technology'. *Organization Science*, 3(3), 383–397.

Laanti, R., Gabrielsson, M. and Gabrielsson, P. (2007). 'The globalization strategies of business-to business born global firms in wireless technology'. *Industrial Marketing Management*, 36(8), 1104–1117.

Lane, P.J., Salk, J.E. and Lyles, M.A. (2001). 'Absorptive capacity, learning and performance in international joint ventures'. *Strategic Management Journal*, 22(12), 1139–1161.

Lewin, A.Y., Massini, S. and Peeters, C. (2011). 'Microfoundations of internal and external absorptive capacity routines'. *Organization Science*, 22(1), 81–98.

Lu, J., Liu, X., Filatotchev, I. and Wright, M. (2014). 'The impact of domestic diversification and top management teams on the international diversification of Chinese firms'. *International Business Review*, 23, 455–467.

Luo, Y. and Peng, M.W. (1999). 'Learning to compete in a transition economy: experience, environment, and performance'. *Journal of International Business Studies*, 30(2), 269–295.

Luo, Y., Shenkar, O. and Nyaw, M.K. (2002). 'Mitigating liabilities of foreignness: Defensive versus offensive approaches'. *Journal of International Management*, 8(3), 283–300.

Lyles, M.A. (1988). 'Learning among joint venture sophisticated firms'. *Management International Review*, 28(4), 85–98.

Lyles, M.A. (1994). 'The impact of organizational learning on joint venture formations'. *International Business Review*, 3(4), 459–467.

Mattes, J. (2014). 'Formalisation and flexibilisation in organisations – Dynamic and selective approaches in corporate innovation processes'. *European Management Journal*, 32(3), 475–486.

McCann, P. and Mudambi, R. (2005). 'Analytical differences in the economics of geography: The case of the multinational firm'. *Environment and Planning*, 37(10), 1857–1876.

Miller, D. and Friesen, P.H. (1980). 'Momentum and revolution in organizational adaptation'. *Academy of Management Journal*, 23(4), 591–614.

Nelson, R. (1993). *National innovation systems: A comparative analysis*. Oxford: Oxford University Press.

Nonaka, I., Toyama, R., and Konno, N. (2000). 'SECI, Ba and leadership: A unified model of dynamic knowledge creation'. *Long Range Planning*, 33, 5–34.

Noorderhaven, N. and Harzing, A.W. (2009). 'Knowledge-sharing and social interaction within MNEs'. *Journal of International Business Studies*, 40(5), 719–741.

Nti, K.O. and Kumar, R. (2000). 'Differential learning in alliances'. In D. Faulkner and M. de Rond (Eds). *Co-operative strategy: Economic, business and organizational issues*. Oxford: Oxford University Press, pp. 119–134.

Park, S.H. and Ungson, G.R. (1997). 'The Effect of National Culture, Organizational Complementarity, and Economic Motivation on Joint Venture Dissolution'. *The Academy of Management Journal*, 40(2), 279–307.

Peng, M.W. and Heath, P.S. (1996). 'The growth of the firm in planned economies in transition: Institutions, organizations, and strategic choice'. *Academy of Management Review*, 21(2), 492–528.

Prahalad, C.K. and Lieberthal, K. (2003). 'The end of corporate imperialism'. *Harvard Business Review*, 81(8), 109–117.

Reuer, J.J. (2000). 'Parent firm performance across international joint venture life-cycle stages'. *Journal of International Business Studies*, 31(1), 1–20.

Shyam Kumar, M.V. (2005). 'The value from acquiring and divesting a joint venture: a real options approach'. *Strategic Management Journal*, 26(4), 321–331.

Senge, P.M. (1990). *The fifth discipline: The art and practice of the learning organization*. New York: Random House Business.

Sosna, M., Trevinyo-Rodríguez, R.N. and Velamuri, S.R. (2010). 'Business model innovation through trial-and-error learning: The Naturhouse case'. *Long Range Planning*, 43(2–3), 383–407.

Spender, J.C. (1994). 'Organizational knowledge, collective practice and Penrose rents'. *International Business Review*, 3(4), 353–367.

Starbuck, W.H. (1983). 'Organisations as action generators'. *American Sociological Review*, 48, 91–102.

Teece, D.J., Pisano, G. and Shuen, A. (1990). 'Firm capabilities, resources, and the concept of strategy'. Centre for Research in Management, University of California, Berkeley, *CCC Working Paper*, pp. 90–98.

Teece, D.J., Pisano, G. and Shuen, A. (1997). 'Dynamic capabilities and strategic management'. *Strategic Management Journal*, 18(7), 509–533.

Todorova, G. and Durisin, B. (2007). 'Absorptive capacity: Valuing a reconceptualization'. *Academy of Management Review*, 32, 774–786.

Tsai, W. (2001). 'Knowledge transfer in intra-organizational networks: Effects of network position and absorptive capacity on business unit innovation and performance'. *Academy of Management Journal*, 44(5), 996–1004.

Tsang, A.H.C. (2002). 'Strategic dimensions of maintenance management'. *Journal of Quality in Maintenance Engineering*, 8(1), 7–39.

Yli-Renko, H., Autio, E., and Sapienza, H.J. (2001). 'Social capital, knowledge acquisition, and knowledge exploitation in young technology-based firms'. *Strategic Management Journal*, 22(6–7), 587–613.

Zahra, S.A. and George, G. (2002). 'Absorptive capacity: A Review, reconceptualization, and extension'. *Academy of Management Review*, 27(2), 185–203.

12
Industry Factors Influencing International New Ventures' Internationalisation Processes

Natasha Evers, Olli Kuivalainen and Svante Andersson

Introduction

There exists a growing body of literature examining firms that internationalise soon after their inception. Such firms are commonly referred to as international new ventures (INVs) and are defined as 'business organisations that from inception seek to derive significant competitive advantages from the use of resources and the sale of outputs in multiple countries' (Oviatt and McDougall, 1994: 49). Although many terms now define the phenomenon, those of 'born global' and 'international new venture' have become somewhat interchangeable, as have the criteria used to categorise them. In this chapter we mostly use the INV term because this can be seen as more encompassing.

The nature of the industry dynamics can be influential in determining the process of new venture internationalisation and their strategic choices (Anderson, Evers and Grigot, 2013; Evers, 2010). However, the impact of industry factors has received limited attention in the international entrepreneurship literature (Zahra and George, 2002; Andersson, 2004, 2006; Fernhaber et al., 2007; Evers, 2010, 2011). This chapter sets out to examine and propose some key factors that can impact a new venture's internationalisation process. The internationalisation process of firms is itself quite complex, and we first define and discuss this process. This is followed by a discussion of literature from which we draw up a research framework supported by propositions for testing and future research focusing on industry factors' effects. The chapter concludes with further research opportunities pertaining to industry factors and INV processes. As this chapter specifically looks at the impact of industry factors on the process in terms of speed, choice of market and market entry mode, we exclude the analysis focusing on the role of the industry on international growth, performance and strategy of the venture.

Deconstructing the internationalisation process of the firm

Firm internationalisation has been defined as the 'the process of adapting firms' operations (strategy, structure, resources, etc.) to international environments' (Calof and Beamish, 1995: 116). In recent years, several authors have attempted to break down the key activities of this process into constructs. Most notably in the domain of international entrepreneurship, Jones and Coviello (2005) suggest three dimensions to define the internationalisation process: time (speed), foreign market selection and entry mode. In this chapter, we select three constructs underpinning a new venture's internationalisation process as 1) speed to internationalisation, 2) entry mode and 3) foreign market coverage strategy. In the case of the last dimension, we extend the construct of foreign market selection to the choices related to geographical scope of the firms' operations – in other words, the geographical market coverage of a firm's operations (Kuivalainen et al., 2012).

Speed of internationalisation

Speed of internationalisation is a central concept in the international entrepreneurship literature. A key assumption of the INV concept is that firms internationalise rapidly in quest of foreign revenues; industry variables may affect the decision to internationalise early in a firm's life cycle and can also speed up its international growth (i.e. pace) from inception (Zucchella et al., 2007; Kuivalainen et al., 2012). Existing studies focusing on INVs from high-tech and low-tech industry sectors have shown that industry variables act as a key determinant in firms' decisions to internationalise rapidly (Andersson et al., 2013; Evers, 2010).

Foreign market coverage strategy: market choice and geographical market scope

In addition to speed of internationalisation, external dynamics in which INVs operate can influence the choice of foreign market and geographical market coverage or scope. With regard to foreign market selection and coverage, the Uppsala model (Johanson and Vahlne, 1990) proposes that psychic distance influences the firm's foreign market choice. As firms gain more knowledge and experience on psychically close markets, they have a tendency to enter more psychically distant markets. However, research shows that psychic distance holds limited relevance for INVs at the time of foreign market selection (Bell, 1995; O'Gorman and Evers, 2011). INVs tend to select foreign markets on the basis of the international knowledge and networks of their founder and to act with devotion to gain an advantage of international opportunities (Andersson and Wictor, 2003). We propose that industry factors which are external to the firm are particularly important in removing the psychic distance because they allow INVs to enter the markets in which their products are in demand (see Evers, 2010). This type of approach to select the markets is often attributed to customer-followership; firms enter the locations in which their customers reside (e.g. Bell, 1995).

Industry variables can also impact geographical market scope. Kuivalainen et al. (2007) give an example of how the degree of global industry integration can influence the market scope by briefly explaining the internationalisation processes of Nokia's mobile phone unit. Nokia initially started with a 'Scandinavian focus' because the existing network technology was jointly agreed and developed in within the firm's home region, namely the Nordic countries. After the introduction of the European-wide GSM standard, first Nokia became a regional player, and later the firm evolved as a global player. What has happened recently, however, such as the sale of mobile phone business to Microsoft, relates naturally to other dimensions of the industry context – that is, industry life cycle and concentration. In the truly global mature industries with prevalent price competition and economies of scale effects, the number of 'global generalist' firms which compete in mass markets on all geographical areas tends to go down to a few (Sheth and Sisodia, 2002). It is difficult for new entrants to compete with the old dominant actors in a mature industry because they have had time to build up economies of scale in production, logistics and marketing.

Entry strategy, mode choices and nature of product category

The Uppsala model describes the way that firms internationalise by increasing their commitment to international operations when they learn about the markets (e.g. Johanson and Vahlne, 1977); in practice this would often mean a change from sporadic export activities with independent representatives to the eventual establishment of a subsidiary. INVs do not necessarily need to create wholly owned subsidiaries abroad; they often manage their operations from headquarters (parent) without physical facilities in the foreign markets. Gabrielsson et al. (2002) and Andersson et al. (2006) found that born globals (INVs) commonly use a combination of different entry modes to enter new markets. The same authors also concluded that born globals often at the same time develop different solutions for different markets. All kinds of developments in communication and transportation technologies affecting many industries (e.g. R&D developments in logistics; see Evers, 2011) have opened up innovative and combined entry mode approaches (e.g. online sales through the Internet), even for smaller firms (Knight and Cavusgil, 1996). Information and financial resources can easily be transferred all over the world with IT solutions. All these developments have given all firms, but especially for those operating in industries driven by digitalisation, more alternatives when making a choice between different foreign market entry strategies. It is clear that the nature of the industry may reduce the need to establish a subsidiary in a market as a prerequisite for quality customer service (see e.g. Blomstermo et al., 2006 for service firms' internationalisation; see Cloninger and Oviatt, 2007 for the internationalisation of INVs). For example, in the case of services the more the elements of production can be unbundled, the more opportunities there are for internationalising different parts of the value chain (e.g. Ball et al., 2008). Our proposition is that industry variables often influence entry mode decisions, and eventually internationalisation patterns tend to differ on the basis of the industry that the firm operates in and the type of the product offering they have.

The role of industry factors in new venture internationalisation

In this section, we first present some insights into the industry idiosyncrasies of INVs. Second, we propose a conceptual framework that identifies several key industry variables with supporting propositions that further aid examination of the role of industry factors in new venture internationalisation processes.

Only a few studies have addressed the influence of industry-specific features on INV internationalisation so far, and thus, theoretical understanding of how industry factors influence the international development and growth of INVs is limited. This lack of research is most likely driven by two factors. First, INV theory has been examined mostly from the perspective of internal firm-specific factors (i.e. from the strategic management perspective). For example, the resource-based and knowledge-based views of the firm have been used as theoretical domains. INV literature has especially advocated firms' heterogeneity to explain these firms' unique resources, strategic decision-making and international competitiveness (McDougall et al., 1994). Thus, firm-specific factors have been seen to matter the most when the focus is on internationalisation at the inception and development of the competitiveness of the new venture. Grogaard et al. (2005) actually suggest that little major differences should exist across industries. Earlier, however, Graham (1978) has pointed out that if industry factors influence firms' internationalisation, similar internationalisation patterns should be found among firms operating in the same industry sector.

Second, the behavioural perspective of the firm underpins the Uppsala model (and other so-named 'stages theories of the internationalisation process'). According to Johanson and Vahlne (1977), the levels of perceived managerial uncertainty, experiential knowledge and risk adversity can moderate the influence of external factors. Grogaard et al. (2005: 3) propose that 'external factors are typically analysed from the perspective of firms and, in particular, decision-makers' perceptions of potential costs or disadvantages of organising and performing activities in various locations. Firms within the same industry may thus be expected to follow fairly different internationalisation paths since external factors become marginalised over time and since their influence is contingent on the perceptions of decision-makers. Andersson (2000) supports this idea: his paper discusses how entrepreneurs operating within the same industry actually interpret the industry environment differently; this would lead to the implementation of different international growth strategies. Therefore, if internationalisation processes and strategies are potentially contingent on the industry in which they operate and also on the managerial perceptions of the environment, then 'the need for a deeper understanding of how industry structure specifically impacts internationalisation in the context of new ventures is imperative' (Fernhaber et al., 2007: 518).

It is still surprising to note how little the industry effects have been studied in the INV context. The article written by Jones et al. (2011) is based on a well-designed and implemented review of the international entrepreneurship literature, which consisted of 323 journal articles published between 1989 and 2009. The largest identified thematic area (96 articles, 30 per cent) in their review focused on patterns and processes in internationalisation. However, only seven of these 96 articles focused on industry and/or environmental influences on the internationalisation process of INVs. Although this is a small number several important notions can be made. First, it is evident that the complexity and variety of environmental variables can motivate a new venture to internationalise (Fernhaber et al., 2007; Evers, 2010). Some firms, for example, may internationalise because of the heavy competition at the domestic market, whereas some other firms' internationalisation is based on perceived market potential abroad (Abouzeedan and Busler, 2007). Second, the impact of the nature of industry on new venture internationalisation suggests the importance of the industry structure as an environmental variable (e.g. Bloodgood et al., 1996; Schrader et al., 2000; Evers, 2010). Third, existing research has also pointed out the possible implications of globalisation processes and internationalisation potential that this creates (Abouzeedan and Busler, 2007). Indeed, industry characteristics may influence a firm's strategies because they define the available strategic options for the firm (Porter, 1986; Ghoshal, 1987; Solberg, 1997). This can also mean making decisions to opt for internationalisation as a necessity or strategic growth. For instance, Porter (1986) notes that industries differ in their international competitiveness along a continuum, from multi-national to global. The success of firms' internationalisation strategies can be highly contingent on industry factors whereby, 'in a multi-domestic industry, company internationalisation is discretionary;...in a global industry, a firm must in some way integrate its activities on a worldwide basis to capture the linkages among countries' (Porter, 1986: 12).

Conceptual framework

Figure 12.1 identifies key industry factors found across the key studies as well as some emergent factors that are worthy of further exploration (Boter and

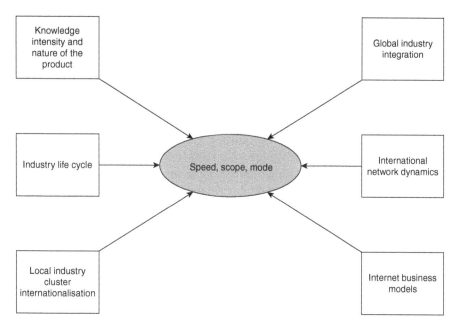

Figure 12.1 Conceptual framework: industry factors influencing INVs' international-isation process

Source: Adapted from Andersson, Evers and Kuivalainen (2014). 'International New Ventures – Rapid internationalisation across different industry contexts'.

Holmquist, 1996; Andersson, 2004; Grogaard et al., 2005; Fernhaber et al., 2007). Figure 12.1 serves as a research conceptual framework identifying some of the key industry variables on new venture internationalisation processes in terms of speed, market scope and entry choices (we acknowledge other industry variables exist but confine our focus to those in Figure 12.1). The constructs underpinning new ventures' internationalisation processes are located at the centre of our conceptual framework (see Figure 12.1). These key factors are: (1) knowledge intensity and product 2) industry life cycle, 3) degree of global industry integration, (4) international network dynamics (within the industry), (5) Internet business models and 6) local industry cluster internationalisation. Our propositions are discussed and presented below.

Degree of knowledge intensity in the industry and nature of product

In her literature review of factors explaining why some new firms move faster towards foreign markets, Evers (2011) conceptualised such factors pertaining to speed of internationalisation into push and pull constructs. She found that industries that are characterised by high degrees of knowledge intensity, in both R&D activity and technology-embedded products, can push firms towards internationalisation early in their life cycle. Such INVs oriented their technology and/or knowledge-based offerings towards international market niches where demand was greater than it was at home. This enabled them to acquire economies of scale, capitalise on their R&D investments and sustain their revenues. Further, ventures operating in industries with short product life cycle, as in the case of technology, need to amortise high R&D costs; thus, early and rapid internationalisation becomes a necessity (Burgel and Murray, 2000).

High-tech INVs tend to internationalise quickly as a result of the rapid, technological and short life cycles in the industry, the dynamic nature of the industry in which they operate and the high R&D costs (Johnson, 2004; see also Knight and Cavusgil, 1996). INV studies tend to focus on high-technology industries because of the role of innovative product characteristics and industry structures in internationalisation (Fernhaber et al., 2007). For example, in Bloodgood et al.'s study (1996) of 61 U.S.-based high-tech international start-ups, they found support for the view that initial international presence was due to the nature of the industry, which required the firm to compete by capitalising on a unique strategy of moving abroad first. High-technology products are often less culture specific and require relatively minimal adaptation to local markets (Andersson, 2006); this also provides a platform for early and rapid internationalisation. Hence, we propose:

Proposition 1: The level of knowledge intensity embedded in a new ventures product offering can determine its internationalisation process in terms of speed, geographic scope and entry mode decisions.

Proposition 2: The product sector in which the new ventures operate can influence internationalisation process in terms of speed, geographic scope and entry mode decisions.

Stage of industry life cycle

Entrepreneurship research suggests that the rate of new venture formation can be directly linked to industry characteristics, such as evolutionary stage, industry life cycle and the level of industry concentration (Dean and Meyer, 1996). The evolutionary stage or life cycle of an industry refers to whether an industry is just emerging (embryonic, growth or mature). In terms of new venture formation, the peculiarities of new industries can make them particularly favourable for the creation of INVs (Evers, 2010). The process of venture creation is initially heavily influenced by the environments in which the ventures reside (Van de Ven and Garud, 1989; Dean and Meyer, 1996). Although new ventures need resources to be able to exploit internationalisation, many resource opportunities exist for new firms in the growth stage of an industry, resulting is somewhat lessened competitive pressures (Eisenhardt and Schoonhoven, 1990; Fernhaber et al., 2007). The so-named 'era of ferment' characterises a time when there are no dominant designs, and this tends to take place when there technology discontinuities exist (see e.g. Tushman and Anderson, 1986; Anderson and Tushman, 1990). When the industry reaches the growth phase, firms that are able to provide customers with desired products or services are able to reap the benefits.

Andersson (2004) discusses also how industry life cycles and the firm's stage in the internationalisation process influence its scale, scope and timing of internationalisation. In growing industries which can bring high levels of volatility, changes can be unpredictable and market opportunities difficult to validate. Market choice in the early international stages is therefore a consequence of the firm's internal resources, for example the knowledge of different markets of entrepreneurs and key personnel, as well as personal networks in different markets. Firms in an early stage of internationalisation in a mature industry can succeed with a relatively slow incremental internationalisation strategy.

Because mature industries are more structured, network relationships are already established, stability ensues and growth is slow. Firms can use the knowledge and experience gained from their first international venture in their subsequent development. These characteristics make it more difficult for INVs to compete in mature industries. That is, firms in this context are constrained by the industry structure, and the internationalisation process is characteristic of a gradual behaviour in which internationalisation begins later, with low commitment entry modes in psychically close markets (Johanson and Vahlne, 1977, 1990).

Hence, we propose:

Proposition 3: The life cycle of the industry in which the new venture enters into in its home country can influence its internationalisation process in terms of speed, geographic scope and entry mode decisions.

Global integration of the industry

Integration of industry or level of internationalisation of an industry sector can inform how INVs compete in the sectors in which they operate (Evers, 2011; Evers 2010). It has also been found that in some cases, industry factors are more influential determinants of the emergence of INVs than international work experience in low-tech sectors (Evers, 2010). Evers's study (2010: 411) highlighted the importance of degree of industry integration concluding that the entrepreneur's international work experience or structured business network 'can be overridden sometimes by environmental factors'.

Another example of global integration of industry on new firm internationalisation is the life science industry. Stremersch and Van Dyck (2009) suggest that the life sciences industry have unique characteristics. For instance, governmental regulations can determine the international behaviour of firms in this industry (Persson and Steinby, 2006). Hence, we propose:

Proposition 4: The degree of global integration of an industry in which the INVs operate, can influence their internationalisation process in terms of speed, scope and entry mode.

Internationalisation of networks in the industry

Another factor is the nature of international network dynamics in some sectors, such as global medical technology (see Evers et. al., 2012; Andersson et al., 2013, Laurell et al, 2013) and the global seafood sector (Evers and O'Gorman, 2011). For example, in the medical technology sector, factors such as cluster location, sectoral type of industry and industry support agencies and institutions can influence the network dynamics in the industry and firm's internationalisation (Andersson et al., 2013; Evers et al., 2012; O'Gorman and Evers, 2011). Further, INV entrepreneurs have been found to work proactively with stakeholders both inside and outside the focal firms to develop marketing capabilities for international development and growth (Evers et al., 2012). Support agencies can have strong international connections that the INVs can leverage. For example, in their study of Irish seafood INVs, O'Gorman and Evers (2011) identified the Irish Seafood Agency as a key network intermediary that accelerated and supported the internationalisation process of Irish export ventures from inception. The international connections of local research institutional networks of INVs in medical technology sector has shown that INVs leverage such networks to mobilise scientific and university networks to promote their products internationally (Evers et al. 2012). In their study, Evers et al. (2012) identified the local medical profession to act as a key opinion leader at international conferences and fairs, promoting and endorsing the case firms' products on global markets (Andersson et al., 2013; Evers and Knight, 2008). Firms in this sector can utilise the fact that universities are part of internationally well-connected networks. Hence, firms need to go beyond being purely market oriented, with a focus on customers and competitors, and include other stakeholders in the network (e.g. universities and local governments). In addition, globalisation of industries such as pharmaceutical and the automotive has been largely driven not only by economic factors but also by international network dynamics between industry actors. Hence, the nature of the industry itself can influence networks dynamics and internationalisation process of the firm (e.g. Coviello, 2006). Hence, we propose:

Proposition 5: The level of international connectivity of networks in an industry in which the new operates can influence their internationalisation process in terms of speed, scope and entry mode.

Internet business models

'Expanding fields of information systems and technologies empower internationally-orientated entrepreneurs to reach remote markets of the world much easier and faster than their traditional counterparts, in spite of time and resource constraints' (Etemad, 2004: 13). The advent of rapid developments in information, communication and digitised technologies created INVs in great number in the 1990s (Hamill and Gregory, 1997; Knight and Cavusgil, 1996; Oviatt and McDougall, 1994, 1995). Since then, more studies on INVs have identified Internet-based technologies as a key driver of new venture internationalisation, with the Internet itself constituting a new mode of foreign market entry for knowledge-based products and services – Amazon, Google and many more. A study by Loane et al. (2004) found that start-ups in Europe and North America were embracing Internet technologies from the outset and adopting e-business models to internationalise globally and rapidly from inception. Furthermore, Internet business models were also found to be led by founders with a global focus at the outset, resulting in early internationalisation from inception (Loane, 2006). Hence, we propose:

> Proposition 6: The level of Internet dependency in an industry will influence a new venture's internationalisation process in terms of speed, scope and entry mode.

Internationalisation of local industry clusters

Formalised locally based industry clusters bridge the gap between INVs and international markets. Giblin (2006) showed how clusters can facilitate the internationalisation of INVs by providing resources, networking opportunities and legitimacy. Further, in some locally based sectors that are internationally market driven, prior international experience of an entrepreneur is not always a required condition for early internationalisation (Evers, 2011; Ghannad and Andersson, 2012). Actors in a cluster may actively connect firms to foreign partners. Location is important because clusters are geographically limited. Research has shown the importance of short geographic distance for firms to be able to effectively exchange information and knowledge. To benefit from the actions of the cluster, firms must be located within geographical limits (Porter, 1990, 1998; Zucchella et al., 2007; Al-Laham and Souitaris, 2008).

Andersson et al. (2013) found that being located in a reputable industry cluster enhanced the international reputation of the medtech firms. Their study examined the internationalisation firms in the Rhone-Alpes region, home to a cluster of firms in the medical industry. They found that industry clusters located in this region served as a magnet for MNC investment to stimulate and refuel needed resources for new venture innovations and their internationalisation processes. They also found that the firm leveraged its relationships with and proximity to the local 'internationally connected' research infrastructure to develop innovation for its global niche markets. Avenel et al. (2005) also identified this region as a factor of growth for firms in the biotechnology industry.

Covolic and Lamotte (2014) also identified the importance of formal clusters for internationalisation of French firms operating in the transportation as well as information and communications sectors.

Hence, we propose:

Proposition 7: The degree of internationalisation of an industry cluster in which a new venture is located will influence its internationalisation process in terms of speed, scope and entry mode.

Conclusions and further research

Industry factors may both push or hinder firms' international growth. One suggested direction for further research that could help us to understand the influence of industry factors over time is the examination of international patterns and performance differences across industries and countries (Fernhaber and McDougall, 2014). Industry can be seen consisting of number of relevant dimensions, however. In Figure 12.1 we have pointed out several of these. For example, the life cycle of the industry the firm enters or is operating in is a significant contextual factor, which should be considered when studying INVs (Hånell et al, 2014). To be able to capture the evolution of the firms' internationalisation patterns and performance in different industry phases or cycles, longitudinal research would be of importance. Especially the later phases of INVs' development in different industrial contexts would be an interesting area to be explored in detail (Kuivalainen et al., 2012; Gabrielsson and Gabrielsson, 2013).

Moreover, as most studies on INVs focus on high-tech industries in developed countries more research on INVs in variety of industries, such as low tech (Evers, 2011), service, trading and agricultural sectors (Knight et al., 2001; Coviello and Jones, 2004; Grogaard et al., 2005) are needed to understand the focal phenomenon better.

More research on how internationalisation theories relate to entrepreneurs (Andersson, 2000; Andersson and Evangelista, 2006) and their interplay with the firm-focused approaches (for the latter, see e.g. Johansson and Vahlne, 1977, 1990) in different industry contexts is also needed. Earlier research on INVs has focused on mostly entrepreneurs (Andersson, 2000) or firm-level theories, such as the resource-based view (e.g. Knight and Cavusgil, 2004) and knowledge-based view (e.g. Kuivalainen et al., 2010). Were it the case that in some industrial domains entrepreneurs would behave differently and consequently the firms would follow different internationalisation patterns? To be able to understand these phenomena, the interplay of the factors should be studied.

Furthermore, it is essential to consider that firms' respective industries may differ from their customer industries, which can significantly affect a firm's internationalisation. The offering (product or service or their combination) may actually serve different types of customers from a number of industries; this might require firms to utilise several business models in parallel, for example. There might also be differences between geographical locations in the case of best functioning business models, and consequently, research from a wide spectrum of countries would help theory development. Most studies in the international entrepreneurship area are conducted in developed Anglo and European economies, with similar institutional and cultural contexts. However, more research is called for to explore our propositions and other emergent factors in different empirical settings such as emergent markets with diverse institutional contexts – for example, China, India and Brazil (cf. Kiss et al., 2012).

Further research should also scrutinise internationalisation strategies and especially strive to define what is meant by INV internationalisation. Strategies could be examined from various perspectives, while keeping in mind the INV context of the speed, scope and modes of internationalisation (Kuivalainen et al., 2012) or the life cycle of INVs (Gabrielsson and Gabrielsson, 2013). As mentioned previously, INVs' life cycles should be examined in parallel to the industry and product life cycles.

Finally, another issue that can occur with INVs is that potential opportunities may exist in horizontal product market across industries. For example, an INV may target its product(s) to customers operating in a specific industry sector, yet the management may later find out that there is potential demand in different industry sectors. For example, several visual imaging products can be used for computer or digital game development, but the product can also fulfil the existing needs in a medical sector. When these contextual, horizontal targeting approaches are studied and taken into consideration, we might be able to better explain international processes and growth patterns of certain INVs. Converging technologies can also lead INVs to reposition themselves (see Evers et al., 2012). One conceptual approach to understand the strategic changes such as these would be to use effectuation and causation logic (see Sarasvathy, 2001; Johanson and Vahlne, 2009; Evers and O'Gorman, 2011; Andersson, 2011; Gabrielsson and Gabrielsson, 2013).

References

Abouzeedan, A., Busler, M. (2007) 'Internetisation management: the way to run the strategic alliances in the e-globalization age'. *Global Business Review*, 8(2), 303–321.

Al-Laham, A., Souitaris, V. (2008) 'Network embeddedness and new-venture internationalization: analyzing international linkages in the German biotech industry'. *Journal of Business Venturing*, 23(5), 567–586.

Anderson, P., Tushman, M.L. (1990) 'Technological discontinuities and dominant designs: a cyclical model of technological change'. *Administrative Science Quarterly*, 354, 604–633.

Andersson, S. Evers, N., Kuivalainen, O. (2014) 'International new ventures: rapid internationalization across different industry contexts'. *European Business Review*, 26(5), 390–405.

Andersson, S. (2000) 'Internationalization of the firm from an entrepreneurial perspective'. *International Studies of Management and Organization*, 30(1), 63–92.

Andersson, S. (2004) 'Internationalization in Different Industrial Contexts'. *Journal of Business Venturing*, 19(6), 851–875

Andersson, S. (2006) 'International growth strategies in consumer and business-to-business markets in manufacturing and service sectors'. *Journal of Euromarketing*, 15(4), 35–56.

Andersson, S. (2011) 'International entrepreneurship, born globals and the theory of effectuation'. *Journal of Small Business and Enterprise Development*, 18(3), 627 – 643.

Andersson, S., Evangelista, F. (2006) 'The Entrepreneur in the Born Global Firm in Australia and Sweden'. *Journal of Small Business and Enterprise Development*, 13(4), 642–659.

Andersson, S., Evers, N., Griot, C. (2013) 'Local and international networks in small firm internationalisation: cases from the Rhône-Alpes medical technology regional cluster'. *Entrepreneurship and Regional Development*, 25(9–10), 867–888.

Andersson, S., Gabrielsson, J., Wictor, I. (2006) 'Born globals' market channel strategies'. *International Journal of Globalisation and Small Business*, 1(4), 356–373.

Andersson, S., Wictor, I. (2003) 'Innovative internationalisation in new firms: born globals – the Swedish case'. *Journal of International Entrepreneurship*, 1(3), 249–276.

Ball, D.A., Lindsay, V.J., Rose, E.L. (2008) 'Rethinking the paradigm of service internationalisation: Less resource-intensive market entry modes for information-intensive soft services'. *Management International Review*, 48(4), 413–431.

Bell, J. (1995) 'The internationalization of small computer software firms – a further challenge to "stage" theories'. *European Journal of Marketing*, 29(8), 60–75.

Bell, J., Crick, D., Young, S. (2004) 'Small firm internationalisation and business strategy: an exploratory study of "knowledge-intensive" and "traditional" manufacturing firms in the UK'. *International Small Business Journal*, 22(1), 23–56.

Benito, G.R.G. (2005) 'Divestment and international business strategy'. *Journal of Economic Geography*, 5(2), 235–251.

Blomstermo, A., Sharma, D.D., Sallis, J. (2006) 'Choice of foreign market entry mode in service firms'. *International Marketing Review*, 23(2), 211–229.

Bloodgood, J.M., Sapienza, H.J., Almeida, J.G. (1996) 'The internationalization of new high-potential US ventures: antecedents and outcomes'. *Entrepreneurship Theory and Practice*, 20(4), 61–76.

Boter, H., Holmquist, C. (1996) 'Industry characteristics and internationalisation processes in small firms'. *Journal of Business Venturing*, 11(6), 471–487.

Burgel, O., Murray, G.C. (2000) 'The International Market Entry Choices of Start-Up Companies in High-Technology Industries'. *Journal of International Marketing*, 8, 33.–62.

Calof J.L., Beamish P.W. (1995) 'Adapting to Foreign Markets: Explaining Internationalization'. *International Business Review*, 4(2), 115–131

Caves, R.E. (1996) *Multinational Enterprise and Economic Analysis*. 2nd edition, Cambridge: Cambridge University Press.

Cloninger, P.A., Oviatt, B. (2007) 'Service content and the internationalization of young ventures: An empirical test'. *Entrepreneurship Theory and Practice*, 31(2), 233–256.

Colovic, A., Lamotte, O. (2014) 'The role of formal industry clusters in the internationalization of new ventures'. *European Business Review*, 26(5), 449–470.

Coviello, N.E. (2006) 'The network dynamics of international new ventures'. *Journal of International Business Studies*, 37, 713–731.

Coviello, N., Jones, M.V. (2004) 'Methodological issues in international entrepreneurship research'. *Journal of Business Venturing*, 19, 485–508

Crick, D., Jones, M.V. (2000) 'Small high-technology firms and international hightechnology markets'. *Journal of International Marketing*, 8(2), 63–85.

Crick, D., Spence, M. (2005) 'The internationalisation of "high performing" U.K. high-tech SMEs: a study of planned and unplanned strategies'. *International Business Review*, 14, 167–185.

Dean, T.J., Meyer, G.D. (1996) 'Industry environments and new venture formations in U.S. manufacturing: a conceptual and empirical analysis of demand determinants'. *Journal of Business Venturing*, 11, 107–132.

Eisenhardt, K., Schoonhoven, C. (1990) 'Organizational Growth: Linking Founding Team, Strategy, Environment, and Growth among U.S. Semiconductor Ventures.' *Administrative Science Quarterly*, 35, 504–529.

Etemad, H. (1999) 'Globalisation and the small and medium-sized enterprises: search for potent strategies'. *Global Focus*, 11(3), 385–104.

Evers, N. (2010) 'Factors influencing the internationalization of new ventures in the Irish aquacultural industry: an exploratory study'. *Journal of International Entrepreneurship*, 8(4), 392–416.

Evers, N., O'Gorman, C. (2011) 'Improvised Internationalisation in new ventures: The role of prior knowledge and networks'. Entrepreneurship and Regional Development, 23(7–8), 549–574.

Evers, N. (2011) 'International new ventures in low tech sectors – a dynamic capabilities perspective'. *Journal of Small Business & Enterprise Development*, 18(3), 502–528.

Evers, N (2011) 'Factors influencing new venture internationalisation: a review of the literature'. *Irish Journal Of Management*, 30(2), 17–46.

Evers, N., Andersson, S., Hannibal, M. (2012) 'Stakeholders and marketing capabilities in international new ventures: evidence from Ireland, Sweden and Denmark'. *Journal of International Marketing*, 20(4), 46–71.

Eerrell, O.C., Tracey L. Gonzalez-Padron, G., Huit, T.M., Maignan, I. (2010) 'Erom Market Orientation to Stakeholder Orientation'. *Journal of Public Policy & Marketing*, 19(Spring), 93–96.

Fernhaber, S., McDougall, P.P., Oviatt, B.M. (2007) 'Exploring the role of industry structure in new venture internationalization'. *Entrepreneurship Theory & Practice*, 31(4), 517–542.

Gabrielsson, M., Kirpalani, V.H.M., Luostarinen, R. (2002) 'Multiple sales channel strategies in the European PC industry'. *Journal of International Marketing*, 10(3), 73–95.

Gabrielsson, P., Gabrielsson, M. (2013) 'A dynamic model of growth phases and survival in international business-to-business new ventures: The moderating effect of decision-making logic'. *Industrial Marketing Management*, 42(8), 1357–1373.

Ghannad, N., Andersson, S. (2012) 'The influence of the entrepreneur's background on the behaviour and development of born globals' internationalisation processes'. *International Journal of Entrepreneurship and Small Business*, 15(2), 136–153.

Ghoshal, S. (1987) 'Global Strategy: An organizing framework'. *Strategic Management Journal*, 8, 425–440.

Gliga, G., Evers, N. (2010) 'Marketing challenges for high tech SMEs'. *Innovation Marketing*, 3(6), 104–112.

Graham, E.M. (1978) 'Transatlantic investment by multinational firms: a rivalistic phenomenon?'. *Journal of Post-Keynesian Economics*, 1(1), 82–99.

Grogaard, B., Gioia, C., Benito, G. (2005) 'An empirical investigation of the role of industry factors in the internationalization patterns of firms'. SMG working paper.

Hånell Melen, S., Rovira Nordman, E., Sharma, D.D. (2014) 'The Continued Internationalization of the International New Venture'. *European Business Review*, 26(5), 471–490.

Johanson, J., Vahlne, J.-E. (1977) 'The internationalization process of the firm – A model of knowledge development and increasing foreign market commitments'. *Journal of International Business Studies*, 8(1), 23–32.

Johanson, J., Vahlne, J.-E. (1990) 'The mechanism of internationalisation'. *International Marketing Review*, 7(4), 11–24.

Johnson, J. (2004) 'Factors Influencing the Early Internationalisation of High Technology Start-Ups: US and UK Evidence'. *Journal of International Entrepreneurship*, 2, 139–154.

Jolly, V., Alahuhta, M., Jeannet, J. (1992) 'Challenging the Incumbents: How High-Technology Start-Ups Compete Globally'. *Journal of Strategic Change*, 1, 71–82.

Jones, M.V., Coviello, N.E. (2005) 'Internationalisation: Conceptualising an entrepreneurial process of behaviour in time'. *Journal of International Business Studies*, 36(3), 284–303.

Jones, M.V., Coviello, N., Tang, Y.K. (2011) 'International entrepreneurship research (1989–2009): a domain ontology and thematic analysis'. *Journal of Business Venturing*, 26(6), 632–659.

Kiss, A.M., Danis, W.M., Cavusgil, S.T. (2012) 'International entrepreneurship research in emerging economies: a critical review and research agenda'. *Journal of Business Venturing*, 27(2), 266–290.

Knight, G.A., Cavusgil, S.T. (1996) 'The born global firm: A challenge to traditional internationalization theory'. *Advances in International Marketing*, 8, 11–26.

Knight, G.A., Cavusgil, S.T. (2004) 'Innovation, organizational capabilities, and the born-global firm'. *Journal of International Business Studies*, 35(2), 124–141.

Knight, J., Bell, J., McNaughton, R. (2001) 'Born globals: old wine in new bottles'. ANZMAC Conference. Proceedings. Bridging Marketing theory and practice, Auckland, New Zealand.

Kotha, S., Rindova, V.P., Rothaermel, F.T. (2001) 'Assets and Actions: Firm-Specific Factors in the Internationalization of U.S. Internet Firms'. *Journal of International Business Studies*, 32, 769–791.

Kuivalainen, O., Lindqvist, J., Saarenketo, S., Äijö, T. (2007) 'International growth of Finnish software firms: starting points, pathways and outcomes'. *Journal of Euromarketing*, 161/2, 7–22.

Kuivalainen, O., Puumalainen, K., Sintonen, S., Kyläheiko, K. (2010) 'Organisational capabilities and internationalisation of the small and medium-sized information and communications technology firms'. *Journal of International Entrepreneurship*, 8(2), 135–155.

Kuivalainen, O., Saarenketo, S., Puumalainen, K. (2012) 'Start-up patterns of internationalization – a framework and its application in the context of knowledge-intensive SMEs'. *European Management Journal*, 30(4), 372–385.

Laurell, H., Andersson, S., Achtenhagen, L. (2013) 'The importance of industry context for new venture internationalisation: a case study from the life sciences'. *Journal of International Entrepreneurship*, 11(4), 297–319.

McDougall, P.P., Shane, S., Oviatt, B.M. (1994) 'Explaining the formation of international new ventures: the limits of theories from international business research'. *Journal of Business Venturing*, 9, 469–487.

Mort, G.S., Weerawardena, J. (2006) 'Networking capability and international entrepreneurship: how networks function in Australian born global firms'. *International Marketing Review*, 23(5), 549–572.

O'Gorman, C., Evers, N. (2011) 'Network intermediaries in the internationalization of new firms in peripheral regions'. *International Marketing Review*, 28(4), 340–364.

Oviatt, B.M., McDougall, P.P. (1994) 'Toward a theory of international new ventures'. *Journal of International Business Studies*, 25(1), 45–64.

Peiris, I.K., Akoorie, M.E.M., Sinha, P. (2012) 'International entrepreneurship: a critical analysis of studies in the past two decades and future directions for research'. *Journal of International Entrepreneurship*, 10(4), 279–324.

Persson, S.G., Steinby, C. (2006) 'Networks in a Protected Business Context: Licenses as Restraints and Facilitators'. *Industrial Marketing Management*, 35, 870–880.

Porter, M.E. (1980) *Competitive Strategy*. New York: Free Press.

Porter, M.E. (1986) *Competition in Global Industries*. Boston: Harvard Business School Press.

Porter, M.E. (1990) 'The competitive advantage of nations'. *Harvard Business Review*, March-April, 73–93.

Porter, M.E. (1998) 'Clusters and competition: new agendas for companies, governments and institutions'. In M.E. Porter (Ed.). *On Competition*. Boston: Harvard Business School.

Preece, S.B., Miles, G., Baetz, M.C. (1999) 'Explaining International Intensity and Global Diversity of Early-Stage Technology-Based Firms'. *Journal of Business Venturing*, 14, 259–281.

Rialp, A., Rialp, J., Knight, G.A. (2005) 'The phenomenon of early internationalizing firms: what do we know after a decade (1993–2003) of scientific inquiry?'. *International Business Review*, 14(2), 147–166.

Rovira Nordman, E., Melén, S. (2008) 'The impact of different kinds of knowledge for the internationalization process of born globals in the biotech business'. *Journal of World Business*, 43(2), 171–185.

Ruzzier, M., Antoncic, B., Hisrich, R.D. (2007) 'The internationalization of SMEs: developing and testing a multi-dimensional measure on Slovenian firms'. *Entrepreneurship and Regional Development*, 19, 161–183.

Sarasvathy, S.D. (2001) 'Causation and effectuation: toward a theoretical shift from economic inevitability to entrepreneurial contingency'. *Academy of Management Review*, 26(2), 243–263.

Sheth, J.N., Sisodia, R. (2002) *The Rule of Three: Surviving and Thriving in Competitive Markets*. New York: Free Press.

Shrader, R.C., Oviatt, B.M., McDougall, P.P. (2000) 'How new ventures exploit trade-offs among international risk factors: lessons for accelerated internationalisation of the 21st century'. *Academy of Management Journal*, 43(6), 1227–1247.

Spence, M. and Crick, D. (2006) 'A comparative investigation into the internationalization of Canadian and UK high-tech SMEs'. *International Marketing Review*, 22(5), 524–548.

Solberg, C.A. (1997) Framework for Analysis of Strategy Development in Globalizing Markets'. Journal of international Marketing, 5(1), 294–306.

Stremersch, S., Van Dyck, W. (2009) 'Marketing of the Life Sciences: A New Framework and Research Agenda for a Nascent Field'. *Journal of Marketing*, 73, 4–30.

Svensson, G. (2006) 'A quest for a common terminology: the concept of born globals'. *Management Decision*, 44(9), 1311–1317.

Tushman, M.L., Anderson, P. (1986) 'Technological discontinuities and organizational environments'. *Administrative Science Quarterly*, 31(3), 439–465.

Van de Ven, A.H. And Garud R. (1989) 'A Framework for Understanding the Emergence of New Industries'. *Research on Technological Innovation Management and Policy*, 4, 295–325.

Zahra, S.A., Ireland, R.D., Hitt, M.A. (2000) 'International expansion by new venture firms: international diversity, mode of market entry, technological learning and performance'. *Academy of Management Journal*, 43(5), 925–950.

Zahra, S., George, G. (2002) 'International entrepreneurship: The current status of the field and future research agenda'. In M. Hitt, D. Ireland, D. Sexton and M. Camp (Eds). *Strategic entrepreneurship: Creating an integrated mindset.* Oxford: Blackwell, pp. 255–288.

Zhou, L. (2007) 'The effects of entrepreneurial proclivity and foreign market knowledge on early internationalization'. *Journal of World Business*, 42, 281–293.

Zucchella, A., Palamara, G., Denicolai, S. (2007) 'The drivers of the early internationalization of the firm'. *Journal of World Business*, 42(3), 268–280.

13
Do Foreign Ownership Modes Matter for FDI Spillovers?

Ziko Konwar, Frank McDonald, Chengang Wang and Yingqi Wei

Introduction

The welfare-enhancing role of spillovers from foreign direct investment (FDI) in a host country generates significant interests and debates among policymakers, long after a wide range of regulatory changes in favour of FDI in the late 1980s and the 1990s. The expectation of positive spillovers reinforces the development of government policies to attract multinational enterprises (MNEs) to the host country. However, as is documented in surveys of the literature on FDI spillovers (Görg and Strobl, 2001; Havránek and Irsová, 2012; Meyer and Sinani, 2009; Wooster and Diebel, 2010), the empirical evidence on FDI spillovers is rather mixed. The surveys highlight two important factors that might offer the explanations of mixed findings. First, the degree of foreign ownership is a primary factor in determining the strength of linkages between domestic and foreign firms and thereby affects spillovers (Javorcik and Spatareanu, 2008). As argued by Görg and Greenaway (2004), MNEs may be effective at preventing spillover effects of firm-specific assets. This is connected to the ownership strategies of MNEs that often use wholly owned subsidiaries (WOS) to better control the technologies they transfer to their foreign locations. Second, absorptive capacity of domestic firms and the strength of linkages between domestic and foreign firms are critical for spillovers. However, studies taking these factors into consideration are sparse. According to Havránek and Irsová (2012), among 1205 horizontal spillover estimates from 52 studies, only 5.7 per cent and 7.8 per cent control for absorptive capacity of domestic firms and the strength of linkages between domestic and foreign firms, respectively.

Three generic foreign ownership modes are possible. Besides WOS, firms can also use majority foreign-owned joint ventures (MAJVs) or minority foreign-owned joint ventures (MIJVs). A few studies that consider foreign ownership mode to be an important factor in influencing spillovers (e.g. Abraham, Konings and Slootmaekers, 2010; Javorcik and Spatareanu, 2008) argue that spillovers from foreign-owned joint ventures (JVs) may be higher than those from WOS because the network connections of domestic partners in JVs to other domestic firms provide effective mechanisms for the diffusion of technologies from foreign-owned affiliates (FOAs) to domestic firms. In the case of WOS, the control of knowledge-based assets (KBAs) limits spillover effects (Javorcik and Spatareanu, 2008). The connection between ownership mode and spillovers is, however, more complicated than is implied by this view. Although the ability of domestic firms to gain access to the MNEs' pools of knowledge is likely to be better in the case of JVs, the pool of knowledge available for spillovers is possibly more conducive in WOS than in JVs. The greater degree of control afforded by WOS is likely to induce MNEs to transfer more and higher quality technologies, thereby creating a larger potential for spillovers. Leakages from knowledge pools are likely to be greater in JVs, but the size and quality of the pools is perhaps greater in WOS. Moreover, there may be differences between MAJVs and MIJVs. The linkages that domestic partners in JVs have to other domestic firms may be stronger in MIJVs than in MAJVs (Ramachandran, 1993) because the domestic partner in a MIJV often has frequent and deeper interactions with domestic agents (domestic competitors, suppliers etc.). As a result, the potential for diffusion of knowledge externalities from MIJVs may be higher. On the other hand, MAJVs may be more likely to receive newer and more advanced technologies than MIJVs are, providing better knowledge pools that permit access to a higher quantity and quality of KBAs than is the case for MIJVs. Existing studies consider either MAJVs vs. MIJVs (Dimelis and Louri, 2004) or WOS vs. JVs without clearly distinguishing between MAJVs and MIJVs (Abraham et al., 2010; Javorcik and Spatareanu, 2008). This study includes all three generic ownership modes and uses a better definition of foreign-ownership mode than existing studies used. The improvement in definition in this study (following Ayyagari, Dau and Spencer, 2009 and Sarkar, 2010) is that the share of foreign ownership is by reference to the dominant shareholder with voting rights. This is an appropriate definition of foreign ownership because promoters (those with voting rights) such as firms or corporate groups possess significant control and decision-making authority, whereas non-promoters (those without voting rights) such as foreign institutional investors, venture capital funds, banks, mutual funds and insurance companies do not exercise direct control (Chalapati and Dhar, 2011). This study uses a more comprehensive method of identifying foreign-ownership mode than the existing literature and thereby improves the prospects of capturing how these modes affect spillovers.

In addition to the knowledge pool of FOAs and their linkages to domestic firms, the role of absorptive capacity is also considered to be of importance in the existing studies (e.g. Barrios and Strobl, 2002; Damijan, Knell, Majcen and Rojec, 2003; Girma, 2005; Griffith, Redding and Reenen, 2003; Haskel, Pereira and Slaughter, 2007; Kokko, 1996; Liu and Buck, 2007; Zhang, Li, Li and Zhou, 2010). Absorptive capacity refers to the ability of an organisation to identify, assimilate and exploit knowledge from the environment (Cohen and Levinthal, 1989). It is contended that firms must have an adequate level of absorptive capacity to benefit from FDI spillover effects. However, the empirical findings are mixed. In many of these studies, absorptive capacity is proxied by the technology gap between the foreign and the domestic firms, R&D intensities of domestic firms or human capital embodied in domestic firms. The strength of such approaches lies in the focus on technological ability or resources required for knowledge absorption. However, whether such measures are effective in capturing absorptive capacity is debatable. Haskel et al. (2007), Girma (2005), Zhang et al. (2010) and Damijan, Rojec, Majcen and Knell (2013) use an alternative approach to control for absorptive capacity by splitting the sample in terms of firm size, and they find smaller firms or plants with a low share of skilled workers in the workforce lack the necessary absorptive capacity to benefit from FDI. Studies using samples of large firms are therefore more likely to capture domestic firms that have absorptive capacity capable of benefiting from spillovers.

This chapter examines the effects of foreign ownership modes on spillovers and, by use of a sample of large domestic firms, takes account of the absorptive capacity factor. A conceptual model explores the possible implications for knowledge pools, linkages with domestic firms and the level of competition associated with different foreign ownership modes. A sample of large firms of the Indian manufacturing industry provides the data to test for the relationship between foreign ownership modes and spillovers. The chapter is organised as follows. Section 2 reviews the existing literature on FDI spillovers in terms of foreign ownership modes, which leads to the development of a conceptual model. Section 3 describes data and research methodology. It is followed by section 4, which discusses how the findings relate to the research propositions along with the theoretical and policy implications of the results. Section 5 provides a conclusion.

FDI spillovers: theoretical review and context-setting

International business theory suggests that MNEs must possess firm-specific advantages (FSAs) in the form of new or advanced technologies and/or marketing and management know-how to overcome '*liability of foreignness*' (Dunning and Lundan, 2008). Such FSAs, particularly in the form of KBAs, imply that there is potential for spillovers because of the public goods nature of non-proprietary knowledge and/or market failures of some form in protecting proprietary knowledge. These FSAs not only exert competitive pressures on domestic firms but also enhance the existing knowledge pool of the host country and thereby increase the potential for spillovers to domestic firms in the host country. In this process, the net impact of competitive pressure and unintended knowledge transfer by FOAs to domestic firms defines spillovers.

The primary channels of FDI intra-industry spillovers are demonstration, labour mobility and competition effects (Blomström and Kokko, 1998). Demonstration effects in the same industry occur when domestic firms imitate product and process technologies possessed by FOAs through 'reverse engineering'. Akin to this *'reverse engineering'*, the domestic firms may also benefit from the presence of FOAs through imitation of managerial and organisational innovation (Ben Hamida and Gugler, 2009). Labour mobility effects arise when skilled employees that are trained in FOAs move away from their employers to commence with entrepreneurial ventures or work for other local employers (Lipsey and Sjöholm, 2004). The entry of MNEs into an industry could also generate *'fresh winds of competition'*. However the net impact could be ambiguous. On one hand, the entry of MNEs may force domestic firms to reduce X-inefficiencies or to upgrade their technological capabilities to remain competitive; as a result, there is an improvement in productivity of the latter (Görg and Greenaway, 2004). On the other hand, the entry of MNEs increases competition in output and input markets. Competition in output market may reduce a domestic firm's market share, forcing them to produce less output and thereby pushing up their average costs (Aitken and Harrison, 1999). Competition in input market such as labour markets may lead to an increase in wages and better employee compensation (Driffield and Taylor, 2000). This is likely to be unfavourable to domestic firms and can have a negative effect on their productivity.

Foreign ownership modes and FDI spillovers

The conventional argument is that spillovers from JVs are higher than those from WOS (Abraham et al., 2010; Javorcik and Spatareanu, 2008). This is because the network connections of domestic partners in JVs to other domestic firms provide an effective mechanism for diffusion of technology and know-how from FOAs to domestic firms, whereas WOS are used by MNEs to maintain control of their KBAs and prevent leakage of know-how (Desai, Foley and Hines, 2004; Ramachandran, 1993), which limits spillovers from WOS. However the link between foreign ownership modes and FDI spillovers is more complicated and will be considered in more depth below.

The empirical evidence on spillovers from foreign ownership modes is scant and the findings are mixed. Dimelis and Louri (2004) detect no significant effect from MAJVs in Greece but find positive effects for *'small'* Greek firms from the presence of MIJVs. Blomström and Sjöholm (1999) reveal insignificant intra-industry spillovers from both JVs and WOS in Indonesia, whereas Javorcik and Spatareanu (2008) show negative spillovers for both JVs and WOS. In the case of China, Abraham et al. (2010) find evidence of positive spillover effects for JVs and negative effects from WOS, whereas in another study on China, Tian (2010) reports positive spillovers from both equity and non-equity JVs and no significant effects from WOS. The inconclusive empirical findings again point out the need for a conceptual model to elucidate the possible effects of foreign ownership modes on FDI spillovers. This requires consideration of the characteristics of knowledge pools, the strength of linkages and the competition effects associated with foreign ownership modes.

Knowledge pools and FDI spillovers

The transfer of KBAs enhances knowledge pools in FOAs, which enable them to offset 'liability of foreignness' when competing in a host country (Dunning and Lundan, 2008). Since WOS enable better internalisation of KBAs and provide greater control over these assets than JVs (Buckley and Casson, 1976), MNEs are likely to transfer technologies of newer vintage through WOS and older technologies through JV (Mansfield and Romeo, 1980). MNEs may also commit more resources to transfer KBAs to WOS (Blomström and Sjöholm, 1999) and thus increase the quality, volume and speed of technology transfer in WOS compared to JVs (Mansfield and Romeo, 1980). Moreover, the source of technological know-how in WOS that is available, albeit imperfectly (because of the low level of localisation), for domestic firms to access and to learn from is more potent (Tortoriello and Krackhardt, 2010).

While WOS receive newer and sophisticated technologies than do MAJVs (Ramachandran, 1993), MAJVs receive more mature technologies than MIJVs (Almeida and Fernandes, 2008; Desai et al., 2004). A JV between a foreign and domestic firm induces threats regarding appropriability of know-how. This threat is higher in the case of MIJVs where the domestic partner has a dominant role. As a result, the capacity and motivation to transfer KBAs is lower in MIJVs. In summary, the volume and quality of transfer of KBAs, and thereby the size of knowledge pools, increase with the degree of foreign ownership in FOAs – that is, pools are smaller in MIJVs, intermediate in MAJVs and larger in WOS.

Linkages and FDI spillovers

The linkages or network connections of FOAs with other domestic firms in an industry can also affect the extent of FDI spillovers. Although knowledge pools play a vital role, the extent of their *'diffusion'* or *'leakage'* is likely to occur when these linkages/network connections are deep enough to permit knowledge diffusion. Linkages are likely to affect FDI spillovers in two ways. First, they provide opportunities for domestic firms to catch up technologically (Meyer and Sinani, 2009) by allowing for richer interactions that are crucial to transfer and absorption of know-how (Kotabe, Martin and Domoto, 2003). Second, they act as information flow conduits that channel non-redundant information benefits to host-country firms – for example, learning about new best practices and techniques (McEvilly and Zaheer, 1999; Podolny, 2001).

The extent of spillovers through linkages is likely to be stronger when FOAs have a higher degree of local embeddedness as this will permit closer and richer interactions between FOAs and domestic firms. WOS have weaker linkages than JVs as their degree of local embeddedness is low, and they also tend to protect their KBAs by minimising threats to the appropriability of know-how. Thus, the opportunities for spillovers from WOS through linkages is likely to be marginal, whereas JVs tend to facilitate spillovers as they are more embedded in the host-country market (Belderbos, Capannelli and Fukao, 2001; Chen, Chen and Ku, 2004; Eberhardt, McLaren, Millington and Wilkinson, 2004; Wei, Liu, Wang and Wang, 2012) and can quickly respond to local conditions (Inkpen, 2000; Zhou and Li, 2008). This is of particular importance for the transfer of tacit knowledge such as management know-how (Inkpen, 2000; Kogut and Zander, 1993). Within JVs, MIJVs have domestic partners with a more dominant role, and therefore, their linkages to other domestic firms in MIJVs are likely to be stronger, relative to MAJVs. For example, as Javorcik and Spatareanu (2008) point out, in an MIJV, the domestic partner can be in charge of hiring policies and place local staff in key technical or managerial positions without taking actions to limit employee turnover. To summarise, the effects of linkages or network connections on spillovers should be highest in MIJVs, followed by MAJVs and (lowest in) WOS.

Competition effects and FDI spillovers

Chen (1996) introduces two firm-specific and theory-based constructs – market commonality and resource similarity. Market commonality refers to 'the degree of presence that a competitor manifests in the market it overlaps with the focal firm', and resource similarity is 'the extent to which a given competitor possesses strategic endowments comparable, in terms of both type and amount, to those of the focal firm'. Chen (1996) posits that the severity of competition co-determines the degree of market commonality and resource similarity. A JV with stronger linkages is likely to facilitate knowledge diffusion and exploit compatible resource/assets between partners (Inkpen, 2000; Kogut and Zander, 1993) than is a WOS. Thus, a JV is likely to tap into the sourcing networks of its domestic partners, leading to high-level resource similarity with other domestic firms (e.g. Belderbos et al., 2001; Eberhardt et al., 2004; Wei et al., 2012).

In terms of market commonality, JVs are more likely to exert stronger competitive pressure on domestic firms than WOS, as JVs tend to have greater degree of embeddedness in the industry and are more familiar with local markets. This effect is more likely to be dominant in a MIJV than a MAJV as the domestic partner of the MIJV has greater control because of its dominant equity share – thus providing better knowledge of domestic markets, which enables the MIJV to engage with and monitor competition more efficiently (Chen and Chen, 2005). Within WOS, greenfield WOS are keen on launching standardised product lines belonging to their corporate parents to better exploit FSAs (Rugman, Verbeke and Nguyen, 2011). This might augment the extent of

Table 13.1 Postulated effects on foreign ownership modes of key factors affecting spillovers

Ownership Modes	MIJV	MAJV	WOS
Knowledge Pool	Low	Intermediate	High
Linkages	High	Intermediate	Low
Competition	High	Intermediate	Low

'liability of foreignness' in WOS, thereby thwarting their efforts to compete for higher sales compared to JVs. WOS established through acquisition are more likely to have higher level local embeddedness than greenfield WOS and could embark on the transfer of KBAs more suited to local conditions, which might stimulate greater degree of industry competition. That said, in terms of market similarity, the competition effect resulted from the presence of WOS is likely to be severe and could be a similar level to that from the presence of JVs if acquisitions account for a majority of WOS in a host country[1].

In the context of FDI spillovers, industry competition is likely to display both positive and negative effects (Blomström and Kokko, 1998). Positive effects emerge when domestic firms are able to adjust input costs *vis-a-vis* their output and respond effectively to growing market share of FOAs, the failure of which leads to the loss of market share, the reduction in profit and ultimately the exit from the market. In line with the discussion above, it is postulated that MIJVs display higher competition effects, followed by MAJVs and then by WOS, subject to the mix of greenfield or acquisition WOS.

The arguments outlined above provide the basis for a conceptual framework on potential spillovers under different foreign ownership modes (see Table 13.1).

Data and methodology

Data sources

The main data source is the Prowess database of the Centre for Monitoring Indian Economy (CMIE). This database provides information on domestic firms and FOAs of MNEs listed on India's Stock Exchanges. It includes large firms that account for 75 per cent of all corporate taxes, more than 95 per cent of excise duty and 60 per cent of all savings of the Indian corporate sector (Marin and Sasidharan, 2010), thus enabling the investigation of spillovers from large FOAs to large domestic firms. Large firms, on average, are better at adopting managerial best practices, including the introduction of new production techniques and the management of human capital, to improve firm productivity (Bloom and Van Reenen, 2007). As a result, knowledge pools of FOAs and absorptive capabilities of domestic firms are likely to be better captured in the case of large firms. Thus, investigation of FDI spillovers with a focus on large firms could be considered as the most plausible scenario. The Prowess database is extensively used, and there is a large number of firm-level published studies using this database (e.g. Balakrishan, Pushpangadan and Babu, 2000; Kathuria, 2002; Kumar and Aggarwal, 2005; Marin and Sasidharan, 2010; Topalova, 2004).

National Industrial Classification (NIC) 2008 code for the manufacturing sector is used in this study to categorise industrial groupings. The definition of foreign ownership is foreign equity is equal to or is greater than 10 per cent of the total equity. To supplement missing information in Prowess on the level of foreign ownership, company websites and annual company reports are used. Furthermore, the adjustment of nominal data for sales, assets and expenditures are deflated using the gross domestic product (GDP) deflator and the wholesale price index obtained from the Reserve Bank of India.

In the data cleaning and inputting process, firms that did not report or that provided insufficient information on key economic activities are excluded. The final dataset contains 1,624 firms with 5,203 observations covering the period of 1991–2008, of which 1,398 firms are domestic firms and 226 are FOAs. The number of FOAs in our sample is in line with other studies using Prowess – for example, Marin and Sasidharan (2010) include 273 FOAs in their sample. Similar studies on the manufacturing sector in Argentina by Chudnovsky, López and Rossi (2008) and Marin and Bell (2006) have 145 and 283 FOAs, respectively, in their samples.

Model estimation

The assessment of FDI productivity spillover effects – that is, productivity growth of domestic firms caused by FDI presence – requires estimates of the total factor productivity (TFP) of firms. Problems arise if firms adjust their inputs according to their expectations about economic conditions, leading to the possibility that idiosyncratic shocks in productivity are captured in the error term (Griliches and Mairesse, 1995). The Levinsohn and Petrin (2003) approach, henceforth the LP method, is commonly used to overcome this potential problem (Javorcik and Spatareanu, 2008; Liu, Wei and Wang, 2009). The LP method is easier to implement than the alternative approach by Olley and Pakes (1996) because there is no requirement for information on firm entry and exit and no information loss that might result from negative values in the proxy investment variable. Very few firms exited the dataset, which provides another reason to use the LP method. The LP method of estimating TFP for two-digit level industry production functions provides the data for the dependent variable.

The control variables include competitive characteristics of industries (industry concentration and import penetration ratios (IMP)) and key conditions in domestic firms that affect absorptive capacity (R&D intensity (RD) and firm scale (SCALE)). Industry concentration is measured with Herfindahl index

(HHI). The RD and SCALE variables are proxies for the firms' own innovation effort and scale effect, respectively.

The baseline model is:

$$\ln TFP_{ijst} = \alpha_0 + \alpha_1 FORFP_{jt-1} + \alpha_2 HHI_{jt-1} + \alpha_3 IMP_{jt-1} + \alpha_4 RD_{ijst-1}$$
$$+ \alpha_5 SCALE_{ijst-1} + \mu_{ijst} \tag{1}$$

$\ln TFP_{ijst}$ is the logarithm of the TFP of domestic firm i in industry j, in state s, at time t. Following Wei and Liu (2006) to maximise the detection of spillovers, three different measures are used to capture FDI spillover effects (FORFP) – the share of MNEs' employee compensation in the three-digit industry (employment); the share of total sales by MNEs in the three-digit industry (total sales) and the share of MNEs fixed assets in the three-digit industry (fixed assets). The study measures spillovers from WOS, MAJVs and MIJVs in the same way as FDI spillovers, by changing the shares of all MNEs to the shares of WOS, MAJVs and MIJVs in the three-digit industry, respectively. The measurement of foreign ownership modes in this study updates Javorcik and Spatareanu (2008) by using foreign ownership levels of promoters' equity share rather than both promoters' and non-promoters' equity share. This definition allows for the determination of the degree of direct control over KBAs that are likely to be exercised by foreign parents. A majority of the existing studies have failed to address this issue and therefore are likely to elicit biases on the extent of control of KBAs in FDI spillover. This leads to the following model:

$$\ln TFP_{ijst} = \alpha_0 + \alpha_1 WOSFP_{jt-1} + \alpha_2 MAJVFP_{jt-1} + \alpha_3 MIJVFP_{jt-1} + \alpha_4 HHI_{jt-1}$$
$$+ \alpha_5 IMP_{jt-1} + \alpha_6 RD_{ijst-1} + \alpha_7 SCALE_{ijst-1} + \mu_{ijst} \tag{2}$$

The introduction of a one-year lag deals with the potential problem that spillovers will not raise instantaneously. Moreover, this lag structure allows for the control of simultaneity bias arising from the fact that MNEs may be attracted to productive industries (Aitken and Harrison, 1999). The appendix provides information on the definition and measurement of the variables used in the study.

Equations (1) and (2) are estimated with corrections for heteroskedasticity and for clustering at the industry-year level to account for correlations between firm observations within the same industry-year (Wooldridge, 2002). The correlation between foreign presence and productivity enhancement in firms may connect to other factors, which can be assumed to be fixed, such as firm, time, industry and region-specific factors. These factors could be connected to things such as organisational and industry culture, technology opportunities, external policy shocks and infrastructure conditions. To control for these fixed effects, use is made of year, industry and region dummies in a fixed effects panel data model. An alternative method to the fixed effects model is first differencing.

Following Aitken and Harrison (1999), Javorcik (2004) and Haskel et al. (2007), the first-differencing model is estimated, which involves the loss of 225 firms from the sample but generates more robust results than the fixed effects model. This is because estimating first differences removes unobserved time-invariant industry and region-specific effects (assuming that the time-varying disturbances in the original equations are not serially correlated) and thereby produces estimates that are no longer biased by any omitted variables that are constant over time (Bond, Hoeffler and Temple, 2001). As argued by Javorcik (2004), 'the examination of longer differences gives relatively more weight to more persistent changes in the variables of interest and hence reduces the influences of noise'. This approach is consistent with previous studies on FDI spillovers, and thus, the discussion involves the use of first differencing.

Another econometric issue is selection bias, which may occur due to firm entry and exit but may simply reflect some firms choosing not to report. To address this issue, we maintain the use of original unbalanced panel, as suggested by Levinsohn and Petrin (2003). The final econometric issue is the multicollinearity between explanatory variables. We checked both the correlation matrix and variance inflationary factors and found this is not a concern. For brevity, the test results are not reported but are available upon request.

Results and discussions

TFP estimation results

Table 13.2 presents a summary of TFP in terms of industry and ownership mode. It is clear that FOAs do not always have higher productivity than domestic firms have. In sectors 11 (beverage production), 13, 14, 15 (textile, wearing apparel, leather and related products), 19 (coke and refined petroleum products), 22 (rubber and plastic products) and 26 (computer electronic and optical products), the average TFP of domestic firms are higher than that of FOAs. This trend is prominent in the case of highly concentrated industries and industries employing low-income and unskilled workers (Chari and Gupta, 2008). A possible explanation is that domestic firms in these industries face weak labour regulations domestically and are therefore in a position to extract higher returns from employees, although the price of labour is the same for FOAs. The FOAs in these industries encounter effective monitoring of labour regulations and therefore are unable to utilise similar strategies.

FDI spillovers estimation results

Table 13.3 reports the results for FDI spillovers. Columns 1–3 present the results without reference to foreign ownership modes and columns 4–6 show evidence with reference to foreign ownership modes. Columns 1–3 reveal that there are

Table 13.2 TFP estimation results

Sl. No.	Sector	No. of obs.	Domestic firms (TFP)	WOS (TFP)	MAJV (TFP)	MIJV (TFP)
1	Food processing	1452	38.744	43.432	52.744	41.325
2	Beverage production	174	0.027	0.005	0.004	
3	Textiles, wearing apparel, leather and related products	148	0.174	0.108		
4	Wood and wood + cork products, furniture, paper and paper products	26	3.803	4.844		
5	Coke and refined petroleum products	212	1.473	1.118	0.795	1.293
6	Chemicals and chemical products	2677	8.449	11.496	12.934	6.237
7	Pharmaceutical, medicinal and botanical products	1531	9.987	22.679	15.166	7.924
8	Rubber and plastic products	1325	3.829	2.584	2.268	3.590
9	Non-metallic mineral products	46	0.068	0.110	0.114	
10	Basic metals, fabricated metal products except machinery and equipment	134	1.007	1.432	0.822	1.593
11	Computer electronic and optical products	415	12.566	6.348	4.719	4.281
12	Electrical equipment	585	4.231	4.309	4.951	9.653
13	Machinery and equipment n.e.c.	705	0.709	0.505	0.790	0.533
14	Motor vehicles trailers and semi-trailers, other transport equipment	40	3.928	5.599		5.235

significant and positive spillover effects on domestic firms' TFP when total sales and fixed assets measures are used. Columns 4–6 reveal the identification of both negative and positive spillovers when using a comprehensive definition of foreign ownership modes that includes WOS, MAJVs and MIJVs. WOS have positive spillovers with total sales and fixed assets measures, and MAJVs have positive spillover effects in all three measures. The findings of positive spillovers from MAJVs are consistent with Abraham et al. (2010) and Tian (2010). However, in contrast to findings of negative effects from WOS in Javorcik and Spatareanu (2008) and Abraham et al. (2010), this study finds that WOS are also

254 Konwar, McDonald, Wang and Wei

Table 13.3 Foreign ownership modes and FDI spillovers

FDI Spillover Variable Measurement	(1) Employment	(2) Total sales	(3) Fixed assets	(4) Employment	(5) Total sales	(6) Fixed assets
FORFP	0.038	0.158**	0.154**			
	[0.059]	[0.063]	[0.066]			
WOS				0.028	0.167**	0.322***
				[0.077]	[0.065]	[0.096]
MAJV				0.136**	0.249***	0.232***
				[0.065]	[0.083]	[0.085]
MIJV				−0.424***	−0.355***	−0.119
				[0.156]	[0.120]	[0.115]
HHI	0.027	0.013	0.019	0.022	−0.001	−0.014
	[0.073]	[0.072]	[0.073]	[0.074]	[0.074]	[0.076]
IMP	0.231**	0.229**	0.240**	0.205**	0.246**	0.234**
	[0.102]	[0.101]	[0.101]	[0.096]	[0.102]	[0.096]
RD	0.116***	0.112***	0.130***	0.115***	0.115***	0.137***
	[0.042]	[0.040]	[0.042]	[0.043]	[0.042]	[0.041]
SCALE	−0.014*	−0.012*	−0.013*	−0.012*	−0.011	−0.012*
	[0.07]	[0.07]	[0.07]	[0.07]	[0.07]	[0.07]
Industry effects	Yes	Yes	Yes	Yes	Yes	Yes
Regional effects	Yes	Yes	Yes	Yes	Yes	Yes
Time effects	Yes	Yes	Yes	Yes	Yes	Yes
N	3652	3652	3652	3652	3652	3652
R^2	0.281	0.281	0.282	0.283	0.282	0.284

Note: 1. Dependent variable is the logged TFP calculated using Levinsohn and Petrin (2003) procedure; 2. Robust standard errors clustered by industry-year in brackets; 3. * $p < 0.10$, ** $p < 0.05$, *** $p < 0.01$

associated with positive spillover effects. Finally, MIJVs display negative and significant effects for employment and fixed assets measures. This contradicts previous studies, such as by Dimelis and Louri (2004), which reveal positive and significant spillovers for MIJVs. The results for MAJVs are perhaps more robust because positive associations were identified for all measures of spillovers, whereas WOS and MIJVs are picked up by two of the measures.

The results for control variables reveal that industry competition effects (Herfindahl index and import penetration) are consistent across all specifications, with the former having insignificant effects and latter being positive and significant. R&D intensity has a positive effect on TFP, whereas the impact of SCALE is negative across all specifications.

Discussion

The findings reported in this chapter add to the literature that suggests that models of spillovers need further development to enable better identification of spillovers (Crespo and Fontoura, 2007; Marin and Sasidharan, 2010). This study finds that spillovers are contingent on foreign ownership modes of MNEs. Positive intra-industry spillovers exist for large Indian firms from WOS and MAJVs, but negative effects arise from MIJVs. The results suggest that accounting for foreign ownership modes, based on a fuller and appropriate classification (promoters rather than non-promoters equity share), enables a more detailed identification of spillovers than seems to be the case in studies that do not account for this factor in deciding on foreign ownership mode.

The results indicate that MAJVs have robust spillover effects on domestic firms compared to WOS. This could be because MAJVs are characterised by well-developed linkages and fairly large and high-quality knowledge pools. It is likely that WOS have larger and better quality knowledge pools than MAJVs, but they perhaps have lower linkages to domestic firms. Moreover, moderate competition arising from the presence of MAJVs also incentivises domestic firms to better adapt to competition and improve their productivity. The results of the positive spillover effects for WOS in Indian industries imply that the large knowledge pools offset the lower level of linkages. The higher level of competition, when compared to MAJVs, that's generated by WOS also favours domestic spillovers from these types of JVs.

The capture of spillovers from WOS through only two measures may arise from differences in protection of intellectual property and in competition, as compared with MAJVs. It is possible that WOS use better protection mechanisms to defend their KBAs in Indian manufacturing sectors, thereby preventing leakage from knowledge pools. In India, due to weak protection of intellectual property, WOS may be associated with the transfer of inferior (non-proprietary) technologies, and therefore, the quality of knowledge pools might be low. On the other hand, the avoidance of MIJVs as a foreign ownership mode may be best because the competition effects from MIJVs are likely to dominate any positive spillover effects (Chen, Kokko and Tingvall, 2011). While the competition effects arise from rivalry between MIJVs and domestic firms for market share, the spillover effect arises from the presence of knowledge pools and linkages with domestic firms (Chang and Xu, 2008). MIJVs are characterised by low-level knowledge pools but significantly well-developed linkages and a higher degree of competition effect on domestic firms. As a result, negative competition effects from MIJVs are likely to outweigh the positive effects that are likely to arise from good linkages with domestic firms and knowledge pools (Merlevede, Schoors and Spatareanu, 2010). Another way of interpreting this is that the high competition effects and the presence of strong linkages in MIJVs are not enough to offset the likelihood of lower knowledge pools in MIJVs, relative to WOS and MAJVs. In essence, the findings provide support for some of the key arguments developed in the conceptual model.

Conclusion

Governments in developing countries, including India, often favour JVs over WOS, believing that the active participation of domestic firms will bring greater benefits to other domestic firms. The findings of this study provide partial support for this. Policymakers, however, also need to understand that restrictions on foreign ownership could prevent accumulation of larger and deeper knowledge pools associated with technology transfer in WOS. Spillovers from these knowledge pools are likely to result in higher benefits to domestic firms when compared to JVs. Our findings reveal that the overall outcomes for knowledge spillovers may depend on whether there is high knowledge transfer potential in WOS, which may outweigh the lower transfer of KBAs but better network linkages in JVs. In the case of India, MIJVs appear to have the lowest prospects of spillovers. This may mean that the strong network linkages to domestic firms by the national partner in FOAs do not, in most cases, overcome the disadvantages of the lower knowledge transfers that MIJVs receive. For MAJVs, however, it is possible that these network linkages compensate or indeed outweigh the benefits of higher knowledge transfers in WOS. The findings undermine conventional wisdom in Indian FDI policy targeted at restricting foreign ownership to JVs in certain industries in order to protect domestic firms from adverse competition. This policy may, however, reduce the quality of technology transfer that is possible in the case of WOS.

The interpretation of the results requires caution. First, our findings draw on a specific spectrum of the Indian economy – that is, large listed firms in the manufacturing sector. Therefore, any generalisation from this in terms of both sector and firm selection needs care. Second, although the study took measures to mitigate the endogeneity issue, a more effective solution involves using datasets that cover a longer period and contain information on effective instrumental variables. Third, the results may be affected by specific characteristics of the Indian business environment arising from the nature of institutional systems leading to particular business and organisational cultures, extensive protection of some industries, low levels of technological dynamism and weak enforcement of some regulations. Fourth, the conceptual model is based on the arguments that both knowledge transfer potential and linkages of FOAs are important for spillovers, and competition effects generated by FOAs influence the extent to which domestic firms will learn and enhance productivity. Unfortunately the data needed to test for the presence and weight of the above qualitative factors for spillovers is unavailable. Therefore, it is not possible to identify the relative importance of these factors.

Despite these limitations, we believe our findings could help discussions on how to improve FDI and related policies in order to enable higher spillovers to domestic firms. Policies to encourage domestic firms to effectively interact with

WOS might enhance the prospects of positive spillovers from the deep knowledge pools that such FOAs are likely to develop in host locations.

Appendix: variable definition and measurment

Variable	Definition and measurement
LTFP	log(TFP)
HHI	The sum of squared firm shares of sales in a three-digit industry
IMP	The ratio of imports to domestic demand in a three-digit industry
RDINT	The ratio of domestic firm's R&D expenses to sales
SCALE	The ratio of domestic firm's sales to average three-digit industry-level sales
FORFP	Foreign spillover variable proxied by the share of FOAs in a three-digit industry total or in a three-digit industry within a region, excluding the focal firm
WOSFP	WOS spillover variable proxied by the share of wholly foreign-owned subsidiary in a three-digit industry total or in a three-digit industry within a region, excluding the focal firm
MAJVFP	MAJV spillover variable proxied by the share of MAJVs in a three-digit industry total or in a three-digit industry within a region, excluding the focal firm
MIJVFP	MIJV spillover variable proxied by the share of MIJVs in a three-digit industry total or in a three-digit industry within a region, excluding the focal firm

Ownership mode is determined using the following classifications:

- Wholly owned subsidiaries (WOS): firms whose foreign promoters' equity share is 100 per cent in the Prowess database and who are defined as a wholly owned subsidiary by the firm's website and secondary sources.
- Majority foreign-owned joint ventures (MAJVs): firms whose foreign promoters' equity share ranges from 51 per cent to 99 per cent in the Prowess database.
- Minority foreign-owned joint ventures (MIJVs): firms whose foreign promoters' equity share ranges from 10 per cent to 50 per cent in the Prowess database.

Information regarding foreign ownership modes is from the equity share datasheet provided by Prowess. However, in the case of some WOS, secondary sources such as websites and company reports are used to complement equity-share information from Prowess database. In cases where the information about a firm is not available in Prowess (whether it is WOS or not) and is also not verifiable from the corporate websites of firms, other secondary sources were used to determine the classification of the firm. Assam Carbon Products, for example, is a foreign firm but has no equity-share information available in the Prowess dataset. It has a website, but it does not report shareholding information. The only information provided is that Morgan Crucible Co. (UK) has a stake in the firm. To validate this information, use was made of government websites such as Securities and Exchange Board of India (SEBI, accessible at http://www.sebi.gov.in/) to provide information on foreign equity. The data gathered from this web site was further supplemented by another reputable website http://www.securities.com to check the information found on the SEBI website.

Note

1. This applies to the knowledge pools, linkages and resource similarity arguments as well but to a lesser extent.

References

Abraham, F., Konings, J. and Slootmaekers, V. (2010). 'FDI spillovers in the Chinese manufacturing sector'. *Economics of Transition*, 18, 143–182.

Aitken, B.J. and Harrison, A.E. (1999). 'Do domestic firms benefit from direct foreign investment? Evidence from Venezuela'. *American Economic Review*, 89, 605–618.

Almeida, R. and Fernandes, A.M. (2008). 'Openness and technological innovations in developing countries: Evidence from firm-level surveys'. *Journal of Development Studies*, 44, 701–727.

Ayyagari, M., Dau, L. and Spencer, J.W. (2009). 'The strategic response of business group affiliates in emerging markets increased inward FDI'. *Academy of Management Best Paper Proceedings*.

Balakrishan, P., Pushpangadan, K. and Babu, S. (2000). 'Trade liberalisation and productivity growth in manufacturing: evidence from firm-level panel data'. *Economic and Political Weekly*, 35, 3679–3682.

Barrios, S. and Strobl, E. (2002). 'FDI Spillovers in Spain'. *Review of World Economics*, 138, 459–481.

Belderbos, R. Capannelli, G., and Fukao, K. (2001). 'Backward vertical linkages of foreign manufacturing affiliates: evidence from Japanese multinationals'. *World Development*, 29, 189–208.

Ben Hamida, L. and Gugler, P. (2009). 'Are there demonstration-related spillovers from FDI?: Evidence from Switzerland'. *International Business Review*, 18, 494–508.

Blomström, M. and Kokko, A. (1998). 'Multinational corporations and spillovers'. *Journal of Economic Surveys*, 12, 1–31.

Blomström, M. and Sjöholm, F. (1999). 'Technology transfer and spillovers: Does local participation with multinationals matter?'. *European Economic Review*, 43, 915–923.

Bloom, N. and Van Reenen, J. (2007). 'Measuring and explaining management practices across firms and countries'. *Quarterly Journal of Economics*, 122, 1351–1408.

Bond, S.R. Hoeffler, A., and Temple, J. (2001). 'GMM estimation of empirical growth models'. *CEPR Discussion Papers 3048*.

Buckley, P.J. and Casson, M. (1976). *The Future of the Multinational Enterprise*. London: Macmillan.

Chalapati, R.K.S. and Dhar, B. (2011). 'India's FDI inflows: Trends and concepts'. *Institute for Studies in Industrial Development Working Paper 2011/01*.

Chang, S.J. and Xu, D. (2008). 'Spillovers and competition among foreign and local firms in China'. *Strategic Management Journal*, 29, 495–518.

Chari, A. and Gupta, N. (2008). 'Incumbents and protectionism: The political economy of foreign entry liberalization'. *Journal of Financial Economics*, 88, 633–656.

Chen, M.J. (1996). 'Competitor analysis and interfirm rivalry: toward a theoretical integration'. *Academy of Management Review*, 21, 100–134.

Chen, T., Kokko, A. and Tingvall, P.G. (2011). 'FDI and spillovers in China: non-linearity and absorptive capacity'. *Journal of Chinese Economic and Business Studies*, 9, 1–22.

Chen, T.-J., Chen, H. and Ku, Y.-H. (2004). 'Foreign direct investment and local linkages'. *Journal of International Business Studies*, 35, 320–333.

Chen, T.T. and Chen, J. (2005). 'Framework of two-mechanism FDI intra-industry spillover on host country internal market'. *China Soft Science*, 10, 137–146 (In Chinese).

Chudnovsky, D., López, A. and Rossi, G. (2008). 'Foreign direct investment spillovers and the absorptive capabilities of domestic firms in the Argentine manufacturing sector (1992–2001)'. *Journal of Development Studies*, 44, 645–677.

Cohen, W.M. and Levinthal, D.A. (1989). 'Innovation and learning: The two faces of R&D'. *Economic Journal*, 99, 569–596.

Crespo, N. and Fontoura, M.P. (2007). 'Determinant factors of FDI spillovers – What do we really know?'. *World Development*, 35, 410–425.

Damijan, J., Knell, M., Majcen, B. and Rojec, M. (2003). 'The role of FDI, R&D accumulation and trade in transferring technology to transition countries: evidence from firm panel data for eight transition countries'. *Economic Systems*, 27, 189–204.

Damijan, J.P., Rojec, M., Majcen, B. and Knell, M. (2013). 'Impact of firm heterogeneity on direct and spillover effects of FDI: Micro- evidence from ten transition countries'. *Journal of Comparative Economics*, 41, 895–922.

Desai, M.A., Foley, C.F. and Hines, J.R.J. (2004). 'The costs of shared ownership: Evidence from international joint ventures'. *Journal of Financial Economics*, 73, 323–374.

Dimelis, S. and Louri, H. (2004). 'Foreign direct investment and technology spillovers: Which firms really benefit?'. *Review of World Economics*, 140, 230–253.

Driffield, N. and Taylor, K. (2000). 'FDI and the labour market: a review of the evidence and policy implications'. *Oxford Review of Economic Policy*, 16, 90–103.

Dunning, J.H. and Lundan, S.M. (2008). *Multinational enterprises and the global economy*, 2nd edition. Cheltenham, UK; Northampton, MA: Edward Elgar.

Eberhardt, M., McLaren, J., Millington, A. and Wilkinson, B. (2004). 'Multiple forces in component localisation in China'. *European Management Journal*, 22, 290–303.

Girma, S. (2005). 'Absorptive capacity and productivity spillovers from FDI: a threshold regression analysis'. *Oxford Bulletin of Economics and Statistics*, 67, 281–306.

Görg, H. and Greenaway, D. (2004). 'Much ado about nothing? Do domestic firms really benefit from foreign direct investment?'. *World Bank Research Observer*, 19, 171–197.

Görg, H. and Strobl, E. (2001). 'Multinational companies and productivity spillovers: a Meta-analysis'. *Economic Journal*, 111, 723–739.

Griffith, R., Redding, S. and Reenen, J. (2003). 'R&D and absorptive capacity: Theory and empirical evidence'. *Scandinavian Journal of Economics*, 105, 99–118.

Griliches, Z. and Mairesse, J. (1995). 'Production Functions: The Search for Identification'. *National Bureau of Economic Research Working Paper Series, No. 5067.*

Haskel, J.E., Pereira, S.C. and Slaughter, M.J. (2007). 'Does inward foreign direct investment boost the productivity of domestic firms?'. *Review of Economics and Statistics*, 89, 482–496.

Havránek, T. and Irsová, Z. (2012). 'Publication bias in the literature on foreign direct investment spillovers'. *Journal of Development Studies*, 48, 1375–1396.

Inkpen, A.C. (2000). 'Learning through joint ventures: A framework of knowledge acquisition'. *Journal of Management Studies*, 37, 1019–1044.

Javorcik, B.S. (2004). 'Dose foreign direct investment increase the productivity of domestic firms? In search of spillovers through backward linkages'. *American Economic Review*, 94, 605–627.

Javorcik, B.S. and Spatareanu, M. (2008). 'To share or not to share: Does local participation matter for spillovers from foreign direct investment?'. *Journal of Development Economics*, 85, 194–217.

Kathuria, V. (2002). 'Liberalisation, FDI, and productivity spillovers—an analysis of Indian manufacturing firms'. *Oxford Economic Papers*, 54, 688–718.

Kogut, B. and Zander, U. (1993). 'Knowledge of the firm and the evolutionary theory of the multinational corporation'. *Journal of International Business Studies*, 24, 625–645.

Kokko, A. (1996). 'Productivity spillovers from competition between local firms and foreign affiliates'. *Journal of International Development*, 8, 517–530.

Kumar, N. and Aggarwal, A. (2005). 'Liberalization, outward orientation and in-house R&D activity of multinational and local firms: A quantitative exploration for Indian manufacturing'. *Research Policy*, 34, 441–460.

Levinsohn, J. and Petrin, A. (2003). 'Estimating production functions using inputs to control for unobservables'. *Review of Economic Studies*, 70, 317–342.

Lipsey, R. and Sjöholm, F. (2004). 'FDI and wage spillovers in Indonesian manufacturing'. *Review of World Economics*, 140, 321–332.

Liu, X. and Buck, T. (2007). 'Innovation performance and channels for international technology spillovers: Evidence from Chinese high-tech industries'. *Research Policy*, 36, 355–366.

Liu, X., Wei, Y. and Wang, C. (2009). 'Do local manufacturing firms benefit from transactional linkages with multinational enterprises in China?'. *Journal of International Business Studies*, 40, 1113–1130.

Mansfield, E. and Romeo, A. (1980). 'Technology transfer to overseas subsidiaries by US-based firms'. *Quarterly Journal of Economics*, 95, 737–750.

Marin, A. and Bell, M. (2006). 'Technology spillovers from foreign direct investment (FDI): the active role of MNC subsidiaries in Argentina in the 1990s'. *Journal of Development Studies*, 42, 678–697.

Marin, A. and Sasidharan, S. (2010). 'Heterogeneous MNC subsidiaries and technological spillovers: Explaining positive and negative effects in India'. *Research Policy*, 39, 1227–1241.

Merlevede, B., Schoors, K. and Spatareanu, M. (2010). 'FDI spillovers and the timing of foreign entry'. *LICOS Discussion Paper 267/2010*.

Meyer, K.E. and Sinani, E. (2009). 'Where and when does foreign direct investment generate positive spillovers? A meta analysis'. *Journal of International Business Studies*, 40, 1075–1094.

Olley, G.S. and Pakes, A. (1996). 'The dynamics of productivity in the telecommunications equipment industry'. *Econometrica*, 64, 1263–1297.

Ramachandran, V. (1993). 'Technology transfer, firm ownership, and investment in human capital'. *Review of Economics and Statistics*, 75, 664–670.

Rugman, A.M., Verbeke, A. and Nguyen, Q.T.K. (2011). 'Fifty years of international business theory and beyond'. *Management International Review*, 18, 1–12.

Sarkar, J. (2010). 'Business groups in India'. In A.M. Colpan, T. Hikino and J.R. Lincoln (Eds). *The Oxford Handbook of Business Groups*. Oxford: Oxford University Press.

Tian, X. (2010). 'Managing FDI technology spillovers: A challenge to TNCs in emerging markets'. *Journal of World Business*, 45, 276–284.

Topalova, P. (2004). 'Trade liberalization and firm productivity: the case of India'. *IMF Working Papers 04/28*.

Tortoriello, M. and Krackhardt, D. (2010). 'Activating cross-boundary knowledge: the role of Simmelian ties in the generation of innovation'. *Academy of Management Journal*, 53, 167–181.

Wei, Y. and Liu, X. (2006). 'Productivity spillovers from R&D, exports and FDI in China's manufacturing sector'. *Journal of International Business Studies*, 37, 544–557.

Wei, Y., Liu, X., Wang, C. and Wang, J. (2012). 'Local sourcing of multinational enterprises in China'. *International Journal of Emerging Markets*, 7, 364–382.

Wooldridge, M.J. (2002). *Econometric Analysis of Cross Section and Panel Data*. Cambridge, MA: MIT Press

Wooster, R.B. and Diebel, D.S. (2010). 'Productivity spillovers from foreign direct investment in developing countries: A meta-regression analysis'. *Review of Development Economics*, 14, 640–655.

Zhang, Y., Li, H., Li, Y. and Zhou, L.-A. (2010). 'FDI spillovers in an emerging market: the role of foreign firms' country origin diversity and domestic firms' absorptive capacity'. *Strategic Management Journal*, 31, 969–989.

Zhou, C. and Li, J. (2008). 'Product innovation in emerging market-based international joint ventures: An organizational ecology perspective'. *Journal of International Business Studies*, 39, 1114–1132.

Index

Printed and bound by CPI Group (UK) Ltd, Croydon, CR0 4YY